The Coming of the Italian-Ethiopian War

The Coming

of the

Italian-Ethiopian War

GEORGE W. BAER

HARVARD UNIVERSITY PRESS

CAMBRIDGE, MASSACHUSETTS · 1967

To Martha

Preface

In May 1936 Benito Mussolini proclaimed the establishment of an Italian empire in east Africa. Ethiopia was annexed to Italy; the last African country free from foreign domination had been conquered by the Italian army. Haile Selassie had fled to England; the king of Italy was invested with the title of emperor. But the conquest of Ethiopia was more than an incident in the later history of European imperialism in Africa. It was also of great importance in the history of Europe after the First World War.

Italy's invasion of Ethiopia in October 1935 posed a direct challenge to the postwar system of collective security as established by the League of Nations. This challenge was not met. The League of Nations failed to protect one of its members; Italy's war of conquest was permitted to succeed; and the League was discredited as a political institution. Its strongest members, Britain and France, instead of upholding the Covenant, withdrew into defensive isolationism and began to pursue policies of appeasement. In these circumstances Germany was encouraged to rearm and to violate the treaties of Locarno and Versailles. Italy, having survived the limited sanctions imposed upon it by the League, was by 1936 moving away from its earlier association with the Western democracies and setting on a course that was to end with the Axis. "The Italian-Ethiopian affair," said Joseph Avenol, secretary-general of the League, was "a European poison."

The purpose of this book is to present an account of the coming of the Italian-Ethiopian war, to examine Italy's preparation for the invasion of Ethiopia and Ethiopia's efforts at defense, and to study the context and nature of the political, diplomatic, and military decisions made by the leaders of the states of Europe as they dealt with the problems posed by Mussolini's decision to invade Ethiopia. For many months before October 1935 this decision was common knowledge. During this period the leaders of Britain, France, the League of Nations, Germany, the United States, and the Roman Catholic Church had time to consider the implications of the impending conflict. How they acted after the war began, and the consequences of the Italian-Ethiopian affair for Europe, reflected the decisions that were made, the positions that were taken, before Italian troops ever crossed Ethiopia's frontiers.

Of those who took an interest in this study I want to express my thanks first to Professor Ernest R. May of Harvard University for his encouragement and assistance. The Henry P. Kendall Foundation generously enabled me to do research in Europe and in Ethiopia. Professor John H. Spencer, who for many years advised the Ethiopian foreign ministry, provided me with helpful information. Professors May, Spencer, Charles F. Delzell, Robert I. Rotberg, and George A. Lanyi read the manuscript of this work. Professor Rotberg at several times helped the manuscript on its way. I am very grateful to these men for their interest, and I valued their comments.

Several men in Europe and in Ethiopia discussed portions of this work with me. Some were themselves participants in the events here recorded; others are historians whose views I was interested to learn. Each was generous with his time, hospitable, and informative. My thanks go to Colonel E. H. M. Clifford, Lieutenant-Colonel A. T. Curle, Professor J.-B. Duroselle, Professor Norman Gibbs, Senator Alessandro Lessona, His Excellency René Massigli, Professor Renato Mori, Professor Richard Pankhurst, Signor Giuseppe Puglisi, Professor Sven Rubenson, Brigadier D. A. Sandford, Sir Geoffrey Thompson, Professor Mario Toscano, and Count Leonardo Vitetti. Dott. Marina Pilotti permitted me to examine the papers of her late uncle, Massimo Pilotti. His Imperial Majesty Haile Selassie I extended several courtesies to me in Addis Ababa. His Excellency Tsahafi Taeszaz Aklilou Abte Wold, Prime Minister of Ethiopia; his secretary, Ato Abitew Gebreyesus; His Excellency Kebbede Mikael, Minister in Charge of the Imperial Chronicle in His Imperial Majesty's Private Cabinet; his secretary, M. Alexandre Belahovsky — each gave me what help he could.

This book was written during a most pleasant stay of fifteen months at Harvard University's Harvard Forest in Petersham, Massachusetts. The director of the Harvard Forest, Professor Hugh M. Raup, and Mrs. Raup, know how much we enjoyed that extraordinary center for research and thought.

G.W.B.

October 1966
Hanover, New Hampshire

Contents

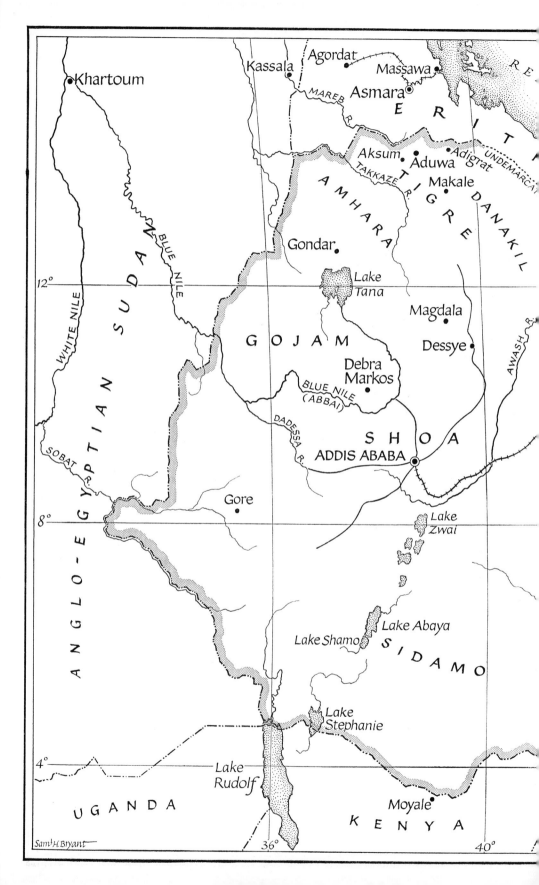

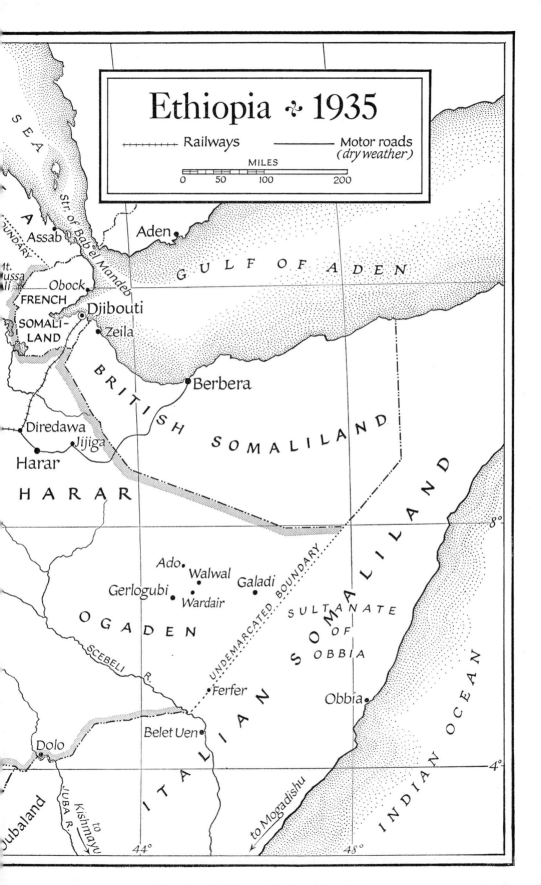

Ethiopia ⚜ 1935

+++++++ Railways   ——— Motor roads
(dry weather)

MILES
0   50   100   200

SEA

Str. of Bab el Mandeb

Assab

Aden

GULF OF ADEN

Mt. ussa li

Obock

FRENCH
SOMALI-
LAND

Djibouti

Zeila

Berbera

B R I T I S H   S O M A L I L A N D

Diredawa

Jijiga

Harar

H A R A R

8°

Ado

Walwal

Gerlogubi

Wardair

Galadi

O G A D E N

UNDEMARCATED BOUNDARY

S U L T A N A T E
O F
O B B I A

I T A L I A N   S O M A L I L A N D

SCEBELI R.

Ferfer

Obbia

INDIAN OCEAN

Belet Uen

Dolo

Jubaland

JUBA R.

to Kishmayu

to Mogadishu

4°

44°   48°

Chapter 1

Italian-Ethiopian Relations, 1889–1934

Italian interest in east Africa was first established in 1869 when a shipping firm of Genoa, taking advantage of the ease of transport provided by the Suez Canal, purchased a strip of land at the port of Assab, just north of the strait of Bab el Mandeb. Preoccupied with domestic affairs, the Italian government refrained from asserting sovereignty there, for the public at home was not prepared to accept the expense and trouble of developing a colony on the Red Sea. But in 1882 control of Assab was transferred to the Italian state and in 1885, frustrated in its designs on Tunis, the government in the hope of imperial gain turned toward this one foothold Italy had in Africa. Encouraged by the British, who after the fall of Khartoum were looking for support against the Mahdists, Italy sent troops to occupy the Turkish port of Massawa. On 1 January 1890 Italy's possessions on the Red Sea were united by royal decree into one province, designated as the colony of Eritrea. The Italians at once looked to the hinterland of their new colony, to the south, and this brought them into direct contact with Ethiopia.[1]

The Ethiopians resented the intrusion of the Italians on the coastal plain and protested their occupation of Massawa. The Ethiopian emperor Yohannis claimed the port, or at least his right to free trading privileges.[2] In 1887 Ras Aloula, the xenophobic leader of Tigre

[1] An official of the Italian foreign ministry wrote in a memorandum in 1932: "The problem of our relationship with Ethiopia in terms of power and our pacific or military penetration in the country was imposed at the very moment of our landing at Assab." Raffaele Guariglia, *Ricordi, 1922–1946* (Naples, 1950), 763 (permission to quote granted by Edizioni Scientifiche Italiane). Guariglia was political director for Africa in 1932, and then in 1935 was appointed to watch over Ethiopian affairs, in the Italian foreign office.

It should be noted at the outset that all translations from French and Italian sources are my own.

[2] G. Portal, *My Mission to Abyssinia* (London, 1892), 159.

and an ally of the emperor's, ordered the Italians to withdraw from the areas claimed by Ethiopia. When they refused, Aloula attacked with a force that outnumbered the troops of Italy by twenty to one. At the massacre of Dogali the Italian force of five hundred men was almost annihilated.

In 1889, upon the death of Yohannis, Menelik of Shoa proclaimed himself emperor. Menelik did not share the xenophobia of the northern rases (chiefs) and lacked their unshakable conservatism. He remained apart from their rivalries and built up his own, overwhelming, power in the far south. It was in the southern province of Shoa that he settled his new and permanent capital, Addis Ababa. Menelik had two political goals. The first was to break down the regional loyalties of the existing feudal system and to unify princes and people behind the centralized government of the emperor. The second goal was to gain international recognition for Ethiopia as a sovereign, independent state.

During his rise to power, Menelik received from Italy the arms and ammunition he needed for his conquests. Though remaining loyal to Yohannis, he had tried occasionally to mediate between the emperor and the Italians. These facts led the Italians, in 1889, to send Count Pietro Antonelli to Menelik to conclude a treaty meant to facilitate Italian expansion inward from the coast and to establish a dominant Italian influence at Menelik's court. In the Treaty of Uccialli Menelik recognized not only Italy's occupation of Massawa but also Italy's right to a large portion of the highlands inland from it, including the town of Asmara.[3] The treaty was copied in both Amharic and Italian. According to the Italian text, in article 17 Menelik agreed (*consente*) to conduct all his foreign affairs through the medium of the Italian government. It was not Antonelli's purpose to create an Italian protectorate over Ethiopia. Nor did he intend to undermine the empire, as General Baldiserra's *politica periferica* (peripheral policy) was meant to do. But the result of his negotiations as expressed in the Italian text inspired Prime Minister Francesco Crispi to use, incorrectly

---

[3] No one knows why Menelik gave Italy the strategically and economically valuable rights to this part of the high plateau, which was closely tied to Ethiopia. Edward Ullendorff suggests, probably correctly, that Menelik agreed to an Italian occupation of this region because the threat of a proximate foe might make the rases of the north more willing to accept his protective leadership. E. Ullendorff, *The Ethiopians* (London, 1960), 92. For a text of the Treaty of Uccialli, see E. Hertslet, *The Map of Africa by Treaty*, 3rd ed. (London, 1909), II, 454–5.

and in bad faith, article 17 as the basis for formally proclaiming Ethiopia a protectorate of Italy.[4] Italy's claim to a dominant position in Ethiopia was accepted by the British. In 1891 British-Italian agreements designated practically all of Ethiopia, including Lake Tana and the western Ethiopian highlands, as an Italian sphere of influence.[5]

When Menelik discovered Italy's use of article 17 and its formulation in the Italian text, he protested at once to Rome. In this he was supported by the French who, as the main rival of the Italians in Ethiopia, resented any assertion of a special position for Italy. Gaining no satisfaction from Rome, in February 1893 Menelik denounced the Treaty of Uccialli and began to unite Ethiopians behind him to withstand Italy's reaction. The danger of Italian encroachment served Menelik's plan of centralization: the need for unity in the face of a foreign threat gave him the opportunity to subordinate the rases to his political direction. Since 1890 the Italians had moved gradually inland. They occupied the Hamasien plateau, including Asmara, and the lands down to the Mareb River, also taking control of the caravan routes to Massawa. After Menelik denounced the Treaty of Uccialli, the Italians, deciding upon war with Ethiopia, turned south toward Ethiopia proper and in so doing "launched themselves against the inner bastions of the Tigrean-Amharic polity," [6] against, in other words, the heart of traditional, "classical," Ethiopia. In their line of advance lay the holy city of Aksum, the spiritual center of Ethiopian civilization. The defense of this territory gave Menelik's campaign a crusading quality, and he mustered men in the name of Ethiopian nationalism. Italian hopes for disunity were not fulfilled — all the great chiefs fell into line behind the emperor. Italy, after all, was trying to destroy Ethiopia's political independence. Nor did any Ethiopian ras expect the Italians to give him part of the sovereignty Italy sought to take from Menelik.[7]

[4] For good discussions of this matter, see C. Giglio, "Article 17 of the Treaty of Uccialli," R. Caulk, trans., *Journal of African History*, 6:221–31 (1965); S. Rubenson, "The Protectorate Paragraph of the Wichale Treaty," *ibid.*, 5:243–83 (1964); C. Jesman, *The Russians in Ethiopia* (London, 1958), 68; C. Zaghi, ed., *Crispi e Menelich, nel diario inedito del conte Augusto Salimbeni* (Turin, 1961), 141–71.

[5] Hertslet, *The Map of Africa*, III, 948–50.

[6] D. Mathew, *Ethiopia, the Study of a Polity, 1540–1935* (London, 1947), 200.

[7] S. Rubenson, "Some Aspects on the Survival of Ethiopian Independence in the Period of the Scramble for Africa," *Historians in Tropical Africa*, Proceedings of the Leverhulme Inter-Collegiate History Conference, September 1960 (Salisbury, Southern Rhodesia, 1962), 263.

On 1 March 1896 the Italian army, prodded by the home government into an incautious advance,[8] met Menelik's troops at Aduwa, the old capital of Tigre. There an Ethiopian army of some 100,000 men routed the Italian force of 17,700 metropolitan and colonial troops, 10,596 of whom were Europeans. Italian casualties amounted to some 6,000 men killed, 2,000 wounded, and 2,000 taken prisoner.[9] For the Ethiopians, Aduwa was the greatest military victory in their history. For the Italians, Aduwa was the greatest military defeat incurred by any European nation at the hands of Africans in all of the nineteenth century.

The results of the battle were received with stunned dismay in Italy. The news of Aduwa shocked the adolescent Benito Mussolini, who said that the figures of "ten thousand [sic] dead and seventy-two cannon lost" hammered in his head for years afterwards.[10] There were severe political repercussions: "Confronted by a wave of national grief and indignation," Crispi resigned.[11] What remained for many Italians was a sense of humiliation, the "shameful scar," Gabriele D'Annunzio later called it. Revenge for Aduwa became a measure of Italian national potency.

> Every other European setback had led automatically to punitive expeditions, which if sometimes costly were always successful. In this case, the defeat of the Italians was followed by peace. This result had two effects: it gave the Abyssinians a new legend and a pride, which was to impede even military modernizations, while on the other hand it left to the Italians a humiliating memory. The defeat and its acceptance formed together a disaster which was not consistent with the record of Italy as a great power.[12]

[8] The Italian government was smarting over the recent defeat at Amba Alagi, and Crispi was staking his political life on a colonial victory. Crispi's telegram to General Baratieri, received on Christmas 1895, reads in part: "This is a military phthisis, not a war . . . We are ready for any sacrifice in order to save the honor of the army and the prestige of the monarchy." G. Berkeley, *The Campaign of Adowa and the Rise of Menelik* (London, 1902), 256.

[9] "In a single day, as many Italians lost their lives as in all the wars of the *risorgimento* put together." D. Mack Smith, *Italy, a Modern History* (Ann Arbor, 1959), 179–88.

[10] L. Fermi, *Mussolini* (Chicago, 1961), 349.

[11] The fate of Crispi might have given Mussolini pause for reflection. Crispi was led to imperial adventure and the need for sudden victory "by his love of the grandiose, by the vision of glory which he dreamed that military triumphs would bring upon himself and Italy . . . Grievous indeed were his last five years. His name, once associated with the glorious expedition of the thousand and the union of Sicily and Italy, was now sullied by the memory of a national disaster." B. Croce, *A History of Italy, 1871–1915*, C. Ady, trans. (Oxford, 1929), 193–4.

[12] Mathew, *Ethiopia*, 226. For an enlightening discussion of how the legend of

The victory served Menelik well. It instilled in Ethiopians a feeling of national pride and power that greatly facilitated the growth of the patriotic self-consciousness necessary to centralize and stabilize the national government. The period after Aduwa also opened a new era in Ethiopia's international relations. Rudinì, Crispi's successor, accepted the Treaty of Addis Ababa, recognizing Ethiopia under Menelik's leadership as an independent and sovereign state.[13] "The defeat of the Italians at Adowa put Ethiopia on the map of the world." [14]

In Europe the question of what country's influence was to predominate in Ethiopia was reopened. Toward the three limitrophe powers, still rivals among themselves, Menelik and his successors adopted a policy of playing one European ambition against another. By rapidly shifting their favors, they tried to achieve a balance of greed, to the benefit of Ethiopian independence. Each bordering power had its own interest in Ethiopia. The British were now aware of the importance to Egypt and the Sudan of the source of the Blue Nile, Lake Tana, and the Nile's tributary, the Atbara River, both under Ethiopia's territorial control. The Blue Nile is the source of the lower Nile's life-giving, silt-laden autumn floods. It has its source in Lake Tana and, like the Atbara, receives almost all its water from the Ethiopian highlands. Because of the rivers' vital importance to Egypt and the Anglo-Sudan, the British were determined to protect the freedom of their courses. The French for their part looked with care to the Addis Ababa–Djibouti railroad line, a monopoly concession they held by grant from Menelik and from which they expected great income and a good opportunity for influence.[15] The Italians,

---

Aduwa and Crispi was kept alive by discontented nationalists, see J. Thayer, *Italy and the Great War: Politics and Culture, 1870–1915* (Madison, 1964), 78, 206–7, 252.

[13] In this treaty, which abrogated the Treaty of Uccialli, Menelik did not press his overwhelming advantage. He left Eritrea in Italy's hands and confirmed the Italians in their possession of the high plateau up to the Mareb line they held before the war. Menelik was criticized in Ethiopia for this generosity, for it put Italy into a position to threaten Ethiopia. Why Menelik did this is uncertain. Most likely, as with Uccialli, he hoped to use the proximity of the Italians to encourage national unity.

[14] Rubenson, "Some Aspects on the Survival of Ethiopian Independence," 265.

[15] Indeed, before Fashoda, some Frenchmen had visions of this railroad as the first section of a great trunkline stretching from Djibouti to the Atlantic. Ethiopia's rulers used monopoly grants to give a specific country interests in Ethiopia. The wider the spread of the grants, the more difficult it would be for any single country to gain total control. The Ethiopians, however, underestimated the willingness of the Europeans to bargain among themselves.

never forgetting Aduwa, continued to assume that their colonial future lay, if anywhere, in expansion into and control over Ethiopia, the hinterland between Eritrea and their possessions on the Somali coast.

In 1906, to prepare for the eventuality of the death of the ailing Menelik and the anarchy expected to follow, Britain, France, and Italy, without consulting Ethiopia, concluded a treaty that defined their respective interests in the country and laid a guideline for any future colonial activity. The treaty's object was to prevent an unregulated scramble for Ethiopian spoils. For the first time Britain and France formally stated the extent of their interests: security for an unimpeded flow of the Nile sources for Britain and the inviolability of the railroad strip for France. The north, south, and east of Ethiopia were left as a potential Italian sphere of influence, all three European countries agreeing that the preservation of Eritrea and Italian Somaliland called for such an extention of Italy's power. Italy was further allotted the right to a "territorial connection" between its two colonies, this connection to run "to the west of Addis Ababa." [16] The three European governments agreed to safeguard each other's interests and, to prevent any unbridled action, decided that all military expeditions in Ethiopia had to be undertaken jointly. Unilateral intervention was ruled out. Despite this limitation, and notwithstanding Italy's ever present suspicion of the French, the treaty of 1906, coming only ten years after Aduwa, was an important diplomatic success for Italy. For the first time Britain and France limited and expressed their objectives in Ethiopia, and for the first time they recognized, and officially accepted, the paramount colonial importance of Ethiopia for Italy. The 1906 agreement, an Italian official wrote in 1932, constituted the "magna charta" of Italian aspirations in Ethiopia.[17]

[16] Hertslet, *The Map of Africa by Treaty*, II, 436–40. Alessandro Lessona later described Eritrea and Italian Somaliland as forming a bow which had to have a string, namely Ethiopia. A. Lessona, "L'Eritrea e la Somali nei fini dell'espansione," *Rassegna italiana*, 35:119 (September–October 1933).

[17] Guariglia, *Ricordi*, 764. H. G. Marcus, "A Preliminary History of the Tripartite Treaty of December 13, 1906," *Journal of Ethiopian Studies*, 2:21–40 (July 1964), fails to consider this side of the matter. The treaty has generally been viewed as a boon to Ethiopia. For example, E. Rouard de Card, *L'Ethiopie au point de vue du droit international* (Paris, 1928), 59–60, wrote that it "put an end to the rivalries which had troubled the Ethiopian empire and prejudiced its development." Menelik did choose to purchase safety at the price of modernization, and refused to allow any single foreign nation sufficient control for a massive introduction of European customs and equipment, but this European rivalry had secured Ethiopia's independence. Now that rivalry was formally ended, by the European powers themselves. It was clear that Italy was, and would be, the only

In the event, though, Ethiopia was spared any immediate threat of foreign domination, for World War I swept the powers of Europe into its vortex. This war came at an opportune time for Ethiopia: upon Menelik's death in 1913, the country was plunged into a state of disorder caused by the political incompetence of the new emperor, Lidj Iyasu, and by his conversion to Islam. Although article 3 of the treaty of 1906 pledged the powers to "observe a neutral attitude, abstaining from all intervention in the internal affairs of the country," the collapse of the central authority and the resurgence of the local power of the rases might have provided an excuse for intervention. This could have destroyed Ethiopia's independence, had not the European powers been otherwise involved.[18]

Civil war abated in 1916 with the deposition of Lidj Iyasu and the ascent to the throne of Queen Zawditu, Menelik's daughter, but the long and tedious process of centralization had to begin again. This time the intiative came from the regent and heir to the throne, Ras Tafari. Tafari started from a much weaker position than Menelik had, for he was young, untried, and without Menelik's large personal following and sources of wealth and military might. Tafari's progressive views were greatly resented and actively resisted by the conservative elements that dominated court, clergy, and country. Until his opponents died or were brought under control, Tafari could move only with the greatest caution. In 1928, after the failure of a palace coup,[19] Tafari proclaimed himself negus, the highest rank below emperor. He proceeded to strengthen his control over the regular imperial army and provided it with modern weapons and European

member of the trio with an interest in asserting its active control over the bulk of the country, and this interest, it appeared, now was recognized by France and Britain.

[18] An example of such an excuse is the Italian claim that in the upheaval following Menelik's death Ras Michael threatened Eritrea with a large force and Italy, in return, had to resort to extensive defensive measures. Another claim that might have provided an excuse for intervention was that the new emperor, by embracing Islam, became a coreligionist of the Turks, and Italy's conquest of Ethiopia could aid the war effort in Europe. See L. Villari, *Storia diplomatica del conflitto italo-etiopico* (Bologna, 1943), 30–1, and G. Fornari, "La Crisi italo-etiopica del 1914," *Rassegna italiana* 28:617–26 (December 1951), and 29:33–40 (January 1952).

[19] This coup is detailed in C. Zoli, *Cronache etiopiche* (Rome, 1930), 234–49. It appears that the revolt was stimulated by the fear that the Italian–Ethiopian treaty of 1928 would give Tafari the power he needed for undisputed predominance. The revolt was a last-ditch effort to topple the regent before he could consolidate his advantages.

instructors.[20] To gain control of the scattered soldiery of the realm, and to spread his power throughout the country, Tafari appointed members of his family to command the armed forces and gave his supporters governorships over potentially troublesome territories. In November 1930, following the death of the empress, Tafari was crowned emperor under his baptismal name, Haile Selassie I.

By the end of 1932, with the defeat by royal troops of an attempt by Gojam's powerful Ras Hailu to reinstate the former emperor, Lidj Iyasu, the centralization of the government was well advanced. The feudal rases were now being replaced as regional leaders by representatives of the emperor. The Ethiopian aristocracy, however, still remained a potent force, and the emperor could not ignore its reactionary sentiment in either domestic or foreign affairs. The aristocracy and the clergy were set against any change.[21] And centralization went only so far. It did not touch the body of tradition by which the people of Ethiopia governed their lives. Indifference to reform among an ignorant populace was a more formidable barrier to the development of a modern state than were the military threats of disgruntled chieftains.

The emperor, who genuinely desired the development of his country, sought to provide his government with some of the accoutrements of a progressive state. A parliament was proclaimed in 1931, but its purpose was to advance public education and to develop a source of legitimacy and support apart from the feudal aristocracy, not to create an alternative to the emperor's autocratic rule. To some extent, too, Haile Selassie's decrees were designed to make a favorable impression in Europe. Slavery was *the* social problem of Ethiopia, as seen from abroad. Its existence, usually exaggerated by foreigners in 1935, was a continual embarrassment to Ethiopia's supporters in the international community and a ready example of Ethiopia's backwardness for its detractors. Laws of 1924 and 1930 looked forward to the

[20] Two military missions were sent from Belgium for this purpose, one in 1930 and the second in 1933. *The Times* (London), 16 January 1930, 21 March 1933. Zoli estimated in 1930 that the imperial government then had at its disposal about half of the total fire power in the country. Zoli, *Cronache etiopiche*, 367.

[21] Haile Selassie was aware of the fate of Amanullah Khan, the reformist Emir of Afghanistan, whose rapid introduction of unpopular innovations in his country caused a conservative reaction that forced him to abdicate in January 1929. Haile Selassie was determined not to give this kind of encouragement to an aristocratic fronde. G. Garratt, "Abyssinia," *Journal of the (Royal) African Society*, 36:37 (January 1937). The clergy, who were also large slaveholders, comprised an estimated one fifth of the adult male population.

abolition of slavery, but a constitution issued in 1931 made no further mention of the subject. A few administrative reforms had some effect, particularly the rationalization of property laws. What was lacking for the success of social and political modernization was the machinery needed to implement the emperor's edicts and make them understood and obeyed throughout the land. The emperor, in his eagerness to centralize the government, important as this was in maintaining political independence, went to the extreme of having every detail of administration pass not only through his office, but through his very hands. His personal decision was needed for permission to purchase firewood outside the market of Addis Ababa, as well for the gravest matters of state policy. Before 1935 he even selected the mules for the army.[22] The emperor steadfastly refused to delegate authority, and he never developed the efficient, dedicated, and extended bureaucracy necessary to relieve congestion in the business of government and to bring about permanent reform. Perhaps, for modernization, what Haile Selassie needed was time, but time is what he was fated not to have. Just as he was completing the task of centralizing the government of his country, from Rome Mussolini was preparing for its conquest.

The first occasion on which Mussolini had to deal with Ethiopia came in 1923, less than a year after the Fascists' march on Rome. In 1923, seeking the protection afforded by the articles of the Covenant, Ethiopia applied for membership in the League of Nations. This was a farsighted move by Tafari, and it was undertaken with the sponsorship of France.[23] Mussolini realized that Italian colonial interests were clearly contrary to Ethiopia's admission,[24] for participation in the League's system of collective security would end Ethiopia's isolation and give to the country a perhaps irreversible guarantee of independence. Mussolini therefore decided to oppose Ethiopia's application.[25]

[22] M. Perham, *The Government of Ethiopia* (London, 1948), 79.

[23] From 1889 to 1935, despite the apparent French permissiveness in 1906, Italy correctly regarded France as its prime rival in Ethiopia. During the world war France had summarily turned down an Italian request for French Somaliland and the Djibouti–Addis Ababa railroad as payment to Italy under the compensation clause, article 13, of the Treaty of London of 1915.

[24] Italy, *I Documenti diplomatici italiani*, 7th ser., II (Rome, 1955), 109, 112, 115.

[25] Minister of Colonies Gaspare Colosimo had presented strong arguments against the seating of an Ethiopian delegate at the 1918 peace conference in Paris, basing his opposition on the argument that Ethiopia was uncivilized and in such a state of disorganization that no representative could be fairly said to

No sooner had he reached this decision than counterarguments were advanced to him by Italy's representative at Geneva, Antonio Salandra, and by Luigi Federzoni, then minister of colonies. Salandra pointed out that, since admission was voted by a two-thirds majority, Italian efforts to prevent the seating of Ethiopia would come to nothing and would only incur the opprobrium of the other member states and increase the enmity of the Ethiopians. In these circumstances he suggested that Italy instead should offer its endorsement. Federzoni thought that, despite Ethiopia's entry into the international community, Italy's special claim to influence could be preserved if Britain and France were encouraged to remain true to the words and spirit of the 1906 treaty.[26]

These practical arguments impressed Mussolini, although he never considered the question of Ethiopia's future a matter for general discussion or for organized interference from Geneva. In his view it was solely the concern of the three powers that bordered Ethiopia, among whom Italy had a paramount interest. Mussolini did not have long to dwell on the problem of what to do, however, for on 27 August 1923 the Italian members of an international boundary commission were slain on the island of Corfu; Mussolini's reaction, "immediata, violenta, intransigente,"[27] took his mind off Ethiopia for the next months. On 19 September Tafari telegraphed the Duce to ask about Italy's intentions toward Ethiopia's application. Mussolini decided to end the uncertainty and offered Italy's unequivocal support.[28] The British alone expressed reservations toward Ethiopia's qualifications. The British delegate objected that the central government of Ethiopia was too weak to constitute an effective governing force; hence, "on the basis of past performances," he expressed doubt that Ethiopia would be able to assume the commitments required by League membership.[29] But Ethiopia was judged worthy and was formally ad-

---

represent the populace. *I Documenti diplomatici italiani*, 6th ser., I (Rome, 1955), 143-5. Mussolini's opposition at this stage, in line with Colosimo's opposition earlier, makes nonsense out of later Italian claims that Italy deserved the credit given France for bringing Ethiopia into the League. For such a claim, see P. Orsini di Camerota d'Agostino, *L'Italia nella politica africana* (Bologna, 1928), 164-6.

[26] *I Documenti diplomatici italiani*, 7th ser., II, 120, 122.

[27] Guariglia, *Ricordi*, 28.

[28] *I Documenti diplomatici italiani*, 7th ser., II, 256.

[29] League of Nations, *Official Journal*, Special Supplement No. 19, Records of the Fourth Assembly, Minutes of the Sixth Committee, Political Questions (Geneva, 1923), 15.

mitted to the society of nations by the unanimous vote of the assembly on 28 September 1923.

But Ethiopia did not enter scot-free. First the Ethiopian representative was required to sign three declarations, two dealing with the arms trade: "Abyssinia declares herself ready now and hereafter to furnish the Council with any information which it may require, and to take into consideration any recommendations which the Council may make with regard to the fulfillment of these obligations, in which she recognizes that the League of Nations is concerned." [30] The hope in Geneva was that, with the League's help, the government of Ethiopia could modernize the country — particularly, abolish slavery — and so arrive more swiftly and successfully at the level of social development expected of League members.[31] Still, in the meantime, Ethiopia had to be considered a member in good standing, and, unless it was formally condemned and expelled for breaking its obligations, Ethiopia had a right to all the privileges of full League membership.

In the first decade of his rule, Mussolini never expressed an interest in extending Italian influence in Ethiopia. The people of Italy, dispirited by a series of defeats in battle in World War I and weary of futile exertions, were not prepared to support active colonialism in east Africa. Mussolini instead turned his attention to establishing his own power, to consolidating his regime, to reviving the morale of Italians, and to asserting Italy's position in European affairs.

Within the foreign ministry and the ministry of colonies, however, interest in Ethiopia remained alive. An opportunity for extending Italian control over east Africa was presented by the terms of the 1915 Treaty of London. According to article 13, "If the other Powers [Britain and France] should increase their African colonies at Germany's expense, an appropriate agreement shall be made to secure to Italy some corresponding and equitable compensation, and that specifically in the regulation in her favour of the boundary questions between colonies of Eritrea, Somaliland and Libya and the contiguous French and English colonies." In 1919 Minister of Colonies Gaspare Colosimo had drawn up a list of claims he hoped would be granted Italy in accordance with the terms of article 13 and as part of the general

---

[30] League, *Official Journal*, Special Supplement No. 19 (1923), 125.
[31] For a critical discussion of how well Haile Selassie fulfilled his obligations, see Perham, *The Government of Ethiopia*, 217–36. Ethiopia's claim to international recognition without qualification is asserted in Rouard de Card, *L'Ethiopie au point de vue du droit international*, 98.

peace settlement. Colosimo wanted, in the words of Robert Hess, to "turn back the clock to pre-Adowa times." [32] He hoped to use the readjustments of power in Europe, and in Ethiopia after Menelik's death, to establish Italian hegemoney over the horn of Africa. With regard to this area, Colosimo's program envisioned the annulment of the tripartite treaty of 1906, thereby giving Italy a free hand in Ethiopia, the cession of French Somaliland and the Djibouti–Addis Ababa railroad by France to Italy, the cession of British Somaliland and Jubaland by Britain, the establishment of a railroad west of Addis Ababa from Eritrea to Italian Somaliland, and the transfer to Italy of control of Ethiopia's central bank.[33]

V. E. Orlando, the prime minister, himself absorbed by the "passione adriatica" and burdened by a debilitating sense of his own, and Italy's, weak position at the end of the war, did not press Colosimo's comprehensive plan with any determination when the Allies met at Paris to settle the peace. Against Britain, Italy's claims eventually boiled down to Kassala and Jubaland.[34] The British refused to part with Kassala. This important district west of Eritrea and north of Ethiopia was in a fertile area of the Anglo-Egyptian Sudan and too close to the Atbara River for the British to want to deliver it into foreign hands. The matter of Jubaland was left unsettled. From France Italy asked for French Somaliland and the Djibouti-Addis Ababa railroad. But France had already turned down these bold requests when they were first made in 1915, and a few minor border modifications

[32] R. Hess, "Italy and Africa: Colonial Ambitions in the First World War," *Journal of African History*, 4:108 (1963). Recent investigations have disproved the traditional view that there were no official Italian colonial claims.

[33] *I Documenti diplomatici italiani*, 7th ser., I, 455–7. Significantly, Colosimo considered that compensation to Italy under the Treaty of London was independent of claims on the mandate system. F. Curato, *La Conferenza della pace* (Milan, 1942), II, 447–52.

[34] Lloyd George claimed he came to the peace conference prepared to concede British Somaliland to Italy, if the French made similar concessions, presumably Obock-Djibouti. D. Lloyd George, *Memoirs of the Peace Conference* (New Haven, 1939), II, 583. But even apart from France's unwillingness to do this, Lloyd George ran into insurmountable opposition from his own colleagues. The Admiralty refused to give up any English African colonies (*ibid.*, I, 70), and Alfred Milner feared for the route to India, the Nile waters, and the cotton industry of the Sudan if Italy should gain complete control of the African horn. "If we give up Somaliland," wrote Milner on 16 May 1919, "we give up the only lever we have got for ensuring the protection of those interests when the Italians proceed to penetrate Abyssinia, as they certainly will do, when they have got possession of all her accesses to the sea." *Ibid.*, II, 584–5.

on the Tunisian frontier and some concessions for Italian schooling in Tunisia were all Italy could get from France at this time.[35]

Italian efforts to capitalize on the colonial clauses of the treaty of 1915 came to nothing at Paris. Italy was left holding an empty bag. Without consulting the Italians, the British and French carved up the old German empire into "mandates" for themselves. Although H. Stuart Hughes is correct in claiming that the basic significance of the peace conference was that it "left the whole nationalist and conservative sector of Italian public opinion the conviction that their country had been swindled of the rewards of victory," and that "this unhappy victory was to overshadow the next two decades of Italian foreign policy," [36] it is important to remember that outside the colonial ministry official Italian attention was not, in 1919, focused with any intensity on the fortunes of Italy's east African colonies. During the world war and its aftermath, the government, interested only in Europe, left these colonies to themselves.

One further overture, concerning Ethiopia directly, was made to Britain. In November 1919 the Italian government, having been unable to acquire a clear right to Ethiopia through the Treaty of London, attempted to activate the advantages held out to Italy by the prewar treaty of 1906. The Italians offered to trade their support for any British effort to build a dam on Lake Tana if Britain would support at the Ethiopian court the Italian claim for a north-south railroad running to the west of Addis Ababa.[37] Such a "territorial connection" between Italy's two coastal colonies would allow Italy to establish a large degree of control over the economically and politically valuable heartland of Ethiopia. By going west of the capital, the Italian line would miss the French-owned railroad which followed the Awash Valley in the east and which then gave Ethiopia its only convenient contact with the coast. Contrary to the spirit if not the letter of the 1906 accord, Italy did not inform France of its offer to Britain. The British, no doubt waiting for the unsettled conditions prevalent in both Italy and Ethiopia in 1919 to become stabilized, did not reply

[35] See M. Toscano, *Francia ed Italia di fronte al problema di Gibuti* (Florence, 1939); M. Toscano, *Il Patto di Londra* (Bologna, 1934), 142–3; Guariglia, *Ricordi*, 765.

[36] H. Stuart Hughes, "The Early Diplomacy of Italian Fascism, 1922–1932," in G. Craig and F. Gilbert, eds., *The Diplomats, 1919–1939* (Princeton, 1953), 212.

[37] League of Nations, *Official Journal, 1926* (Geneva, 1926), 1519.

to the Italian overture and the matter was dropped.[38] Seeing no threat from Ethiopia and no reason at the time to curry Italian favor, the British followed their usual practice of ignoring Italian demands until they served some British purpose.

Three years later, having nothing to hope for from the French and not wanting the 1906 agreement to die of neglect, the Italian ministry of foreign affairs instructed Raffaele Guariglia again to approach London in search of reassurance for Italy's claim to a large sphere of influence in Ethiopia. Nothing came of this step, and the British continued to remain silent on the Italian offer of 1919.[39] The Italians now took a more independent line. The governor of Eritrea, Iacopo Gasparini, began a policy of wooing the northern Ethiopian chieftains. This was a return to General Baldissera's pre-Aduwa "peripheral policy," the plan of divide and conquer, and it was undertaken just as Ras Tafari was starting his efforts to centralize the government of Ethiopia.

In 1923 Ethiopia was admitted to the League. The next year Ramsay MacDonald's Labour government agreed to the transfer of Jubaland to Italy, thereby liquidating, however late and unsatisfactorily, Italy's colonial claim on Britain under the 1915 Treaty of London. Although it was less than desired, Jubaland was not a bad acquisition for Italy. Kismayu is the true port of the southern part of Italian Somaliland, and the only spot along the thousand miles between Cape Guardafui and the Juba River where ships can load and unload safely throughout the year.[40] In addition to the port, Italy gained the banks of the Juba River for 300 miles inland, an important means for extending Italian influence into the interior.

That Italy looked to Britain as an ally in the three-cornered rivalry

---

[38] The British did not definitely refuse to consider the Italian proposal, but simply created the conditions for postponement. A. de La Pradelle, *Le Conflit italo-éthiopien* (Paris, 1936), 112. A later official explanation was that the Italian "offer was not entertained at the time, chiefly owing to the strong objection felt to the idea of allowing a foreign Power to establish any sort of control over the headwaters of rivers so vital to the prosperity and even the existence of Egypt and the Sudan." League, *Official Journal, 1926*, 1519.

[39] Guariglia, *Ricordi*, 43. There is some evidence to indicate that a reason for British silence is that just at this time the British government was offering Ethiopia the port of Zeila in return for a concession on the Tana waters. If true, this would mean that Britain sought to gain this advantage without Italian help. Ethiopia turned down the British offer. See M. Rava, "L'Inghilterra e l'Etiopia, date e fatti," *Nuova antologia*, 303:76 (1 September 1935).

[40] M. Macartney and P. Cremona, *Italy's Foreign and Colonial Policy, 1914–1937* (London, 1938), 72.

for influence in Ethiopia is a reflection of the friendly state of British-Italian relations. Mussolini and the career diplomats in the foreign ministry also realized that Italy, at least for the present, had to keep on good terms with the country that controlled both outlets to the Mediterranean Sea. There was the shock of the Corfu incident, not to mention what seemed to Mussolini to be Britain's dog-in-the-manger attitude over the Mediterranean.[41] But during the first dozen years of the Fascist regime, "Anglo-Italian relations were marked by the utmost cordiality. At no other period since Italy had ceased to be the mere client of Great Britain were the policies of the countries marked by such general harmony and close co-operation." [42]

In December 1924 the council of the League of Nations met in Rome, and the British foreign minister, Austen Chamberlain, took the occasion to have a series of talks with Mussolini. In one of these discussions, evidently distressed by a British note of 1923 which claimed that the 1906 agreement was no longer valid,[43] Mussolini brought up the subject of Ethiopia and the respective interests of Britain and Italy. The talk appears to have been informal, an exploratory conversation of the sort Guariglia had fruitlessly undertaken two years before in London.[44] This time, however, the British were ready to listen, for an issue was at hand on which they desired Italy's support. The peace treaty with Turkey left unresolved the question of who owned the zone of Mosul. The British wanted the Turks to recognize the British mandate of Iraq, and this the Turks did not want to do.[45] To support Britain's effort in forthcoming negotiations to settle the matter, the British government wanted Italy to exercise a discreet military pressure on Turkey. The British would then take up the Italian claims of 1919 concerning a sphere of influence in western Ethiopia.[46]

---

[41] G. Christopoulos, *La Politique extérieure de l'Italie fasciste* (Paris, 1936), 94.

[42] Macartney and Cremona, *Italy's Foreign and Colonial Policy*, 174.

[43] Villari, *Storia diplomatica del conflitto italo-etiopico*, 34. Curzon's note was evidently based on the assumption that the agreement lapsed with the entry of Ethiopia into the League. The Italians rejected any unilateral repudiation of the treaty.

[44] The topics listed on the agenda were the possibility of revising the 1906 treaty, the question of importing arms to Ethiopia, and a clarification of the 1906 accord on Lake Tana. *I Documenti diplomatici italiani*, 7th ser., III, 364-5.

[45] For their reasons, see G. Gathorne-Hardy, *A Short History of International Affairs, 1920-1939*, 4th ed. (London, 1950), 122-3.

[46] P. Quaroni, "Le Diplomate italien," in K. Braunias and G. Stourzh, eds., *Diplomatie unserer Zeit* (Graz, 1959), 191-2.

It is difficult to know whether or not a bargain was struck along these lines. But Italy did exercise a helpful pressure on the Turks, and in return, in gratitude or for whatever reason, in the summer of 1925 there arrived at Rome a British note taking up the dormant Italian proposal for Ethiopia.[47] Accord was swiftly reached: "in the event of His Majesty's Government, with the valued assistance of the Italian Government, obtaining from the Abyssinian Government the desired concession on Lake Tsana, they [the British] will also recognise an exclusive Italian economic influence in the west of Abyssinia and in the whole of the territory crossed by the [Eritrea-Somaliland] railway [to be built west of Addis Ababa]."[48] This bilateral agreement was deemed not to conflict with the treaty of 1906, even though it was made without consulting France. It also said nothing of Ethiopia's independence being maintained, recognized large areas of exclusive privilege, and gave an order of precedence to the attainment of particular European goals. After a considerable delay, copies of the agreement were sent to the governments of France and Ethiopia.

French reaction was surprisingly subdued.[49] The French held that the tripartite treaty of 1906 gave each of the signatories equal rights to Ethiopian territory, and that this agreement could be modified only with the consent of all three parties. But, perhaps sensing that the British-Italian agreement would meet opposition elsewhere, the French refrained from the outspoken criticism they could have made.[50]

[47] The question of why the British note came at this time is not clear. Did the British act on their own initiative or as part of a prearranged agreement? Guariglia saw the British note as arriving "like a lightening-bolt from a clear sky" (*Ricordi*, 44), but the Italian foreign ministry, or some of its officials, might not have been informed of any Chamberlain-Mussolini agreement. Lending credence to the *quid pro quo* explanation is the fact that the question of establishing a common line of conduct toward Turkey appears in the outline of subjects discussed by Chamberlain and Mussolini at their December 1924 meeting. It does appear that, however much it was encouraged by a more general British-Italian rapprochement at this time, the British move was triggered by the Mosul negotiations.

[48] The agreement was concluded in the summer of 1925 and a formal exchange of letters took place in December between Mussolini and the British ambassador in Rome, Ronald Graham. League, *Official Journal, 1926*, 1519–22. It may be worth noting that this exchange took place on 14 and 20 December 1925; on the 16th the League council gave Mosul to Iraq along the favorable "Brussels line." The British and Italian ministers in Addis Ababa presented the terms of the agreement to the Ethiopian government on 9 June 1926. Four days before, on 5 June, the Treaty of Amhara formally ceded Mosul to Iraq.

[49] See, e.g., *I Documenti diplomatici italiani*, 7th ser., IV (1962), 258–9, 274–5, 371, 435.

[50] A. Toynbee, *Survey of International Affairs, 1929* (London, 1930), 223. Briand

It was the Ethiopian government that found its tongue. On 15 June 1926 Tafari addressed identical notes to Britain and Italy, protesting their apparent intention to infringe on Ethiopia's independence and best interests. To the British Tafari added a further complaint: Ethiopia would "never have suspected that the British Government would come to an agreement with another regarding the lake." [51] Four days later, on 19 June, Tafari took his case to the League of Nations.

> We have been profoundly moved by the conclusion of this agreement concluded without our being consulted or informed . . . [At the time of] our admission to the League of Nations we were told that all nations were to be on a footing of equality within the League, and that their independence was to be universally respected . . . We were not told that certain Members of the League might make a separate agreement to impose their views on another Member . . .

Lest the members of the League ignore the danger facing Ethiopia or forget Ethiopia's determination to resist encroachments, Tafari added:

> The people of Abyssinia are anxious to do right, and we have every intention of guiding them along the path of improvement and progress; but throughout their history they have seldom met with foreigners who did not desire to possess themselves of Abyssinian territory and to destroy their independence. With God's help, and thanks to the courage of our soldiers, we have always, come what might, stood proud and free upon our native mountains.[52]

Response to Ethiopia's complaint was soon in coming. The British on 3 August 1926, and the Italians on the 7th, sent notes to the secretary-general of the League protesting that neither country had any aggressive designs on Ethiopia. Italy's note that that the matter of "an exclusive sphere of Italian economic influence" constituted

> an agreement which is binding solely on the Italian and British Governments; it cannot detract from the right of the Abyssinian Government to take such decisions as it may think fit or limit the

---

tried to dampen Italian hopes for exclusive privileges by stating that the agreement did not alter the open-door policy in economic matters. R. Woolbert, "Italy in Abyssinia," *Foreign Affairs*, 13:506 (April 1935). The Germans, incidentally, believed that the agreement was meant to exclude them from Ethiopia. *I Documenti diplomatici italiani*, 7th ser., IV, 254.

[51] League, *Official Journal, 1926*, 1520.

[52] League, *Official Journal, 1926*, 1517. Two lines of the Ethiopian national anthem, in the then current French translation, read: "Tes monts seront tes défenseurs, / Ne crains donc pas les agresseurs," or, in the more prosaic present English rendering, "Thy mountains a fortress, / Fear not Thine enemies!"

possible action of third parties. It is a guarantee of an economic nature obtained for Italian enterprises as against British enterprises in order to avoid competition which might imperil the success of these enterprises.[53]

The two countries' representatives in Addis Ababa assured Tafari of their governments' desire for friendly relations with Ethiopia.[54] For the Ethiopians, Tafari's appeal to the League seemed to demonstrate in a striking way how a weak state could use the international organization as protection against the machinations of the great powers.[55]

In Italy the agreement of 1925 reopened the Ethiopian question. Britain's formal recognition of Italy's "exclusive" economic interest in western Ethiopia put virtually the entire country in Italy's sphere of influence.[56] There was, however, no consensus in Rome on how to take advantage of this opportunity. Until 1934 Mussolini was preoccupied with events in Europe. Lacking the resolute leadership of the Duce, lacking indeed a clear definition of purpose in Ethiopia, weakened by departmental rivalries and indecision, the Italian government had no long-range plans for a consistent Ethiopian policy. The career officials in the foreign ministry were certain of only one fact: the fate of Ethiopia would be settled in Europe. Their diplomatic goal was "to repeat the operation which [Italy] had followed at the time of the occupation of Tripolitania: a series of accords by means of which the principal powers accorded to [Italy] the right of going there, which would be done, at a favorable moment, with the most limited military jar." [57] For the present, in its dealings with the Ethiopian government, Italy vacillated between two policies — friendly cooperation and calculated subversion. The first course was urged on

[53] League, *Official Journal, 1926*, 1523–5.

[54] See, e.g., *I Documenti diplomatici italiani*, 7th ser., IV, 137, 190, 260, 268.

[55] Tafari was opposed in his plan to appeal to the League by the conservative minister of war, Fitaurari Hapte Gorghis, who feared that such a step would antagonize the Italians. *I Documenti diplomatici italiani*, 7th ser., IV, 256, 259. Hapte Gorghis died in 1926, and with his death Tafari's strongest opponent within the Ethiopian government passed away. Tafari's appeal to the League did in fact annoy the Italians, and the government postponed a proposed visit to Ethiopia by the Duke of the Abruzzi. *Ibid.*, 313.

[56] In an interview with the *Petit Journal* of Paris on 29 September 1935, Mussolini reportedly said: "After all, England just recently considered Abyssinian independence as absurd. In 1925 Sir Ronald Graham and I signed an accord which practically partitioned Abyssinia." Quoted in G. Salvemini, *Mussolini diplomatico, 1922–1932* (Bari, 1952), 113. This quotation is not found in B. Mussolini, *Opera omnia di Benito Mussolini*, E. and D. Susmel, eds., 36 vols. (Florence: Casa Editrice la Fenice, 1951–1963).

[57] Quaroni, "Le Diplomate italien," 192.

the foreign ministry by Giuliano Cora, minister to Addis Ababa since 1926, a patient, optimistic diplomat and an old friend of Tafari's. Cora believed, in the tradition of Antonelli, that Italy's best interest lay in the development of a strong and united Ethiopia. If Italy supported the regent's efforts to modernize his country, Italy could gain the political influence in Addis Ababa then held by France. Tafari, Cora thought, would repay Italy's friendship with economic concessions, thus enabling Italy to undertake the peaceful penetration and development of Ethiopia. Cora saw no long-term profit for Italy in intriguing with the undisciplined rases against the central government, no advantage in promoting instability and uncertainty throughout the country.[58]

The argument for this last course was that Italy might be able to use the internal confusion of the kingdom to exert pressures on individual rases and thereby carve out areas of Italian influence entirely apart from the control of the central government. This had been the policy of General Baldissera and Gasparini, the peripheral policy. Its new exponent was Corrado Zoli, made governor of Eritrea in 1928 and an impulsive, intolerant, and shortsighted man — a good Fascist. Zoli, in his advice to Luigi Federzoni, head of the ministry of colonies, called for the assertion of Fascist "prestige" in east Africa by displays of armed strength and by the use of threats to cause individual rases to desert the central government and throw in their lot with Italy.[59]

Now, if the British would actively support the establishment of Italian influence in the west of Ethiopia, Italy might find it advantageous to follow a peripheral policy, hoping to benefit from the disorganization of the empire to increase its share of Ethiopian spoils. But, unexpectedly, in November 1927 the Ethiopian government gave an American company permission to survey for the establishment of a dam on Lake Tana,[60] and this appeared to eliminate the condition

[58] See Cora's memorandum of April 1927, published by G. Vedovato, *Gli Accordi italo-etiopici dell'agosto 1928* (Florence, 1956), 59–66. The cooperative "policy of Antonelli" received considerable support in writings of the 1920s. See, e.g., Agostino Orsini di Camerota, *L'Italia nella politica africana*, 33, a book published in 1928.

[59] See Zoli's letter to Federzoni of 19 July 1928, printed in Vedovato, *Gli Accordi italo-etiopici*, 140–56.

[60] See *The Times* (London), 4 November 1927. This permission, accorded the J. G. White Engineering Corporation of New York, was an obvious counter to British ambition as expressed in the British-Italian agreement of 1925. It was in keeping with Ethiopia's effort to involve as many countries as possible with an interest in maintaining the independence of the country.

of British support as defined in the accord of 1925. The Italian government thereupon turned to what appeared to be a policy of good will toward the Ethiopian government. Cora was encouraged to engage in amicable negotiations with the regent, and on 2 August 1928 Italy and Ethiopia signed a twenty-year treaty of "Friendship and Arbitration." [61]

But despite the hard work and honorable intentions of Cora, the appearance of détente was illusory. The purpose of the Italian government was to expedite the economic and political penetration of Ethiopia. Article 3 of the treaty of 1928 pledged each country to increase its trade with the other. Cora called this article the "fulcrum" of the treaty.[62] An economic convention was signed providing for the construction of a road from Dessye to Assab, each nation undertaking to build the stretch that passed through its territory. About 50 miles of the proposed route were in Eritrea; the remaining 430 miles were in Ethiopia. The Ethiopians were also to be given a lease of land for a wharf and a free zone at Assab. The economic convention was doomed to failure. Even apart from political considerations, it was difficult to imagine that the Ethiopians could have, without foreign aid, the technical capacity and economic resources to construct their portion of the road.[63] The conflict of policies between Cora and Zoli flared out, and Zoli, backed by the new minister of colonies, Emilio De Bono, used his position as governor of Eritrea to obstruct the project at every turn.[64] Cora's own superiors in the foreign ministry failed to support his efforts to make the project successful. An important member of the foreign ministry suggested that Ethiopia's failure to fulfill the terms of the agreement would give Italy "a certain basis for warlike action." The value of the road project, he noted, was its "utility in a negative sense." That is, it created an issue filled with "material for discussion and political action." Moreover, Italian engineers and explorers considered a Dessye-Assab road impractical. Italy's real interest lay in the north and in the west, and the Italian government, in the guise of a private firm, began pressuring the Ethiopian government for a road-building concession on a route running from Gondar to the Takkaze above

[61] Vedovato, *Gli Accordi italo-etiopici*, 102–5.

[62] G. Cora, "Il Trattato italo-etiopico del 1928," *Rivista di studi politici internazionali*, 15:214 (April–June 1948).

[63] Road building in Ethiopia was no small job, as the Italians later discovered. See F. Quaranta, *Ethiopia: An Empire in the Making* (London, 1939), 77.

[64] The fascinating story of this conflict is related in Vedovato, *Gli Accordi italo-etiopici*, 198–204.

Lake Tana. But Tafari held firm against this Italian attempt to penetrate the region.[65]

Cora's position in Addis Ababa soon became untenable, for the government in Rome began to withdraw its support from Tafari and to encourage his enemies. At the end of 1929 the Italian government turned down a plea from the regent for aid against insurgent rases — to whom Italy was again making overtures — and it was France that gave Tafari help.[66] Italy's excuse was that Tafari had a limited political future.[67] At the end of 1930 Cora was removed from his post, and his efforts to establish a policy of rational, peaceful collaboration for mutual benefit to both countries came to an end.[68]

During the years 1930–1933, official Italian interest in Ethiopia waned. There was no sense of common purpose among the ministries in Rome, and as a result no coherent policy was created for dealing with Ethiopia. Minister De Bono failed to get the Duce's approval for any program of development, and in the face of Mussolini's indifference the colonial ministry neglected the east African colonies. Italian interests in Eritrea and Italian Somaliland drifted into decay.[69] Only in the foreign ministry was any thought given to the possibility of future Italian action in east Africa. Raffaele Guariglia, who was political director for Europe, the Near East, and Africa and a close adviser to Minister of Foreign Affairs Dino Grandi during these years, has given us a glimpse of how the Ethiopian question was viewed from the Palazzo Chigi, home of the Italian foreign ministry, before Mussolini's purge of the career diplomats in the summer of 1932.

[65] Guariglia, *Ricordi*, 56, 767–8; La Pradelle, *Le Conflit italo-éthiopien*, 141.

[66] The Italians supported Tafari at the time of the palace revolt following the conclusion of the treaty of 1928 and helped to establish him on the throne. Zoli, *Cronache etiopiche*, 248n. Before stopping shipment in 1930, the Italians sent Tafari arms and ammunition on credit worth 1.9 million lire. League of Nations, *Official Journal, 1935* (Geneva, 1935), 1388.

[67] Vedovato, *Gli Accordi italo-etiopici*, 210.

[68] See Cora, "Il Trattato italo-etiopico del 1928," 217–33.

[69] For an example of the lack of any unified colonial policy, or even any general concern, see Guariglia, *Ricordi*, 142–3. The Palazzo Chigi, concerned for political reasons with the "weakness and inferiority" of Eritrea, which in 1931 had only "two or three" airplanes, asked the air ministry to send out some additional units. This request was turned down with the comment that, if any planes were sent to Eritrea, funds for them would have to come out of the budget of the foreign ministry. Things were at such a pass that an Ethiopian aircraft was used to transport the body of an Eritrean religious leader who had died in Addis Ababa, "with what increase to Italian prestige it is easy to imagine."

For reasons of history, geography, and political opportunity, Guari-glia observed, Ethiopia was the only region available to Italy in Africa for fresh colonial expansion.[70] Guariglia thought that Ethiopia might be of some economic importance to Italy as a source of raw materials, and that it might become valuable in absorbing Italian emigrants. He imagined the possible development of a native army there as well. In the event that the Italian government decided to use Ethiopia in its effort to become a major colonial power in east Africa, Guariglia presented what he believed to be the most successful formula for achieving this. To win the greatest amount of international prestige, Italy should gain its colonial empire by itself. Furthermore, Ethiopia should be mastered not by gradual economic or political penetration, but by military conquest, by an independent military campaign "di grande stile.[71] By the sacrifice of blood and treasure, Guariglia hoped a close bond would be created between the Italian homeland and its new empire. Before Italy embarked on its preparations for invasion, however, Guariglia warned that Italy must first gain prior approval from Britain and France. No east African empire could be established or maintained in the face of active British opposition, and no colonial hold-ing was worth the price of Italy's alienation in Europe. The best way to avoid such disasters, and the best way to assure Italy's success, was to come to a clear and comprehensive agreement with the two political leaders of Europe. The Tripolitanian War of 1911–12 had been preceded by years of diplomatic preparation and, as a result, was won for Italy almost before it was begun. This was the example Guariglia held up for Italian diplomacy, and it had great merit. Britain and France controlled the League of Nations, and only they could minimize the disturbing effects in Europe of a war against Ethiopia. British and French interests in east Africa would have to be guaranteed protection, and Italy's extreme vulnerability along its extended line of communica-tion would have to be safeguarded by diplomatic agreement. The sea route to east Africa, through the Suez Canal, stretched some 2,100

[70] The long struggle to control the native populations of Tripolitania and Cyrenaica in north Africa ended with the occupation of the oasis of Kufra in January 1931 and the suppression of the rebellious Senussi by General Rodolfo Graziani a year later. The two colonies were fused into a single unit, Libya, in 1934. To that date, however, in the absence of strong governmental encourage-ment and aid, few Italians had been willing to emigrate there.

[71] The career diplomats of the Italian foreign ministry were not averse to an aggressive Fascist foreign policy, for they saw its value in asserting Italy's position in international affairs. See Hughes, "The Early Diplomacy of Italian Fascism," 226-7; D. Varè, *The Two Impostors* (London, 1949), 116.

miles from Naples to Massawa and some 3,700 miles from Naples to Mogadishu. It was controlled by the British all the way. The Italian general staff also feared that an African campaign would weaken Italian forces on guard in the Alps.[72] Better relations with France were a necessity both for gaining French permission to act in Ethiopia and for ensuring the stability of Europe during a period of conquest. To compensate France, Guariglia thought that Italy might have to give up, temporarily, its "sentimental" claims in Tunisia. Italy might also offer France an "implicit guarantee" to oppose any attempt by a rearmed Germany to seek hegemony in Europe.[73] What the professionals in the Italian foreign office hoped to do, in other words, was to make "the Abyssinian enterprise an episode rather than a new departure," and to prevent "a development which would constitute a definite and final break with the traditional system of Italian foreign policy."[74]

On leaving the foreign ministry in the summer of 1932, Guariglia warned that indecisiveness of purpose and feebleness of action were destroying Italian prestige in east Africa. He called for a return to the policies of Baldissera, Gasparini, and Zoli. Guariglia noted that Ethiopia was no longer a weak, decentralized state but rather, under Haile Selassie, an armed and unified nation. As such, he claimed, Ethiopia presented a new and potent danger to Italy's east African possessions. To counter this threat Italy must take a strong military and political stand on the Ethiopian frontier. Further, this display of firmness and power, combined with a renewal of the peripheral policy, would so impress the "oriental mentality" of the border chiefs that in the event of an Italian invasion they would turn to cooperation with Italy against the central government.[75]

Efforts were now initiated to infiltrate Ethiopia. To the Italian legation in Addis Ababa and the consulate in Diredawa there were added, in 1932, four new consulates on the northern and western parts of the high plateau, at Gondar, Aduwa, Debra Markos, and Dessye. The Ethiopians were rightly suspicious of this move, for there were no Italian traders or settlers in these areas and hence no need for con-

---

[72] E. De Bono, *Anno XIIII, The Conquest of an Empire*, B. Miall, trans. (London, 1937), 11.

[73] For Guariglia's opinions on the Ethiopian question, including his important memorandum written in August 1932, see *Ricordi*, 141–73, 763–73.

[74] F. Gilbert, "Ciano and His Ambassadors," in Craig and Gilbert, eds., *The Diplomats, 1919–1939*, 513–72.

[75] Guariglia, *Ricordi*, 769–72.

sulates. In June 1932 an Italian army colonel, Alfredo Peluso, formerly commander of the army corps at Massawa, was accidentally killed on the shore of Lake Tana. Peluso had been acting as a political agent of the Italian government, and his activities in the two previous years in western Ethiopia had been such as to cause concern among the British, who wanted to keep the area around Lake Tana free from Italian control.[76]

By what authority this political subversion was begun is not clear. Mussolini probably knew of the activity and encouraged it. It did indeed represent a quickening of Italian interest in Ethiopia, and alarmed the Ethiopians accordingly. But still it was not part of a defined policy whose purpose was known throughout the government. Whatever Mussolini's own thoughts or plans were at this time, the policies of the Italian ministries, despite Guariglia's warnings and advice, remained as vague and uncertain as ever. Up to 1934 the ministries had accomplished nothing to advance significantly Italy's position in Ethiopia. As of July 1934, according to Mussolini's "head of cabinet" in the foreign ministry, a systematic application of the peripheral policy had not even begun.[77] No single program of action was devised until Mussolini himself manifested an interest in Ethiopia, and took complete and forceful command of the formulation and execution of Italian colonial policy in east Africa.

[76] La Pradelle, *Le Conflit italo-éthiopien*, 150-1 609-10. Villari represents Peluso as a simple man of commerce. Villari, *Storia diplomatica*, 43.

[77] P. Aloisi, *Journal, 25 juillet 1932—14 juin 1936*, M. Vaussard, trans. (Paris, 1957), 201 (permission to quote granted by Librairie Plon). Aloisi was "head of cabinet" in the Italian foreign ministry and led the Italian delegation to the League during the Ethiopian affair.

Chapter 2

Mussolini Turns to Ethiopia, 1934

In the early 1930s, now in control of the political apparatus of the nation, Mussolini turned his attention to the development of Italian prestige abroad and the assertion of Fascist Italy's claim to a place among the great powers of Europe. Until 1934 Mussolini's major ambition was to create a "grande politica europea" in which Italy, and hence the Duce, would become a more active participant in the determination of European affairs.

Mussolini sought to prove Fascism by way of Italy's ability to act autonomously as a major power. He refused to conduct foreign policy through the League of Nations. Fascism rejected the principle of the equality of nations, and Mussolini viewed the League as an unnatural and unmanageable institution wherein petty states were given an influence entirely incommensurate with their actual importance. This exaggerated influence of the lesser states, Mussolini feared, increased the possibility of discord among the greater powers.[1] The League's insistence on unanimity, and the rigid formulas and overriding morality of the Covenant, hindered the development of a system of flexible political control over Europe by the great powers and formed a barrier to Italy's revisionist policy, designed to improve Italy's political standing in Europe and to enable Italy to extend its sphere of influence into the basin of the Danube and onto the eastern shore of the Adriatic. Mussolini was convinced that the League as constituted would never be able to solve the dynamic problems of the world or permit Italy to satisfy its European or colonial ambitions.[2] Mussolini removed Dino

[1] Aloisi, *Journal*, 80.

[2] A proof of this, for Italians, was that Italy's plea at the first assembly for "justice and equality in the sphere of economics" was ignored by the League. "It is certain that the principle of unanimity has condemned the League of Nations to impotence . . . the principle of unanimity renders particularly void the

Grandi from his post as foreign minister in July 1932, and took the office himself, because he objected to Grandi's pro-League inclination at a time when he wanted freedom to assert Italy's independent authority.[3] Although he did not then consider withdrawing from the League, Mussolini henceforth cooperated with it only to achieve specific advantages for Italy. Other events, from the diplomatic settlement of the Corfu incident to Japan's invasion of Manchuria, seemed to indicate that the League could be ignored with impunity.

As the means for establishing Italian leadership in Europe, Mussolini proposed a four-power pact, to include Britain, France, Germany, and Italy. The purpose of the pact, as stated in his original draft, was to create a common line of conduct "in all questions, political and non-political, European and extra-European, and also as regards the colonial sector." Here was the alternative to the League.[4] Mussolini envisioned a directorate of the great powers, gathering at Italy's instigation, sitting in conference to establish the direction of the future of Europe, able to prevent the expense of an arms race that Italy could ill afford, able to iron out disputes before they gave rise to war, and above all able to assure, through its coordinated, centralized power, the peaceful development of Italian interests in Europe and a sympathetic hearing for Italy's ambitions abroad. Short of this, by extending Italy's friendship to Germany and by breaking through Germany's isolation, Mussolini hoped to gain leverage against the French, who might then be compelled to divert their attention from central Europe.[5]

---

possibility of applying article 19." Latinus (pseud.), *L'Italia e i problemi internazionali* (Milan, 1935), 191–2. For a good indictment of the worth of article 19 of the Covenant, see G. Gathorne-Hardy and D. Mitrany, "Territorial Revision and Article 19 of the League Covenant," *International Affairs*, 14:818–36 (November–December 1935).

[3] Guariglia, *Ricordi*, 177. Mussolini's explanation of why he fired Grandi is found in B. Mussolini, *Storia di un anno* (Verona, 1944), 161. With the purge of the career diplomats in the summer of 1932, Mussolini assumed complete control of Italian foreign policy. As the *tono fascista* took hold in the foreign office, a quest for the heroic, dramatic, and audaciously independent action replaced the old policy of careful diplomatic preparation. Only a few moderates were allowed to remain. Grandi was sent to London, Guariglia to Madrid, and Augusto Rosso to Washington.

[4] Mussolini described the pact as "the only logical and rational historical attempt to reach an understanding with the Western powers so as to coordinate Europe's political and social evolution." Mussolini, *Storia di un anno*, 191, 214. The Italian press hailed the pact as "the opening of a new era," "the new pivot of European politics," and lavished praise on Mussolini as "the pacifier of Europe."

[5] J. Gehl, *Austria, Germany, and the Anschluss, 1931–1938* (London, 1963), 65.

But there was no suport for Mussolini's proposal among the powers of Europe.[6] The British, absorbed in economic crises and political changes at home, were withdrawing into a shortsighted isolationism. France would not consider an alteration of the status quo. Both countries were suspicious of Italy's motives in drawing Germany into the pact. Even Hitler, who was now setting his own course for Germany, at first refused to subscribe to Mussolini's scheme.[7] The four-power pact was signed on 6 June 1933, but the text of the agreement had been watered down by the French who feared becoming a minority of one and had heeded the terrified protests of Poland and the nations of the Little Entente (Rumania, Czechoslavakia, Yugoslavia).[8] The final text made no mention of the colonial sector. The Council of Four never met. Treaties retained their "marble immobility," and there seemed no hope for Mussolini's plans for peaceful revisionism in Europe.

Mussolini's disillusionment with conference diplomacy was confirmed by the failure of the Disarmament Conference in the late spring of 1934. Mussolini would have welcomed a disarmament agreement, since he hoped to achieve his own goals in Europe through peaceful means. An upward-spiraling arms race would severely strain the Italian budget,[9] and there was much to gain by a system of arms control. Mussolini thought that, in the face of Hitler's claim to international equality in arms, this was the only way other than war to prevent a perhaps unstoppable German expansion along the Danube.[10] But in

[6] Mussolini bitterly reproached France and Britain for failing to take the pact seriously. G. Roux, *Mussolini* (Paris, 1960), 204.

[7] Aloisi, *Journal*, 128. Mussolini was angered at Hitler's hesitation.

[8] E. Cameron, "Alexis Saint-Léger Léger," in Craig and Gilbert, eds., *The Diplomats, 1919–1939*, 384. This French tour de force is described by Joseph Paul-Boncour in France, Assemblée Nationale, 1947 session, *Rapport fait au nom de la commission chargée d'enquêter sur les événements survenus en France de 1933 à 1945* (Paris, n.d. [1951–1952]), III, 790–1. Paul-Boncour then wrote to reassure the Little Entente nations, and they replied that they were satisfied. Poland's fears are detailed in R. Debicki, *Foreign Policy of Poland, 1919–1939* (New York, 1962), 71.

[9] L. Salvatorelli and G. Mira, *Storia d'Italia nel periodo fascista*, 3rd ed. (Rome, 1959), 738. On 16 January 1934 the Italian finance minister told the Senate, "the government has made economy one of the principal concerns of the regime." Recent budgets showed a decline in military spending, and, interestingly, this trend publicly continued in the budget projected for 1935–36, presented on 15 January 1935.

[10] So he told Aloisi on 2 September 1933. Aloisi, *Journal*, 143. In late 1933 and early 1934 the Italian air ministry, near Milan, secretly trained over 100 German airmen in bombing techniques. Germany, *Documents on German Foreign Policy, 1918–1945*, ser. C, III (Washington, 1959), 766n. Such aid ended in 1934 when Mussolini became alarmed and disenchanted with Hitler.

May 1934 the Disarmament Conference ended unsuccessfully, as had the Naval Conference, the World Monetary and Economic Conference of 1933, and the four-power pact. These failures exhausted the alternatives to unilateral action that Mussolini was willing to consider. Already in 1933 he had suggested that the discredited term "conference" be stricken from the vocabulary of diplomacy.[11]

Mussolini saw the failure of the Disarmament Conference as the opening of a new arms race in Europe and the start of a new era in international affairs. On 28 May 1934 he published an article entitled "Verso il riarmo" (Toward Rearmament). The collapse of the conference, Mussolini wrote, meant the end of the prestige of the League of Nations and the beginning of a "prewar" scramble for alliances in preparation for war. In this new international anarchy it was necessary for Italy to rearm, in order to assure its own national survival. Italy had done its best, Mussolini said, to throw a bridge "over the historic, profound, and fearful discord which separates Germany from France." Now Italian diplomacy was able to do no more.[12]

Mussolini's "Verso il riarmo" marked a new departure in his foreign policy. The failure of his grand European plan and the feebleness of conference diplomacy caused Mussolini to decide that the success of Italy's foreign policy, the success of his own ambitions, would now have to depend on Italy's acting alone to maintain its position in the world. And for Italy to act alone, Italy must be rearmed. Mussolini's prediction of 1927 seemed fulfilled, that the only way Italy could make its "voice felt" and have its "rights recognized" was by backing its demands with an armed and powerful state. In the middle of 1934 Mussolini thus launched Italy on a course of independent nationalistic militarism. Despite his claim in "Verso il riarmo," however, he was not undertaking rearmament for Italy's protection in the face of the impending European storm. On the contrary, rather than use what he considered the few years of peace remaining to Europe to strengthen Italy's economy and to develop some capacity for military defense, Mussolini now began to prepare for colonial expansion in Africa. Frustrated by the complicated affairs and inhospitable political climate of Europe, Mussolini put aside his plans to establish Italy's influence there and looked now across the Mediterranean for the field on which to assert the power and prestige of Fascism.

---

[11] Article entitled "Dopo Londra," *Il Popolo d'Italia*, 29 July 1933.
[12] Mussolini, *Opera omnia*, XXVI, 224–6.

An announcement of the new course came in Mussolini's speech to the second quinquennial assembly of the Fascist Party on 18 March 1934:

> Italy is more an island than a peninsula . . . it stretches to the shore and heart of Africa . . . The historical objectives of Italy have two names: Asia and Africa. South and east are the compass points toward which the interest and will of Italians are directed. To the north there is little or nothing to do, to the west nothing either, either in Europe or beyond the sea. Of all the great western powers of Europe, the closest to Africa and to Asia is Italy . . . But there must be no misunderstanding of this centuries-old task assigned to this and future generations of Italians. There is no question of territorial conquests — this must be understood by all, both far and near — but of a natural expansion which ought to lead to collaboration between Italy and the peoples of Africa and the nations of the near and middle east . . . Italy in the first place is able to introduce Africa more fully into the circle of the civilized world. Italy's position in the Mediterranean, the sea which has regained its historic function of joining the east and west, gives it the right and duty to accomplish this task. We demand no privileges or monopolies, but we require and wish those who are "arrived," satisfied, and conservative to refrain from blocking this cultural, political, and economic expansion of Fascist Italy.[13]

From this time on, then, Mussolini prepared for a war against Ethiopia,[14] the only area, it seemed, where Italy might still act freely and decisively.

Why did Mussolini at this time decide to undertake an aggressive colonial war in Africa? The answer is not clear. Available evidence does not give us a conclusive explanation. To approach an understanding of this decision, I believe consideration must be given to the condition of Italy in the early 1930s — the nature of Italian Fascism, the mind of Mussolini, and the needs of his dictatorship.

Mussolini based his rule on a combination of political machination, massive propaganda fictions, economic concessions to property owners and employers, and, above all, the ubiquitous power of the Fascist Party. Fascism, as a political ideology, did not sustain itself with a clear program for the improvement of civilized life. What passed for its doctrine ignored fundamental matters of social welfare and economic

[13] Mussolini, *Opera omnia*, XXVI, 190–2.
[14] See M. Toscano, *Lezioni di storia dei trattati e politica internazionale* (Turin, 1958), 364, and introduction to Aloisi, *Journal*, xii.

development. The main code of conduct on which Fascism insisted was strict obedience to the party leader. Lacking greater principles, Fascists substituted primitive slogans for social programs, surface style for substance, rhetoric for ideology, and emotional excitement for reason.[15] General De Bono, in his book on the Ethiopian campaign, expressed his personal philosophy: "Better a thousand times those who rush headlong forward, even with their eyes shut." [16] Life was a struggle, Fascism proclaimed, and the battle for existence would be won by the most audacious, the most dynamic. There was, there had to be, incessant action. To give this action form, military values and practices were assiduously cultivated throughout all levels of Italian life.

In his article on the doctrine of Fascism, published in 1932, Mussolini wrote:

> Fascism does not, generally speaking, believe in the possibility or utility of perpetual peace. It therefore discards pacifism . . . War alone keys up all human energies to their maximum tension and sets the seal of nobility on those peoples who have the courage to face it . . . Fascism carries this antipacifist attitude into the life of the individual. "I don't give a damn" — the proud motto of the fighting squads . . . sums up a doctrine which is not merely political: it is evidence of a fighting spirit which accepts all risks. It signifies a new mode of Italian life.[17]

By 1935 all of Italy was being pressed into the militarist mold. In February 1935, for example, a program was instituted in the schools to imbue the children with "military culture," to interest them in the "heroic and adventurous qualities of war." On 30 March 1935, General Federico Baistrocchi, speaking to the Italian Senate, said that "Italy has become a military nation in which the functions of citizen and soldier are inseparable." [18] You can do everything with bayonets except sit on them; war is a most likely consequence of militarism. In 1934 and

---

[15] For an example of the use of vague and highly charged words to express the mystical quality of Fascism, see G. Pesenti, "Alcuni aspetti de mondo nuovo," *Gerarchia*, 15:389–402 (May 1935), in which the author deals with the "revolt of the Telluric force" whose hidden logic directs the energy of men toward the development of "grandi condottieri politici."

[16] De Bono, *Anno XIIII*, 21.

[17] B. Mussolini, "La Dottrina del fascismo," *Enciclopedia italiana di scienza, lettere ed arti* (Milan, 1932), XIV, 846–51. The Fascist propagandist Giovanni Gentile should probably be given credit for the organization, if not the wording, of this "doctrine."

[18] *Gerarchia*, 15:189–90 (February 1935); *Le Temps*, 31 March 1935.

1935, what Mussolini was preparing Italy for was a war against Ethiopia.

What I have described indicates the basic sterility of Fascism. Indeed, this was its problem as it faced the world economic crisis of the 1930s. Without a broad and viable program for the peaceful development of Italy, Mussolini came to lean more and more on the pursuit of militant nationalism to give the appearance of direction and energy to his regime. The Ethiopian adventure was almost certainly contrived, at least in part, as an alternative to social reform: it was a way to glorify the Duce and, correspondingly, to divert public attention from domestic problems.

In 1934 Mussolini found himself faced with intensifying popular discontent, which called for release before it could become a threat to the dictatorship. The world economic crisis of the early 1930s hit Italy with great force. It became clear that, although Fascism had benefited those with substantial property, the Fascist state was no guarantor of security for workers or peasants. Agriculture, in which half the population was involved, suffered a collapse in prices. Whereas the "battle for grain" had succeeded in producing enough wheat for national consumption, this had been an uneconomic victory: the battle for grain was primarily a political device meant to garner support for the regime. In the long run it was not wise economically, for it emphasized wheat production at the expense of more profitable areas of agriculture (such as citrus fruits and olives, vineyards, or meat). Had these been encouraged, the terms of trade may have enabled Italy to purchase grain from abroad more cheaply than it cost to produce at home.[19] With the depression, grain prices fell, and the earnings and then the savings of farmers disappeared.

There were similar problems in industry. Fascism had favored capital at the expense of labor, and the state provided few welfare provisions by which to cushion the shock of depression. By 1933 industrial production was off by over 30 percent, with the percentage even higher among important textile firms, and some plants were operating at only 20 percent capacity.[20] Wages fell sharply for those who did remain at work. In January 1935 there were 1,011,711 unem-

[19] Salvatorelli and Mira, *Storia d'Italia*, 526; C. T. Schmidt, *The Plough and the Sword* (New York, 1938), 45–72, and *The Corporate State in Action* (New York, 1939), 97–105.
[20] Salvatorelli and Mira, *Storia d'Italia*, 540.

ployed Italians.[21] International trade declined well over a third from its 1929 level, and before exchange controls were imposed in December 1934 Italy's foreign reserves underwent a catastrophic plunge.[22]

The result was a demand for constructive national leadership, and it fell at the doorstep of the Duce. The depression seemed to represent the collapse of the laissez-faire system, which Mussolini had often denounced as moribund.[23] Could the vaunted "synthetic" abilities of Fascism now present an alternative to capitalism, an alternative to socialism, "an alternative solution to the problem of an industrial society"? [24]

The trouble with Fascism was that it had not developed a successful program to achieve full employment or improvements in the general welfare. Far from having solved the problems of an industrial society, Fascism permitted owners of capital to grow in wealth as industrial workers became impoverished. And to the stress of unemployed factory and farm workers was now added the strain of unemployment within the urban middle class: small businessmen were squeezed out by larger concentrations of capital; holders of government bonds suffered from a lowered interest rate; and members of professions and university graduates could not find jobs. Fascism had originally received much support from these groups, and in the expanding party bureaucracy in the early years of the regime educated men had found employment. Men who had grown up under the Fascist system had been trained for service in the party and were fired with expectations for a career in the state apparatus. But in the 1930s they found themselves out of work, in a society whose economy was not working, and without a clear future in a party hierarchy whose offices were already filled by the first generation of Fascist supporters. Inside or outside the party organization, there were simply not enough positions open to provide outlets for the talents and ambitions of this younger group. Instead of enjoying

[21] League of Nations, *Statistical Year-Book of the League of Nations, 1935–36* (Geneva, 1936), 60. Officially registered as wholly unemployed: in 1932, 1,006,442; in 1933, 1,018,955; in 1934, 963,677. Out of a total population of 43 million, these are high figures; it is probable that the true number of unemployed Italians, including those not registered was far higher.

[22] League, *Statistical Year-Book, 1936–37* (Geneva, 1937), 212, 236; O. Mosca, *Nessuno volle i miei dollari d'ora* (Naples, 1958), 252; S. B. Clough, *The Economic History of Modern Italy* (New York, 1964), 246–50.

[23] At the end of 1932 Mussolini told Hugh Dalton: "Individualistic capitalism has completely broken down." H. Dalton, *The Fateful Years: Memoirs, 1931–1945* (London, 1957), 34.

[24] K. Polanyi, *The Great Transformation* (New York, 1944), 243.

benefits under Fascism, the urban middle class of Italy, like many workers and peasants, was living in conditions of growing insecurity. This was, of course, a source of possible danger to Mussolini, who had exploited similar social tensions after the war in his own seizure of political power.[25]

Many of these younger men were growing increasingly disgruntled with Mussolini's permanent personal dictatorship and with Fascism's failure to begin a widespread program of social reform.[26] In democratic countries it was possible for the electorate to vote out governments deemed unresponsive to the crises of depression. Mussolini's dictatorship gave no allowance for nonrevolutionary political change. It was up to Mussolini to find some way to prevent the discontent of these difficult times from going against his government. The future of Mussolini's regime depended on how successfully he could provide a safety valve for this mounting social and economic stress.

Some of the more thoughtful Fascists were champions of social reform through what was known as the corporate state. Corporatism had long been a part of the Fascist rhetoric. It involved the establishment of twenty-two "corporations" embracing all categories of the nation's working people. Representatives of the various groups would meet to deliberate in a National Council of Corporations. Within this council, conflicting class interests would be reconciled and national solidarity achieved. The Council of Corporations was meant to become the supreme arbiter of Italy's economic life. Mussolini ostensibly accepted the notion of a corporate state, and by February 1934 corporatism was formally installed in Italy. On 10 November 1934 Mussolini stated its domestic aim as "higher 'social justice.'" As for its foreign purpose, "the object of the corporation is to increase constantly the global power of the nation to further the ends of its expansion in the world." [27]

In this last goal Mussolini revealed his true interest: by 1934 he was

[25] In 1922, however, Mussolini had been able to place his Fascists in thousands of positions that opened when he took control of the state. For an outstanding discussion of "The Legacy of Fascism: The Corporate State," see H. Stuart Hughes, *The United States and Italy* (Cambridge, Mass., 1953), chap. 4. For further indication of Mussolini's political troubles in 1935, see G. Stolper, "European Kaleidoscope," *Foreign Affairs*, 14:225–6 (January 1936).

[26] As Giuseppe Bottai expressed it, it was "il Mussolinismo contro il Fascismo" — G. Bottai, *Vent'anni e un giorno*, 2nd ed. (Rome, 1949), chap. 4. For a good criticism of Fascism's political weakness, see F. Deakin, *The Brutal Friendship: Mussolini, Hitler and the Fall of Italian Fascism* (London, 1962), 49.

[27] Mussolini, *Opera omnia*, XXVI, 379.

less concerned with programming social justice than in expanding Italy's global power. He had permitted the Council of Corporations to be established because of its propaganda value in giving the appearance of social progress, but he never allowed corporatism, in its institutional form, to become powerful. Mussolini would tolerate nothing that undermined his personal direction of Italian political life.[28] All moves that Mussolini made to improve the economy were taken with the purpose of strengthening his rule. But his actions, such as supervising finance and trade, did not help the workers or reduce industrial unemployment, especially since entrenched capital and the interests of the employers were left untouched.[29] Nor were well-publicized public-works projects, such as the draining of the Pontine marshes and the monumental construction of the "Roma di Mussolini," effective in solving the problem of unemployment: most were in or near the capital and thus readily observable by influential Romans and by foreign newsmen. Their purpose was to enhance the popularity and renown of the regime. Mussolini, not corporatism, ran Italy, and Mussolini aimed less at social justice than at protecting his regime and, from 1934 on, preparing Italy for war.

We come here to the great turning point in the history of Italian Fascism. When Mussolini failed at this juncture to work out a comprehensive program of social and economic reform for Italy, all that was left to him was a reassertion of the sterile slogans of Fascism: activism, militarism, combative nationalism. All hopes for the peaceful development of Italy vanished when Mussolini decided that the basis of his, and Italy's, prestige lay in a powerful militaristic state that could pursue an aggressive foreign policy. Mussolini's "Verso il riarmo" was a reflection of this new turn. Frustrated in his designs for Europe, Mussolini in 1934 turned to African imperialism as a field for dramatic action. To avoid the consequences of his failure to solve the domestic problems of Italy, Mussolini sought to involve the nation in the conquest of Ethiopia.[30]

[28] From 1932 on, e.g., Mussolini bypassed the Council of Ministers as a policy-making organ. Henceforth, as he wrote, they would not "waste any more time in useless discussion. The Ministers are soldiers. They stand or go where the leader tells them to go." B. Mussolini, *Memoirs, 1942–1943*, R. Klibanski, ed., F. Lobb, trans. (London, 1949), 156n.

[29] Salvatorelli and Mira, *Storia d'Italia*, 519–20.

[30] See F. Chabod, *A History of Italian Fascism*, M. Grindrod, trans. (London, 1963), 76. From 1922 on, Mussolini had made an effort to use successes in foreign affairs to support the consolidation of the Fascist regime, but for a decade

The demands of an Ethiopian campaign would absorb the idle energies of the population. Preparations for war would revive the economy, increase profits, provide employment, and raise wages. Army service would drain off more of the unemployed. According to Alessandro Lessona, his undersecretary for colonies, Mussolini hoped that the creation of a warrior state would educate Italians in a sense of responsibility, duty, and national purpose.[31] Mussolini's insistence that Italy must act alone could be used to inspire a deeper spirit of patriotism which would overcome internal social divisions. The fear or hatred of a foreign enemy would silence domestic opposition and draw support to the regime. Victorious battles overseas, particularly the avenging of Aduwa, would renew the glory of the Duce and enable his regime to share in the mythic grandeur of imperial Rome. And no doubt also in Mussolini's mind was the hope that Ethiopia would become a land of settlement for Italian farmers and a source of wealth, of raw materials and food, for Italy. The Ethiopian campaign suited Mussolini's needs in all respects. It repeated the classic maneuver of dictators, to try for success abroad to take people's minds off troubles at home.[32]

We do not have sufficient evidence to determine the exact date of Mussolini's decision to precipitate a conflict with Ethiopia. We do know that the first time he gave serious consideration to the prospect of military action there was in September 1933. Before this time Mussolini had been content to stop at political subversion. In 1931 he reacted furiously to a suggestion by the secretary-general of the French foreign ministry, Philippe Berthelot, that Italy might have a future in Ethiopia, for Mussolini viewed this as a French scheme to involve Italy in Africa and thereby impede his efforts to extend Italy's influence in Europe.[33] Until 1933 Mussolini was preoccupied with European affairs, and the question of Italian action in east Africa was virtually ignored by the Italian government at large. In January 1933 Count Luigi Vinci-Gigliucci was sent to Addis Ababa as the new Italian minister, with instructions to maintain a friendly front in order to

---

these attempts were held in check by the career diplomats at the Palazzo Chigi and by his own uncertainty. Guariglia, *Ricordi*, 39–40. Mussolini's commitment to aggressive war and the creation of a military state under his unrestrained control marked a new departure for Fascism.

[31] See A. Lessona, *Memorie* (Florence, 1958), 171–2.

[32] See Chabod, *History of Italian Fascism*, 77.

[33] Guariglia, *Ricordi*, 144.

conceal any hostile policies that Italy might decide upon.[34] But, as we have seen, ministerial lethargy and disinterest held back the full development of a "peripheral policy," although enough political propaganda was undertaken to alarm the Ethiopian government. In an article written in the late summer of 1933, Undersecretary of Colonies Alessandro Lessona asserted Italy's historical right to political and economic predominance in Ethiopia. This statement indicated that official interest in Ethiopia was increasing, and it probably was an effort to establish some degree of legitimacy for later Italian action.[35] But how and when a campaign against Ethiopia would be conducted awaited the decision of the Duce.

Mussolini's developing interest in Ethiopia was encouraged by Emilio De Bono, the minister of colonies. General De Bono was a frustrated old man. His record in the world war was not particularly outstanding, and he had been reprimanded for his Fascist politics. Like many others, he sought to fulfill his ambition by joining the Fascist movement, and he was one of the original quadrumvirs of the march on Rome. Thereafter he made his career in Fascist service. Part of the responsibility for Giacomo Matteotti's murder was laid at his door, and Mussolini removed him from his posts as chief of police and commander-in-chief of the Fascist militia. He spent the years 1925–1929 in unnoticed semiexile in the governor-general's mansion in Tripoli. In 1929 he returned to Rome as minister of colonies. Eager to show a success, throughout 1931 and 1932 De Bono implored Mussolini to pour men and money into developing Italy's foreign possessions. Italy, he said, languished behind the colonial progress of Britain and France. If Italy did not commit itself to massive colonial development, it would lose its colonies through neglect. But De Bono's pleas did him no good.[36] Italian east Africa remained ignored, and the credit for the pacification and consolidation of Libya went to generals Pietro Badoglio and Rodolfo Graziani. The impressive economic and social achievements there of a later governor, Italo Balbo, far outshone De Bono's

[34] Aloisi, *Journal*, 45.

[35] A. Lessona, "L'Eritrea e la Somalia nei fini dell'espansione," *Rassegna italiana*, 35:119–27 (September–October 1933). Lessona himself makes it appear that his new interest in Ethiopia was a product of boredom and the need to fill time in the colonial office after the conquest of Libya. *Memorie*, 131, 145.

[36] Personal Papers of Benito Mussolini, etc., National Archives, Washington, D.C., Microcopy No. T-586, Job (Series) No. 329, sect. 5, frames 112801–69.

own accomplishments and earned his envy.[37] But in 1933, taking advantage of the "peculiar weakness" [38] Mussolini had for him, De Bono seized upon the Ethiopian campaign as the opportunity he had long sought.

For De Bono a war against Ethiopia, if he could command it, would be the satisfaction of a great personal ambition, the final chance to close his career in a blaze of military glory. De Bono did not consider the further implications of an Italian-Ethiopian conflict. As a first step, De Bono began presiding over a committee of military men to study possible plans of action.[39] In the autumn of 1933, resolved "to lose no time," he presented himself to the Duce:

> "Listen," De Bono said to Mussolini, "if there is a war down there — and if you think me worthy of it, and capable — you ought to grant me the honor of conducting the campaign."
> "Surely," Mussolini replied.
> "You don't think me too old?"
> "No, because we mustn't lose time."

A promise given is usually a promise accepted and, according to De Bono, "from this moment the Duce was definitely of the opinion that the matter would have to be settled no later than 1936.[40] Being settled did not, at this stage, necessarily mean a full-scale war and total conquest. But the decision for action in Ethiopia, already growing in Mussolini's mind and encouraged by the eager De Bono, could hardly lead to any other conclusion when it coincided with Mussolini's desire for a dramatic military action. For a while the decision to move on Ethiopia remained the secret of the two men. In early 1934 various military leaders were let in on the gradually developing plan when their advice was sought.[41] But the undersecretary at the ministry of

[37] De Bono, like many older Fascists, was envious of successful younger men. Balbo, thirty-six years younger than De Bono and two grades higher in military rank, also had succeeded him as commander of the militia.

[38] Lessona, *Memorie*, 151.

[39] Aloisi, *Journal*, 43.

[40] De Bono, *Anno XIIII*, 13.

[41] Robert L. Hess has published the report of a meeting held on 31 May 1934 between Mussolini, De Bono, Chief of Staff Badoglio, and Fulvio Suvich, undersecretary of foreign affairs. The plan outlined there stated that first defensive arrangements for Eritrea should be completed and then a study should be made of how Ethiopia could be provoked, indirectly, into taking action against the Italian colony to provide Italy with an excuse for war. Until Italian military preparations were completed, however, relations with Ethiopia should be main-

colonies, Lessona, did not learn of the change of policy until its "decisive phase" in July 1934, and Pompeo Aloisi, "capo di Gabinetto" in the foreign ministry, does not appear to have been informed that war was being considered until the late summer of 1934.[42]

At the beginning of 1934, the commander of the Royal Corps of Eritrea and the military attaché in Addis Ababa, Colonel Vittorio Ruggero, were brought to Rome for consultation.[43] Colonel Ruggero was told to return to Addis Ababa and begin a program of political subversion within the empire. When Italy was ready for military action, Ruggero was to create an incident that would give Italy its excuse for war. In February 1934 the undersecretary for war, General Federico Baistrocchi, who had previously engaged in planning the defenses for Eritrea and Somalia, was asked by Mussolini to give an accounting of the problems of a military action in east Africa and especially to provide a plan for a swift and decisive offense against Ethiopia. Baistrocchi was an ambitious man, who himself later schemed for the Ethiopian command. He was a party stalwart, suspected by the king of wanting to "fascistize" the Italian army.[44] But the thought of a full-scale war in Ethiopia staggered him, and he at once raised the most obvious objection, which bothered all the professional military men save De Bono (who was not a good strategist and who was unwilling to let anything interfere with his own ambition). To embark on a major campaign thousands of sea miles from Italy was difficult enough, Baistrocchi noted, but, when the only channel of communication to east Africa ran through two seas and a canal controlled by a possibly hostile British navy, the risks for Italy became enormous and the dangers to the enterprise became prohibitive. Mussolini did not blink an eye. He replied that "the order to march will be given only when, by political action, neither the democracies with their dependent, the Little Entente, nor Germany will be able to be the slightest nuisance to us." [45] Baistrocchi was not convinced and began to study the problem; but he did this in a desultory fashion, considering it more of an academic exercise than a preparation for a future reality.

---

tained on a friendly basis in line with the treaty of 1928. In no case should Italy's military plans be admitted to the governments of France and Britain. R. Hess, *Italian Colonialism in Somalia* (Chicago, 1966), 172–3.

[42] Lessona, *Memorie*, 149; Aloisi, *Journal*, 224.

[43] De Bono, *Anno XIIII*, 16.

[44] N. D'Aroma, *Vent'anni insieme: Vittorio Emanuele e Mussolini* (Rome, 1957), 213.

[45] D'Aroma, *Vent'anni insieme*, 229–30.

Mussolini was not to be put off, however, and in July 1934 he was jolted into an awareness that events in Europe demanded swift action in Africa. The incident that introduced the "decisive phase" of his plans for Ethiopia was the attempted Nazi putsch in Vienna.

Italy was interested in the independence of Austria for two reasons. One was the defensive need to have a friendly country on the north side of the Brenner Pass. Italy was accordingly reluctant to allow Germany to gain control there. Second, for years it was Mussolini's ambition to extend Italy's sphere of influence into the "heritage of the Habsburgs." [46] In early 1933 he told Count Ernst von Starhemberg that the Danube basin was Italy's "European hinterland. That is why we seek a firm position there. Without it we shall be forced to play the insignificant role of a peninsula on the edge of Europe. We might even be pushed to Africa." [47] Mussolini had not won the Habsburg legacy for Italy, but Austria remained important for Italy's position in Europe even after Mussolini's hopes for his "grande politica europea" faded. Indeed, Mussolini hoped to see a Fascist government on the Italian model established in Vienna, and to these ends financial subsidies and moral support crossed the Alps.

Mussolini's disillusionment with Hitler's Germany was well advanced by the summer of 1934. Hitler was no mere pupil of the Duce, and many differences of opinion grew up between the two leaders. Mussolini felt that National Socialism was a contradiction in terms, and he scorned the racial theories of the Nazis. The Reichstag fire, the Roehm purge, the Fuehrer's lack of finesse, all disgusted Mussolini.[48] This bitterness was increased when Hitler at first refused to sign the four-power pact and when Germany withdrew from the Disarmament Conference and from the League of Nations in October 1933.[49] A

[46] J. Bastin, *L'Affaire d'Ethiopie et les diplomates, 1934-1937* (Brussels, 1937), 22–9.

[47] Quoted by E. Wiskemann, *The Rome-Berlin Axis: A History of the Relations between Hitler and Mussolini* (London, 1949), 31.

[48] For an example of Mussolini's contempt of Nazism, see his speech of 6 September 1934: "Thirty centuries of history permit us to look with supreme pity on certain doctrines held beyond the Alps by the descendants of people who were wholly illiterate in the days when Caesar, Virgil, and Augustus flourished in Rome." *Opera omnia*, XXVI, 319. See also his attack on Nazism and his description of Hitler as "a horrible sexual degenerate, a dangerous fool," in E. von Starhemberg, *Between Hitler and Mussolini* (London, 1942), 170. The Vatican was also growing cool toward Nazism at this time. L. Salvatorelli, *Vent'anni fra due guerra* (Rome, 1941), 451.

[49] Mussolini had hoped to have the German card in his hand at Geneva. He was informed beforehand of Germany's intention to withdraw from the dis-

meeting in June 1934 between the two dictators was a further disappointment to Mussolini. Colonial matters were not discussed at Venice, and all that came out in the talks, as Foreign Minister Konstantin von Neurath said in a circular of 16 June, was the hope that "the Austrian question must not be allowed to hinder the development of German-Italian relations." [50] But their opposing aims in Austria remained a contentious matter between the two countries. Germany was a threat to Italian interests in Austria and the Tyrol, and from the time of the introduction of the Gleichschaltung policy in the spring of 1933 there was acute mistrust and suspicion in Rome.[51]

On 25 July 1934 Nazis attempted a coup d'état in Vienna and shot to death the Austrian chancellor Engelbert Dollfuss, who was on the eve of departing for Italy to spend a vacation at Mussolini's Adriatic villa. This apparent threat to the independence of the Austrian government worried Mussolini, and the Nazis' brutal actions enraged him. Starhemberg, the acting chancellor, was put aboard an Italian airplane and flown to Vienna, and a forceful telegram asserting Italy's national interest in Austria's independence followed him.[52] The Italian ambassador and the papal nuncio were the first to offer their condolences at the Austrian embassay in Berlin. Most important and dramatic of all, Mussolini ordered the troops of the Arditi to the Brenner and the Carinthian border. It may have been, as General Carlo Favagrossa maintains, that Mussolini's military display was only a "bluffistico," because the logistical support of the troops was inadequate to back up a movement into Austria let alone to defend the country against invasion.[53] We know now, with later evidence, that Hitler was not in fact prepared then for military action against Austria, and, the putsch having failed, he disowned the rebels.[54] In 1934, however, Mussolini's actions were considered instrumental in protecting Austria from a German invasion. Regardless of his real intentions, the Duce's prompt actions did serve to shore up the authority of the Austrian government in an hour of crisis.

---

armament conference, but Hitler's withdrawal from the League was kept a secret from him. The news reached him only after the public announcement in Berlin. Mussolini was furious at what he considered an act of deliberate disloyalty. *Documents on German Foreign Policy*, ser. C, IV (1962), 106–7.

[50] *Documents on German Foreign Policy*, III, 19, 50.

[51] See Gehl, *Austria, Germany, and the Anschluss*, chaps. 3, 4.

[52] Starhemberg, *Between Hitler and Mussolini*, 152, 168.

[53] C. Favagrossa, *Perchè perdemmo la guerra* (Milan, 1946), 4.

[54] Gehl, *Austria, Germany, and the Anschluss*, 99.

The conclusion Mussolini drew from the events in Vienna was that Hitler meant to bring war to Europe. His suspicions of Germany were aroused as never before. He told Starhemberg: "Hitler will create an army. Hitler will arm the Germans and make war — possibly even in two or three years." [55] A month after Dollfuss's death, Mussolini told Aloisi that a war, meaning evidently a European war, was not far off and that it was necessary to be ready for it.[56] In the middle of August 1934, speaking from an open armored car at army maneuvers, Mussolini declared that Italy must prepare for war "not tomorrow but today." [57] This concern that Germany would rearm and would soon become a serious threat to the peace of Europe meant that Mussolini could not afford to delay if he were going to win a colonial victory. He would have to turn away from Europe, and from Austria, to strike at Ethiopia while he still had time. For the present, Britain and France would have to share in the responsibility of protecting Austria's independence; if this could be arranged, Austria would have to stand alone.[58] Mussolini warned the Austrians that they had to fend for themselves and that in the near future they could count on Italy only for limited support. As he told Chancellor Kurt von Schuschnigg in August 1934, a conflict with Ethiopia seemed inevitable.[59]

Mussolini had reached the "decisive phase" of his planning for war against Ethiopia.[60] In July 1934 he sent General Pietro Badoglio, longtime chief of the general staff, and an Italian military commission to Eritrea to investigate the prospects of a campaign. After observing the total lack of Italian preparedness in the colony, Badoglio submitted what appears to have been an exceedingly pessimistic report. The general staff was concerned that an African expedition would weaken Italy's own defenses by taking troops away from the Alpine frontier. Musso-

---

[55] Starhemberg, *Between Hitler and Mussolini*, 171.

[56] Aloisi, *Journal*, 211.

[57] Mussolini, *Opera omnia*, XXVI, 308.

[58] Despite French and Italian efforts, it was impossible to create either an effective tripartite guarantee or an agreement by France or Britain to let Italy act for them. See Gehl, *Austria, Germany, and the Anschluss*, 112–13. For Mussolini's hopes, see Starhemberg, *Between Hitler and Mussolini*, 171. Mussolini expressed discouragement at the failure of Britain and France to come to his aid in defending Austria's independence. V. Mussolini, *Vita con mio padre* (Rome, 1957), 61.

[59] K. von Schuschnigg, *Ein Requiem in Rot-Weiss-Rot* (Zurich, 1946), 220, 238.

[60] Massimo Magistrati, then an official in the Italian foreign office, emphasizes the influence of Mussolini's apprehensions toward Germany in bringing about the Ethiopian undertaking at this time. M. Magistrati, "La Germania e l'impresa italiana di Etiopia (Ricordi di Berlino)," *Rivista di studi politici internazionali*, 17:564–70 (October–December 1950).

lini's talk about being back in the Brenner before a European war broke out was not entirely convincing, for no one could estimate the length of time Italy might be involved in Africa or the amount of men and matériel needed to win against the Ethiopians. Mussolini rejected these cautions. Planning for the campaign went ahead regardless. On 29 August 1934 the American military attaché in Rome reported to Washington that the general staff had drawn up plans for "the military conquest and occupation of Abyssinia . . . to be undertaken whenever Abyssinia commits an 'overt act.' " These plans called for an expeditionary force of 100,000 men and the expenditure of not less than two billion lire.[61] De Bono and his ministry staff were also working on a plan of campaign.[62]

The skepticism of the general staff was shared by the king of Italy. Victor Emmanuel III disapproved of a war in east Africa. For one thing, as he told Governor Rava on his visit to Italian Somaliland in November 1934, "it is necessary to have eyes and hands ready in Europe." [63] The king had other arguments against an Ethiopian campaign. He was much impressed by Somalia and the work of Rava, he told Marshal Enrico Caviglia when he returned from his trip. Yet there were problems involved in any extensive Italian settlement there: "The colony has all the elements to become wealthy. Good land, water, and high temperature. All the animals are large. Plants grow fruitfully and reproduce rapidly. But . . . there are three buts. The great distance from the nearest Italian port, Brindisi; [the high cost of transportation charges through] the Suez Canal; the lack of a port, which could only be remedied by the expenditure of a hundred million lire." The same factors had to be considered in maintaining troops in east Africa. Further, "the difficulties of a great war are many and elaborate, especially considering the distance of the base of operations." Such factors, the king thought, would limit "the use of the preponderant force which we possess, and the use of air power would have only minor moral and material effects on the [Ethiopian] population." No doubt recalling Menelik's defense of fifty years before, the king continued: "It is an illusion that Abyssinia will divide up into civil war between the various rases. Instead, if we go to war against them, they

[61] U.S. Department of State, *Foreign Relations of the United States, Diplomatic Papers, 1934*, II (Washington, 1951), 754; hereafter referred to as *U.S. Diplomatic Papers*.

[62] De Bono, *Anno XIIII*, 37.

[63] D'Aroma, *Vent'anni insieme*, 230.

will unite against us." [64] But opinions change with the times. Ultimately Victor Emmanuel did not oppose Mussolini's east African adventure, and tears of pride came to his eyes when the Duce later proclaimed him emperor of Ethiopia.[65]

Mussolini, in any event, was not to be deterred by such arguments. Having set Italy on the course for war, he was prepared to go ahead at all costs. The protests of those who opposed military action in Africa grew weaker and finally ceased. On 1 October 1934 the undersecretary for foreign affairs, Fulvio Suvich, told Aloisi that Mussolini was reckoning on the war's beginning in two years, at the end of the Ethiopian rainy season in 1936. The two diplomats hoped that these two years might provide time for a change of mind and that somehow the conflict would not materialize.[66] But preparations for war were under way and they were now hard to stop. Rumors of a coming invasion of Ethiopia were current already in Rome.[67] They were noted by the American ambassador, Breckinridge Long, who reported in September that some factories were working three shifts a day in the production of war matériel. Orders for cloth for uniforms had been placed, and a factory near Milan had received an order for 500,000 sun helmets. American consuls, at watch in Italian ports, reported considerable activity. Ammunition of Swiss origin was being shipped to east Africa marked as "wire nails." Banana boats, usually empty on their way out, were reported to carry war supplies, as did commercial ships with spare room.[68]

At this time, too, the Ethiopians began to express their concern in Rome. The Ethiopian chargé requested a reaffirmation of the Italian-Ethiopian treaty of friendship. The Italian government, for propaganda purposes, agreed, and a joint statement of mutual amity was issued in Rome on 29 September 1934. The Italian section of the communiqué read in part: "Italy does not have any intention that is not friendly toward the Ethiopian Government with whom we are bound by the treaty of friendship of 1928." [69]

[64] E. Caviglia, *Diario, aprile 1925 — marzo 1945* (Rome, 1952), 126–8.

[65] C. de Chambrun, *Traditions et souvenirs* (Paris, 1952), 214; Great Britain, Foreign Office, *Documents on British Foreign Policy, 1919–1939*, 3rd ser., III (London, 1950), 496.

[66] Aloisi, *Journal*, 224.

[67] See, e.g., the witness of Viscount Cecil, *A Great Experiment* (London, 1941), 264.

[68] U.S. Department of State, *Peace and War, United States Foreign Policy, 1931–1941* (Washington, 1943), 29, 235–6; *U.S. Diplomatic Papers, 1935*, I, 759.

[69] *New York Times*, 30 September 1934.

It is clear, however, that Italy was preparing for war. The schedule of operations, on the other hand, was still unclear. What Mussolini lacked was an "overt act" by Ethiopia to provide the excuse for an immediate invasion and an agreement with France analogous to the exchange with Britain of 1925, which, in his opinion, would give Italy an assurance of freedom in any Ethiopian action. These two requirements were soon met. The Walwal incident of 5 December 1934 was used to provide the excuse to invade; conversations on 6–7 January 1935 with Pierre Laval, the French foreign minister, provided Mussolini with the expectation that France would not oppose his war.

Chapter 3

December: The Walwal Incident

The border between Ethiopia and Italian Somaliland had never been formally delimited. The general conditions defining the border were laid down in a treaty between Italy and Ethiopia that was signed on 16 May 1908.[1] North of the Scebeli River a set of fairly clear directions governed the demarcation of the frontier line, which was to be marked out on the ground "as soon as possible." Article 4 of the treaty read: "From the Uebi Scebeli the frontier proceeds in a northeasterly direction, following the line accepted by the Italian Government in 1897;[2] all the territory belonging to the tribes towards the coast shall remain dependent on Italy; all the territory of the Ogaden and all that of the tribes towards the Ogaden shall remain dependent on Abyssinia." Article 6 declared that Italy, like Ethiopia, would refrain from any interference beyond the frontier line.

In 1911, in compliance with the terms of the treaty, a joint commission began laying a boundary, starting from Dolo on the upper Juba River, but mutual distrust and unwillingness to compromise doomed the project to quick failure.[3] No further border negotiations ensued, and the frontier remained undemarcated. In the following years maps of all nations, including Italy's own, maps official and unofficial, dotted in a tentative border that conformed roughly to the 180-mile parallel. The watering spot of Walwal was at least fifty miles inside this line, regardless of the scale used, and was universally regarded as being well

[1] R. Brant and W. Maycock, eds., *British and Foreign State Papers, 1907–1908* (London, 1912), CI, 1000–1. Hertslet, *Map of Africa by Treaty*, III, 1223–5, presents an inferior and misleading translation.

[2] The agreement of 1897 declared that the borderline was to run, following the curvature of the coast, "at a distance of 180 miles parallel to the coast of the Indian Ocean." Endless trouble stemmed from the fact that the Ethiopians interpreted this as signifying statute miles while Italians contended that the reference was to nautical miles.

[3] League of Nations, *Official Journal, 1935* (Geneva, 1935), 1420–3.

within Ethiopia's territorial limits. As late as January 1929 the Italian minister in Addis Ababa, Giuliano Cora, wrote to the Ethiopian foreign ministry concerning "tribes subject to the Ethiopian Government, in the locality of Wal Wal." [4] On all the evidence, Walwal belonged to Ethiopia.

For many years the government of Ethiopia had neglected this area of the outer Ogaden, the semiarid part of Harar province over which nomadic Somali tribes wandered. In 1895, shortly after the region was annexed, an expedition of 7,000 men had been sent into the Ogaden and was led by natives into the waterless wastes. Only seven men of the Ethiopian force returned, and with this disaster the central government lost interest in the distant lowlands, for thirty-five years. Preoccupied with problems of centralization and control, unable to spare men to send to the Ogaden, and more concerned with the Italian menace pressing on the high plateau from Eritrea in the north, neither Menelik nor Haile Selassie bothered with the tribes of herders drifting across the remote region beyond the eastern escarpment. Every five years or so, the governor of Ogaden sent down a force to collect taxes in kind, camels and a few cattle that were sold for cash in Jijiga. Other than this, the subject tribes in the Ogaden were left alone.

For the Italians in Somalia, however, one part of this region had immediate importance for their control of the coastal colony. The significance of Walwal and its neighboring points of Wardair, Afdub, and Ado was that these spots, along with Gerlogubi, offered the greatest supply of water in the Ogaden. For years the 359 wells at Walwal were a source of life for the region's nomadic tribes, a prize fought for by local chiefs. On an arid plain, control of the waterholes gives control of the population.

In October 1926 the governor of Italian Somaliland, the quadrumvir Cesare De Vecchi, decided to push the confines of the colony westward and to take control of the line of water spots, including Walwal and Wardair; these would be claimed, in terms of the 1908 treaty, as the eastern boundary of the sultanate of Obbia, whose subjects drifted "towards the coast." One purpose of this policy was to claim Walwal as a dependency of Italy. De Vecchi did not at the time carry out his plan of expansion, but before he left Somaliland in 1929 he revived the scheme and his successors, Guido Corni and Maurizio Rava, put it into action. From 1929 on, Italian officers commanding armed native

[4] P. Potter, *The Wal Wal Arbitration* (Washington, 1938), 38.

Somali troops in mobile patrols were in effective control of this part of the Ogaden. In the spring of 1930 a garrison post was built at Walwal, establishing the Italians in permanent occupation. A sector command position was installed at Wardair, about nine miles from Walwal, and the Italians began to propagandize the native population of the border.[5]

The Italians were in *de facto* occupation of Walwal. An attempt by Haile Selassie to regain control of the area was thwarted in September 1931, and he had to recall a large force of armed men sent out from Harar under Deputy-Governor Dedjazmach Gabre Miriam.[6] Another effort to stir up trouble for Italy in the Ogaden, this time by Fitaurari Mezlekia, also failed; it was called off in March 1933 because of a strong diplomatic stand by Italy and a shrinking of Ethiopian troops because of illness.[7] No further efforts were made by the Ethiopian government to assert its sovereignty, and Ethiopia did not even officially protest the Italian penetration.[8] In 1932 the governor of the Ogaden, an uncle of the emperor, died in a plane crash; this put a halt to Ethiopian patrols in this region.[9] Italian control seemed complete. No Ethiopian or British-protected person was allowed to go to the wells of Walwal without first obtaining the permission of the Italian authorities at Wardair. The water there was primarily for the use of those tribesmen claimed as Italian dependents. On 18 March 1932 Captain Roberto Cimmaruta, an Italian officer on border duty, informed the British-Ethiopian commission surveying the frontier between Ethiopia and British Somaliland that the same rules applied to it — permission to use the wells must be received from Italian authorities on the scene. The Italians in Somalia had begun a policy of "inflexible reciprocity" in

[5] R. Cimmaruta, *Ual Ual* (Milan, 1936), 54, 64; I. Lewis, *The Modern History of Somaliland* (London, 1965), 107-9. The process of control was selective. A Somali dubat testified: "The officer commanding at Galadi had ordered us to challenge any person coming from that side [west], whatever his tribe, and to send him into Italian territory with his live-stock. Persons without property did not interest the Italians. Others, if they refused, when they had once entered the territory, to become Italian nationals, were despoiled of their belongings and sent back." League, *Official Journal*, *1935*, 750-1. Galadi is some 80 miles to the east of Walwal, proof that the Italians did not consider their territory to begin until even farther to the east — along the old 1897 line.

[6] See League, *Official Journal*, *1935*, 1382, 1446; Potter, *Wal Wal Arbitration*, 101-2; Cimmaruta, *Ual Ual*, 48.

[7] League, *Official Journal*, *1935*, 1384-5, 1460, 1463, 1471, 1539.

[8] This surprising fact is noted in Potter, *Wal Wal Arbitration*, 29-30. Potter's explanation is highly speculative.

[9] Information of Marcel Griaule, a student of Ethiopia, in La Pradelle, *Le Conflit italo-éthiopien*, 151.

dealing with Ethiopia. On 1 August 1932 an order went out from Mogadishu instructing Italian authorities on the Somalia border to re-organize the military police and to prepare Somalis there for auxiliary military service. Talk was current of solving the "Italian colonial ques-tion" by expanding into adjacent parts of southern and western Ethiopia.[10]

The general hardening of Italian policy throughout 1934 caused a resurgence of virulent suspicion against Italy. On 16 November 1934 the French chargé d'affaires in Addis Ababa said that Italian-Ethiopian relations were "infinitely" more acute than two years previously.[11] From the meager evidence available, it appears that during 1934 Haile Selassie decided to confront the problem of Italian penetration in the Ogaden in two different ways — by direct military display and by a diplomatic flanking movement. Both plans, by chance or design, con-verged to meet over the issue of Walwal, in November 1934.

The emperor's first step was to commence the active harassment of the Italian positions in the Ogaden. At the beginning of 1934, according to Italian documents, the Ethiopian government made an offer to a renegade of the area, Omar Samantar: he would be paid to lead an armed band of Ethiopians and Somalis to occupy Gerlogubi, from this nearby base to attack and capture Walwal and Wardair. Omar Samantar held out for a higher price and, in early 1934, the Ethiopians broke off negotiations. In the middle of March, the Italian consul in Harar reported that Omar Samantar had decided to accept the original Ethiopian offer and was on his way to Addis Ababa to conclude an agreement. At the beginning of April, the consul at Harar and Gov-ernor Rava reported that two armed bands of a thousand men each were forming in the border region and at Jijiga, under the command of Omar Samantar and a sultan of the Makail; the men, armed by the Ethiopian government, were preparing for an assult on Walwal. In June, July, and August, telegrams went from the government of Italian Somaliland to the colonial ministry in Rome, reporting the existence of hostile forces in the Ogaden and noting the threat to Italy's outposts.[12]

[10] Cimmaruta, *Ual Ual*, 54; Hess, *Italian Colonialism in Somalia*, 172.
[11] *U.S. Diplomatic Papers, 1934*, II, 765.
[12] The account of the exploits of Omar Samantar is based primarily on the Italian memorandum presented to the League of Nations on 21 June 1935, in League, *Official Journal, 1935*, 1542–5, and on Governor Rava's testimony before the Walwal arbitration commission at Bern in August 1935, in Potter, *Wal Wal Arbitration*, 95–6.

The strategy followed here by the Ethiopian government appears as a repetition of the plan of frontier skirmishes carried on by Fitaurari Mezlekia the year before. In such cases the Ethiopian government could disclaim knowledge of or responsibility for the trouble caused by mercenaries, and any tactical success could be immediately followed by official action, forces for which were being prepared in 1934 under the command of Fitaurari Shiferra and Ato Ali Nur. Unofficial action by irregular forces was the safest way of harassing the Italians and testing their strength without becoming involved in the endless intricacies of European law and diplomacy. As it had handled the Italian complaints against Fitaurari Mezlekia, the Ethiopian foreign ministry could maintain its initiative in the face of protest by contrived delays, the search for "information," and the denial of official connection with any border incidents.

In April 1934 Count Vinci, Italy's minister to Addis Ababa, delivered a protest to the Ethiopian foreign ministry against what he claimed was the hostile behavior of Dedjazmach Gabre Mariam, deputy-governor of Harar, mentioning the "impropriety of . . . entrusting a military command to an Italian refugee sentenced for murder." [13] No Ethiopian response is recorded. In May, as foreseen, an Ethiopian garrison was established at Gerlogubi, and in July Omar Samantar and a substantial number of armed men were patrolling the Walwal area. In August illness and a shortage of supplies was reported among these irregulars, but an account book kept by their leader reveals that he was well supplied with modern ammunition during the recruiting months of October and November 1934. Some of this ammunition was given under the promise that the remaining cartridges would be returned "when the war was over." [14]

[13] League, *Official Journal, 1935,* 1544. In 1925 Omar Samantar killed an Italian army captain at a frontier station. He fled, and the Italians forgot about him until they discovered that he was in Ethiopia's pay. They then put a price of 25,000 lire on his head in an effort to discredit the Ethiopian government. Most anti-Italian activity in the south was mounted from Harar, the special preserve of Haile Selassie and his family. The emperor had long been governor of the province and now, in these circumstances, in May 1934 gave the nominal governorship to his son.

[14] League, *Official Journal, 1935,* 1538. The procurement of ammunition was a matter of utmost importance to the Ethiopians, especially with the rising fear of an Italian invasion. At the end of October 1934, the emperor requested permission from the German government to send a representative to Germany to purchase military supplies, including aircraft. The Germans politely turned this request aside. *Documents on German Foreign Policy,* III, 543. Overtures for the purchases of arms were also being made to firms in other European countries.

In early November, the movements of these armed bands became more marked. They were now joined by a strong force of Ethiopian regular soldiers under the command of the governor of Jijiga and Ogaden, Fitaurari Shiferra, who brought his men down from the north. These troops, the regulars led by Shiferra[15] and the Somali levies commanded by Ato Ali Nur, which now absorbed Omar Samantar's mercenaries, numbered around 600 men altogether. They were prepared for war and thought of themselves as on a military expedition. On 20 November 1934, at Ado, eighteen miles from Walwal, this force met the British-Ethiopian boundary commission, which had been traveling for two weeks down from the north with its own escort of 44 men. Until the commission reached Ado, it traveled in regions where the inhabitants were under British protection and subject to British patrols; as a result, a platoon of the Somaliland Camel Corps was judged sufficient protection. Past Ado, the possibility of Italian-inspired trouble provided one possible reason for having a larger escort. Ethiopians always feared a Somali attack when in the Ogaden. But a larger escort had not been requested by the British section of the commission, and the Englishmen were surprised to encounter these new Ethiopian troops. At any rate, the large Ethiopian force now became the commission's escort, and together the groups moved toward Walwal and the Italian garrison.

We do not know what specific orders were directing the Ethiopian military force. It is likely that its general had no clear instructions. Most probably the soldiers were simply meant to be on hand when the commission confronted the Italians at Walwal, to add force to whatever requests the commission might make, to gain a certain legitimacy from the commission's presence, to fight if the occasion arose — to reap, in other words, whatever advantages might accrue to Ethiopia from the confrontation. Evidently a straightforward offensive action against Italy was not planned.

The presence of the British fit perfectly into the emperor's plan for a military display, and may well have motivated it in the first place. The British were interested in who controlled the lowlands, for over

[15] Shiferra, a relative of the empress', brought some 60 men from Jijiga. The second-in-command of the Ethiopian force was Fitaurari Alemayehu, also related to the empress. He joined Shiferra on 20 November, the same day the mixed commission arrived and met the combined force at Ado. On 20 November Shiferra greeted Alemayehu with the message: "Let me know at once the number of men who have come with you under orders for the military expedition." Alemayehu had about 300 men. League, *Official Journal, 1935,* 1538.

the Ogaden passed the protected tribes from British Somaliland. British interest was such that the Italians suspected London of preparing an "encirclement of Italian Somaliland." According to Governor Rava, for years before 1934 the British had tried to create "a kind of zone of influence on the other side of the frontier land between the Ogaden and Italian territory." [16] Rava claimed that the British sent out armed bands of natives from British Somaliland to cross Ethiopian territory and exert their influence on the native populations along the Italian frontier. This constant movement of subject peoples across the Ogaden made control of the vital water spots important to all three nations whose representatives were now converging on Walwal. Britain and Ethiopia were each content to let the other have the wells; both disliked Italian control, especially the Ethiopians in their new assertion of sovereignty.

For some time, a joint British-Ethiopian commission had been at work to the north marking out the border between Ethiopia and British Somaliland in accordance with a long-standing treaty. Since January 1934, the British section of the commission had planned to make a survey of the migration of tribes in the Ogaden after completing the task of demarcation. In July the British minister in Addis Ababa, Sir Sidney Barton, suggested that the Ethiopian section accompany them. In September the Ethiopian government gave its permission, and on 20 October 1934, the same day that Fitaurari Alemayehu entered the Ogaden with his troops, the commission, finished with its work of demarcation, received a formal request from the Ethiopian and British governments to move to the south; they were "to survey on the spot the grazing-grounds of the Ogaden" as part of an effort to determine rights of joint jurisdiction of migrating tribes. The job was carried out, and extensive reports were submitted.[17]

This investigation of the situation in the Ogaden was of such a nature that it could be used by the British government in the event of any transfer of Ethiopian territory to Britain. Haile Selassie had been toying with the idea of ceding to the British lands bordering on the hinterland of British Somaliland in exchange for a corridor of land providing Ethiopia access to the sea. The area considered for the transfer ran south and east of what was later known as the "red line," running

---

[16] Potter, *Wal Wal Arbitration*, 97.
[17] League, *Official Journal*, 1935, 756–9; E. H. M. Clifford, "The British Somaliland-Ethiopia Boundary," *Geographical Journal*, 87:289–302 (April 1936).

from Jijiga near Harar southeast to Wardair where it turned south to Ferfer. This vast crescent included almost half the Ogaden, almost two thirds of the area bordering Italian Somaliland, and all the disputed well areas around Walwal.[18] Such a transfer would increase the size and value of British Somaliland by a considerable degree and, above all, end the danger to Ethiopia of Italian penetration into the low-lying southeast. This plan for eliminating the threat of an invasion from Italian Somaliland reflected Haile Selassie's growing concern over Italy's new encroachments after 1930. An investigation for such a purpose was not part of the formal terms of reference for the work of the British section of the commission, but it was understood that the section's report would be the foundation for any diplomatic discussions in which the transfer might be negotiated. The British section had been asked earlier, while it was in the hinterland of Zeila, to draw up maps for three possible land corridors of varying widths, which would form the basis for bargaining with the Ethiopian government.

The joint commission had worked its way south, through Daggah Bur, then to Ado where, on 20 November 1934, it was joined by the new Ethiopian force sent ostensibly to act as an escort. The combined party now set its sights for Walwal and those crucial 359 wells. The British government was aware that Walwal was under Italian occupation: Anthony Eden, in a reply in the House of Commons on 21 February 1935, stated that the existence of an Italian garrison at Walwal was known to the British government at least since 1932.[19] This occupation was considered illegal. The acting chief of the Egyptian department in the British Foreign Office said on 15 October 1934 that the wells of Walwal were "clearly" in Ethiopian territory under any interpretation of the 1908 treaty.[20] The head of the British section of the boundary commission, Lieutenant-Colonel E. H. M. Clifford, stated in a report of 30 November that he was aware of Captain Cimmaruta's warning of March 1932 that Italian permission should be

---

[18] John H. Spencer, who advised the Ethiopian foreign office in this period, helped me to determine the area considered for transfer.

[19] *Parliamentary Debates*, 298 H.C. Deb. 5s., cols. 537–8.

[20] *U.S. Diplomatic Papers, 1934*, II, 760. Curiously, Sir Samuel Hoare, writing long after the event, states that Walwal was "situated in what had been recognized in fact as part of the Italian colony." Viscount Templewood (Samuel Hoare), *Nine Troubled Years* (London, 1954), 150. (Published by Wm. Collins Sons and Co. Ltd.; permission to quote granted by Curtis Brown Ltd.)

requested to draw water at Walwal,[21] but he made no effort to acquire such permission. Almost simultaneous with the arrival of the British mission at Walwal, the secretary of the British embassy in Rome verbally informed the Italian foreign ministry that a British mission "intended probably" to visit the wells of Walwal and Wardair. For some reason, perhaps a bureaucratic delay in Rome, this information did not reach Governor Rava in Mogadishu or Cimmaruta at Wardair until after the joint commission had arrived.[22]

Between 20 and 22 November 1934, the rendevous took place between the commission and the military force of Fitaurari Shiferra. On the 22nd, Shiferra and Omar Samantar, with their 600 troops, arrived before the Italian fort at Walwal "to prepare the camp." The activity, and the possibility of an armed clash at the wells, was immediately reported to Rome by Governor Rava. The next day, setting out from Ado, the commission arrived and joined its escort. The Italians were surprised at the appearance of the "expedition" at Walwal, the objective of which they did not know. However, Cimmaruta told Clifford, for three weeks they had been expecting an Ethiopian force (of undetermined size) to arrive in the vicinity. In the Italian garrison there were some 160 native soldiers, *dubats*. Rava in Mogadishu was alarmed by the size of the Ethiopian force. Fearing at worse the beginning of an Ethiopian march to the sea, he made arrangements to have the post adequately reinforced, but at the moment there was no Italian national on the scene. The garrison troops, commanded by a Somali noncommissioned officer, refused to evacuate the territory needed by the three British and Ethiopian camps. They were pushed back, without violence, by the far greater numbers of the Ethiopian escort force. Camps were established, and the Union Jack was raised over the British camp at the suggestion of the Ethiopian section. The flag was raised from a can on the ground, not planted in the soil, to signify British recognition of Ethiopia's territorial sovereignty. On the same day, 23 November, Clifford sent a formal protest to Cimmaruta, objecting to the fact that the commission was "prevented by force from moving about freely in Abyssinia

[21] League, *Official Journal, 1935*, 264. Clifford comments on this warning of 1932: "It goes without saying that the British Government did not even reply to such a communication."

[22] Potter, *Walwal Arbitration*, 129–30.

by the Italian authorities in the Walwal region." [23] Cimmaruta arrived at Walwal on the following day and declared that as a soldier he was not competent to discuss the subject of the British protest, "a problem which concerns only the political authorities." The matter rested for the moment, but upon the arrival of two Italian planes from Wardair, which flew threateningly over the camps of the commission, to the "great indignation" of Clifford and his party, Clifford decided to withdraw the British section. The Italians had not requested the withdrawal, but he was unwilling to become directly embroiled in any Italian-Ethiopian argument over rights to Walwal. On the 25th both sections of the commission and their personal escorts left Walwal for Ado, eighteen miles away. The 400 men of Shiferra stayed in position at the wells.

For the next ten days the two sides faced each other along a line of brushwood often not more than six feet across, and the state of tension grew. Ethiopian reinforcements arrived, the force soon numbering, it was said, between 1,400 and 1,600 men.[24] Rava sent more equipment to Wardair and wrote instructions to the officers of the sector that "so long as the armed Ethiopians do not use arms against our military post, refrain from any hostile act whatsoever." [25] At last, however, during the afternoon of 5 December 1934, a shot of indeterminate origin broke out from the ranks, and a short but fierce battle followed. It was over by dawn on the 6th, with the Ethiopians routed and in flight to Ado, and the Italians still in command of Walwal. Ethiopian losses were 107 dead and 45 wounded; the Italian *dubats* suffered 30 dead and about 100 wounded.

At no time during the incident did the British or the Ethiopians

[23] League, *Official Journal, 1935*, 258.

[24] This figure, originally an Italian estimate, is probably too high, although it is generally and officially used. Clifford reported at the time that Shiferra's Ethiopian force was around 550 men. They were opposed by some 430 men under Italian leadership.

[25] League, *Official Journal, 1935*, 1545. Rava did caution restraint, but it must be noted that both he and Cimmaruta were good Fascists and were no doubt aware of the potential importance of the Walwal confrontation. Although they were not immediately responsible for the outbreak of fighting, for reasons of personal reputation, national prestige, and orders from Rome, neither man wanted to see the Walwal incident end in other than an Italian victory. The incident followed close upon the November visit of the king of Italy and the highest colonial officials. Rava won the king's praise for his firm hand and control in Italian Somaliland. Caviglia, *Diario*, 126. Cimmaruta returned to Wardair and the crisis directly after the excitement of leading his camel corps past the royal visitor; he was himself about to leave for Italy after his tour of duty. Cimmaruta, *Ual Ual*, 89–90.

admit to the legality of the Italian occupation of Walwal. Throughout, the Italians were treated as trespassers and Ethiopian sovereignty over the territory was affirmed.[26] Ethiopia had decided to assert its territorial rights. This stand was important. If Ethiopia hoped to cede the Ogaden to Britain, it had to do so under a clear title of ownership. This meant an intransigent stand against Italy's occupation of Walwal, and no discussion whatever of its legitimacy. The wells were too important to Ethiopia to allow any admission of disputed ownership. But the Ethiopian force did not make an offensive onslaught against the Italian garrison. The emperor had ordered caution, and Shiferra was a mild little man who may have been selected to command the escort because he could be relied upon to hold back the more bellicose Ethiopian leaders.[27] On the other hand, for the reasons noted above and on the grounds that he would lose necessary prestige by withdrawing, Haile Selassie refused to order the force to retire, against the nearly unanimous advice of his counselors.[28] The time for a showdown had come. The Ethiopian troops did not retreat until the military balance was tipped away from their more numerous force by the presence at Walwal of Italian machine guns, armored motor vehicles, and planes.

The decision of the Italian government to stand firm at Walwal, no less intractable than the emperor's, was a manifestation of Mussolini's resolve to embark on an Ethiopian campaign. From the summer of 1934 on, Italy acted uncompromisingly in all incidents with Ethiopia. To be sure, the Italian plan was to provoke an incident that could be used as a justifiable reason for war only after Italy's military preparations had been completed and when a swift response would be

[26] See, e.g., Clifford's letter to Cimmaruta on 29 November 1934, which reads in part: "the Italo-Abyssinian Convention, signed on May 16th, 1908, at Addis-Ababa, stipulates that the whole of the Ogaden territory shall remain an Abyssinian dependency. As the Commission's terms of reference in that region merely concern the Ogaden territory and the tribes under British protectorate, there has never been any question of the Commission's entering Italian territory." League, *Official Journal, 1935*, 261.

[27] General Eric Virgin, *The Abyssinia I Knew*, N. Walford, trans. (London, 1936), 139. Virgin was the emperor's military adviser, and very well informed. A. T. Curle, who with Clifford was a member of the British section of the mixed commission and present at the Walwal incident, knew Shiferra and made this suggestion about him to me. I am grateful to Lieutenant-Colonel Curle and to Colonel E. H. M. Clifford for sharing with me their personal recollections of the events in the Ogaden. The responsibility for all interpretations is mine alone.

[28] *U.S. Diplomatic Papers, 1934*, II, 766.

possible. Since military preparations were just beginning, it seemed to some premature to use the Walwal episode in this way. A later provocation secretly engineered by Colonel Ruggero in Addis Ababa would provide a better diplomatic and legal justification for action. Still, Walwal was the most important confrontation yet, and a strong stand was called for as ground work for future action. To admit Ethiopian sovereignty in the Ogaden, to withdraw from the wells, would be an ignominious retreat. The Italian government therefore decided to challenge Ethiopia by a show of force on the scene, to assert Italy's claims and to deny Ethiopia's, and to make of the Walwal encounter the first step on the road to conquest.

Immediately following the Walwal incident, the Ethiopian foreign minister and the Italian chargé d'affaires in Addis Ababa exchanged protests, each accusing the other's government of responsibility for the fighting.[29] The Italian note demanded a full apology and reparations of an amount to be specified later. These steps opened the diplomatic phase of the coming Italian-Ethiopian conflict. On 9 December the Ethiopian government, "desirous of reaching a settlement in accordance with law," invoked article 5 of the Treaty of Amity, Conciliation, and Arbitration signed on 2 August 1928, providing for the settlement by "conciliation or arbitration" of disputes which the ordinary processes of diplomacy could not resolve. On 11 December, making no reference to Ethiopia's statement, the Italian government demanded moral and material satisfaction for the Walwal incident, including a formal apology from Ethiopia, recognition of Italy's right to occupy Walwal by paying homage to the Italian flag there, the surrender of Omar Samantar to Italian hands, and compensation in the sum of 200,000 Maria Theresa dollars.[30] On 14 December Italy

<hr />

[29] Minister Vinci, it is curious to note, was on a return trip to Rome at this time of crisis. Vinci left Addis Ababa on 30 November knowing, as the American chargé in Ethiopia reported, of an impending critical situation at Walwal. U.S. Department of State, Diplomatic Correspondence, Foreign Affairs Branch, National Archives, Decimal File No. 765.84/111; hereafter referred to as U.S. Diplomatic Correspondence.

[30] There was a precedent for such a demand. In November 1934 a civil disturbance had broken out in Gondar, in the course of which a person at the Italian consulate was killed. The Ethiopian government, on demand, paid an indemnity and offered its apologies. The prompt settlement of this matter showed a desire on the part of the Ethiopian government to prevent Italy from using the incident as an excuse for reprisals. The Italians were quick to proclaim the Gondar incident, in which the Ethiopian government was in no way involved,

refused to submit the dispute to the arbitration required by the treaty.[31]

The British and French ministers in Addis Ababa were anxious to bank the incident before it burst into a larger conflagration. They pressed the Ethiopian government to accept the Italian demands.[32] This Haile Selassie could not do, for he realized it would only encourage Italy in further actions and lead to the loss of the Ogaden. The rases were urging the emperor to take immediate action against Italy as a reprisal for the incident.[33] The problem Haile Selassie faced was how to keep the peace and at the same time maintain Ethiopia's prestige and security.

The emperor had one important factor in his favor. Walwal was in his country, and so Ethiopia had a case that would stand adjudication. In the face of veiled pressure from the representatives of Britain and France, who wanted the matter settled swiftly even if it would benefit Italy,[34] Haile Selassie turned to the one court that could not deny him a hearing, the one institution that, by its own laws, could not put individual advantage above general principles, the one body that, though it did not love, could not harm Ethiopia, the one body that had proved its worth once before in 1926. On the night of 14 December 1934, the day the Italians formally rejected the arbitration clause of the treaty of 1928, Ethiopia, acting under paragraph 2, article 11, of the Covenant, formally brought the Italian-Ethiopian question before the council of the League of Nations.[35]

---

as an example of Ethiopia's belligerency and a precursor of the "aggression" at Walwal. See "Sull'incidente di Ual Ual," *Affari esteri*, 1:9–10 (20 December 1934).

[31] Texts of the notes are found in League, *Official Journal, 1935,* 270–4.

[32] Virgin, *Abyssinia*, 156.

[33] Aloisi noted in his journal on 24 December 1934 that the Italian colonial office told him that the rases wanted to dethrone Haile Selassie because the emperor was against any action "in the grand style" against Italy. *Journal*, 239.

[34] Already wary of the French minister, the emperor also viewed his friend Sir Sidney Barton, the British minister, with some reserve at this time. The British embassy in Addis Ababa gave no help to Ethiopia at this critical hour, despite the presence of the British mission at Walwal and the British interests at stake in the Ogaden. The British government informed the emperor that Britain desired to have no connection whatsoever with the affair. *U.S. Diplomatic Papers, 1934*, II, 770, 773. In June 1935 Haile Selassie revealed to the American chargé in Addis Ababa that, shortly after the Walwal incident, he applied to the British government for a British frontier police force. U.S. Diplomatic Correspondence, 765.84/535.

[35] The text of paragraph 2 reads: "It is also declared to be the friendly right of each Member of the League to bring to the attention of the Assembly or of the Council any circumstances whatever affecting international relations which threatens to disturb international peace or the good understanding between nations upon which peace rests."

The Italians were chagrined by this move. Naturally Italy did not want the League to take cognizance of the dispute, for this would put in train endless political, legal, and moral complications, sure to embarrass Italy and perhaps to raise grave difficulties. Mussolini wanted to be left alone to devour Ethiopia in his own way in his own time, without the interference of anyone. The Italian government thus tried to discount the League's interest or authority in the dispute and to underplay the incident's significance. An often officially inspired journal, Milan's *Corriere della sera*, which did not comment on the Walwal incident until 18 December, said then: "The League of Nations has nothing to say and ought to say nothing . . . No juridical questions ought to be resolved in this specific case. To complicate things will not help relations between Italy and Ethiopia, which, until now have been excellent and which ought not to be troubled by one incident." [36]

In Rome the Walwal incident and the emperor's quick refusal to bow to Italian demands galvanized Mussolini's plans. Here was the "overt act," the spur to action. From this time on, Italian preparations for war began in earnest. On 20 December Mussolini drew up a lengthy "Directive and Plan of Action for the Resolution of the Italian-Abyssinian Question," secret copies of which were issued on 30 December 1934 to his closest advisers.[37] The fourteen-point memorandum, with its spelled-out intentions and precise instructions, governed Italy's course for the year to come.

(1) The first paragraph, reflecting the mood of decisiveness after Walwal, claimed that diplomacy could no longer solve the "problem" of Ethiopia, and that force of arms remained the only way to deal with the country.

(2–4) These paragraphs echoed the warnings of Guariglia and Zoli, that Ethiopia under Haile Selassie was becoming centralized, modernized, politically adept, and hence a more powerful state. European technicians were improving the efficiency of the Ethiopian army.

(5) The above facts led to inescapable conclusions for Italy: "Time

---

[36] Quoted in A. Cohen, *La Société des Nations devant le conflit italo-éthiopien (décembre 1934–octobre 1935), politique et procédure* (Geneva, 1960), 57n. Reports on the incident appeared in the Italian press by 8 December, and moderate editorials on the episode, such as the one noted here, began appearing by the 12th.

[37] The full directive, which the present point-by-point discussion follows, is printed in A. Lessona, *Memorie*, 165–71. See also De Bono, *Anno XIIII*, 116.

works against us . . . it is necessary to resolve the problem as soon as possible."

(6) The problem of relations with Ethiopia could be solved in only one way: "The destruction of the Abyssinian armed forces and the total conquest of Ethiopia."

(7) What mattered most for Italy was to be granted a free hand by the powers of Europe. No war in Ethiopia could be carried on in the face of active opposition from Britain or France. Mussolini did not believe there would be trouble from Europe, so long as the Italian action took place soon, while the political climate was favorable and before the impending storm in Europe broke. There was a significant precedent in Morocco. There, a few years before, the French, using aircraft and tanks, had defeated the "republic" of Abdel Krim in a clear-cut colonial war. The French took advantage of a moment when Germany was not yet armed, and this fact alone gave them freedom to act. The French had made a modern colonial conquest, without stirring up the slightest criticism or hindrance from the nations of Europe.

(8) As far as Mussolini could see, Europe would remain tranquil at least through the middle of 1937 — until Germany was strong enough to take the initiative. The Nazi government for the present wanted peace, to build up its armed forces and to consolidate the regime. The one complication would occur if European weakness inspired Hitler to march into Austria.[38] But an accord between France and Italy would be a keystone for European stability at least while Italy was engaged in Africa.

(9) To the political need for quick action was added the danger that the Italian colonies would face when Ethiopia became militarily stronger. If Ethiopia was not conquered as soon as possible, and if Italy became involved in a renewal of the struggle for mastery in Europe, the Italian colonies would lie defenseless, at the mercy of Ethiopia.

(10) Mussolini foresaw at least 100,000 metropolitan soldiers em-

[38] In December 1934, it was reported later, Mussolini telephoned Vittorio Cerruti, the Italian ambassador in Berlin: "I have decided to take revenge next year for Aduwa." Cerruti said that Hitler would support this because it would weaken Italy's opposition to the Anschluss. Mussolini asked how long before Hitler would be ready to invade Austria. Cerruti said two years. Good, said Mussolini, for "by then I will have conquered Ethiopia. This campaign will last only seven months." Report in *Il Tempo*, 20 April 1959, quoted in Roux, *Mussolini*, 215.

ployed in the war against Ethiopia. They, as well as native African troops under Italian command, would have to be prepared to march in October 1935. Complete preparations were essential, for the war had to be short and decisive: "The more rapid our military action the less will be the danger of diplomatic complications. No one in Europe will raise any difficulties for us if the conduct of military operations rapidly creates an accomplished fact. It will be enough to declare to England and France that their interests will be recognized." Mussolini contemptuously dismissed the League of Nations. The League would do nothing; if it did, no matter, for its action would not be sufficient to impede the conduct of the war.

(11) A renewed "peripheral policy" should begin at once, to impress both Eritreans and Ethiopian chiefs with the might and determination of Italy. The aim of this political subversion was to weaken Ethiopia's power to resist invasion, by dividing the emperor's forces and demoralizing the populace.

(12) The crucial task for policy planners and diplomats was to regulate the timing of the program of military preparation and developments in international and domestic politics. The campaign was now set to begin at the end of the rainy season in the autumn of 1935. Italian diplomacy was to make certain that no incident caused this date to be put off or advanced.

(13) Military supplies were to be reallocated without, the Duce hoped, a diminution of the army's "global efficiency."

(14) The last point in Mussolini's directive was an assurance that Fascists were convinced of the inevitability of a conflict with Ethiopia, and that the morale of Fascist youth was high.[39] He did not put forward any of the economic, demographic, or social arguments later contrived to befuddle the naive at home and abroad. He based Italy's

---

[39] Mussolini did not claim that all the Italian people were behind him, and, except in the negative sense of providing a safety valve for popular discontent, he ignored public opinion in making his decision to go into Ethiopia. See *Documents on British Foreign Policy, 1919–1939,* ser. 3, III, 496. The Italian populace was interested in and increasingly aware of Italy's new activities in international affairs, but Mussolini kept the people largely ignorant of the true implications of his foreign-policy decisions. G. Bastianini, *Uomini, cose, fatti* (Milan, 1959), 46. The Ethiopian campaign did not become popular until British opposition made itself felt. Then the small war of colonial expansion was transformed into a war of national survival and honor. Chabod, *A History of Italian Fascism,* 77–8. C. F. Delzell, *Mussolini's Enemies: The Italian Anti-Fascist Resistance* (Princeton, 1961), 137–40, discusses the various reactions against the coming war as expressed by anti-Fascist Italians in exile.

claim to Ethiopia on pure imperialist lines: "This problem has existed since 1885. Ethiopia is the last part of Africa that is not owned by Europeans. The Gordian knot of Italo-Abyssinian relations is going to become increasingly entangled. It is necessary to cut it before it is too late."

With the directive of 20 December 1934, the Italian government established its intention to undertake a war of colonial conquest nine months later. The strategic goal was defined — the establishment of Fascist control in east Africa by the invasion and conquest of Ethiopia. The date was set for the beginning of operations — October 1935. The second step now, and a crucial one, was to come to an agreement with France. On 24 December Mussolini told Aloisi that the Ethiopian affair would "mature" when Italy concluded an accord with France, and that it was therefore necessary to hurry this project along.[40]

[40] Aloisi, *Journal*, 239.

Chapter 4

January: The French-Italian Entente

During the late 1920s and early 1930s, relations between France and Italy ranged from cool at best to downright hostile. No great common need or danger brought the two countries together, and important differences in interest and policy kept them apart. France, exhausted and passive, its ideals, treasure, and manhood spent in the world war only just over, needed quiet in Europe to recover its strength. With its allies in the Little Entente, France insisted on a maintenance of the postwar settlement, and the "Versailles system" was created to encircle Germany and hold the peace. Mussolini, on the other hand, not content to accept the status quo, vaunted the ideals of belligerent activity, "dynamism," expansionism, and revisionism in the foreign affairs of Italy. His attitudes and plans came into conflict with France's interests in central and southeastern Europe. Mussolini wanted to establish Italy's influence in the region of the Danube. He made overtures to Hungary. His proprietary movements toward Albania and his friendship with Bulgaria and Rumania were manifestations of his hope for some control in the Balkans. And his ambitions were sharpened by the fact that Italy now had a good port on the eastern side of the Adriatic.

Italy's activities alarmed and annoyed the French. Italian revisionism threatened the Versailles system, and Mussolini's expansionism threatened the vital interests of at least one of the nations of the Little Entente. Yugoslavia feared an Italian encirclement. Fronting on the Adriatic, with Italy in control of Trieste and Fiume, surrounded by Albania, Hungary, and Bulgaria (all of whom Italy tried to win over), bitter at Italian aid to Croatian terrorists, Yugoslavia saw Italy as a determined foe. As long as Mussolini continued his policy of opposition to any stable, coordinated system of cooperation or understanding among these various states on the outskirts of Europe, and until he refrained from forcing Italian ambitions into the interstices left by their own restless rivalries, no peace could come to these areas. France could not help but view the situation dimly.[1]

Two other problems, exclusively French-Italian, strained relations between the two countries. One concerned the status of Italians in Tunisia. The other was the matter of colonial compensation due Italy according to the terms of article 13 of the Treaty of London of 1915.

French-Italian friction in Tunisia was long-standing. No part of Africa is closer to Italy than Tunisia, and Italians by the thousands emigrated to its shores, forming the largest European group in the country. In 1868 Italy and the Bey of Tunis signed an agreement giving juridical rights and civil guarantees to the Italian citizens there. In 1881 France, encouraged by Bismarck, imposed a protectorate on the country and, although Italy did not recognize the validity of this new arrangement, France agreed to respect the privileges accorded the resident Italians in 1868. Then in 1896, profiting from Italy's unfavorable diplomatic position after Aduwa, France compelled the bey to renounced the 1868 agreement. Immediate Italian protests led to a compromise: Italy recognized Tunisia as a French protectorate and France established the Conventions of September 1896, which in substance reproduced the guarantees given by the bey. Under the conventions Italians preserved the right to maintain and perpetuate their own nationality, to have their own Italian-language schools, and various other special privileges.[2] But the tensions remained. French restrictions gradually infringed on the Italians' freedom and, in September 1918, in the wake of changes brought on by the war, France denounced two of the three conventions dealing with the economic and commercial privileges of resident Italians. This angered the Italians, even though the French eventually agreed, pending a final settlement, to renew the conventions for periods of three months at a time. Italians by now considered their compatriots in Tunisia as part of *Italia irredenta*. Since Tunisia was only a French protectorate, not a colonial possession, Italy never gave up its claim to full Italian citizenship for its overseas nationals. But the temporary trimonthly renewals con-

---

[1] "The reorganization of Central and South East Europe raises perhaps the only real problem which brings French and Italian policy directly to grips." M. Pernot, "Franco-Italian Relations," *International Affairs*, 13:520-1 (July-August 1934).

[2] Macartney and Cremona, *Italy's Foreign and Colonial Policy*, 126.

tinued to govern their status, and the situation was made more acute by French laws that made any child born in a French protectorate *ipso facto* a French citizen and by Fascist Italy's exaggerated nationalistic demands supporting the rights of its cross-channel nationals. France became increasingly suspicious of Tunisia's Italians, for the growing Italian population, which outnumbered the French by some 30,000 persons, might cause a serious threat to French control. Nice and Savoy seemed like dead letters compared to the persistent Italian claims in Tunisia.

The second strictly French-Italian problem, also an old bone of contention, was the debt owed Italy under the Treaty of London. This 1915 agreement, it will be recalled, was the bribe offered Italy to enter the war on the Allies' side. It promised Italy "equitable compensation . . . specially in the regulation in her favour of the boundary questions between the colonies of Eritrea, Somaliland and Libya and the contiguous French and English colonies," to be commensurate with the spoils from the former German empire received by Britain and France. In 1924 the British ceded Jubaland to Italy to liquidate their side of the debt. France's contribution had never been settled.

From France, in 1919, the Italians demanded French Somaliland, control of the Djibouti–Addis Ababa railroad,[3] and boundary rectifications on the south and west of the Libyan frontier. The first demands had already been turned down in 1915, and all that France was willing to concede at the end of the war was a small adjustment of the western Libyan border, giving Italy greater control over some caravan watering holes, and a few improvements in the status of Italians in Tunisia. These meager gains did not satisfy Italy and, as time went on, as Italy consolidated and expanded its position in Libya, greater demands were pressed upon the French.[4] By the 1930s Italian claims in this area had extended southward into the area north of Lake Chad. The Italian request was not exorbitant, but the French, fearful of any hindrance to the communications between their great African holdings to the west and south of the region, refused to consider it. They maintained that, by an agreement of 1902, Italy had no claim to the Libyan hinterland further south than the Tummo area, and there the

---

[3] An excellent study of French-Italian negotiations with regard to Djibouti and the railroad is M. Toscano, *Francia ed Italia di fronte al problema di Gibuti* (Florence, 1939).

[4] Macartney and Cremona, *Italy's Foreign and Colonial Policy*, 128-9.

matter rested. Italian demands for compensation under the 1915 agreement remained unfulfilled.

France and Italy were thus separated by conflicts of policy and of interest. But after 1933, in the face of a resurgent Nazi Germany, new needs emerged, and the two Latin sisters began to come closer together at last. In 1934 France's worst fears were realized. The specter of a rearmed Germany turned into a reality that would have to be dealt with. Across Europe went Louis Barthou, negotiating and persuading in an effort to contain Germany with a ring of watchful states. Poland wavered, keeping to its own devices, but the Little Entente went along with France. Still this was not enough. To give real strength to his policy of defensive encirclement, the French foreign minister saw that he must associate the Soviet Union and Italy in his system of alliances. Russia, pariah among nations, was brought into the League under French sponsorship in September 1934, with a permanent seat on the council, and a French-Russian treaty of mutual assistance was signed in May 1935 by Laval, Barthou's successor.

At least as early as 1932, the French had seen the value in an understanding with Italy. In December of that year Henry de Jouvenel was named ambassador to Rome with instructions to search out, with the Italian government, "the basis of an entente which would not put in peril [France's] Mediterranean interests or other alliances." [5] The mission was not a success because Mussolini discounted its importance in France's over-all planning. Also, in the first flush of excitement over his four-power pact, he was in no mood to see a French-Italian agreement muddled by objections from the states of the Little Entente. This would surely happen (as indeed it did with the pact), since Mussolini insisted to Jouvenel that Hungarian revisionism must be endorsed. Italy viewed with skeptical suspicion French efforts to build up a security system. Why was the four-power pact not good enough for France? Why should Italy sacrific its *dinamismo* in the Balkans to France's interest? With the Soviet Union as well Mussolini wanted to steal a march on France, and in September 1933 he signed a treaty of friendship and neutrality with Russia, designed "to neutralize the action of Herriot and the French." As long as Mussolini was absorbed in his own, rival, plans for Europe, France could make no progress toward the desirable entente with Italy. We have already seen, for

[5] J. Paul-Boncour, *Entre deux guerres* (Paris, 1945), II, 338–9.

instance, the suspicion with which Mussolini received Berthelot's suggestion in 1931 that he interest himself in Ethiopia, a suggestion Mussolini considered a Machiavellian attempt by France to embroil Italy in Africa to the detriment of its European position.[6]

This stalemate moved toward a solution in 1934. Discouraged by the failure of his enterprising attempts to install himself as arbiter among Europe's contending powers, Mussolini turned his sights to Africa. Disillusioned and dismayed by Hitler, and needing peace now in Europe, Mussolini became increasingly receptive to the idea of an accord with France. It was just at this time that the French, insistently encouraged by Jouvenel's successor, Count Charles de Chambrun, renewed their efforts to bring Italy into the anti-German camp. There were, after all, areas of agreement between the two countries. Both opposed any German movement into Austria. Both feared for Europe when a restive Germany had rearmed itself. Even as early as March 1933, Mussolini admitted that two French-Italian issues, the statute governing Italians in Tunisia and the question of frontier rectification in Libya, were not insoluble.[7]

In 1934 Raffaele Guariglia set out the advantages of a settlement with France. In the first place, Guariglia said, Italy stood in a strong bargaining position. It was France that now sought an accord with Italy, not, as in the past, vice versa. Furthermore, there was a new factor: Italy could not move into Ethiopia without some prior approval from France, similar to that received from Britain in 1925. Without the consent of all the partners in the 1906 treaty, any full-scale Italian expansion in east Africa ran the serious risk of leading to a conflict in Europe. France now wanted Italian support in Europe and seemed willing to sacrifice its sphere of influence in Ethiopia to get it. The time was ripe for Italy to take advantage of this French-inspired opportunity.

Only one difficulty stood in the way of such an agreement: the Italian claims in Tunisia. France, as Guariglia saw it, demanded Tunisia in return for Ethiopia. The eventual goal was to turn Tunisia from a mere protectorate into a full-fledged French colony. This was impossible as long as the large Italian population there, with its special privileges, constituted something of an empire within an empire. For

---

[6] Aloisi, *Journal*, 46, 79–80, 143; Guariglia, *Ricordi*, 114, 144.
[7] Aloisi, *Journal*, 79.

the present Italy was not strong enough to challenge France for Tunisia, but the opportunity was at hand to create a vast Italian empire in east Africa. Cold reason thus demanded that, to gain the reality of control in Ethiopia, Italy would have to give up its strong but at present less important claims to privileges in Tunisia. This renunciation did not have to be permanent, nor the sacrific complete. By means of shrewd diplomacy, Italian privileges could be prolonged until Italy, stronger in its new empire, could take an army to Tunisia, win it as a prize of war, and establish Italian sovereignty. The conquest of Ethiopia, however, was the major and immediate goal, and an understanding with France was a *sine qua non* of an Ethiopian campaign.[8]

In 1934 Italy followed such a line in settling a colonial difference with the British. By the early 1930s Italy had completed its conquest of Tripolitania and Cyrenaica with the subjugation of the Kurfa oasis in the southeast of the territory that became Libya. Italian desert patrols then had pushed further to the southeast into the area where Egypt, the Sudan, and Libya come together. The Libyan-Egyptian frontier was long fixed, but the border between Libya and Anglo-Egyptian Sudan had not been established. No problem arose until Italy found itself strong enough to make expansionist claims in the region, which were argued in terms of the compensation still owing to Italy under the Treaty of London. In November 1933, to offset the possibility of serious conflict, the British proposed a conference in London to settle on a Libyan-Sudanese frontier. At the conference the Italians arrogantly demanded territory far to the south of Libya in the Sudan, reviving many vague claims and presuming a great deal on British patience. The result was a stalemate. Then, in mid-July 1934, the Italians reversed their stand and accepted the delineation of the frontier proposed by Britain.[9] The reason behind the about-face was obvious: if the Ethiopian campaign was to succeed, British favor must be curried. This was the "ulterior significance" of the Italian "climb-down," as one of the British negotiators, Maurice Peterson, discerned. Peterson warned London at the time "that the way was being cleared for Mussolini's descent upon Abys-

[8] Guariglia, *Ricordi*, 150, 164–8.
[9] For details see the Stefani agency dispatch of 22 July, reprinted by the French Ministère des Affaires Etrangères, *Bulletin périodique de la presse italienne*, 302:14 (Paris, 1935).

sinia." [10] The Italians, for their part, were well satisfied. Concession of a remote and unimportant desert frontier was a small price to pay if the reward was better relations with the British. Fulsome praise was heaped upon the "straightforward and correct policy of Great Britain," which "never regarded Article XIII of the Pact of London as a scrap of paper." And a broad hint was dropped to France: "There remains an open account with other contracting parties to the Pact of London." [11]

In the late summer of 1934, France and Italy drew closer together. Germany's threat to Austria strained relations between Hitler and Mussolini and pushed Italy toward France. Mussolini needed French accord for his African plans, as we have seen. Louis Barthou had maintained his interest in bringing Italy into his "grand alliance," and plans were made for the French foreign minister to go to Rome for talks, a date finally being set for 6 November. Preliminary conversations in Rome between Chambrun and the Palazzo Chigi began in July 1934, with the stated intention of regulating the differences over Tunisia and the Libyan frontier. From the beginning the Italians accepted French resistance to their claims on the Lake Chad region, agreeing that it would be preferable to "round out [their] empire in east Africa." This was part of Italy's effort at "adequate diplomatic preparations" for the Ethiopian campaign.[12] In expectation of Barthou's visit, Mussolini, speaking in Milan on 6 October 1934, announced that French-Italian relations had improved: "An entente with France would be very useful and very fruitful." [13] Cultural exchanges between the two countries also took place, and the Comédie Française performed in the Roman Forum.

Barthou had one job to do before leaving for Rome. He had to placate Yugoslavia, for he hoped on his trip to Italy to patch up the Italian-Yugoslav quarrel, a weak link in his "iron ring." King Alexander was invited to France, but the visit ended in tragedy. On 9 October, meeting at Marseilles, Barthou and the king were killed by a Croatian assassin.

Barthou's successor as French foreign minister was Pierre Laval,

---

[10] M. Peterson, *Both Sides of the Curtain* (London, 1950), 94-9, 115. It was Peterson who in August 1935 was given charge of a new department in the British Foreign Office dealing exclusively with Ethiopian affairs.

[11] Corrado Zoli, quoted in *The Times* (London), 24 July 1934.

[12] Aloisi, *Journal*, 205, 224.

[13] Mussolini, *Opera omnia*, XXVI, 358.

who approached the problem of French security in a rather different fashion.[14] Barthou had bent his energies to a single goal: the organization of multinational pacts for the containment of Germany. His negotiations were governed by this master plan, clearly defined, systematically blueprinted, frankly presented.[15] But Laval, lacking a "synthèse politique dans l'esprit," [16] distrusted "preconceived systems," which he believed forced people and facts into inflexible, and hence unmanageable, positions. Because they were too large, too diffuse, too unwieldly, Barthou's plans ran the chance of running aground. Instead of dealing with blocs, Laval preferred to deal individually with single nations. Agreements reached bilaterally could be tailor-made to fit particular needs, could be given closer attention and kept in better repair, and they offered more advantages than large general agreements among many often unruly nations. In addition, when dealing bilaterally the subtle art of personal diplomacy was most effective, an art in which Laval excelled.

Laval brought to the conduct of diplomacy the methods of mediation that he had used with such success as minister of labor. He believed in the process of conciliation and compromise. The diplomatic techniques best suited to his experience and ability were direct personal negotiation, talks tête-à-tête, discussions between leaders unimpeded as far as possible by the rigidities of predetermined doctrine, unburdened by popular pressures, and unhindered by the binding formalities of professional diplomats. The advantage of applying these methods in bilateral negotiation was that it allowed differences to be

---

[14] The change was welcome, for different reasons, in both Germany and Italy. Goering said: "We hope Barthou's German policies will disappear with him. We are confident M. Laval will adopt a more conciliatory policy." Quoted in H. Torres, *Pierre Laval*, N. Guterman, trans. (New York, 1941), 190–1. Aloisi wrote: "Laval's nomination is good for us" — *Journal*, 227. The British, according to Eden, found the change "unwelcome." Earl of Avon (Anthony Eden), *The Eden Memoirs: Facing the Dictators* (London, 1962), 111 (permission to quote granted by Cassell and Company Ltd. and Houghton Mifflin Company).

[15] However, there is evidence that Barthou favored a conciliatory reply to Germany's offer to return to the League if rearmament was allowed. Barthou was superseded in committee, and the French reply of 17 April 1934 refused all German claims, thus ending any hope for success in the Disarmament Conference. It made the French increasingly dependent on their allies for protection, and antagonized the British by its intransigence. G. Tabouis, *They Called Me Cassandra* (New York, 1942), 200–2. This is confirmed by Anthony Eden, in *Facing the Dictators*, 89. The result of this for British-French relations was, as the French statesman Edouard Herriot said, "at bottom England always reproached us for the note of 17 April." E. Herriot, *Jadis* (Paris, 1952), II, 561.

[16] G. Tabouis, *Vingt ans de "suspense" diplomatique* (Paris, 1958), 220.

ironed out before they could mature into irreversible conflicts. Laval's "fundamental desire was to keep international relations in the realm of diplomatic manoeuvre and subtle negotiation." [17] To achieve this, to keep issues from solidifying into the uncompromising positions from which war came, any means was valid. Yet the content of Laval's foreign policy was determined by more important things. He was a pacifist. Along with most Frenchmen, still stunned and fatigued by the great bloodletting of the nation during 1914–1918, Laval knew that no greater tragedy could befall France than another war. Laval had one goal, one purpose: France must be kept from war so that it could recover its strength in peace.

In 1935 France was entering the *années creuses*, the lean years. Between August 1914 and February 1917 one French soldier died for every minute, and a generation of men was destroyed. In 1934 there were 42,840 more births than deaths, but in 1935 there were 19,476 more deaths than births. The French army faced an acute manpower shortage; for several years after 1935, the usual annual call for 230,000 recruits fell to an average of only 118,000 men. Total French metropolitan troops in 1935 numbered only some 265,000 men.[18] Even with the new "two-year law," Marshal Pétain estimated that France's army total for 1936 could rise only to 405,000, whereas Germany would by then have some 600,000 men under arms.[19] The French army was weak in other regards as well. Modernization of equipment was desperately overdue. No *plan d'armement* was seriously applied before 1934, and innovations such as Charles de Gaulle's idea of a specialized mobile offensive corps were officially discouraged. The Maginot Line was France's sole strategic military plan, and the general staff completely accepted its purely defensive implications. The training of the army was substandard: the much anticipated field maneuvers at Rethel in September 1935, the first held in two years, were

---

[17] D. Thomson, *Two Frenchmen, Pierre Laval and Charles de Gaulle* (London, 1951), 51.

[18] M. Gamelin, *Servir* (Paris, 1946), II, 148–9. In 1914 France had 735,000 men under arms. Herriot, *Jadis*, II, 518.

[19] Marshal Pétain, "La Sécurité de la France au cours des années creuses," *Revue des deux mondes*, 1 March 1935, i-xx. There were also 87,000 North Africans, 16,000 Legionaires, and 109,000 colonials, making a grand total of some 577,000 men. But these additional forces were needed for use overseas. Pétain warned that the African troops might have to be sent back to repress the foreign-inspired insurrections which might result in the colonies in the event of a European war. Herriot, *Jadis*, II, 503.

undistinguished and disappointing.[20] The French were prisoners of their own weakness, and indifference or hostility toward making further preparations for national security pervaded the nation. Tired with war, weak and defensive, the French nation seemed to lack the will actively to resist the renewed threat from Germany. These were the governing conditions and limiting factors for Laval as he sought to save France from war.

Laval was not a defeatist, and he never gave up all hope of coming to a conciliatory understanding with Germany.[21] But his eye never left the menace presented by the country across the Rhine, and his main problem was to find a way to forestall a German attack on France. No less than Barthou, Laval sought France's security. For the nation's defense, Laval thought, the realities of power pointed not to an endless accumulation of weak friends in vague alignment in the east of Europe or to complete dependency on the up-to-then ineffectual League of Nations, but to direct agreements with those countries whose strength gave them immediate and substantive value as allies. This meant Britain and Italy. Accord with Britain was the first essential, and from this opinion Laval never wavered. The problem was that the British government persistently refused to come to a formal engagement with France. Nonetheless, where the islanders led, France had to follow. The next best means to French security was to have strong continental allies that stand up to Germany. This meant an agreement with Italy and, to a lesser degree, with the Soviet Union. These countries must be brought to France's side and prevented from joining Hitler's camp. Laval sought to prevent "la conjonction des dictateurs"[22] and at the same time to gain a powerful friend below the Alps.

The roads to both Moscow and Rome were already pointed out when Laval installed himself at the Quai d'Orsay in October 1934. A rough draft for an accord with Italy lay in the files of the foreign office.[23] Plans for the trip to Rome were postponed so that the new

---

[20] J. Fabry, *De la Place de la Concorde au course de l'Intendance* (Paris, 1942), 68, 80–2. General Pietro Badoglio, Italian army chief of staff, came to the Rethel maneuvers as an observer on the invitation of General Maurice Gamelin, head of the French army. Gamelin, *Servir*, II, 172.

[21] On 28 December 1935 Laval told the French Chamber that, failing a French-German rapprochement, there could be no peace in Europe. *Journal officiel, débats parlementaires*, Chambres des Députés, 29 December 1935, 2866.

[22] A. Mallet, *Pierre Laval* (Paris, 1955), 58–60.

[23] France, Haute Cour de Justice, *Procès du Maréchal Pétain* (Paris, 1945), 183.

foreign minister could acquaint himself with the relevant proposals and problems. In the meantime, putting his conciliatory diplomacy to work, Laval tried to settle the troublesome aftereffects of the Marseilles assassinations. France would use its influence with Yugoslavia to keep that country from implicating Italy in the crimes, to stem an anti-Italian reaction, and to encourage Yugoslavia to blame only Hungary. "In return Italy would do nothing to support Hungary in the League. Yugoslavia was to be told that she could not look for French military support." [24] This plan succeeded in forestalling a possible explosion, although of course it was resented by the Yugoslavs. It did, however, please Mussolini, and from Italy came paeans in the Fascist press on the subject of French-Italian brotherhood.[25]

Negotiations for a French-Italian entente opened on 1 November 1934. On 15 November Laval revealed to the French Council of Ministers his instructions to Chambrun in Rome. What France wanted from Italy was a guarantee for support if Germany broke the treaty stipulations prohibiting its rearmament, a general agreement with all adjacent states governing the independence and integrity of Austria, cooperation in the search for an economic settlement in central Europe, and the amelioration of Italian-Yugoslav relations. In Africa, France offered a rectification of the frontier in the south of Tripolitania. Italian hopes for expansion toward Lake Chad were given up.[26] But Italy had other demands: the extension for ten years of the advantages of the Convention of 1896 and the cession of French Somaliland to Italy, France being allowed to keep the port of Djibouti. These concessions would liquidate the compensation France owed under the treaty of 1915.

France could not accept these extreme demands. The colonial disagreements, however, were secondary to the greater differences of opinion regarding policies in Europe. Until late in December, negotiations were bogged down over questions of Italian relations with Yugoslavia and the degree of cooperation over the matter of Austrian independence. Negotiation was difficult, and Laval worked hard. He

[24] A. Johnson, *Anthony Eden* (New York, 1939), 234. Yugoslavia in any case was becoming a weaker reed, for the successors of King Alexander were less firmly in control and increasingly opposed to the notion of a French rapprochement with Russia. D. Brogan, *The Development of Modern France* (London, 1940), 690.

[25] See G. Salvemini, *Prelude to World War II* (London: Victor Gollancz Limited, 1953), 170.

[26] Herriot, *Jadis*, II, 484.

refused to go to Rome until definite results were obtained in the preliminary talks. Laval said on 20 December that he did not want a *solution de façade*. On the 31st negotiations came to a dead end, and Aloisi feared that the talks would have to be called off. Chambrun, the prime mover behind the negotiations, was utterly discouraged. Laval's report to his Council of Ministers on 2 January 1935 was very pessimistic: all the problems still had to be worked out; the negotiations remained confused and unsettled.[27]

Yet both sides wanted an agreement, and time was running out. Laval was in a hurry to have it done with and be back in Paris in the event a crisis arose from the certain victory of Hitler in the coming Saar plebescite.[28] In December he asked the British foreign minister, Sir John Simon, to use his good offices, and Simon confidentially advised Mussolini that Laval would come to Rome if he could be assured of success. Mussolini was impressed by Simon's information and, at the turn of the year, gave Laval this assurance.[29] Mussolini was also worried that a victory in the Saar might encourage Hitler to hasten his plans for expansion in Europe.[30] And other matters were impinging: the Walwal incident took place on 5 December, Ethiopia went to the League on the 14th, and on the 30th Mussolini circulated his fourteen-point directive "for the resolution of the Italian-Abyssinian question." War against Ethiopia was decided upon, and for its success France's friendship had to be won. Mussolini now decided to realize an accord "at all costs," and if professional diplomats with their "interminable arrangements and their endless chinoiseries" could not succeed, direct talks between the two foreign ministers were called for.[31]

These facts explain Laval's hasty and unexpected departure from Paris on the night of 3 January. Laval on his own took up the responsibility for the diplomacy of France, leaving the Quai d'Orsay largely in the dark on what was to come.[32]

[27] Herriot, *Jadis*, II, 492–3; Aloisi, *Journal*, 240. An account of some of the differences with regard to Europe is given in A. J. Toynbee, *Survey of International Affairs, 1935* (London, 1936), I, 101–3.

[28] E. Cameron, *Prologue to Appeasement* (Washington, 1942), 99.

[29] *U.S. Diplomatic Papers, 1935*, I, 189.

[30] H. Lagardelle, *Mission à Rome*, (Paris, 1955), 102–3.

[31] E. Cameron, "Alexis Saint-Léger Léger," in Craig and Gilbert, eds., *The Diplomats*, 384; Aloisi, *Journal*, 241. Mussolini was foreign minister as well as head of government. Since 1933 he was also minister of war, minister of the air force, and minister of the navy.

[32] Pierre-Etienne Flandin, who was then prime minister of France, states the following: "I personally insisted to a large extent on the conclusion of these agreements, and even forced Laval in the end to leave for Rome in order to

Laval and Mussolini met in Rome for four business meetings. At the end of the second, it was announced that an agreement had been reached on the Austrian question but that African problems had yet to be settled.[33] This thorny matter was tackled by the experts on the afternoon of 6 January, and some measure of agreement was hammered out.[34] But the leaders had not given their approval, and by 10:00 P.M. there was talk of the failure of the negotiations.[35] That same night Laval gave a formal dinner at the Palazzo Farnese. Mussolini appeared rather preoccupied at the meal. At 11:00, after dinner, Laval and Mussolini withdrew for an hour for a private conversation.[36] When they emerged at midnight Laval, smiling, said to a French journalist: "C'est fini." During that decisive hour a French-Italian rapprochement became a reality, and on the following day the two countries signed a treaty, a

put an end to the sabotaging which officials in every quarter of both foreign ministries were indulging." P.-E. Flandin, *Politique français, 1919–1940* (Paris, 1947), 105n. Mme. Tabouis "quotes" from the Quai d'Orsay: "The trip to Rome has not been properly prepared. Il Duce will certainly question Laval about Ethiopia and North Africa, and Laval will not know the proper answers. We haven't even begun to discuss these questions at the Quai d'Orsay." Tabouis, *They Called Me Cassandra*, 225. The matter was further complicated by the fact that Chambrun was conducting his own negotiations with Mussolini, without informing Léger and Saint-Quentin, a French African expert. *Ibid.*, 227–8. Actually, a draft on the African question was at the time being worked on at the Quai. Léger claims that Laval was more interested in the voyage to Rome than in the substance of the agreement, and that the minister insisted on leaving before the diplomatic preparations were completed. Léger almost resigned in protest at this time. Cameron, "Léger," 384.

[33] Toynbee, *Study of International Affairs, 1935*, I, 103.

[34] Chambrun gives the following report on the work of the 6th: The terms in which Laval spoke of an economic *désistement* in the regions of Ethiopia other than the hinterland of French Somaliland and the railroad zone "made a visible impression on Mussolini and effectively prepared the way for the entente which was established in the evening, following long discussions between Léger and Saint-Quentin and Chergueraud on the one side and Suvich and the Italian experts on the other. A definitive accord was signed at the end of the afternoon, at the same time that the other texts were already decided." Chambrun, *Traditions et souvenirs*, 197. Full discussions took place, no doubt, and ground work was being done, but it is too much to claim that an agreement was concluded. Mussolini would probably not have accepted the African clauses without Laval's later assurances.

[35] E. Reale, *La Politique étrangère du fascisme des accords de Rome à la proclamation de l'Empire* (Paris, 1937), 10.

[36] Chambrun, *Traditions et souvenirs*, 203, 205. It has usually been stated that Mussolini and Laval were closeted alone during this hour. But *Il Popolo d'Italia*, 7 January 1935, reported that Suvich, Chambrun, and Léger joined the conversation. Mussolini, *Opera omnia*, XXVII, 328. Chambrun stated that the two statesmen never met "without either myself or M. Léger being present." Gamelin, *Servir*, III, 530–1. Yet Léger asserts that he had no idea of the extent of Laval's private concessions to Mussolini — but that he was sure they existed. *Ibid.*, II, 172; Cameron, "Léger," 385.

protocol, several declarations, and a secret agreement concerning Ethiopia.

The questions of Austria and German rearmament were dealt with in the declarations. France and Italy agreed to go into consultation if Austrian independence was menaced and jointly to recommend a convention for reciprocal nonintervention between Austria and other "particularly interested states," including Yugoslavia. The French, but not the Italian, résumé stated that these agreements would be reached within the procedures of the League of Nations. Touching on the question of rearmament, both countries affirmed that no state had the right unilaterally to modify its treaty obligations with regard to an increase in its arms, and they agreed to consult in case of violations.[37] The agreement over Austria is worthy of note for two reasons. On the one hand, in Aloisi's words, it represented for Italy "an absolute change of front because we will enter, with regard to Austria, into the framework of the League and into cooperation with the Little Entente." This was a diplomatic victory for France. On the other hand, and of greater significance for the future, the French now in effect gave their recognition to Italian predominance in Austrian affairs.[38]

Three agreements concerning Africa were made available to the public view. First came a treaty that gave Italy a rectification of its southern Libyan frontier, with the addition of 44,000 square miles of arid and unpopulated desert, and some 13.5 miles of Eritrean coastline that fronted on the strait of Bab el Mandeb and included the off-lying barren islet of Dumayrah. Second came a declaration of economic collaboration, which provided that 2,500 shares, about 7 percent, of the French-owned Djibouti–Addis Ababa railroad could be bought by Italy. The third instrument was a protocol for the progressive liquidation of Italian rights and privileges in Tunisia.[39]

[37] J. Wheeler-Bennett and S. Heald, eds., *Documents on International Affairs, 1935* (London, 1936), I, 23–4. Germany was not mentioned by name in the official public communiqué. But a secret protocol on disarmament was also signed by Mussolini and Laval on 7 January, obliging France and Italy to consult if Germany should "modify by unilateral actions its obligations in the matter of armaments." See D. C. Watt, "The Secret Laval-Mussolini Agreement of 1935 on Ethiopia," *Middle East Journal*, 15:75–6 (Winter 1961).

[38] Aloisi, *Journal*, 240; Gehl, *Austria, Germany, and the Anschluss*, 114.

[39] By 1965 all children born of Italian nationals in Tunisia were to be under French law and considered as French citizens. Italian schools were to retain their present status until 1955 when they would become private schools subject to French legislation. Italian nationals admitted to the liberal professions before 1945 would have their rights retained until their death. Those entering after 1945 would be subject to French law and jurisdiction.

The extent of Mussolini's colonial concessions is remarkable. For all their previous demands over the 1915 debt, on 7 January 1935 the Italians peacefully accepted the humiliating sop of a small and worthless portion of desert and a minuscule stretch of Red Sea coast.[40] The 2,500 shares in the Djibouti railroad were a trivial token and did not give control. Laval later said that not only was a speck of Libyan desert used to pay off the terms of the Treaty of London but it was given "in exchange for the cancellation of rights in Tunisia." And nothing is more striking in the agreements of 7 January than this capitulation, this apparent renunciation of the Italian dream to control Tunisia. Laval aptly summed up the sacrifice: "Tunisia is for Italy what Alsace-Lorraine was for France." Now these old claims, so long a part of Italian thinking, these claims to privilege or at least to national identity in the nearby land of Tunisia, were publicly given up.[41]

For what? Nothing in the public documents provided an adequate basis for the Italian toasts that greeted the agreements of 7 January. Nothing listed in the treaty or the declarations had a value corresponding to the claims Mussolini had renounced. The Duce seemed to have sold out to France — and for no apparent reason. The Fascist press made much of the accord; its main theme of "relief and joy" was justified by the idea that the entente was filled with future possibilities.[42]

[40] In the area south of Libya, Laval said later, there was not a "single inhabitant or a tree; it is completely sand and rocks." *Procès du Maréchal Pétain*, 183. Mussolini claimed that there were only 62 inhabitants in "that desolate area," and "they had to be searched for like a needle in a haystack, and were eventually found tucked away in an isolated valley which happened to have enough water to be cultivable." Quoted in Toynbee, *Survey of International Affairs, 1935*, I, 105n. Actually there were almost 900 souls in the area. The new Eritrean acquisition of 309 square miles had 1,000 inhabitants.

[41] P. Laval, *The Diary of Pierre Laval* (New York, 1948), 19; *Procès du Maréchal Pétain*, 183. Recall Guariglia's proposal discussed above, in which this Italian renunciation was to be used merely as a device in the short run to gain immediate advantages for the east African campaign. It is interesting that in 1938–39, under the clumsy hand of Galeazzo Ciano, the Italians called the agreements invalid, "historically out of date," denied they had ever been put in force, and reopened the whole question of Italian colonial claims on France going back to 1915. France rejected these contentions and saw Italy as attempting to make Tunisia "a second Czechoslovakia," with Italian nationals there playing the part of Sudetenland Germans. For these events, see *Documents on British Foreign Policy, 1919–1939*, 3rd ser., III, 470ff; IV, 293–4; V, 570, 611 613. See also A. François-Poncet, *Au palais Farnèse, souvenirs d'une ambassade a Rome, 1938–1940* (Paris, 1961), 20–40.

[42] See, e.g., Latinus (pseud.), *L'Italia e i problemi internazionali* (Milan, 1935), 309. V. Gayda in *Il Giornale d'Italia*, 9 January 1935, dwells on the spiritual aspects of the rapprochement, and *Politica*, 39:22–9 (January 1935), has a "poetical intermezzo" to *latinite* and Franco-Italian friendship. Not all writers appear so

But Italian diplomats were angry and distressed; some Italian school-children in Tunisia took Mussolini's portrait from the wall, threw it on the ground, and spat upon it; and it was said in Rome that if there had been a parliament in Italy Mussolini would have fallen.[43]

Mussolini, of course, had a sound reason for his apparent renunciation of claims that had long been the keystone of Italian colonial policy and for his acceptance of France's design for European stability. The French entente created invaluable advantages for the Fascist regime. For reasons of politics and security, in Europe he needed France as a counterweight against Germany. Mussolini needed at least tacit French approval of his Ethiopian plans, and he could not get this while France was suspicious and hostile. These advantages were worth far more to Mussolini than control of a stretch of Libyan desert or Italian rights in Tunisia.[44]

Apart from questions of power politics, the entente gave Mussolini great personal satisfaction. The chief of the Italian police, Carmine Senise, wrote in his memoirs that the French-Italian understanding was "the fact to which Mussolini held most closely during his regime. This type of endorsement of his regime, coming from a country of ancient democracy and the cradle of a revolution which renovated the world, was for him like conferring a patent of nobility on Fascism." [45] Guariglia noted that Mussolini believed that his new alliance would be able to surmount any crises resulting from the coming war in Ethiopia. Even Mussolini's later anger with France was said to carry the mark of

---

naive. *Ottobre*, 17 January 1935, saw the agreement only as a point of departure for new enterprises: "The protocols of Rome are not the end but the beginning of the main highway to our ardent desire for Empire. Glory to the Duce, constructor of Italian Africa." Quoted in Reale, *La Politique étrangère du fascisme*, 11.

[43] Aloisi, *Journal*, 246; Herriot, *Jadis*, II, 494; *Procès du Maréchal Pétain*, 184. It was Mussolini who had to make the concessions that broke the deadlock on the night of the 6th. Laval was overheard saying to Mussolini then: "You are the undisputed chief of Italy. I am a French minister. If you want these negotiations to come to a happy conclusion, it is you who will have to concede." Mallet, *Laval*, I, 69.

[44] Laura Fermi sees an inconsistency in that Mussolini "who bid for an empire so that Italians would not have to lose their nationality in foreign countries was willing to give up some 100,000 Italians in Tunisia." Fermi, *Mussolini*, 314. This assertion is based on two misunderstandings of the reasons behind the Ethiopian campaign. The demographic and nationalistic arguments for conquest were latter-day justifications contrived for propaganda purposes. Further, there is no reason to assume that Mussolini intended a permanent renunciation of the Tunisian claims. There may well have been a plan, as Guariglia suggests, to take future action to regain Italian privileges or to slow up the abrogation of the conventions.

[45] Quoted in Mallet, *Laval*, I, 74.

"amour deçu" and "amour refoulé." Mussolini found particular satisfaction, too, in dealing with Pierre Laval. Laval was the first French minister to make an official journey to Rome since the war.[46] The two men got along well: they were the same age; Laval spoke of the two, and Stalin, as "un fameux cru." They had similar backgrounds and tastes: their humble origins, their "tormented youths" as socialists, their disdain for rigid ideologies and for regular diplomatic procedure.[47] Léon Blum pointed this out in an editorial in *Le Populaire* of 5 January 1935: "The two statesmen will recognize each other at first glance. In order to assure a 'contact' of an intimate character, all they will have to do is exchange their memories." [48] Such recollections were in fact exchanged and formed a fertile ground for the discussions. The talks began with an understanding, Laval said, instead of a misunderstanding.[49] This is what made *l'ambiance romaine*, and it made agreement between the two men easier.

Above all, Mussolini wanted the assurance that France would give Italy freedom of action in Ethiopia. This assurance alone would permit and justify the Italian concessions.[50] The fact that such concessions were made is the best proof we have that Laval did promise to gratify Mussolini's desires. Lack of evidence makes it impossible to ascertain the precise content of the assurances Laval gave Mussolini during their meetings, and especially during the "straightforward talk" at the Palazzo Farnese on the night of 6 January, but there is sufficient evidence to point to the significance, if not the nature, of the all-important secret promises.

Strictly speaking, the only formal assurance Laval gave Mussolini was that France would no longer claim its rights under the tripartite

[46] Cohen, *La Société des Nations*, 33–4; Lagardelle, *Mission à Rome*, 4, 291; G. Bottai, *Vent'anni e un giorno*, 2nd ed. (Rome, 1949), 87. Léon Blum, in an editorial in *Le Populaire*, 5 January 1935, wrote: "For the first time a French minister is the guest of the assassin of Matteotti. For the first time a representative of the French republic recognizes the tyrant of Italy as a chief of state by the deferential initiative of his visit." L. Blum, *L'Histoire jugera*, 2nd ed. (Montreal, 1943), 100. It is important to remember, in reference to later events, that Blum was Laval's successor as prime minister, save only for the interregnum of Sarraut, in the first half of 1936.

[47] Lagardelle, *Mission à Rome*, 106. See also D. Bardens, *Portrait of a Statesman* (New York, 1956), 136.

[48] Blum, *L'Histoire jugera*, 101.

[49] J. Romains, *Seven Mysteries of Europe*, G. Brée, trans. (New York, 1940), 229.

[50] See Fulvio Suvich's testimony in F. Suvich et al., *Il Processo Roatta* (Rome, 1945), 18.

treaty of 1906 to seek economic concessions in Ethiopia and would
henceforth confine its influence to the zone necessary to maintain the
French-owned railroad to Addis Ababa from Djibouti.[51] The corollary
to this was that France would raise no obstacles to the peaceful development of Italian interests in Ethiopia. This act, Laval ingeniously
asserted later, corresponded to the arrangements Italy had already made
with the British in 1925.[52] Now this assurance alone constituted a
massive diplomatic victory for Italy. Together, the British and French
willingness to disengage themselves from Ethiopia meant that Italy was
able to claim an uncontested sphere of economic influence over the
entire country, subject only to the preservation of Britain's hydraulic
interests on the Nile and France's privileges in the railroad zone. For
the first time Italy had unrivaled claim to the economic potentiality of
Ethiopia. Never before had full freedom been given to Italy to develop
and exploit the resources of the empire.

But, as we know, Mussolini wanted more than the mere economic
domination of Ethiopia. In a letter to Laval on 25 December 1935,
Mussolini argued that economic privilege could not be made effective
without the further step of political control. He asserted that Laval
had given his consent to this in their talks at the beginning of the year.
Mussolini claimed that, "par la nécessité d'une entente verbale," Laval
had in fact promised him a "free hand" in Ethiopia. This did not necessarily mean control won through war — and Mussolini expressly ab-

[51] This promise was contained in a secret letter, written by Laval to Mussolini
on 7 January 1935 and confirmed by Mussolini in writing on the same day. The
crucial portion of the letter reads: "After an examination of the situation of Italy
and France in East Africa . . . the French Government declares to the Italian
Government that, on the application of the arrangement of December 13, 1905
[1906], and all the agreements mentioned in Article I of the aforesaid Treaty,
the French Government does not look to Abyssinia for satisfaction of any interests other than those economic interests relating to the traffic of the Jibuti-
Addis Ababa railway in the zone defined in the annex thereto. Nevertheless,
the French Government does not by this renounce the rights which its subjects
and protected persons enjoy under the Franco-Abyssinian Treaty of January
10, 1908, nor the concessions which it has obtained over parts of Abyssinia situated outside the zone mentioned above, nor the renewal of the aforesaid concessions." The existence of this letter, long suspected, and the object of much
conjecture, was discovered in documents captured from France by the Germans
in 1940. It was published in Watt, "The Secret Laval-Mussolini Agreement of
1935 on Ethiopia," 69–78.

[52] This clever point deserves notice. Laval stated the nature and extent of
this promise in a speech before the Chamber of Deputies on 28 December 1935.
Journal officiel, débats parlementaires, 29 December 1935, 2865. See also Laval's letter to Mussolini of 22 December 1935, printed in Lagardelle, *Mission à Rome,*
275–8.

solved Laval of supporting a conquest by force. What Mussolini needed, and what he claimed Laval had in fact given him in the Rome talks, was "adherence and sympathy" to the principle of political as well as economic predominance in Ethiopia. Often during the conversations, Mussolini said, Laval had recognized "my being able to have 'free hands' in Abyssinia." Mussolini "never doubted for a single instant" that Laval was aware of the political dimension required by Italy. In Laval's "spirit of understanding of the needs of Italy," he surely recognized that the acceptance of the few acres of sand in Libya and Eritrea did not in the slightest degree constitute a "solution" for Italy's pressing need for space and raw materials. The solution was to be sought in Ethiopia. On 6 January, Mussolini claimed, Laval had granted France's "sympathy" with the undertaking, and this assurance, said Mussolini, was the "point of departure" for the Ethiopian campaign.[53]

Mussolini's assertions, though not false, do not tell the whole story. Mussolini did not only want full control over Ethiopia, conditions that peaceful diplomacy might bring to pass if Britain and France co-operated as Mussolini had reason to expect they would. In addition he wanted an Italian military campaign and a Fascist military victory in Africa. For this he needed further guarantees that he could count on France not to interfere when the Italian-Ethiopian conflict was turned into war. Despite his disclaimer in the letter just discussed, Mussolini believed that Laval had directly or indirectly given him this assurance in Rome. This was Mussolini's definition of a "free hand." His belief that he had secured this vital condition for success is the only explanation one can give for his willingness to renounce all other Italian colonial claims on France and to submit to the French proposals for Europe.[54]

A year after the event, at a time when he was fighting for the life of his government, Laval spoke to the Chamber of Deputies and denied that he had ever approved an Italian war against Ethiopia.

There was nothing either in the agreements or in the conversations which preceded or followed them that could encourage Italy to

---

[53] Mussolini's letter to Laval of 25 December 1935, a reply to Laval's letter of the 22nd, is printed in Lagardelle, *Mission à Rome*, 279–83.

[54] The significance of such a counterpart agreement is noted by Herriot, *Jadis*, II, 558, and M. Toscano, "Appunti sulla questione tunisiana," *Quaderni dello studio fiorentino di politica estera*, no. 4 (quoted in Cohen, *La Société des Nations*, 34). Aloisi, in his diary for 6 January 1935, refers to the "felicitous" formula arrived at for a "political *disinteressement*." *Journal*, 246.

resort to war. I am too deeply attached to peace not to want it to be universal and not to be aware that it is fragile. How can it be imagined that I should not have estimated the consequences, for the peace of Europe and the security of France, of a warlike enterprise in a distant theatre? At the moment when I was signing a treaty of friendship with Italy, with the object of reinforcing collective security in Europe by a Franco-Italian collaboration that was to be a reality, I should have been imprudent, and perhaps even culpable, if I had smoothed the path for some adventure or other in Africa which would deprive us of the presence, and the assistance, of our neighbor in Europe.[55]

It is correct that in a formal sense Laval did not make any secret arrangements concerning the political future of Ethiopia, and it is true also that he did not give Mussolini any formal French approval of a war of aggression. Other than that, Laval's denials cannot be accepted at face value.[56]

The truth is that in Rome Laval was willing to give Mussolini a free hand in Ethiopia, to give him Ethiopia for that matter, because

[55] Laval's speech of 28 December 1935 is found in *Journal officiel, débats parlementaires*, 29 December 1935, 2863–6. Laval's is not a fully convincing argument. As I shall show, there were military advantages simply in having Italy as a friend, for it freed France's southern flank and gave France security in the Mediterranean. Ensconced behind the Maginot Line, France did not need Italian troops for its own defense system, and was not prepared to march to Austria's aid in any case. Hitler was unlikely to invade Italy in the near future, and it was possible to take Mussolini at his word that Italian troops would soon be back after a swift African campaign. It was hard to believe, after the maneuvers following the murder of Dollfuss, that Mussolini would desert the continent and his Alpine frontier. There was also the belief in France that Italian military preparations in east Africa were part of a bluff, an imitation of Marshal Lyautey's tactic of having on hand more troops than he intended to use, to overawe impressionable Africans. In any event, the extent of Mussolini's commitment was underestimated, and the French could see few alternatives beyond alliance with Italy.

[56] See Laval's further denial before the French Senate on 26 March 1935. *Annales du Sénat . . . débats parlementaires*, 1935, CXXII, 395, and his interpretation of the January conversation contained in a letter to Mussolini of 23 January 1936, replying to Mussolini's letter of 25 December 1935, printed in France, Ministère des Affaires Etrangères, *Documents diplomatiques français, 1932–1939*, 2nd ser., I (Paris, 1963), 145–7. See also Flandin, *Politique française*, 105n, and a letter of Chambrun's in Gamelin, *Servir*, III, 530. Cf. Cohen, *La Société des Nations*, 30–4. Laval's caution in admitting his concessions to Mussolini, quite apart from the occasion of his politically inspired speech on 28 December 1935, came from a fear of antagonizing the anti-Italian French left and from warnings by the Quai d'Orsay not to cause suspicion and irritation among the British. See the evidence of Soulier, vice president of the Committee of Foreign Affairs of the French Chamber, and the statement of Chambrun to Italian Ambassador Pignatti in Villari, *Storia diplomatica del conflitto italo-etiopico*, 184.

he considered this a price worth paying for Italian friendship. Ethiopia, for Laval, was merely an unfamiliar and unimportant African country, which he was willing to see sacrificed if by this means he could assure a greater degree of security for France in Europe.[57] He surely recognized that in January 1935 Mussolini was preparing for war against Ethiopia. The seriousness of the Walwal incident was described to him by the Ethiopian delegate to the League in December 1934.[58] Yet, in January, it seemed folly to Laval to anger Mussolini because "of that measly little spring . . . at the end of the field." [59] No doubt international complications would result from an Italian-Ethiopian conflict, and a war against Ethiopia would violate the Covenant of the League. But at the beginning of 1935, the principles of the League meant less to France than the degree of security to be gained from an entente with Italy. Should France throw away this opportunity to end its long history of dissension with Italy just to protect remote, unknown, and ineffectual Ethiopia, or to forestall a distant and unclear threat to an idealistic organization whose practical assistance in containing Germany might well be ineffective? Any Italian action in east Africa was still some time off, and ways could doubtless be found to attenuate the repercussions. The British were not ranged in opposition to Mussolini, were not championing the League, and would probably help in the task of reconciliation. So there seemed no reason why Italy's colonial ambitions in distant Africa should be allowed to disrupt the search for stability in Europe. The important thing for Laval was to take advantage of the immediate opportunity to win Italy over to the side of France. If French "adherence" to Mussolini's imperial pretensions was the price to be paid for this major diplomatic victory, the price did not at the time, or later, seem too great.

Laval, nonetheless, did not encourage or desire to see an Italian war of aggression. In fact he sought to give some direction to Mussolini's

[57] Eden describes Laval's amusement at learning the alliterative name of Ethiopia's capital city in December 1934 after the Walwal incident. Avon, *Facing the Dictators*, 193. Michael Foot tells the probably apocryphal but richly ironic story that, when someone reminded Laval that Ethiopia was a member of the League, Laval replied: "Good God, is it really?" M. Foot, *Armistice, 1918–1939* (London, 1940), 164.

[58] Avon, *Facing the Dictators*, 193.

[59] Laval's expression, in Romains, *Seven Mysteries of Europe*, 229. René Massigli of the French foreign office took a more somber view and, in December 1934, saw the Walwal incident as possibly the beginning of another "Manchuria." Avon, *Facing the Dictators*, 193.

"free hand" in Ethiopia. Laval told the Duce in Rome that he hoped Mussolini would imitate the example of Marshal Lyautey in Morocco.[60] This suggestion implied that, as Italy fulfilled its now conceded claim to economic influence in Ethiopia, it could also begin to develop a corresponding degree of political influence, all the while leaving Ethiopia's formal independence intact. This would enable Mussolini to gain the substance of his demands (as interpreted by the French) while avoiding the legal and moral complications that would arise from an unprovoked Italian attack. If force then had to be employed to achieve political control, the prior use of this procedure might make it appear in some sense "legitimate" and in this way avoid, as the French had in Morocco, serious international results.[61]

Thus, although Laval did not endorse an aggressive war against Ethiopia, he did not disapprove of some Italian use of force. The deliberate vagueness, the ambiguity, the calculated imprecision of Laval's behavior in this matter allowed him to be strictly correct in his denials of having endorsed war; at the same time, Mussolini could draw the equally correct conclusion that Italy had France's adherence and sympathy. Joseph Paul-Boncour describes one fashion in which Laval's approval might have been delivered to the Duce: "By a shrug of the shoulders, or a wink . . . Laval was able to convey to Mussolini that he would not be too critical if the latter attempted a military expedition." [62] Whatever the means, Laval's behavior convinced Mussolini that France would not stand in the way of the Ethiopian campaign. One way or another, Laval established this impression and allowed Mussolini to accept the broadest, most generous, interpretation of his "wink." It

[60] *Procès du Maréchal Pétain*, 184.

[61] Ciano later told the British ambassador in Rome that in May 1935 he had been sent to Paris to see Flandin. Ciano claimed that the prime minister of France gave him advice on how Italian military operations could best be started in Ethiopia. Flandin suggested that Italy try to stir up the rases against the emperor. The unrest would give Italy a good pretext for intervention. On the other hand, Flandin warned that if Italy made a direct attack France's position would become more difficult. *Documents on British Foreign Policy*, 3rd ser., III, 490; G. Ciano, *Diario, 1937–1938* (Bologna, 1948), 313. This is an entirely plausible story, although it is doubtful that Laval could give Italy such a perspicacious warning in January.

[62] Paul-Boncour, *Entre deux guerres*, III, 16. At a meeting of the French Council of Ministers on 10 January 1935, at which Laval commented on the Rome accords, Herriot noted to himself: "My impression of the Franco-Italian accord: we agreed on the word 'sì,' but in Italian it means yes and translates a reality. In French, it signifies perhaps and expresses a hope or an illusion." M. Soulie, *La Vie politique d'Edouard Herriot* (Paris, 1962), 457.

was enough to satisfy Mussolini and to bring about the French-Italian entente of 7 January 1935.[63]

Laval's diplomacy had achieved a great success. France won a major victory over the Tunisian question. The debt of 1915 was painlessly liquidated. Italian expansionism was turned away from central Europe and the Balkans.[64] If Mussolini was going to disturb the peace, it would be in Africa not Europe — and, if in Africa, in Ethiopia not Tunisia.[65] The conflict between Italy and the Little Entente was tempered. Agreements were made that at least claimed to protect Austrian independence. Italy was on record as objecting to German rearmament. All these benefits were gained merely by giving Mussolini to understand that he had French sympathy for his (undefined) ambitions in Ethiopia.

Of prime importance as well were the military advantages Italy's friendship gave to France. As Hitler's Germany became increasingly menacing, as German rearmament became more obvious, as France's eastern allies faded into the distance, as Britain hardened its isolationism, Rome was France's new continental point of support. Italy's friendship meant freedom in the use of the French army in the Alps. With Italy as a buffer on France's exposed southern flank, along which the Maginot Line did not extend, ten divisions of infantry and two brigades of cavalry were freed to be moved north.[66] Italian friendship meant assured tranquillity in the Mediterranean, which granted safety to the southern coast and allowed the secure transport of troops from Africa. Mussolini and Laval, in their conversations in January, contemplated a scheme of French-Italian military cooperation in Europe and agreed that talks between their military leaders should begin.[67] In the spring

[63] Paul Reynaud records that, when Laval was leaving the French Council of Ministers after his report on the January talks, he was asked: "Didn't Mussolini demand anything of you?" Laval replied: "No . . . poor Abyssinia!" P. Reynaud, *La France a sauvé l'Europe* (Paris, 1947), 157.

[64] This was a strong motive behind Laval's support of Italian imperialism in Africa, according to one French writer. See Cameron, *Prologue to Appeasement*, 102.

[65] "By directing Italian dynamism to Ethiopia, Laval thought he was diverting the sword of Damocles which hung over French Africa." J. Bastin, *L'affaire d'Ethiopie et les diplomates* (Brussels, 1937), 90.

[66] Fabry, *De la Place de la Concorde*, 67, 93. A similar advantage had come in World War I, when Italian neutrality released four French divisions from guard duty on France's southeastern frontier. B. Tuchmann, *The Guns of August* (New York, 1962), 126.

[67] Gamelin, *Servir*, II, 166. General Gamelin had been in officially approved "close and confidential" relations with Badoglio ever since the two men had been in Brazil at the same time in the early 1920s. *Ibid.*, 163.

and summer of 1935, air and military conventions were signed by the two countries. These enabled France to benefit from the Italian air force which, although in fact more effective in display than as a fighting arm, was considered in France to be "probably the best in Europe." [68] All these advantages were integrated into the French strategic design, representing factors that could not be given up without leading to change in the entire security system. Loss of the Italian connection would mean a serious weakening of France's position in the event of trouble in Europe.[69] Alexander Werth claims that "the whole of France's foreign policy during 1935 was dominated by [the] widespread belief in the value of the Rome agreements and in the strength of Franco-Italian friendship." [70] A community of interest was created and maintained throughout 1935. For one year following the entente, Pierre Laval controlled French foreign affairs and remained consistently faithful to the spirit of the Rome accords and to the appeasement of Italy.[71]

This new direction in French policy had important results for eastern Europe and for France's old allies. Laval claimed that he had advanced the policy of encirclement of Germany. Military conventions signed later, he said, provided a "bridge" to central Europe, over which French troops could march to the aid of their eastern allies.[72] But, quite the reverse, after the Italian entente France became increasingly inward-looking. Despite much diplomatic talk to the contrary, France would not, and could not, go to the aid of its friends and dependents on the other side of Germany. Italy was not desired as a potential military highway to reach the armies of France's allies in the east, but as a necessary defensive zone on France's own southern frontier. As part of its new position, France now recognized Italy's role in Austria. France was giving up the contest with Italy for influence in central Europe. The eastern allies were cut adrift and left helpless, and France became

---

[68] Flandin, *Politique française*, 172n. The Italian air force suffered from critical weaknesses. Its commander, General Giuseppe Valle, said it was in a "state of crisis," and Badoglio said the majority of airplanes would be out of action after a couple of days of hard use. V. Vailati, *Badoglio risponde* (Milan, 1958), 259. See also Aloisi, *Journal*, 349.

[69] Fabry, *De la Place de la Concorde*, 69. Fabry was Laval's minister of war for the last half of 1935.

[70] A. Werth, *The Twilight of France* (New York, 1942), 39.

[71] This fact was recognized and appreciated by Mussolini. See his letter to Laval of 25 December 1935 in Lagardelle, *Mission à Rome*, 279, and an even more gracious appreciation, *ibid.*, 144–5.

[72] P. Laval et al., *Le Procès Laval* (Paris, 1946), 56.

more than ever dependent not on the old system of an encircling alliance, not on the fair words of Versailles and the League, but on the security offered by the wholly defensive Maginot Line.[73] This made Italy's friendship important, and here was the other side of the coin: France was now to a large degree dependent on Italy for its European position. In this circumstance Mussolini could exercise some subtle blackmail in order to hold France to a line of noninterference in Ethiopia.

Hence an essential political condition for Mussolini's success in Ethiopia was fulfilled — the French would not resist.[74] Mussolini said that the understanding with France was "one of the directing lines of the international policy of Italy," and on this basis he now turned all of Italy's energies toward Africa.[75] On 7 January, the day the public and secret agreements were signed, Mussolini spoke to the press in his office in the Palazzo Venezia. "The crucial year" was beginning, he said, "under the propitious sign of the Franco-Italian accord." [76] On this

[73] The French minister of war, General Maurin, replied on 16 March 1935 to a speech by Reynaud in favor of De Gaulle's plan for a permanent *corps cuirasse:* "How is one able to believe that we dream yet of the offensive when we have spent billions to establish a fortified [defensive] barrier? Would not we be mad to go, beyond that barrier, to I know not what adventure?" Reynaud comments: "This was public and cynical notice that France was not going to honor the engagements which she had taken toward her allies." P. Reynaud, *Mémoires: Venu de ma montagne* (Paris, 1960), I, 434.

[74] Official efforts helped to create and maintain cordiality between the two nations. After the accord, Italian agents in France enjoyed an immunity equal to that of diplomatic officials. Torres, *Laval*, 198. Italy was said to have scattered 60 million francs among the notoriously venial French press during the Ethiopian campaign. Tabouis, *They Called Me Cassandra*, 263. The French government did its part as well. Cameron, *Prologue to Appeasement*, 152–4. This propaganda had its effect. Arnold Toynbee writes: "This intensive cultivation of emotional links of friendship between two peoples who had been profoundly estranged from one another before the beginning of the year 1935 was a characteristic incident of international politics in a generation in which the politicians were minutely studying and cold-bloodedly putting into practice the science of propaganda." Toynbee, *Survey of International Affairs, 1935*, I, 117–18.

[75] Mussolini's letter to Laval of 25 December 1935. Lagardelle, *Mission à Rome*, 279–80. See also Herriot, *Jadis*, II, 558. In a secret memorandum on the political situation of France, prepared at the end of 1935 by the Italian foreign office for the use of high Italian officials, the following paragraph occurs: "The fate of Ethiopia and of all the French position on the question of east Africa was virtually already decided at the end of the Mussolini-Laval talks at Rome. With the draft of the letter of 7 January and Laval's verbal assurances, the French government was bound to accord Italy a free hand for the satisfaction of its needs of expansion in east Africa and for the settlement once and for all of any questions with the Ethiopian government." Extracts from this memorandum are printed in W. C. Askew, "The Secret Agreement between France and Italy on Ethiopia, January 1935," *Journal of Modern History*, 25:47–8 (March 1953).

[76] Mussolini, *Opera omnia*, XXVII, 9.

same day General Emilio De Bono, minister of colonies and field commander of the Ethiopian campaign, sailed from Italy for Eritrea.[77] The first stage of active preparation for war with Ethiopia was under way.

From the beginning of 1935, two related problems faced Italian diplomats. One was to maintain the good will of Britain and France. The other was to prevent the League of Nations from acting on Ethiopia's appeals for help. If Britain and France were sympathetic, the League could be immobilized with no difficulty. For the League followed without much question wherever the two great Western democracies led.

Despite some disenchantment,[78] Mussolini's confidence in the French-Italian entente turned out to be well placed. France supported Italy throughout the conflict, up to one crucial point at any rate. That point was reached when the shortcomings of Italian diplomacy and the boldness of Mussolini's ambitions met Britain's unexpectedly renewed interest in international morality. Should a decisive choice have to be made, France, as the French always knew, would have to opt for Britain. As General Gamelin said, "for us Italy is important; England is essential." [79] On the other hand, the effects of this situation might be altered for Italy's behalf, and in such tacking Laval excelled. But this troublesome situation was not yet in the offing, and for the present it appeared that Britain was steering the same course as France. To keep the active sympathy of French officials, all Italian diplomacy had to do, it seemed, was not to alienate Britain.

By the end of January, as we shall see, Italy had won an important diplomatic victory over Ethiopia at Geneva. Following the Walwal incident, Ethiopia made an effort to invoke article 11 of the Covenant, declaring that a threat to the peace was at hand. To prevent the League from taking formal jurisdiction in the matter, Italy proposed as an

---

[77] De Bono, *Anno XIIII*, 56.

[78] Mussolini at first had exaggerated hopes for the entente. According to Guariglia, he believed that the accord obliged France to help Italy "unguibus et rostris" — with claws and beak — against any protest the British might raise. French-Italian solidarity was such, Mussolini thought, that it could surmount any crisis brought about by even the most extreme action in Ethiopia. This hope was swiftly modified when it became apparent that Laval was not able to handle French foreign policy in the same dictatorial manner as Mussolini directed Italy's, and when France's ultimate dependence on Britain became evident. Guariglia, *Ricordi*, 220–1.

[79] Gamelin, *Servir*, II, 175.

alternative that direct arbitration only over the Walwal conflict take place. By this tactic the Italians sought to bypass the League, to bypass the larger questions of war or peace and Italy's intentions in Ethiopia. Italy's proposal was accepted by Ethiopia at the urging of France and Britain. In the wake of this success, on 29 January 1935, three weeks after the accord with France, Italy approached the British government on the matter of Ethiopia.

There was a marked contrast between the two Italian moves. With France, Italy entered into a new era of diplomatic relations, the friendship sealed by apparently extravagant Italian concessions. Mutual need bound the two nations together, and the entente was cemented by careful diplomatic attention in the months that followed. Toward Britain, Italy's behavior seemed almost casual. On 29 January Leonardo Vitetti, counselor to the Italian embassy in London, visited the Foreign Office for an informal conversation. Vitetti was instructed to let the British government know that Italian interest in east Africa was quickening and that agreement on its general direction had been reached with France. He informed the British of the secret understanding between Mussolini and Laval for a French economic *désistement* in Ethiopia.[80]

Mussolini did not want the British to think they had been duped by a French-Italian understanding made behind their backs. It was important that the British learn of the French permissiveness, for this information might have an influence on future British policy. But the Italians did not at this time seek specific British approval of their plans, nor did they look for promises of a free hand. They did not even seek "good will" as such. Mussolini merely wanted to put London *au courant*, to maintain the illusion that Italy had acted in open frankness with its partners in the 1906 treaty and to assure Britain that its interests in Ethiopia would be protected. The British were not informed that Mussolini was planning to use force in Ethiopia, and Vitetti deliberately kept the Italian plans vague.

Vitetti was also instructed to suggest informally that an exchange of views might take place concerning the claims of Britain and Italy in east Africa. This was, Mussolini asserted later, an invitation to the British "to consider the possibility of specific agreements" for harmonious development of the two countries' interests in Ethiopia.[81] But

[80] See the Maffey report, *New York Times*, 20 February 1936; Lagardelle, *Mission à Rome*, 128.

[81] From an interview published in the *Morning Post* of London, 17 September 1935. Mussolini, *Opera omnia*, XXVII, 139.

the invitation was casually tendered and Italy did not extend its exploratory démarche. The Italian purpose was not to initiate negotiations so much as to inform the British that lines of communication were open if the British cared to make use of them. Mussolini watched carefully for Britain's reaction. One object of broaching the subject at this time was to give the British an opportunity to clarify their own position on the matter of Ethiopia, for themselves as well as for Italy. There was general uncertainty in Rome as to what Britain's future policies would be both toward Europe[82] and toward a conflict between Italy and Ethiopia. As long as the government seemed uncertain of its own course, any negotiation to bring Britain into prior agreements seemed unlikely to succeed. Mussolini also lacked the opportunity to bargain with the British that he had with the French. He made no further effort to open negotiations, but an invitation for discussion had been put forth. It remained for the British to accept.

Guariglia, in his speculation on Mussolini's motives, surmised that the Duce did not want to run the possibility of stirring up serious opposition in Britain before his own plans and preparations had been fully developed. Mussolini knew that an Italian war against Ethiopia would be very unpopular in Britain. What effect public opinion might have on the government was uncertain. For the moment, the British government was friendly enough toward Italy. Indecision was better than opposition, and, if this indecision lasted long enough, perhaps Italy might be able to present the British with a *fait accompli*. Mussolini therefore preferred to leave unsaid those facts which might cause premature hostility and force the British into a recalcitrant stand. He eschewed frank discussion and wanted to "let the sleeping dog lie." [83]

This tactic of equivocation rested on the assumption that the British were, at least in the short run, friendly or indifferent enough not to interfere, or that, despite their feelings, they were unwilling to un-

---

[82] The uncertainty that most impressed the Italians was caused by what appeared to be a conflict within the Foreign Office between the "soft" line of Simon and the "hard" line of Vansittart toward a rearmed Germany. Guariglia, *Ricordi*, 200. However, contrary to Italian belief, this debate did not extend to Italy. The intense and single-minded animosity that Vansittart held toward Hitler's Germany did not apply to Mussolini's Italy. Vansittart in fact saw Italy as an important element in containing the Reich and sought its friendship. Simon at this time was beginning a policy of shortsighted, irregular, and unwary appeasement, "through getting a recognition of [Germany's] rights and some modifications of the Peace Treaties," as he told the king on 14 January 1935. H. Nicolson, *King George the Fifth* (London, 1952), 522.

[83] Guariglia, *Ricordi*, 215.

dertake large-scale resistance to the Italian invasion of Ethiopia. While waiting for a statement of governmental intention on which negotiations might be based, Mussolini counted on the pacifism of the British people to offset any hostile reaction against Italy. Before beginning his plans for the conquest of Ethiopia, Mussolini had ordered a statistical study of the age groupings of British citizens. The conclusions of the survey were that British society consisted mostly of "static" elements, the elderly and women, and that the British would seek peace and compromise rather than interrupt a quiet life for military resistance.[84] With this in mind Mussolini judged that, once France had accepted Italian ambitions in east Africa, Britain's government would not create a stumbling block. The long tradition of compromise over Ethiopia might still be counted on as a guide to British policy. The treaty of 1906, recognizing most of Ethiopia as Italy's sphere of influence, was still in force, as was the bilateral agreement of 1925, and their import clearly was that Italy would be allowed to extend its influence throughout Ethiopia so long as no blatant violation of international law took place and no specifically British interest was endangered.

It was true that the British government wanted to keep Italy's friendship. Despite Mussolini's own confidence, however, it was not certain Italy could count on Britain once the design on Ethiopia was revealed not merely as economic penetration but as military conquest, a violation of the League Covenant. Aggression against Ethiopia, in the current context of international affairs, would be a direct challenge to the principles of the League. It was now difficult to separate a specific colonial action from its repercussions on the international scene, and a violation of the Covenant was not endorsed by any British-Italian agreement over Ethiopia. Although the British government may have been willing to give Mussolini as much latitude in Ethiopia as it could, it dared not act too far in opposition to British public opinion. Here is where Mussolini's assumptions and his policy of purposeful ambiguity ran into danger. The British people did not want war, as Mussolini correctly perceived, but they did feel strongly about the

---

[84] Ciano, *Diario*, 12; Aloisi, *Journal*, 386. Mussolini heaped contempt on the British. He claimed that the country was old, without creative ideas, stagnating after a libertine past and covering this decline with a pose as a teacher of wisdom and virtue. Mussolini was impressed by what he claimed to see in statistics on Britain's population: "the number of celibates, of unmarried people, the number of deaths [over] births, the spread of alcoholism and sexual perversion." G. Bastianini, *Uomini, cose, fatti* (Milan, 1959), 49.

League. This fact was of the utmost importance, for it placed the League in the forefront of British policy making. Just because at the start of 1935 British public opinion appeared quiescent and peace-seeking, no one could be certain that, in the case of an unprovoked Italian war of conquest, a popular inclination to stand behind the League would not outweigh the pacifism. If it should and if the British government, uncommitted in prior agreements with Italy, should allow itself to be pushed into upholding the principles of the League and imposing military sanctions, the consequences for Italy and for Fascism would be disastrous.

This possibility worried the more prudent Italian diplomats. The risks of conducting a war fought on the far side of the Suez Canal, in the face of British control of the Mediterranean, the canal, the Red Sea, and the Indian Ocean, were enough to daunt even the most sanguine of Italians. The military risk, as Neville Chamberlain later expressed it, was like tying a noose around one's neck and leaving "the end hanging out for anyone with a Navy to pull." [85]

These dangers, however, still remained only possibilities. In January 1935 Mussolini deemed it sufficient diplomatic preparation merely to inform the British of his renewed interest in Ethiopia and to suggest further discussions as a matter of mutual colonial interest. This done, he left the next move up to Britain.

The decision on how to treat the Italian overture of 29 January rested with Sir John Simon, minister of foreign affairs. Simon realized, as he told Geoffrey Thompson in January, that "the Italians intend to take Abyssinia." [86] Simon had no special love for Ethiopia,[87] and he did not want to oppose Mussolini. He feared that British resistance would bring about the Duce's fall and leave Italy open to the Bolsheviks.[88] For Britain's strategic needs, too, there was great value in

[85] K. Feiling, *The Life of Neville Chamberlain* (London, 1946), 273. (Permission to quote granted by Macmillan and Co. Ltd.)

[86] G. Thompson, *Front-Line Diplomat* (London, 1959), 95.

[87] "Having written a preface a few years previously to Lady Simon's unanswerable exposure of the Abyssinians' foul methods of slavery [Simon] would have found it difficult to express much sympathy for them — even though they were members of the League of Nations." B. Roberts, *Sir John Simon* (London, 1938), 302. Actually, Lady Simon's chapter on Ethiopian slavery gave credit to the reforming efforts of Haile Selassie and considered that these efforts could be furthered with League help. K. Simon, *Slavery* (London, 1929), chap. 1. But her description of Ethiopian slavery constituted a serious enough indictment to make Roberts' comment valid, especially given Simon's disinterest in the League.

[88] A. Rowse, *All Souls and Appeasement* (London, 1961), 26; see also C. R. Attlee, *As It Happened* (London, 1954), 79.

having Italy as a friend. Simon did not believe that the protection of a remote and primitive African kingdom was worth the cost of losing this friendship, to say nothing of the much greater cost of a British-Italian war. Simon's overriding concern, then, as he told King George in February, was to handle the Italian-Ethiopian conflict "in a way which will not affect adversely Anglo-Italian relations." [89] This approach to the coming crisis was conditioned by expedience, not by broader principles.[90] Mussolini's plans for the conquest of Ethiopia were a direct and vital challenge to the ideals and political existence of the League of Nations. But to champion the League meant to oppose Italy and hence endanger Britain's interest in a stable and peaceful Mediterranean. This Simon was not willing to do. He did not believe enough in the principle of collective security or in its value to Britain to make a national sacrifice on its behalf.

On the other hand, Simon was not prepared to undertake an effective appeasement of Mussolini by asserting British strength, despite the fact that such a course would benefit both Britain and the cause of European peace and security. Mussolini later claimed that at this time he had been willing to "table his case." [91] The door to negotiation was opened by Italy on 29 January, and there was a very real possibility that at this early stage, if the British took the initiative, a bargain for the peaceful settlement of Mussolini's colonial ambitions might be struck. Such an effort would enable the British to keep Italy's friendship and to prevent a major Italian challenge to the League. Robert Vansittart, the permanent secretary of the Foreign Office, saw Italy as a vital element in containing a rearmed Germany. Germany had to be deprived of "the one thing she needed to precipitate [a] conflict" — Italy as an ally. Mussolini was potentially trustworthy, Vansittart thought, and he could be bought. The question was: How, and at what price? Vansittart was furious with the French for giving Mussolini concessions so broad as to make it impossible for Britain to accept them.[92] Yet something might be worked out, as far as the British were concerned, to appease the Fascist appetite. Mussolini refused to help the British along by suggesting a plan of his own for a modus vivendi with Ethi-

[89] Nicolson, *King George the Fifth*, 528.

[90] A. Rowse, *The End of an Epoch* (London, 1948), 12.

[91] *Morning Post* interview, published 17 September 1935. Mussolini, *Opera omnia*, XXVII, 139.

[91] R. Vansittart, *Lessons of My Life* (London, n.d. [1943]), 48; R. Vansittart, *The Mist Procession* (London, 1958), 479, 502, 516.

opia,[93] but this did not mean that a solution could not be found if the British government had the will, the nerve, and the skill.

For example, the British as a first step might give Mussolini quiet and forceful warning that they would not tolerate military aggression against Ethiopia. This would be in line with the moral and political ideals of the League, and British control of the seas would lend substance to the warning. Stated at the outset before Mussolini had publicly committed his prestige to a military imperium, such a warning might deter Italy from invasion, give Mussolini sufficient reason to back down, and force him to limit his demands to claims which could be met either by the peaceful cession of territory in east Africa, parts of Ethiopia or British Somaliland, or by the peaceful economic penetration of Ethiopia with British and French cooperation. In the last instance the Ethiopians could be pacified with, say, the gift of an outlet to the sea at Zeila and further British guarantees of their territorial and political integrity. Such a plan would have been worth a try. If successful, an unjust war would be prevented. A critical challenge to the League would be forestalled. Britain would not have to choose between Rome and Geneva. And, with proper diplomatic care, Italy's friendship need not be irrevocably lost. As it was, no such plan was then proposed or even considered. The times cried out for creative statesmanship on the part of the British. But farsighted, imaginative, and courageous diplomacy was simply absent from the Foreign Office. "What we needed to steady [Mussolini] at this stage was a British statesman who would impress him, and we had not got one," wrote Vansittart.[94] Sir John Simon let this opportunity slide by without any action on his part.

The British response to the overture of Vitetti on 29 January was to postpone a decision on the matter. Italy did not request an immediate or specific reply to its informal proposal, and so Britain did not offer any.[95] Mussolini interpreted British muteness as tacit consent: "In the face of that silence there was only one road which remained open to me and I took it." [96] From this time on, the development of the dispute put a reasonable diplomatic settlement increasingly out of reach. Mus-

---

[93] Ambassador Drummond's interview with Mussolini at the end of February, reported in Avon, *Facing the Dictators*, 200.

[94] Vansittart, *The Mist Procession*, 502.

[95] *Parliamentary Debates, Official Report*, 305 H.C. Deb. 5s., col. 25.

[96] *Morning Post* interview, 17 September 1935. Mussolini, *Opera omnia*, XXVII, 140.

solini hurled his army beyond Suez and thereby cut off the possibility of retreat. Positions moved to extremes and hardened. The British government thus missed the best opportunity to exercise effective diplomacy that the Italian-Ethiopian conflict was to offer.

Only Dino Grandi, the Italian ambassador in London, made a further effort at this time to have the Ethiopian question treated as an object of colonial agreement between the interested powers and not, as it was threatening to become, a subject of policy bound up in the anti-colonialist strictures of the new international morality. Grandi was a good Fascist who had come during his time at the Palazzo Chigi to think like an old-line diplomat, and he was eager to maintain British-Italian friendship. In February 1935, on his own initiative, he spoke several times with British officials. The British government, however, did not take up his proposals for negotiations, even though Grandi told Vansittart that he did not believe Mussolini had yet come to an irrevocable decision over Ethiopia. Anthony Eden considered this news "hopeful, almost a hint," [97] but no action was taken. Another opportunity to reach a negotiated settlement with Mussolini was passed up, though Vansittart did give Grandi some cautions for the future.[98] At a meeting on 27 February, Vansittart said that British public opinion would be hostile to any Italian colonial war in Ethiopia. Such a war would seriously jeopardize the new and important possibility of cooperation among Britain, France, and Italy to keep the peace in Europe. Simon in his turn made a small effort to point out a danger to Italy and informed Grandi that Britain would continue to allow Ethiopia to import arms across British Somaliland.[99] Obviously rebuffed, Grandi

[97] Avon, *Facing the Dictators*, 201.

[98] *Ibid.*, 199–201.

[99] Guariglia, *Ricordi*, 216. On the other hand, De Bono found the British governor at Khartoum and the British resident at Kassala "extremely obliging" when, during February, Italy sent its military aircraft out to east Africa over British-controlled territory from Cairo to Kassala. E. De Bono, *La Preparazione e le prime operazioni*. 3rd ed. (Rome, 1937), 74. Nonetheless, from March 1935 on, the Italians took the precaution of shipping their planes rather than flying them over British lands. For all regular civil air traffic to Asmara, Italy remained dependent on the British until Ala Littoria created a regular service from Khartoum. This line, however, did not go into operation until the end of July 1935 and was still dependent on British service between Brindisi and Khartoum. Not until 1 December 1935 was a direct all-Italian air route established between Rome and Asmara. De Bono, *Anno XIIII*, 145–6. It is to be noted, though, as Hoare told the House of Commons on 30 July 1935, that during the first six months of 1935 the Italian government requested permission for eleven aircraft only to fly over Egyptian territory and that in four instances the flights did not occur. *Parliamentary Debates*, 304 H.C. Deb. 5s., col. 2482.

did not press his proposals any further. The British were not ready to enter into negotiations, and he could not let it seem that British approval was considered a necessary preliminary to Italian action. Italy had decided to maintain as free a hand as possible in this affair.

At the beginning of March 1935, it became obvious that some policy had to be formulated by the British Foreign Office in the increasingly serious Italian-Ethiopian situation. And so the issue was referred to a committee. On 6 March a special interministerial commission under Sir John Maffey was secretly established to study the question of British interests in Ethiopia.[100] The Italian preparations for invasion pushed forward. Mussolini had no assurance that Britain would allow him his conquest, but, all things considered, he did not fear the British, and English silence seemed as good as the French wink.

---

[100] Maffey was a former governor of the Sudan and then permanent under-secretary to the minister of colonies. In a speech of 22 October 1935, Hoare maintained that the Italian overture of 29 January "was most seriously considered and that a special committee was set up to review the whole field of Anglo-Abyssinian relations and British interests in that country, in order that we might decide our course of action . . . No instantaneous reply was possible [to the Italian overture] and none was asked; indeed there could have been no occasion for special haste if no special Italian activities had been contemplated." *Parliamentary Debates,* 305 H.C. Deb. 5s., col. 25. Over a month passed, however, before the Maffey commission was even established.

Chapter 5

January-March: Ethiopia Turns to the League

During these early months of 1935, while Mussolini was clearing the deck in Europe, bargaining with France and sounding out Britain, general international attention was focused on the aftermath of the Walwal incident. The diplomatic activity of this period, December 1934 to April 1935, is significant, for it led to the ignominious failure of the first British and French efforts toward conciliation, the inception of Italy's plan of tactical delay, and above all the critical involvement of the League of Nations.

The fighting at Walwal took place on 5 December 1934. Protests were exchanged at once, each side claiming unwarranted aggression by the other. Confident of Ethiopia's legal and political position, the more so since British officers had been present in the Ethiopian camp, the Ethiopian foreign minister, Blattengeta Herouy Wolde Selassie, on 9 December 1934 invoked article 5 of the bilateral treaty of 2 August 1928, which called for the submission "to a procedure of conciliation and arbitration any question" between Italy and Ethiopia that it was not possible "to settle by the usual diplomatic means, without having recourse to force of arms." An Italian reply on 11 December made no mention of this proposal and instead demanded from the Ethiopians an extraordinary list of reparations, which included honors to the Italian flag at Walwal (that is, recognition of Italy's right to possession) and a totally unreasonable monetary compensation. Ethiopia immediately restated its proposal for arbitration, to reach a solution "in conformity with law," and reserved comment on the Italian demands.[1] On 14 December an Italian response rejected arbitration outright, blamed the Ethiopians for all that had occurred, and repeated the insistence that apologies and reparations be forthcoming. Counsel was

[1] League, *Official Journal, 1935*, 271–3; Virgin, *Abyssinia*, 144.

taken in Addis Ababa, and it was decided on the 14th to send a tele-gram that night to the secretary-general of the League, drawing the "Council's attention to the gravity of the situation." [2]

This move was not a request for specific action by the League. Acting only in reference to the terms of paragraph 2 of article 11, the Ethi-opians hoped to call attention to the dispute, to appeal to world opinion through the open forum at Geneva, and to indicate that they would invoke the assistance of the League if bilateral negotiations failed.[3] Haile Selassie would have been better advised, as Herbert Feis writes, to take a strong stand early. "But he felt it best to give proof of patience to those countries whose influence would decide whether the League *ever* gave his country protection." [4] Throughout the last part of De-cember and during the early days of January 1935, the Ethiopian gov-ernment strove only for a negotiated resolution of the Walwal incident, confident of its position and hopeful that successful arbitration would forestall further Italian aggression. This was a vain hope and reliance on arbitration was a dangerous tactic, for it focused attention on a minor incident rather than on the greater threat of Italian imperialism. Nonetheless, Ethiopia had now appealed to the League, and that was a most significant step.

Ethiopia continued to hold open the door to arbitration. On 15 December, Foreign Minister Herouy told the Italians that the notice

[2] Claiming an unprovoked surprise attack at Walwal, "The Italian Government does not see how the settlement of an incident of that kind can be submitted to arbitration procedure." League, *Official Journal, 1935*, 273–4. Eden writes that the Foreign Office told Barton that, while Simon "agreed to the Emperor doing all he could to reach agreement by direct negotiation, it seemed probable that the co-operation of the League would be needed in the end. We would do anything we could to help." Avon, *Facing the Dictators*, 193. Fair words, but limited solely to mediatory action within the League: the British legation in Addis Ababa was "at pains specifically to inform the Ethiopian Government that Britain desired to have no connection with the affair." *U.S. Diplomatic Papers, 1934*, II, 773. For Britain, as Eden said, the Walwal dispute as such "was certainly not one which should be allowed to do any harm to Anglo-Italian relations." Avon, *Facing the Dictators*, 192.

[3] Feeling isolated, the Ethiopians were casting about. They considered applying to the American government, asking the United States to draw attention to the Kellogg-Briand Pact of 1928, and perhaps to create an international com-mission to investigate and establish responsibility for the Walwal incident. The United States refused to become involved, citing Ethiopia's connection with the League as a more appropriate channel for action. *U.S. Diplomatic Papers, 1934*, II, 770, 774–5.

[4] H. Feis, *Seen from E.A.: Three International Episodes* (New York, 1947), 199. Feis adds: "So often in history the suppliant has tried to merit help by patient endurance of injustice and suffering — and usually only given the impression that he was by nature made to bear them."

to the League was sent without wanting to prejudice "in any way the continuance of our diplomatic negotiations." The move was also accepted in this sense by Italy. The Ethiopian government stood ready to "satisfy Italian demands, if its responsibility [for the Walwal battle] is proved" by investigation and arbitration. The British, and others, were impressed by what Simon called the "very conciliatory and constructive attitude" of Ethiopia.[5] But this was no help to Addis Ababa.

The Italians for their part steadfastly refused to accept arbitration, and a stalemate greeted the new year. At this stage, Italy was stalling for time. The Italians were not yet sure of their position in Europe, and these early skirmishes, and Italy's intransigence, were delaying actions until their standing with Britain and France could be clarified. Minister Vinci was greatly uneasy when he left for Addis Ababa on Christmas of 1934, for no one in the government in Rome could tell him what Italian policy was or what line he should follow. Mussolini was unwilling to move until after an accord was concluded with France. Only then, he rightly believed, could the Ethiopian affair "mature." Mussolini told Vinci to be patient. All would become clearer, he said, when he himself took over the ministry of the colonies.[6]

This Italian indecision was naturally viewed in Addis Ababa as deliberate evasion. Sporadic incidents were still occurring in the Ogaden, where the withdrawing Ethiopian troops were harassed by Italian aircraft. At Afdub, Ado, and Gerlogubi, bombs were dropped on Ethiopian soldiers. It seemed that Italy was planning to establish another permanent camp in this region, further violating Ethiopia's territorial rights. No progress was being made toward getting Italy to accept arbitration of the incidents in accordance with the treaty of 1928, and no help came to Ethiopia from any outside quarter. It was obvious that something more than an appeal to world opinion was needed. Ethiopia therefore turned to other provisions of the Covenant of the League.

On 3 January, the same day Laval left Paris for Rome, Herouy cabled the secretary-general requesting full "application of Article 11 of the Covenant that every measure effectually to safeguard peace be taken."[7] The eighty-fourth meeting of the council was scheduled for 11 January, and the Ethiopian communication was forwarded to the

---

[5] League, *Official Journal, 1935*, 274, 726–7; Avon, *Facing the Dictators*, 195.
[6] Aloisi, *Journal*, 239.
[7] League, *Official Journal, 1935*, 252.

council's members. According to the terms of paragraph 2, article 11, which Ethiopia had already invoked on 14 December 1934, each member of the League had the right "to bring to the attention of the Assembly or of the Council any circumstance whatever affecting international relations which threatens to disturb international peace or the good understanding between nations upon which peace depends." The League was now a second time officially informed of the Italian-Ethiopian conflict. A further dimension was added by paragraph 1, article 11, which Ethiopia now invoked as well. This paragraph stated:

> Any war or threat of war, whether immediately affecting any of the Members of the League or not, is hereby declared a matter of concern to the whole League, and the League shall take any action that may be deemed wise and effectual to safeguard the peace of nations.

Under this clause the more general questions of peace or war, territorial protection, national safety, and the fulfillment of treaty obligations were stated as the League's province. On 3 January the Ethiopian government informed Italy that, as far as it was concerned, the decision of "all the questions involved" in the incidents of the Ogaden were now under the League's official jurisdiction.[8]

The normal procedure was that, when a member invoked article 11, the problem as a matter of course was put on the agenda of the council or a special meeting of the council was called. This possibility worried the Italians, for it could complicate their plans. Mussolini did not want to give up anything to Ethiopia, but most of all he did not want the League of Nations to take the conflict under its jurisdiction. The immediate task of Italian diplomacy was to prevent this from happening, and with this in mind Aloisi was sent to Geneva. The Italian preparations for war continued unabated in the meantime. On 30 December 1934 Mussolini issued his fourteen-point "Directive and Plan of Action for the Resolution of the Italian-Abyssinian Question." On 7 January De Bono sailed for east Africa to create the necessary base of supply for the invasion force. On 10 January De Bono was named "High Commissioner for East Africa."[9] On 16 January, the day De Bono

---

[8] League, *Official Journal, 1935*, 728.

[9] On the same day the Ethiopian chargé in Rome, Megodras Afework, was received by both the king and Mussolini. They assured him of Italy's peaceful intention towards Ethiopia. Afework was a poor example of a diplomat. He had an Italian wife, and he believed what the Italians told him. He considered himself "almost" an Italian and described his position as "between the hammer and the

landed at Massawa, Mussolini took over the post of minister of colonies. At last the Ethiopian campaign was under a single authority — the Duce himself. These events, wrote "Romulus" in the *Nuova antologia* of 1 February 1935, constituted a clear prelude to Ethiopia's becoming the "most suitable field for Italy's civilizing mission." [10] The disquiet grew at Geneva.

The problems raised by the Italian-Ethiopian conflict presented a crucial test of the League as an organization meant to ensure world peace. Italian colonial ambitions challenged directly, and dramatically, many of the fundamental tenets of the Covenant. The Covenant was based on the ideals of open diplomacy, the equality of nations, collective protection for all members, and the predominance of the principles of international law over particularist ends. It established a civilized procedure for the settlement of international disputes. But the League was only a framework providing the means to realize these ideals. Practical success depended on the absolute willingness and determination of all League members to support these principles and to follow these means.

At the beginning of 1935 the most important members of the League, Britain and France, were hesitant to commit themselves to such systematic devotion. Although their governments paid lip service to the League, their leaders did not really believe that the outstanding political problems of Europe could be solved by appeal to the League alone. Frightened by their weakness in the face of a rearming Germany, Britain and France looked outside the League in seeking their security in Europe. Total adherence to the principles and procedures of the League appeared a luxury they could not afford.

This did not mean that the governments of Britain and France were prepared to jettison the League. Despite their doubts and qualifications, they saw that the League still held advantages for them, and public opinion in each country insisted on at least a titular pro-League policy. But it did mean that Britain and France would think twice before alienating Italy. They were pursuing two policies simultaneously: trying to conciliate Italy while upholding the authority of the League.

---

anvil." Afework was also dependent on the Italian foreign office for swift communication with his government, and the Italians occasionally decoded his radiograms for him. After Walwal, he had asked Aloisi to send a telegram to Haile Selassie requesting permission for Afework to make an on-the-spot investigation. Aloisi, *Journal*, 240; G. Waterfield, *Morning Will Come* (London, 1944), 66.

[10] "Cronaca politica," *Nuova antologia*, 308:452.

With the Ethiopian affair these two policies not only diverged; they threatened to come into direct conflict. The only way to avoid a forced choice between Geneva and Rome was to keep the Italian-Ethiopian controversy out of the League.

To this end they were aided by Joseph Avenol, who in 1933 became Eric Drummond's successor as secretary-general of the League of Nations. Avenol was not a professional diplomat, although for the previous ten years he had been assistant secretary-general. Avenol inherited and followed the lead set by Drummond, and he inclined even more toward the primarily administrative content of his office, rarely taking any initiative to strengthen the political bases of the League. This lack of leadership was a serious source of weakness for the international body, although such passivity was what self-serving member states often wanted. What the League needed was a far-seeing politician, a statesman, at its head, a man who would be a forceful supranational leader in the service of peace and justice.[11] Avenol was not such a man, and his idea of the purpose of the League was radically different from that of its founders. He did not believe in the enforcement machinery of the League, its very heart, the basis of the system of collective security. He considered this unworkable and thought that article 16 should be abandoned by amendment. In Avenol's view, the League had a future only if the whole conception of its nature were changed. What should be emphasized was not the political and security machinery of the Covenant, but the less controversial and hence more widely acceptable elements conducive to economic and social cooperation.[12] Avenol wanted the League revamped, made nonpolitical.

There was an argument for such a position. If, as many feared, the League was too weak to stand up to the political test posed by the Italian-Ethiopian dispute, then perhaps there was a risk of discrediting the entire organization by involving it in a controversy that it could not resolve according to the hope of its founders and the letter of its statutes. Perhaps, as Avenol thought, it was better to solve the conflict by diplomatic action outside the League's framework. But it had not yet been proven that the League as a political organization would fail the current test; to evade the issue too long, until a crisis arrived in

[11] E. Ranshofen-Wertheimer, *The International Secretariat* (Washington, D.C., 1945), 48–9.
[12] J. Avenol, "The Future of the League of Nations," *International Affairs*, 13:142–58 (March–April 1934); S. Schwebel, *The Secretary-General of the United Nations* (Cambridge, Mass., 1952), 215–24.

which the League was forced to become involved, would only make the issue more dangerous, the failure all the more serious. Avenol was within his rights to try to find a compromise solution by the means of traditional diplomacy, when it appeared that disputes could be satisfactorily resolved in such a way. But it was not the job of the secretary-general to maintain that the League was helpless, to keep a desperate member state from appealing to the apparatus of the League's system of collective security, or to create obstacles to the working of the League's machinery. For, despite Avenol's wishes, the League in 1935 was still functioning under its original mandate, and to put off Ethiopia's appeal was contrary to the interests and purposes of the organization. From the first instance, in the middle of January, with the support of the Italians Pompeo Aloisi and Massimo Pilotti, and Eden and Laval, Avenol was the key person in the effort to keep Ethiopia from inscribing its complaint on the agenda of the council.[13]

There was a further clue to Avenol's behavior. The position was based on the idea of an international civil servant, neutral in office and dedicated to the purposes of the organization, but Avenol remained a loyal Frenchman who, in the mid-1930s, was susceptible to pressures from the French foreign ministry. What made this particularly damaging to the League was not only the influence on him of France's compromising policy during these years, but the fact that Avenol's own "sympathy with the reactionary forces" in his own country "made him less than half-hearted with regard to the League."[14] Avenol never took an unequivocal stand against aggression.[15] Like Laval, he did not want to antagonize or humiliate Italy by involving it in the web of League procedures and publicity. More specifically, Avenol showed all communications from Ethiopia to the assistant secretary-general, the Italian jurist Pilotti, in advance of circulation, so that the Italian government would have ample time to formulate an appropriate response when the matter arose formally. Pilotti was in close touch with the Italian delegation at Geneva and maintained a direct connection with Italian officials in Rome through his assistant, Alberto Berio.[16] It was through these channels that advice and comment flowed. Rome

---

[13] Aloisi, *Journal*, 251–2; J. Whitaker, *And Fear Came* (New York, 1936), 247.
[14] F. P. Walters, *A History of the League of Nations* (London, 1952), II, 810. (Published by Oxford University Press, under the auspices of the Royal Institute of International Affairs; permission to quote granted.)
[15] D. Cheever and H. Haviland, Jr., *Organizing for Peace* (Boston, 1954), 358.
[16] Tabouis, *They Called Me Cassandra*, 264–5; A. Berio, "L' 'Affare' etiopico," *Rivista di studi politici internazionali*, 25:182 (April–June 1958).

was kept informed of the workings of the League while Pilotti represented Italy's interest in the secretariat.

The council of the League convened in Geneva on 11 January, as scheduled. The Ethiopian delegate, Tecle Hawariate (also minister to Paris), discovered at once that the incertitude of Britain and France was the major obstacle for Ethiopia. Tecle Hawariate could start up the League machine, but its direction, and the speed and success of its operation, depended on Britain and France. "Uncertain and apprehensive," writes F. P. Walters, "the other Council Members and the Secretariat looked to London and Paris for a lead. And here began a sort of dual procedure which in the end proved fatal to the League . . . the proceedings of the Council were made to alternate with conversations between Britain, France, and Italy, in which the Covenant was often forgotten and the interests of the League were treated as of small account." [17]

Behind the scenes, a series of near frantic negotiations took place. Laval, fresh from his success in Rome, Eden, Aloisi, and Avenol did all they could to change the Ethiopian delegate's intention to put the dispute on the agenda. They were eager to have the matter settled swiftly and beyond Geneva. Laval was the chief mediator with the Ethiopians. Simon and Eden for their part presented naive proposals to both Mussolini and the emperor.[18] These proposals came to nothing, for they assumed that the issue was simply the solution of the Ogaden dispute, that there were valid arguments on both sides, and that there was an equal desire for a peaceful and equitable settlement. Mussolini quickly disabused the British. He stood firmly on his earlier demands and refused to negotiate with Ethiopia.[19] The Italian position placed all the blame and responsibility squarely on Ethiopia, and this stand admitted no room for arbitration.

The concerted pressures on Tecle Hawariate, on the other hand, had some effect. The Ethiopians hesitated, eager not to offend the British on whom all their hopes depended.[20] At the opening private

[17] Walters, *History of the League*, II, 628.

[18] Virgin, *Abyssinia*, 146; Avon, *Facing the Dictators*, 194–6; *U.S. Diplomatic Papers, 1935*, I, 595–6.

[19] Mussolini's interview with Drummond on 14 January. Avon, *Facing the Dictators*, 195.

[20] The Ethiopians placed their confidence in the belief that Britain would not, in the last analysis, allow Italy to conquer their country. "The Emperor was misled partly by taking too seriously [British] speeches at Geneva and elsewhere, and partly by the Ethiopian minister in London, Dr. Martin [Azaj Wargneh C. Martin]. Ethiopian officials before the defeat had a certain naivity, an almost

meeting of the council on 11 January, Avenol announced with the air of a magician performing the impossible that, "as the Members of the Council could see, this question had not been placed on the agenda." Any Italian joy was premature. "We have succeeded for the moment in suspending its inscription on the agenda," wrote Baron Aloisi in his diary that night, "but will it be possible to evade it definitely . . . ?" The Ethiopian envoy carefully reserved the right to insert the matter on the agenda during the current session.[21]

The next few days were filled with further efforts by Laval, Eden, Avenol, and Aloisi to get the issue dropped. But the Ethiopians were determined, and the very mechanics of the League were set up to prevent this kind of stymie. For a month the Ethiopian government had been gathering reports on the Walwal incident.[22] On the night of 15 January Tecle Hawariate presented the memorandum to Avenol and made a formal request that the matter be placed on the current agenda. Despite a last-minute effort to stem the tide, Avenol had to comply. On the 17th he presented Ethiopia's request to the council; the matter was scheduled for discussion on the 19th; and the Ethiopian memorandum was circulated.

Things looked grave for Italy. Aloisi's first reaction was to continue the effort to silence Tecle Hawariate. In this he was joined by Eden, Laval, and Avenol — the League was run by *couloir* diplomats. Their plan was to allow Tecle Hawariate to make his complaint before the council, but not to discuss it then. Laval and Eden would also continue to press Tecle Hawariate to moderate his stand.

Then, between the 17th and 19th of January, the Italian government made a sudden and unexpected change in tactics. The impetus behind it seems to have come from Eden, who was rapidly cooling toward any further postponement of the Ethiopian complaint. Rather than all this work to frustrate the League openly, a better idea was to create an alternative to League action: Italy should accept the procedure of arbitration under the terms of the treaty of 1928, with the arbitration to deal only with the incidents in the Ogaden. Mussolini at first op-

---

Victorian confidence in public opinion and international law, and above all, an overwhelming belief in England's ultimate domination in North Africa. In all this they were confirmed by their representative in England, a man who served his full time as a Civil Surgeon in India . . . The whole basis of Ethiopian policy was that England would see them through." G. Garratt, "Abyssinia," *Journal of the (Royal) African Society*, 36:42 (January 1937).

[21] League, *Official Journal*, 1935, 87; Aloisi, *Journal*, 249.

[22] Virgin, *Abyssinia*, 145–6.

posed any such concession, despite Aloisi's urgings. Nonetheless, over the 18th and 19th, working against the deadline of 19 January when Tecle Hawariate would take the council floor and the League would be committed to the conflict, Mussolini gave in. A "last minute reprieve," Eden called it.[23]

Laval and Eden met at once with Aloisi, Tecle Hawariate, and Avenol, and letters were drafted which Avenol presented to a private meeting of the council on the 19th. The Italian letter noted, "it is in conformity with the spirit of the Covenant and with the tradition of the League of Nations to encourage direct negotiations concerning disputes that may arise between two States Members." The whole thrust of Ethiopia's argument was turned aside. Italy asserted its good faith: "it does not regard [the incidents] as likely to affect the peaceful relations between the two countries." This was a patent falsehood, but evasion of the truth was more comfortable to Britain and France than facing a troublesome situation. Then the Italian note presented Italy's about-face: "the settlement of the incident might be advantageously pursued in accordance with Article 5 of the Treaty of 1928." Ethiopia's retreat was simply stated, and its letter confirmed the government's willingness to arbitrate. Ethiopia agreed "to the postponement of the discussion of its request to the next session of the Council." Both sides pledged to avoid fresh incidents. The council was only too glad to be rid of the problem and, with an almost audible sigh of relief, resolved to postpone the Ethiopian request for discussion.[24]

The Ethiopians won a skirmish — arbitration would ensue. But they lost a battle — no discussion of the Italian-Ethiopian conflict took place at that session of the council. Ethiopia found itself caught in Britain's and France's conflict of interest. Ethiopia needed the League, but the League was nothing without Britain and France. This is why Tecle Hawariate was so susceptible to the pressures of Laval and Eden. All he could hope was that their two governments would guarantee the success of arbitration,[25] and assure Ethiopia's security during the interim. Yet the Ethiopians made a mistake in not forcing their demand

[23] Aloisi, *Journal*, 251–2; Avon, *Facing the Dictators*, 196–7.
[24] League, *Official Journal, 1935*, 162–3.
[25] The British government telegraphed its representatives in Rome and Addis Ababa, instructing them to do all within their power to bring about the success of the projected negotiations. Thompson, *Front-Line Diplomat*, 95; Simon to the House of Commons, 13 February 1935, *Parliamentary Debates*, 297 H. C. Deb. 5s., col. 1904.

for League action, despite the obvious fact that the council sought nothing more than "to avoid taking up any attitude towards the dispute itself." [26] It was vitally necessary to Ethiopia to focus attention on Italy's ongoing military preparations, which clearly portended a direct threat to Ethiopia, a danger to the peace, a challenge to the principles of the League. In bilateral arbitration these fundamental concerns would be bypassed, while the Italian military build-up proceeded and Mussolini's commitment to war hardened. Arbitration would deal only with the Ogaden incidents, treating these frontier disputes as the only issue of the conflict, and isolating them from far graver matters of which they were only symptoms.

For Italy the agreement of 19 January was a diplomatic victory. Time was gained for Italian preparations, free from outside interference, and a new way was found for diplomatic distraction. Beside these advantages, agreement to arbitrate was a minor concession. Indeed, arbitration became the very means by which the tactic of calculated evasion was to be achieved. Above all, Britain and France had acted amiably. They supported Italy; pressure from them brought about the Ethiopian retreat; their eager search for a compromise created the formula for delay. The significance of this support was well noted in Rome. By late January, Mussolini, who had now gathered to himself full control of the political and military aspects of the campaign, was completely absorbed in the matter of Ethiopia. His decision to conquer the country appeared "irrevocable," wrote Aloisi, and "put *en cause* the future of the regime." [27] Increasingly, Mussolini saw his government standing or falling on the outcome of his Ethiopian plans; increasingly, all other things became subordinated in his mind.

On 29 January, we have seen, Mussolini tested the ground with his overture to Britain and apparently found it firm. On 1 February he decided to integrate the Fascist militia with the regular army. The Duce proclaimed: "I want to make a nation of workers and of soldiers. Relations between nations are founded on force, the force of arms." [28] Workers to build roads, soldiers to fight — these were the two manpower needs for the invasion of Ethiopia. No sooner had these words been uttered than the flow of workers and soldiers to east Africa began. During 1934, to maintain secrecy, Italy had relied on local labor in the

[26] Virgin, *Abyssinia*, 147.
[27] Aloisi, *Journal*, 253.
[28] Aloisi, *Journal*, 254.

colonies. After the events and decisions of January 1935, when speed of preparation became more important than concealment of purpose, laborers were sent directly from Italy. In February 1935, 10,000 Italian workers arrived in the east African colonies, sent for one purpose: the construction of military roads to carry the means of offensive war directly to the Ethiopian frontier.[29] Soldiers followed soon after. On 6 February Mussolini told his undersecretary for foreign affairs, Fulvio Suvich, "that a nation, to remain healthy, should make war every twenty-five years." [30] Between 5 and 11 February two divisions of the regular army, totaling 30,000 men, were placed on a war footing. The recall of young men whose age put them in the so-called class of 1911 of the Fascist militia was begun, causing a strong reaction in the foreign press.[31] These troops were designated expressly for use in Ethiopia, and the first contingents sailed on 17 February. On 16 February the Fascist Grand Council approved "with enthusiasm" the military measures taken to that date and gave its support to any that might follow.[32] On 20 February the Supreme Defense Committee declared that the resources of Italy were ready for war, and on the 27th the government announced that it was prepared for "any eventuality." [33] These preparations were not for colonial defense; from the beginning of 1935 the Italian general staff planned only in terms of an offensive campaign. The invasion was scheduled for September

[29] De Bono, *Anno XIIII*, 21, 67.

[30] Aloisi, *Journal*, 255. The last colonial war waged by Italy began in 1911. Mussolini, then a socialist, opposed the Italian-Turkish war over Libya, calling it an imperialist crime. He organized an antiwar strike in Forli and was imprisoned for five months as a result. On the eve of the war, which he described as a manifestation of "nationalistic delirium tremens," Mussolini, in the 23 September 1911 issue of *La Lotta di classe* (The Class Struggle), wrote a passage of interest in the light of events twenty-five years later. He asserted that "millions of workers . . . are *instinctively* opposed to the African colonial undertakings. The slaughter of Abba-Garima [Aduwa] is still very much alive in the memory of the people. The adventure of Tripoli was to be for many a 'red herring' that would distract the country from posing to itself and solving its complex and very grave internal problems." Cited in G. Megaro, *Mussolini in the Making* (Boston, 1938), 253.

[31] Mussolini, *Opera omnia*, XXVII, 335; Aloisi, *Journal*, 255.

[32] One should not be misled by the resolution. At this stage there was no real popular support for the coming conflict, which was viewed as a personal enterprise of Mussolini's. A revealing illustration of this is the acknowledgment in Mussolini's own journal, *Gerarchia*, 4 April 1935, of the complaints and unwillingness of men who were called into service. Their reluctance stemmed evidently from a disapproval of the purpose behind the conscription. *Gerarchia*, in reply, claimed that the defense and prestige of "nostro Impero Coloniale" should be justification enough for their services.

[33] Mussolini, *Opera omnia*, XXVII, 23–6; *Bulletin périodique de la presse italienne*, 307:19.

or October. Although some effort was made to conceal the extent of the preparations, the activity and its purpose were evident to observers in Rome. Aloisi was correct when he asserted to the League council in May that Italy "has demonstrated the nature of its intention by accompanying its measures with an unprecedented publicity." [34] Italy's plan of action for the first stage of the war was to recapture the area around Aduwa and Aksum in the northern sector, and to remain on the defensive in the south. Rodolfo Graziani, Italy's famous colonial general, was sent to Italian Somaliland at the end of February to take command of the southern sector. On 26 February Mussolini wrote De Bono that the Ethiopians would not attack and that, "should the Negus have no intention of attacking us, we ourselves must take the initiative." [35]

Only those who wanted to be deceived were fooled. There was no excuse for mistaking Italian intentions, except wishful thinking. The British government kept its head buried in the sand. Despite the fact that every one of the Italian troops, each of the Italian workers, and every pound of matériel had to pass through the Suez Canal, the British continued to accept the spurious Italian claims that the increase in military strength was purely precautionary and defensive.[36] The British foreign minister repeated these Italian assertions in the House of Commons on 13 February, the same day the American ambassador in Rome informed Washington that Italy was preparing for an "extensive campaign" using between 200,000 and 300,000 troops, 30,000 of which had already left Naples.[37] The French were no more willing to allow the truth to come out, with the troublesome consequences

[34] League, *Official Journal, 1935*, 641; *U.S. Diplomatic Papers, 1935*, I, 599; P. Badoglio, *La Guerra d'Etiopia* (Milan, 1936), 9–10, 28.

[35] R. Graziani, *Il Fronte sud* (Milan, 1938), 25, 31, 88; De Bono, *Anno XIIII*, 117–18.

[36] Drummond accepted this without much question in the early months of 1935. He thought that "on financial and general grounds" public opinion in Italy was unfavorable to any military adventure. This is a good example of what Emile Giraud, for twenty years in the service of the League and its legal counselor, has listed as the first cause of the failure to keep the peace: misunderstanding by the democracies of the spirit and aims of the totalitarian states. Lack of critical curiosity, a willingness to be lulled into the acceptance of propaganda statements, lack of psychological acuity, unwillingness to face unpleasant realities — these were products of the democracies' isolationism, pacifism, and good will, and were crucial factors in the diplomacy of the 1930s. For Giraud's analysis, see his *La Nullité de la politique internationale des grandes démocraties, 1919–1939* (Paris, 1948), xiii–xiv.

[37] *U.S. Diplomatic Papers, 1935*, I, 599.

that it would have. Suvich's disclaimers and hopeful comments were also accepted by Chambrun. No more than the Foreign Office did the Quai d'Orsay inquire further or ask embarrassing questions. On 19 February the French informed the British that they considered all Italian-Ethiopian negotiations to be proceeding satisfactorily.[38] Nothing could have been further from the truth.

According to the agreement reached at Geneva on 18 January, direct bilateral negotiations were to be undertaken in accordance with article 5 of the treaty of 1928, leading to the formation of a commission to settle the Ogaden dispute. For Italy this agreement offered a most valuable opportunity for keeping the Italian-Ethiopian conflict outside the jurisdiction of the League. It created the illusion that Italy was seeking a peaceful settlement through acceptable diplomatic channels. It concentrated all formal action on a minor side issue while diverting official attention from Italy's preparations for aggressive war. With a little diplomatic skill, before and after a commission was formed, Italy could prolong the negotiations indefinitely — until October at least, Aloisi hoped.[39] Such negotiations, never finally succeeding but always kept in motion, were the perfect means for a policy of diplomatic delay and diversion.

Diplomatic exchanges began in February. At Geneva the British and French delegates had suggested that both sides withdraw their forces from the disputed area to prevent further clashes. This was unobjectionable to the Ethiopians, and in a series of notes in the first half of February they invited the Italian government to enter into negotiations for the establishment of a neutral zone.[40] The Ethiopians did not consider this a necessary preliminary, but merely a useful adjunct for the later discussions. The Italian minister ignored these notes. Around the middle of February, however, Rome saw the advantages of using this matter as a stalling device. The Italians now began to assert that a neutral zone must be established before any substantive negotiations even began. The Ethiopian government[41] bowed part way to this

---

[38] Avon, *Facing the Dictators*, 197–8.

[39] Aloisi, *Journal*, 255. For this reason Mussolini treated possibly troublesome further incidents lightly and did not use them as an excuse to break off talks by claiming infractions of the Geneva agreement. See *ibid.*, 254; League, *Official Journal, 1935*, 731–4; Virgin, *Abyssinia*, 150.

[40] Ethiopian notes of 1, 9, 12 February in League, *Official Journal, 1935*, 733–5.

[41] Haile Selassie had at this time three principal advisers on foreign affairs, two Europeans and one American. This trio, who called themselves La Trinité, Société

insistence as an earnest of its good will. Protracted negotiations on the zone ensued, lasting a full month. Agreement was reached on 13 March, and the neutral zone was located entirely within Ethiopian territory.[42]

Still the formal main issue, resolution of the Walwal incident by conciliation or arbitration, remained untouched. Time after time the Ethiopian government demanded in notes to the Italian minister that a commission be set up in accordance with the treaty provision and the Geneva agreement.[43] All that the Ethiopians received in reply were verbal comments by Minister Vinci, speaking, he claimed, in a private capacity. He ignored the matter of the neutral zone. With a stubbornness born, no doubt, of directives from Rome, Vinci insisted that the demands in the Italian note of 14 December 1934, for compensation and apologies, were a necessary precondition to any discussion of the Walwal incident. This was clearly contradictory to the agreement of 19 January, and the Ethiopian government had to reject the renewed demands. Any other course would put Ethiopia's diplomatic position back to where it was before the appeal to the League. To accept responsibility for the incidents would admit an Italian standing in the Ogaden, weaken Ethiopia's position before the League, create serious discontent among the rases, and encourage Italy to take further steps of aggression. In a note of 8 March 1935 the Ethiopians declared that, in no circumstances, would they pay an indemnity or other reparations unless judged liable by an impartial tribunal. They would enter into no further discussions along these lines. They demanded once again, for the last time, to know whether or not Italy was prepared to abide by the Geneva agreement and the 1928 treaty and set up the prescribed commission.[44] Italy kept its silence.

Anonyme, "Counsiels en tous genres . . . Ouvert dimanches et fêtes," was composed of General Eric Virgin of the Swedish army, whom the Swedish government had sent to Ethiopia as a military adviser; M. Auberson, a Swiss who was the emperor's legal adviser; and Everett Colson, an American who was the emperor's financial adviser and the most important member of the Trinity. These shrewd men guided Haile Selassie through the shoals and quicksands of European diplomacy and were responsible for the masterful diplomatic notes that brought Ethiopia's plight to the highest courts of international jurisprudence. For an account of how the three worked, see Colson's comments in G. Steer, *Caesar in Abyssinia* (Boston, 1937), 28n–29n.

[42] Virgin, *Abyssinia*, 148; League, *Official Journal, 1935*, 742–3.

[43] See the Ethiopian notes of 20, 21, 27 February in League, *Official Journal, 1935*, 735–7.

[44] Virgin, *Abyssinia*, 150–1; League, *Official Journal, 1935*, 738–9.

Throughout these tedious and frustrating weeks the Ethiopian government acted with great patience, skill, and dignity. It remained conciliatory and showed itself ready to begin negotiations. Italy's behavior, on the other hand, was marked by a highly insulting insouciance. The Italians consistently refused to enter into any negotiations on the issue formally before them. Vinci's casual replies offered no hint of interest or cooperation, and the Italians turned deaf ears to every Ethiopian overture. This was bad diplomacy, for the Italian government gained little by its obstructionism and did not take proper advantage of Aloisi's clever maneuvering at Geneva.[45] All the Italians succeeded in doing was to provoke the Ethiopian government beyond its already extraordinary patience. And during this time the real intentions of Italy became obvious to all observers. There was a speed-up in military praparations in Eritrea and Somaliland. On 7 March General Graziani was named governor and commander of the forces in Italian Somaliland.[46] The number of bellicose statements coming from Rome increased. In these circumstances, exasperated by Italian diplomatic intransigence, the Ethiopians, to break the deadlock, returned to their only haven, the League.

On 16 March 1935 Ethiopia informed Italy and the secretary-general that it would submit to the council a formal request for examination of the Italian-Ethiopian dispute. The government would request the council not merely to consider the Walwal incident, but to undertake a full study of Italian-Ethiopian relations in the face of Italy's military threats and the absence of replies from Italy to Ethiopia's repeated requests for arbitration.[47] The following day, 17 March, Tecle Hawariate submitted Ethiopia's invocation of article 15 and an appeal to article 10 of the Covenant. The Ethiopian government claimed

> in consequence of the mobilization ordered by the Royal Italian Government and of the continual despatch of troops and war material to the Italo-Ethiopian frontier, there now exists between Ethiopia and the Royal Italian Government a dispute likely to lead to a rupture.

[45] Perhaps it is relevant to note that, from 28 February to 7 March, Aloisi was on a tour of Germany. On the other hand, he did not have an important role in policy making in Rome, and it was no doubt Mussolini's own dislike of the concession of 19 January which caused Italian diplomats to resume their intransigent stance.

[46] Mussolini, *Opera omnia*, XXVII, 289–90.

[47] League, *Official Journal, 1935,* 571, 740.

This "imminent danger," with extremely serious international consequences, was aggravated by the failure of direct negotiations and Italy's unwillingness to engage in arbitration. Ethiopia feared for its national survival. "The independence of Ethiopia, a Member of the League of Nations, is in peril." Ethiopia invoked paragraph 1, article 15, of the Covenant:

> If there should arise between Members of the League any dispute likely to lead to a rupture, which is not submitted to arbitration or judicial settlement in accordance with Article 13, the Members of the League agree that they will submit the matter to the Council. Any party of the dispute may effect such submission by giving notice of the existence of the dispute to the Secretary-General, who will make all necessary arrangements for a full investigation and consideration thereof.

To underscore the gravity and urgency of the situation, Ethiopia also made appeal to article 10, the "heart of the Covenant":

> The Members of the League undertake to respect and preserve as against external aggression the territorial integrity and existing political independence of all Members of the League. In case of any such aggression or in case of any threat or danger of such aggression, the Council shall advise upon the means by which this obligation shall be fulfilled.

No appeal to the principles and machinery of the League could have been clearer. The responsibility for peace and justice finally and formally rested with the League of Nations. Arbitration was not ruled out, but the larger problem of national security was now at issue. Ethiopia "solemnly" undertook "to accept any arbitral award immediately and unreservedly, and to act in accordance with the counsels and decisions of the League of Nations." [48]

No action was taken by the League for the moment. Another event, graver and more pressing, compelled the attention of Europe. On 16 March the proclamation in Berlin of a law to build up a German conscript army of twelve corps and thirty-six divisions revealed to a dismayed world Germany's sensational violation of the Treaty of Versailles. France, Italy, and Britain lodged protests with Berlin. France and Italy joined, according to the agreement of 7 January, in rejecting Germany's unilateral repudiation of the treaty. Events then moved

---

[48] Ethiopian appeal of 17 March 1935 in League, *Official Journal, 1935,* 572.

swiftly. On 20 March, three days after Ethiopia had invoked article 15 of the Covenant, Laval appealed to the secretary-general of the League to call, under the terms of paragraph 2, article 11, an extraordinary meeting of the council to consider Germany's treaty violation. Two days later, the president of the council, Rüstü Aras of Turkey, announced that an extraordinary session would be held in the first week of April to deal with the French request. The League selected its topics of concern according to its own priorities; Ethiopia's appeal of 3 January under the terms of the same article had resulted only in strenuous moves of evasion by the leading League members. On 23 March, Laval, Suvich, and Eden met in Paris and agreed that the foreign ministers of France, Italy, and Britain would meet in the Italian resort town of Stresa, on 11 April, for consultations on Germany's action. The conferees noted "with satisfaction the complete unity of purpose of their governments." [49] This was an overstatement, though, and France and Italy viewed with perplexed astonishment, justified suspicion, and concealed anger the ensuing journey that Simon and Eden made to, wonder of wonders, Berlin itself.[50] Nonetheless all, and the Italians not the least, wanted, in Mussolini's words, to "take steps immediately to stop the rot." It was Mussolini who particularly wanted the Stresa conference, for he was genuinely disturbed by German remilitarization. He feared for Italy's exposed position after Italian troops had been drained off to Africa. His revisionist interest in Europe was gone, and now he wanted a stable continent to allow him the freedom to conquer Ethiopia. Nothing could be more upsetting than a dynamic, rearmed Germany. France and Italy were at one over the German problem — the only equivocation came from Britain. On 24 March it was announced in Geneva that the date of the extraordinary session of the League council, called by France, would be governed by the timetable of the Stresa meeting.[51]

Meanwhile, still pending was Ethiopia's request of 17 March for League action. On 22 March Italy sent a note to the secretary-general denouncing the Ethiopian appeal as inaccurate and inappropriate. The Italian note concluded, however, in a conciliatory vein. Italy did not

---

[49] Avon, *Facing the Dictators*, 132. Aloisi optimistically wrote that this "re-established Franco-Anglo-Italian solidarity." *Journal*, 261.

[50] The journey was viewed in Italy as an "act of weakness." Guariglia, *Ricordi*, 219.

[51] Avon, *Facing the Dictators*, 132; Toynbee, *Survey of International Affairs, 1935*, I, 146.

consider the stage of direct negotiations ended, it said, but if this phase closed without settlement Italy would be prepared to "take steps forthwith with a view to the constitution of the commission provided for." The Italians were trying to regain the initiative, to refloat their tactic of delay, and, above all, to route the conflict away from the League. In their note of the 22nd, the Italians contended that if arbitration was entered into as provided by the agreement of 19 January and under procedures laid down in the treaty of 1928, then "Article 15 of the Covenant cannot be applicable in this particular case." [52]

Delays won by diplomacy were sought, as before, only to gain time for military preparation. On 23 March, despite the Italian claim to the League on the 22nd that "it is not true that Italy has mobilized a class," Mussolini issued an order mobilizing the class of 1911, which had been called up the previous month for action in Ethiopia. Although an argument can be raised for the Duce's assertion that he took this step as the "best way to stop Germany," [53] the real reason was that Mussolini needed all the men he could get for Ethiopia, and needed them at once. There was no doubt where the class of 1911 would be sent (and soon it did go to east Africa).[54] Two weeks before, on 8 March, Mussolini had written De Bono:

> It is my profound conviction that, we being obliged to take the initiative of operations at the end of October or the end of September, you ought to have a combined force of 300,000 men (including about 100,000 black troops from the two colonies) . . . You ask for three divisions by the end of October; I intend to send you ten, I repeat, ten: five from the regular army, five of volunteer formations of Blackshirts, who will be carefully selected and trained. These divisions of Blackshirts will be the guarantee that the undertaking will obtain popular support . . . In view of the possible international controversies (League of Nations, etc.) it is wise to speed up our tempo. For the lack of a few thousand men we lost Adowa! I will never commit that error. I am willing to err in excess, but not in deficiency.[55]

[52] League, *Official Journal*, *1935*, 573.

[53] Aloisi, *Journal*, 261; Reale, *La Politique étrangère du fascisme*, 19. This move did not disconcert the Germans. Neurath claimed to be totally puzzled over the reasons behind the Italian mobilization. *Documents on German Foreign Policy*, *1918–1945*, ser. C, IV, 10.

[54] De Bono, *Anno XIIII*, 123.

[55] Mussolini, *Opera omnia*, XXVII, 276-7.

The Ethiopian government, aided by surveillance in Eritrea and a close reading of the Italian press, saw the threat to their country as obvious beyond doubt.[56] On 29 March the government submitted a long note to the secretary-general of the League, once more appealing under article 15. Reviewing the course of the dispute, the Ethiopians pointed out that the problem was no longer one of arbitrating a border clash. As a result of Italian mobilization and the dispatch of troops to east Africa, a new and far more critical phase of the conflict had begun. Arbitration could no longer solve the basic problem between the two countries, and it held inherent dangers for Ethiopia. Shrewdly surmising Italy's intentions, the Ethiopian note read:

> the appointment of arbitrators, and the drafting of the arbitration agreement fixing the questions to be referred to arbitration and the procedure to be followed, must not be the occasion of fresh delays in the pacific settlement of a very simple dispute. These delays must not be utilized for the continuation of military preparations and of despatches of troops and war munitions, as has been the case hitherto. Otherwise, once these preparations had been completed, nothing would be easier than to create incidents and, with the help of a Press campaign, to find pretexts for an aggression. Ethiopia possesses no military force comparable with that of her powerful neighbor. She has no newspapers, no means of propaganda to influence public opinion and to present all the circumstances, whatever they may be, in a light favourable to herself. To defend her rights, her only remedy is appeal to the League of Nations. She cannot therefore renounce this last resort for protecting her independence and the integrity of her territory.[57]

The warning to the League was clear: the technique of arbitration could be used against the cause of peace as well as for it. The Ethiopians, still resolving to follow "any fair arbitration procedure capable of restoring the friendly and confident relations with Italy," proposed that a time limit of thirty days be established in which to complete all preliminaries, such as appointment of the arbitrators and agreement on procedures. If the full arbitration process was not under way in thirty days, the League itself should undertake arbitration,

[56] De Bono had a high opinion of the success of Ethiopian espionage, but the success was due mainly to the fact that Italian actions were so obvious. De Bono, *Anno XIIII*, 92–3. Ethiopia, in its note of 29 March, made the point that the Italian press was "inspired by the Government and publishes nothing which has not been approved."

[57] Ethiopian note of 29 March in League, *Official Journal, 1935*, 573–6.

its conclusions to be binding. During this time, neither Italy nor Ethiopia should pursue any actions that could be construed as military preparation. The Ethiopian government presented these proposals as adjuncts to the invocation of article 15, as a spur to League action.

So far Ethiopia had received no assurance that the League would take up the dispute. To force the issue, Ethiopia on 3 April requested the secretary-general to ask the council to consider the matter at its forthcoming extraordinary session in mid-April. Avenol replied formally, noting that it was up to the members of the council to decide what items would be included on the agenda of an extraordinary session. He would place Ethiopia's request before them when the session opened.[58]

Italy's reaction was soon in coming. Despite the confusion in international affairs at this time, Italy's diplomatic aim in the Ethiopian conflict remained the same: the dispute must be kept away from the League. At the beginning of April a new office was opened in the Palazzo Chigi, headed by Raffaele Guariglia and concerned exclusively with Ethiopian affairs. The Italians realized that the second phase of their long stall was now over. Until 19 January, Italy refused to consider the possibility of arbitration. Ethiopia threatened to take the issue to the council, and so Italy agreed to arbitrate. For two and a half months, Italy succeeded in dragging its feet, thwarting all attempts to establish the arbitral commission it had agreed to. Now the choice was: either arbitrate, or Ethiopia would submit the problem to the council for decision. Despite the unwillingness of the League to antagonize Italy, it seemed certain that the council could no longer avoid formal consideration of the Ethiopian appeal. The Italians therefore entered the next phase of their delaying policy. On 10 April, on the very eve of the Stresa conference, Italy informed the secretary-general that, contrary to the Ethiopian contention, Italy did not consider that "the stage of ordinary diplomatic methods referred to in Article 5 of the Italo-Ethiopian Treaty of 1928 is exhausted," and that Italy was now prepared to begin the direct negotiations toward the establishment of a commission of conciliation. The dispute, the Italians asserted, could be settled along the lines of existing bilateral agreements. Italy was now ready to proceed to the nomination of arbitrators.[59]

[58] League, *Official Journal, 1935*, 577.
[59] Italian note of 10 April in League, *Official Journal, 1935*, 577-8.

The success of these Italian maneuvers depended on the willingness of France and Britain to allow the evasion to work. More important for Italy, as in the spring military preparations approached a point at which there could be no turning back, was the need for reassurance that France and Britain would not balk at the invasion of Ethiopia. The leaders of the three countries were preparing to meet in private at Stresa between 11 and 14 April. The Ethiopian question was not on the agenda of the Stresa conference, which was called to discuss the means of presenting a united front toward Germany. Still it was an auspicious time for Italian soundings or for some discussion of Ethiopia. The extraordinary meeting of the League council was scheduled to open immediately after the conference, and Ethiopia's request of 3 April was pending. Italian intentions toward Ethiopia were clear enough. Britain and France had had time to consider their reactions and, it might be supposed, time to formulate their policies. If there were objections to Italy's plans, one might reasonably assume that they would be aired at Stresa.

The Italians were confident of French support.[60] A rearmed Germany drew the two countries closer together. On 22 March the French Chamber of Deputies ratified Laval's agreements of 7 January by the overwhelming vote of 555–9. On 26 March the French Senate ratified them unanimously. Pierre-Etienne Flandin, the prime minister and head of the French delegation, came to Stresa with the expressed purpose of regulating any outstanding differences and creating an "intimate accord" with Italy. Laval came as foreign minister. France had not changed its view of Italy as its main support on the continent and was still unwilling to jeopardize the new friendship. On the other hand, as the Italians knew, France dared not move in opposition to Britain. Despite all Italian efforts at Stresa to convince the French that Britain was not indispensable to contain Germany, that a French-Italian coalition was sufficient, the French were not persuaded.[61] For Italy, then, Britain remained the key to success, and on the eve of the Stresa conference British intentions were the great unknown.

[60] Guariglia, *Ricordi*, 225–6.
[61] Quaroni, "Le Diplomate italien," 123.

Chapter 6

April: The Stresa Conference and After

The British delegation to Stresa was headed by Ramsay MacDonald, the erstwhile Labour prime minister of the Tory "National" government, and the foreign secretary, Sir John Simon, fresh from the conference in Berlin. These were no men to face Mussolini. MacDonald was infirm: "his mind was no longer equal to public tests." He relied on Robert Vansittart for all his needs and was prevented by the Foreign Office's permanent undersecretary from dealing with the inquiring press. Simon, who had not wanted to go to Stresa, was Eden's replacement. Simon's problem, as he told Eden, was that "he never knew what people were thinking." [1] Eden was home in bed, recovering from a heart attack brought on by a stormy air flight after the meetings in Berlin and Warsaw.[2] Eden saw Stresa as an "exceptional opportunity for a direct approach to Mussolini" on the Ethiopian affair, and before the British delegation left London he received the agreement of MacDonald and Simon that "Mussolini must be confronted on this subject." [3] Within the Foreign Office the British ambassador in Rome, Eric Drummond, had urged Vansittart to warn Mussolini specifically of British anger in the case of an attack on Ethiopia.[4]

Mussolini came prepared to discuss the subject of Ethiopia if, as he expected, the British should bring it up. He was, after all, curious to find out what Britain's intentions were, for the British government

[1] Avon, *Facing the Dictators,* 175.
[2] "So Stresa was deprived of the one man who could have given its deliberations perspective," says an admiring biographer. A. Campbell-Johnson, *Eden: The Making of a Statesman* (New York, 1955), 107. For a similar sentiment, see Thompson, *Front-Line Diplomat,* 96.
[3] Avon, *Facing the Dictators,* 179.
[4] Vansittart, *The Mist Procession,* 520.

had never replied to the Italian overture of 29 January. On the other hand, Mussolini did not want to undertake a second initiative to open the discussion. He still believed in following a line of equivocation toward Britain: as long as British indecision over Germany prevented the government from formulating a definite position on the Italian-Ethiopian controversy, Mussolini had leeway for action. Rather than force a conversation that might compel the British to decide on an unfavorable response, Mussolini preferred an uncertainty that he did not fear. He thought that, before the British could make up their minds, he might be able to present them with an accomplished fact. In the meantime, if the British wanted to maintain a silence on the subject, this was good enough for Mussolini, for he read silence as consent.

One Italian who did want a full-scale discussion of the issue was Dino Grandi, Italy's ambassador in London. Grandi fought hard for British-Italian friendship. He was genuinely disturbed by the danger of a widening breach between the two countries, and he sought to bring about frank talks at Stresa in order to arrive at some mutually acceptable solution before the crisis came. Grandi led Mussolini to believe that the British would come ready to discuss the Ethiopian question. He persuaded Rome to send to the conference Giovanni B. Guarnaschelli, head of the African desk at the Palazzo Chigi. In London Grandi was at first rebuffed by the British and told that no English expert would be sent. At the very last moment Grandi persuaded the Foreign Office to send out Geoffrey Thompson, an expert on Egypt now keeping his eye on Ethiopia. Thompson, however, was told to go under the condition that his conversations be limited to examining the question of pasturage in the Ogaden. He was expressly prohibited from discussing the major issues of the Italian-Ethiopian controversy.[5]

The only chance for initiating substantive talks, once the conference opened, lay with the heads of the British delegation. The French were not going to rock the boat, and Mussolini waited expectantly for some British opening. None came.

On the afternoon of 12 April, Thompson and Guarnaschelli, shepherded by Counselor Leonardo Vitetti, met for three hours of informal but frank talk. Thompson, as instructed, made no effort to clear the

---

[5] Guariglia, *Ricordi*, 226–7; Thompson, *Front-Line Diplomat*, 96.

way for compromise bargaining.[6] The Italians on their side made it plain that they "could not exclude the possibility of solving the Abyssinian question by force." Thompson found this fact "of the highest importance," for in diplomatic language and in the circumstance, such a statement was tantamount to an admission that war was being considered; this was the first time the Italian officials had made such an admission. The meeting adjourned at six. Thompson reported his significant news to Vansittart and prepared a memorandum on the conversation. Thompson recalls:

> Late that night after dinner I received a message from Sir John Simon inviting me to breakfast with him at eight the next morning. This pleased me greatly, for it suggested that the Secretary of State wished to be fully briefed on what had occurred before setting out with the Prime Minister [MacDonald] for the next day's sessions of the main conference in its medieval castle setting on Lake Maggiore. On the stroke of eight the following morning I was ushered into his suite and we sat down to a tête-à-tête breakfast. Exactly five minutes later, as I was listening to some opening comment on my memorandum, Horace Seymour, Sir John's chief private secretary at that time, entered the room and made some remark to my host which I did not catch. A conversation then ensued between the two which, whatever it may have been about, was certainly far removed from Ethiopia. At 8:30 Sir John Simon intimated that he had to get ready to leave for the island and I made my exit, having enjoyed a good but silent breakfast. It was indeed a sad anti-climax. The Stresa Conference ended gloomily the next day. From the moment that I had left the Secretary of State's suite after my unrewarding breakfast I had no work of any kind.[7]

Frustration was felt by the Italian staff as well. "We were all trying to get the talks going," wrote Pietro Quaroni, a member of the Italian delegation. Thompson and Guarnaschelli sat waiting, each in his armchair, and talked of irrelevant matters. They expected an order from above to begin serious conversations dealing with the dispute, but none was issued. Three members of the Italian delegation took the two experts out to lunch on the Isola dei Pescatori, an event much noted by the journalists. Quaroni recalls: "I don't know what good thing we hoped for, perhaps that by one trick or another to get some

---

[6] Simon on 1 May 1935 described the conversation to the House of Commons as "informal . . . on matters connected with watering and grazing rights of nomadic British Somali tribes in certain zones outside the boundary of British Somaliland." *Parliamentary Debates*, 301 H.C. Deb. 5s., col. 348.

[7] Thompson, *Front-Line Diplomat*, 97–8.

word which would permit us to say to our superiors that it was necessary to talk because there was something new." [8] Nothing came of the luncheon, and no delegation head appeared willing to make an opening move.

On the 14th the conference wound up with, as Mussolini had predicted, a communiqué which represented "a least common denominator between three powers and able to be — short of a surprise — only a general or consultative nature, 'consultation' being the last resource of indecision in the face of reality." [9] Still, even this appeared to be a positive, if limited, accomplishment. The three powers had exchanged views on the European scene. The "Stresa front" was established to present a "common line of conduct" in the coming League meeting on German rearmament. Britain and Italy adopted a joint declaration reaffirming their intention to fulfill their obligations under the Treaty of Locarno. Agreements hitherto taken bilaterally with regard to Austria were renewed in the presence of all three nations, and consultation on Austrian independence was pledged. But there was no discussion of any kind among the heads of government or their foreign ministers on the Ethiopian problem or its critical consequences for the future of European diplomacy and the Stresa front. The Ethiopian question was not mentioned in the communiqués. The final declaration of the conference read:

> The three Powers, the object of whose policy is the collective maintenance of peace within the framework of the League of Nations, find themselves in complete agreement in opposing, by all practicable means, any unilateral repudiation of treaties which may endanger the peace of Europe, and will act in close and cordial collaboration for this purpose.[10]

And yet the Ethiopian question was not entirely absent from the upper reaches of the Stresa conference. Indeed, in the wording of the final declaration lies our key to understanding the significance of Stresa.

Mussolini waited in vain, throughout the conference, for the British

---

[8] Quaroni, "Le Diplomate italien," 124–5.

[9] From an article by Mussolini that appeared in *Il Popolo d'Italia* on the morning the conference opened, 11 April 1935, cautioning Italians against "facile and inconclusive optimism." Mussolini, *Opera omnia*, XXVII, 53–4. There were no "surprises" at Stresa.

[10] Wheeler-Bennett and Heald, eds., *Documents on International Affairs, 1935,* I, 82.

leaders to make some mention of Ethiopia. Their silence, it would appear, had to be a matter of official British policy; there could be no mistaking the fact that Italy's military preparations were meant for the invasion of Ethiopia. British silence must have a reason, and the reason could not be ignorance of Italian designs. Mussolini decided to put this to a final test in the last moments of the conference. When the final declaration was drawn up for signing it read: "The three Powers, the object of whose policy is the collective maintenance of peace within the framework of the League of Nations, find themselves in complete agreement in opposing, by all practicable means, any unilateral repudiation of treaties which may endanger the peace . . ." As Mussolini read the statement, at this point he paused and asked: was it not necessary to add the words "of Europe" to the text? Twice he repeated the words "of Europe," and he looked around the table at which he as the host presided. Africa had not been mentioned at the conference, although it was in everyone's thoughts. Here was a clear invitation, whose import could not be misunderstood, to bring up the question of Italy's intentions in Ethiopia. Mussolini waited for some protest. MacDonald and Vansittart looked at Simon. Simon sat absolutely still. Flandin and Laval watched them as carefully as Mussolini did. The French would not make a move unless the British led. The British leaders did not say a word. The French and Italians drew an identical and instantaneous conclusion: the silence was a tacit consent given by the British government to Italian ambitions in Ethiopia. The words "of Europe" were inserted by Mussolini's own pen, and the Duce thought he had achieved an official assurance that Great Britain would not oppose his conquest of Ethiopia.[11]

What is the explanation, and where the responsibility, for the British

[11] Bottai, *Vent'anni*, 125; Flandin, *Politique française*, 178; Guariglia, *Ricordi*, 781–2; Mussolini, *Opera omnia*, XXVII, 140; Quaroni, "Le Diplomate italien," 125; G. Ward-Price, *Extra-Special Correspondent* (London, 1957), 242; I. Colvin, *Vansittart in Office* (London, 1965), 60–1. Alberto Pirelli, sent to Britain by Mussolini a few weeks later to "fathom Britain's future," told Arthur Salter: "We thought we had your tacit acquiescence. We went to the Conference of Stresa . . . expecting to learn England's real attitude. We had assured ourselves already of Laval's acquiescence. We knew that you knew that our military stores were already going through the Suez Canal. We knew that you wanted us to be on your side in an issue with Hitler, and we thought it likely that you were prepared to acquiesce in our Abyssinian venture as the price. When your Ministers said nothing, we thought we could rely at least on being safe from active intervention." A. Salter, *Personality in Politics* (London, 1947), 236–7. Fulvio Suvich said that the war in Ethiopia was made under a gentleman's agreement with England. Suvich et al., *Il Processo Roatta*, 19.

silence at Stresa? Hugh Dalton condemned it as "one of the most criminal blunders in the whole course of British diplomacy in these disastrous years . . . because evidently Signor Mussolini was expecting that this subject would be raised." [12] Responsibility rests above all with John Simon and his conception and execution of British foreign policy. Simon, as we have seen, was not willing or prepared to antagonize Mussolini. At no time was this reluctance more acute than at Stresa. What was being decided there was a common front to put forward at Geneva a few days later. The matters under discussion were purely European, and Simon intended to keep it so. He tended to see each issue in international affairs in isolation from its precedents and its consequences.[13] What Simon wanted at the moment was to attach Italy to the British-French side in the face of the German threat.

One way to do that, in the European context, was to give Mussolini the security he sought on the Austrian frontier, the assurance that Britain would cooperate in containing Germany to the south and west and in guaranteeing the independence of the Austrian republic. Vansittart, looking for a way to moderate Mussolini's ambitions in Ethiopia, saw the possibilities in a scheme that used an Austrian guarantee to "land Mussolini first and lecture him later. Get an agreement, I suggested, make it look valuable if we can — and there is the rub — then tell him all will go for nothing if he embroils himself for nothing." [14] The "rub" was in making an Austrian guarantee effective. It necessitated a firm British commitment in Europe, and this the British, in their "horror of commitments," were unwilling to give.[15] Furthermore, as Simon had told Hitler, the British government was essentially uninterested in Austria. In accordance with its hope of coming to a settlement with Germany, the government wanted to avoid any commitment directed against Berlin.[16] These factors militated against

[12] Dalton speaking to the House of Commons on 6 May 1936. *Parliamentary Debates*, 311 H.C. Deb. 5s., col. 1721.

[13] Walters, *A History of the League*, II, 612.

[14] Vansittart, *The Mist Procession*, 520.

[15] Vansittart, *Lessons of My Life*, 46. Simon said there was a general feeling in Britain against accepting "undefined obligations in undefined circumstances." A. C. Temperley, *The Whispering Gallery of Europe* (London, 1938), 329. But the British were already bound by a variety of such commitments under the League and under the Locarno Treaty. In the present case "circumstances" were easily definable. What was lacking was a desire by the British government to become involved in central Europe where it did not appear to the government that there was a direct threat to vital British interests.

[16] Gehl, *Austria, Germany, and the Anschluss*, 114. For Vansittart's warnings on the shortsightedness of such a policy, see *ibid.*, 63.

a British guarantee of Austria's independence. Only a month before, on 1 March, just prior to Simon's and Eden's visit to Hitler, Mac-Donald issued a statement on Britain's European policy in which he noted that "proposals for increasing the security in Eastern Europe and the Danube basin, with special reference to the maintenance of the independence and integrity of Austria . . . involve no military commitments, direct or indirect, by this country." [17] As far as Europe was concerned, then, all the British would offer Mussolini was a series of general platitudes which, as Mussolini predicted, settled nothing and did not aid Italy. The British thought to relieve themselves of the necessity of binding themselves to future action by relaying further responsibility to the League. This merely confirmed Mussolini's belief that the British, lacking the continental concern over a rearmed Germany, were not going to back Italy in Europe. The Stresa front, in its European framework, was as a result only a temporary and tenuous grouping created for the imminent League meeting. The Stresa agreements accomplished little, and Britain's attempt to buy Italy cheap was not enough to "land" Mussolini.

To accomplish this, another bait was needed. If Britain would not commit itself over Austria or against Germany, the bait would have to be found in Mussolini's interest in Ethiopia. But this fact immediately revealed new and serious problems, for to consider the question of Ethiopia meant no less than weighing the nature and degree of Britain's interest in Italy against the nature and degree of Britain's interest in the League of Nations. In this broadened context, three main lines of action were open to the British.

One was to adopt a strong stand in favor of the League's concept of collective security, to warn Mussolini clearly and firmly against any violation of the Covenant. This would establish Britain as the champion of the League, but it also meant heavy burdens. For example, a corollary of this position was that the British government would have to accept, at the worst, the possibility of war against Italy. But such an awful conclusion was not inevitable, and in the circumstances the British navy's control of the Suez Canal would probably make a definite British warning decisive in bringing an end to the Italian military build-up in Africa. Although the time was not as opportune

[17] Cited in J. Ganterbein, ed., *Documentary Background of World War II, 1931 to 1941* (New York, 1948), 294.

as it was in January, it was not too late for such a warning to have effect. Mussolini had not yet openly proclaimed his purpose as military conquest, no matter how clear the signs were. He could not begin his campaign until the rains had ended in the Ethiopian highlands. He had not yet irrevocably committed the prestige of his regime or the wealth and men of his country. Mussolini was in fact anticipating such a warning, which would open the way to a negotiated agreement.

Such a move would take conviction, courage, and skill, and would have to be followed by careful appeasement if Mussolini were to be kept on Britain's side. The British policy makers were not prepared for this alternative at Stresa. Hoare, trying to justify his predecessor's action, told the House of Commons on 22 October 1935 that at Stresa "the hope of an amicable settlement between Italy and Abyssinia was still strongly entertained, while the immediate and all-important objective was to secure unity between France, Italy, and the United Kingdom in Europe. Indeed, it was hoped that this object, not lightly achieved, would be regarded as a precious inducement to do nothing which might imperil it." [18] All the more cautious for not having supported Mussolini's interests in Europe, the British were reluctant "to force an issue that might break the Allied front." [19] They shunned the matter of Ethiopia at Stresa because they did not have a plan for dealing with it. Above all they were not prepared to threaten Mussolini with resistance.[20] The British knew that if Mussolini raised the issue of Ethiopia at Stresa they would have to discuss it, even though they had not prepared a policy. Mussolini's indirection, his insertion of the phrase "of Europe," was sufficiently inexplicit to allow the

[18] *Parliamentary Debates*, 305 H.C. Deb. 5s., col. 26. Eden gave two other official explanations. One was that "in the face of the assurances we had received . . . and in light of the fact that the conference had been called to deal solely with the complexities of the European situation," there was no reason to discuss Ethiopia. The other was that at the time "the Abyssinian dispute was then almost entirely confined to this minor frontier incident [Walwal] . . . and the wider aspects of the dispute had not then begun to loom so seriously on the horizon." Eden in the House of Commons on 23 October 1935, *ibid.*, col. 213.

[19] Templewood, *Nine Troubled Years*, 156.

[20] Some Englishmen evidently believed that they could exert sufficient pressure on Mussolini to deter him at a later time, not realizing that time was swiftly closing in on events, that Italy was more determined and stronger than they thought, and that the supposed Ethiopian potential for effective resistance was a myth. "We thought we could push them about, as they thought they could push the Abyssinians. 'We shall have to use the Boy Scouts on the dagos' became a frequent phrase." Vansittart, *The Mist Procession*, 515.

British an escape, and they let the matter pass, delighted to have avoided the necessity for choice or discussion.[21]

A second line of action open to the British at Stresa was to begin negotiations for a compromise settlement, to satisfy Italian ambitions with a substantial bribe. Various alternatives could have been offered which, coupled with a strong stand against military aggression, might have succeeded in keeping the matter out of the League, in maintaining at least the greater part of Ethiopia free, and in not alienating Italy. Despite British willingness to allow Mussolini some measure of colonial gain, the statecraft necessary for this to be achieved was not even considered, let alone attempted, at Stresa. Mussolini came expecting to enter into negotiations. He claimed later that he was "especially disposed" to discussion at this time, and he was annoyed when no British overture was forthcoming.[22] Once again the British let slip an opportunity to prevent the coming war. They were to see the advantages of negotiation only when its chance for success was past.

Both of these options open to the British, a firm warning or a compromise, offered, in April 1935, good prospects of success. Neither was taken. A third line was played out, in one of the most inept diplomatic moves of the period. The bait Simon dangled in front of Mussolini was silence — silence over Ethiopia. The British themselves adopted the diplomacy of equivocation. It is impossible to discover what significant benefit Simon's evasiveness could bring to Britain. In no sense could it be an effective tactic to gain Italian friendship, and it is difficult to imagine an ultimately more ineffective device for winning the favor of or gaining control over Mussolini.

If there was no real danger to Ethiopia and to the Covenant from Mussolini's military preparations, if Mussolini was bluffing, if the

[21] So Vansittart told Grandi in late April. Guariglia, *Ricordi*, 232. Vansittart told Randolph Churchill that "a few minutes" after the term "of Europe" was inserted he, Vansittart, pointed out to MacDonald that this phrase did not cover African affairs. MacDonald replied: "Don't be tiresome, Van, we don't want any trouble. What we want is an agreement that we can put before the House of Commons." R. Churchill, *The Rise and Fall of Sir Anthony Eden* (London, 1959), 85.

[22] *Morning Post* interview of 17 September 1935. Mussolini, *Opera omnia*, XXVII, 140. Thompson states that Mussolini almost dismissed Grandi for misleading him into believing that the British would have something to say at Stresa. Thompson, *Front-Line Diplomat*, 99.

League could handle the issue, if Ethiopia could protect itself, then the British need not have said anything. Or if the British government was prepared to allow Mussolini his conquest without future protest, and the silence was *meant* to be interpreted as tacit consent, then it is understandable. But none of these conditions existed. On the basis of available information and with a minimum of foresight, it was clear that there was a danger to Ethiopia; Italy was contemplating aggression; this would be a direct and flagrant violation of the Covenant, and Britain was the leader of the League. The British government, responsive to the opinion of its electorate, could not overtly condone Italian aggression without disgrace. The government might be tolerant of the ends of Mussolini's ambitions, but it could not for long approve his means. This distinction was not made clear to the Italians at Stresa.

Even if Mussolini interpreted Britain's silence correctly as consent, for that fleeting moment, neither he nor British officials had assurance that such a position could be maintained as a policy of the government. A coalition based on unsubstantial ambiguity could not persist, and the British had already rejected the chance to tie Mussolini to a Western alliance by providing him with security in Europe. The future clearly foretold a choice for the British government between support of the League and Mussolini's friendship. Until this choice was made, the British silence could not be assayed as to its true worth, and hence as a bribe it was of little value. Even in the short run Britain's timidity gave the government no opportunity to modify Mussolini's ambitions. The government's only hope was somehow to avoid a clash between two potentially conflicting interests. What leverage could there be in applying pressure on Mussolini to halt his plans for invasion when the very fulcrum of Britain's position was a silence interpreted as acquiescence? Simon's empty and neglectful diplomacy was the very negation of Vansittart's concept of "land Mussolini first and lecture him later."

Although most of the responsibility for Britain's stand rested with Simon, some of it belonged to Vansittart and the staff of the Foreign Office. Diplomacy, Anthony Eden has written, "has to determine which difficulties will resolve themselves and which will spread their rot when shoved under the rug." [23] The Foreign Office did not make

[23] Avon, *Facing the Dictators*, 181.

this distinction at Stresa. They failed to keep the foreign secretary fully informed or to force upon him the implications of events, and they failed entirely to explore alternative lines of conduct. For example, the French were not consulted about the possibility of presenting a warning to Mussolini. It was simply assumed that they would not join one, and this in turn was accepted as reason enough not to make an effort to sound them out.[24] Vansittart failed to convey Drummond's warnings to Simon or to transmit the ambassador's suggestion that Mussolini should be warned of the consequences of any aggressive action.[25] Thus, though the major blame for Britain's carelessness must remain with the foreign secretary, to a degree failures in the intelligence system and inadequacies in the dispersal of advice and information played their role in the Italian-Ethiopian conflict.[26] They were in part responsible for the late awakening to the serious implications of the conflict, and for the length of time many Englishmen harbored the comfortable notion that Mussolini's armies could not easily conquer the Ethiopian empire.

As MacDonald left the Stresa conference, Alexander Werth of the *Manchester Guardian* asked him if the matter of Ethiopia had been discussed. "My friend," MacDonald replied, "your question is irrelevant." [27]

As Mussolini bade farewell to the members of the British delegation he turned fiercely to Dino Grandi. "You are a futile ambassador," he said. "You told me that on Austria the English answer would be

---

[24] Vansittart, *Lessons of My Life*, 46.

[25] Vansittart let Drummond shoulder the burden. "I advised Eric to press his views on our two Ministers and let them choose. No trace of such action was visible . . . Either the advice was not pressed, or it was ignored, or simply forgotten." Vansittart, *The Mist Procession*, 520–1.

[26] For a scathing but perhaps exaggerated attack on the Foreign Office's organization, see W. Selby, *Diplomatic Twilight, 1930–1940* (London, 1953), 50, 52–4, 136–40, 183–9. Walford Selby was the British minister in Vienna during these years. For a corresponding complaint on the French side, against the failure of the Quai d'Orsay to pay attention to its ambassadors in the field, see François-Poncet, *Fateful Years*, xii. See also G. Young, *Stanley Baldwin* (London, 1952), 182–3, and V. Lawford, *Bound for Diplomacy* (London, 1963), 271–3.

[27] R. Dell, *The Geneva Racket, 1920–1939* (London, n.d. [1940]), 111. A few weeks after this, Arthur Salter went to MacDonald's home and asked him directly whether he had said anything about Ethiopia at Stresa. MacDonald replied that Foreign Office experts had made contact with their Italian opposite numbers, but that he himself was "completely preoccupied with the main problem, that of Germany. Simon . . . was also at the Conference. I do not know if he raised the question of Abyssinia." Salter, *Personality in Politics*, 237.

'yes,' and on Africa 'no.' As it happens their answer on Austria was 'no,' and on Africa 'yes.' " [28]

The Stresa conference ended on 14 April, and the French and British ministers and the Italian delegate, Aloisi, entrained for Geneva and the League council meeting scheduled for the next day. Laval's progress through northern Italy was in the nature of a triumphal procession. He was welcomed at each stop by enthusiastic Fascist officials. Simon, traveling on the same train, was pointedly ignored by the Italians on these occasions.[29] Mussolini's exasperation with the British had begun.

The first matter of business presented to the extraordinary session of the council when it met in private session on the afternoon of the 15th was Ethiopia's message of 3 April, referring to its earlier notes of 17 and 29 March, that the seriousness of the Italian-Ethiopian conflict had reached a point where it warranted consideration by the council. To this end Ethiopia requested the council formally to consider the affair under the terms of article 15 and to bring up the subject for discussion. These requests, if accepted, would mean that the League would formally commit itself to the maintenance of peace, the protection of Ethiopia as a member state, and a full investigation of the dispute, complete with recommendations for its solution. This the Italians were determined to prevent, and in their obstructionism they had the support of Britain, France, and the secretary-general.

F. P. Walters, a former deputy secretary-general, has given us an account of the mood of Geneva.

Everybody knew that the Ethiopian appeal was justified and that the Italian answer[30] was a falsehood. Italy's colonies were not threat-

---

[28] I. Kirkpatrick, *Mussolini, a Study in Power* (New York, 1964), 303. A different version, perhaps less trustworthy since Kirkpatrick got his story directly from Grandi, goes that, when the conference was over, Mussolini turned to Grandi and said: "You see, you were all wrong; the English are not going to make any difficulties over Abyssinia." Grandi could only reply: "Don't be too sure; they are queer people, and might still be tiresome at Geneva." Mussolini responded, referring to the notion that the Ethiopians emasculated their captives: "Anyhow these feeble creatures can't give us any serious trouble — I expect the Abyssinians caught them young." L. S. Amery, *My Political Life* (London, 1955), III, 166. (Permission to quote granted by Hutchinson Publishing Group Ltd. and David Higham Associates Ltd.)

[29] Thompson, *Front-Line Diplomat*, 99.

[30] This was the answer of 22 March saying that article 15 was inapplicable because bilateral arbitration was to be undertaken.

ened; her warlike measures were intended for attack, not for defense; her promise to submit the Wal-Wal incident to arbitration was a diplomatic screen to cover her real purpose. The issue before the League was not who was responsible for the fight at Wal-Wal, but whether there was to be war or peace between two Members of the League. Italy's attempt to remove the question from the Council's consideration could not have stood for a moment against a serious challenge from any of her fellow Members. But such a challenge would mean incurring the anger and hostility of the Italian dictator; and Britain, France, and even Russia, had special reason to wish for his friendship and support . . . No one felt inclined to take the risk of pushing Mussolini once more into that attitude of sympathy with Germany which he had long displayed but, as it seemed, had lately abandoned.[31]

The method adopted to circumvent Ethiopian persistence was "evasion in technique." This tactic, defined by Emile Giraud as "formalism . . . a system which substitutes rite for action, which is satisfied with appearance and neglects reality," [32] was henceforth the guiding diplomatic formula of Italy and the Western democracies in handling the Italian-Ethiopian conflict at the League. The application of this formula was to make it appear that article 15 could not be invoked at this time and to use the argument of invalidity to thwart the Ethiopian request to put the dispute onto the agenda of the current session of the council.

Hedging and evasion had begun already. Immediately after the first Ethiopian requests, the League secretariat had solicited an opinion from its judicial section as to their relevance. The opinion was returned on 8 April, a full week before the council session opened. The judicial section asserted that the Ethiopian notes of 17 and 19 March, although demanding "full investigation and consideration" of the dispute under article 15, did so only because arbitration had been unsuccessful up to then, and that League action was requested only "pending the arbitration contemplated by the Treaty of 1928 and the Geneva Agreement of January 19th, 1935." This was technically true, even though the note of 17 March had also informed the League of the "immediate danger" of a "rupture" between the two countries, called the League's attention to Italian military preparations, and appealed to article 10 as well as to article 15. The Ethiopian diplomats

[31] Walters, *History of the League*, II, 632.
[32] Giraud, *La Nullité de la politique internationale*, 143.

had made an awkward presentation of their case. They had, as the judicial section quickly noted, allowed the issue to be focused formally on the minor problem of the Walwal incident and not on the more serious and now more immediate problem of an Italian military threat to their national independence. This provided an excuse for those who chose to ignore the real issue, which was whether a war of colonial conquest would be allowed. Time was running out for Ethiopia, and arbitration, even successful arbitration, was no longer an effective means of containing Italian ambitions. Worst of all, concentration on the resolution of this minor issue permitted the League itself to take the line of least resistance, of narrow legality, and, by following the letter but not the spirit of the Covenant, to disassociate itself from the dispute.

The opinion of the judicial section, submitted to the secretary-general on 8 April, stated that if arbitration was undertaken, and Italy had declared itself ready to submit the Walwal incident to arbitration on 19 January, then the secretary-general ought to suspend all action for the moment. Bilateral arbitration, it was judged, excluded simultaneous examination by the council and, if arbitration were proceeding, article 15 would be inapplicable to the dispute — that is, inapplicable to the settlement of the Walwal incident. On the other hand, so long as arbitration had not commenced, or was not proceeding in a regular manner, Ethiopia did have a right to invoke article 15: "The mere existence of an obligation to arbitrate and the alleged willingness of both parties to the dispute to execute this obligation is not . . . a bar to the application of Article 15 but merely a circumstance which must be taken into account by the Council." [33] The report concluded with the recommendation that if the council chose to consider the dispute, "since under Article 15 the Council's first duty is to conciliate," what the council might most advantageously do would be to encourage the arbitration proceedings.

Thus on 8 April the law still allowed Ethiopia the opportunity to invoke article 15 and, second, to bring its complaint, in all its broader aspects, to the forthcoming council meeting, if the council itself agreed to accept the matter on its agenda. But the chance to invoke article 15 was blocked by two events. One was the last-minute agreement of Italy to proceed with the Walwal arbitration. This agreement was made known by Italian notes to the League on 10 and 14 April, one on the

[33] Cohen, *La Société des Nations*, 69.

eve of the Stresa conference and the other on the eve of the council meeting.[34] These moves gave the Italians the argument that, since bilateral negotiations leading to arbitration were about to begin, article 15 was inapplicable. The argument was invalid, but it was enough to afford the British and French an excuse to undertake the second of the blocking tactics: direct pressure on the Ethiopian delegate at Geneva, applied by Simon and Avenol, to prevent him from carrying through his plan to invoke the article.[35]

Cowed by this pressure, Ethiopia withdrew its attempt at invocation but continued its effort, initiated on 3 April, to insert the dispute on the agenda for 15 April. The question now was whether the council would agree to accept the matter for discussion; the answer was not long in coming. At the private meeting before the session opened, Aloisi argued that, since arbitration was about to begin, article 15 had no force in the dispute and the council need not concern itself formally with the matter. Tecle Hawariate meekly limited himself to noting that Italian military preparations were contrary to the treaty of 1928 and that Ethiopia had already chosen its arbitrators. He hoped arbitration would begin as soon as possible with the exchange of the names of the two countries' nominees. There was no movement of support on his behalf. The council president, Rüstü Aras, unaccountably spoke of "the perfectly clear declarations as to their pacific intentions" made, he mistakenly claimed, by the two countries and of their desire "to settle the question in conformity with the stipulations of the Treaty by which they were bound." He noted that the council's ordinary session was scheduled for 10 May, a month away, and that the matter was already scheduled for discussion then in virtue of the resolution of 19 January. Therefore, he proposed that "there was no reason to place this item on the agenda of the present extraordinary session." The council adopted the president's proposal.[36] Once again the Italians had won a victory of delay at Geneva. They had prevented discussion within the framework of the League; they had forestalled an invocation of the terms of the Covenant; they had prevented the League from becoming a party to the Italian-Ethiopian conflict.

[34] League, *Official Journal*, 1935, 577, 749.

[35] " 'They threw it in a wastebasket,' said Tecle Hawariate in perplexed terror," after he had presented his country's plan to Simon and Avenol. Whitaker, *And Fear Came*, 247–8.

[36] The private meeting of the council on 15 April is recorded in League, *Official Journal*, 1935, 546–60.

And yet the Italian victory was not unalloyed. In the middle of this discussion there occurred an event which reopened the nagging and all-important question that had seemed at least temporarily settled only the day before: what in fact was Britain's attitude toward Italian designs on Ethiopia?

Britain's silence at Stresa seemed to confirm Mussolini's own assumptions, that the indecisive and pusillanimous British would not offer serious resistance to the conquest of Ethiopia. Britain would be, at worst, neutral in the coming conflict. Other Italians were less convinced and were as much puzzled as assured by the Stresa silence. The Italian delegation that came to the council meeting on the 15th, "greatly interested and nervous" about what the council would do, was most of all preoccupied with the British attitude, about "what had happened, or rather what had not happened" at Stresa.[37] Could they count on the British, count even on British indifference, now that the Ethiopian question was becoming an acute public concern?

The discussions were going along smoothly during the meeting of 15 April. Italy's plan of evasion seemed on its way to success in precluding any action by the council. If Italy could delay the actual arbitration proceedings until the very last moment, without ever renouncing the intention to conclude bilateral negotiations, then, when the council next met in May, the matter of arbitration could still be presented as a possible means of settling the dispute; further, the process would be so far from completion that any interference by the League could be claimed as prejudicial to its success. This would enable Italy, with British and French support, to argue that the matter was being settled by regular diplomatic means, as yet unconcluded of course, and the argument of inapplicability and noncompetence, so successful in January and April, could again be used to prevent the League from considering the broader reaches of the dispute. Italian diplomacy at Geneva was based on focusing the issue only on the Walwal incident and dragging out arbitration until the invasion in October.

During the meeting on the 15th, even the Ethiopian delegate offered no serious objections. Then, without warning, Simon made two "improvised and unexpected" interruptions, his only comments at the discussion. Simon proposed that the Italians and the Ethiopians offer assurance then and there to the council that "the conciliators on both

[37] Berio, "L' 'Affare' etiopico," 188.

sides would be appointed before the May session and that the terms of reference would be fixed." Twice he repeated his proposal, to the end that the "Council would then be in a position to know that, when it met in May, something practical could be undertaken." The Ethiopian delegate "readily accepted the proposal," with the condition that military preparations cease during this time. Baron Aloisi turned the proposal aside with the comment that Italy "would do its utmost to see that the procedure of conciliation and arbitration was opened as readily as possible." Laval stepped into the breach with a strong support of Italy and the matter was passed over, although Simon "returned to the charge" in conversation with Avenol after the meeting adjourned.[38]

Now Italy's confidence in Britain was shaken. Simon's proposal cut into the very foundation of Italian policies. If the British pushed further, their proposal would force arbitration proceedings to begin almost at once and bring the issue quickly before the League. The British had given public notice of their concern about unnecessary delay and evidence of their interest in treating the issue within the League. Simon's completely unexpected proposal shocked the Italian government. Aloisi considered the British intervention "underhanded." Mussolini later described it as evidence of what he called the British "inclination to block off every just demand of Italy's for satisfaction." [39] Alberto Berio, an Italian member of the League secretariat whose unofficial job was to maintain a liaison between the secretariat and the Italian government, gave the best statement of its significance. Berio wrote: "the improvised and unexpected intervention by the British minister produced a sense of dismay in the ranks of the Italian delegation. This intervention so soon after Stresa constituted an extremely clear warning. It shattered all illusions that the Ethiopian enterprise would be able to be undertaken with even the tacit accord of England." [40]

The Italians took little comfort from the fact that the Stresa front acted to present and pass the joint resolution condemning German

[38] League, *Official Journal, 1935,* 549; Berio, "L' 'Affare' etiopico," 188; Aloisi, *Journal,* 266.

[39] Aloisi, *Journal,* 266; Mussolini, *Opera omnia,* XXVII, 140.

[40] At Simon's proposal of 15 April, Berio continues, "opened the hostility between Italy and England, a hostility which . . . was not to end until 8 September 1943." Berio, "L' 'Affare' etiopico," 188. Anti-British sentiment in Italy did not become really serious until May and June, though its beginnings can be traced to April.

rearmament. Nor were the effects of Simon's bombshell undone by his action on 17 April when, in a much noted exchange with the Soviet delegate Maxim Litvinov, the British foreign secretary made a point of adhering to the purely European pertinence of the resolution which condemned a unilateral treaty violation and insisted that such repudiation "call into play all appropriate measures on the part of Members of the League and within the framework of the Covenant." [41] Although Litvinov in his protest to this European limitation was probably trying to extend the provisions of the resolution to the Far East, "there must have been many present whose minds were on Africa and Abyssinia," [42] and on these the implications of Simon's careful limitation were not lost, despite Simon's additional comment that "nobody is withdrawing or denying the authority and force of the obligations which attach to the rest of the world."

During the last two weeks of April, the Italians sought to weigh the threat of the unexpected and ominous British démarche of the 15th.[43] Guariglia and Suvich, with the approval of Mussolini, telegraphed

[41] The exchange is in League, *Official Journal, 1935*, 563–4. The passage in the resolution stated that the repudiation leading to League action was related only "to undertakings concerning the security of peoples and the maintenance of peace in Europe" (551). This was a clear repetition of Mussolini's addition to the Stresa declaration.

[42] Avon, *Facing the Dictators*, 182. See Gathorne-Hardy, *A Short History of International Affairs*, 398, for the assertion that "it seems clearly mistaken to read into the words [of Litvinov] a hidden reference to the Abyssinian situation." This disclaimer cannot be applied to Simon.

[43] Guariglia's immediate reaction, expressed in a memorandum of 16 April, was that Britain might use an extended conflict as an excuse to send British troops from the Sudan and British Somaliland into Ethiopia to secure Wallo lands and Harar. Such moves, he feared, would be taken as only "provisional" in the face of the Italian threat in the north, but would in fact become permanent. Guariglia, *Ricordi*, 229–30. This reflected Italy's mistrust of British activity in its colonial hinterland, though the suspicion was not valid in this case. With the imminent threat of a great conflict, the British dropped any interest they might have had in extending their influence into Ethiopian lowlands. In fact, in January the British had been concerned that too much pressure might make the Italians suspicious. Avon, *Facing the Dictators*, 196. Hoare gave as a reason for not replying at once to Mussolini's overture of 29 January that the British did not want to appear as if they were acting to preserve British interests in Ethiopia by agreeing to spheres of influence at Ethiopia's expense. Speech of 22 October to the House of Commons. *Parliamentary Debates*, 305 H.C. Deb. 5s. col. 25. The Maffey commission, on the other hand, had been appointed in March to ascertain the interests of Britain as a preliminary to the formation of future policy. A good deal of published opinion in France and Italy assumed that British sympathy toward Ethiopia was motivated solely by a desire to secure British interests there. In regard to British action at Geneva, this section of opinion held that the initials "S. d. N." referred more to "Source du Nil" than to "Société des Nations."

Grandi on the 20th, to the effect that the time had come to speak more openly to the British and to put aside the policy adopted in January of artful equivocation. Grandi, long an exponent of the frank approach under the auspices of the 1906 and 1925 accords, agreed at once, suggesting that not only should Simon and Vansittart be approached "in a more explicit and more clear fashion" concerning Italy's "necessary objectives" in Ethiopia, but also that other influential Englishmen, in and out of the government, should be contacted and Italy's position explained to them. Italian preparations could no longer be glossed over; the time for straight talking had come.[44] Italian officials realized that the British government, for reasons of internal politics, could not publicly approve an Italian invasion or fail to support in some degree the Ethiopian position at Geneva.[45] But this did not require the British to give open aid or encouragement to Ethiopia or to take the initiative at the League. The Italians hoped to find some middle way which would give the British some freedom to protest but at the same time provide Italy with the assurance that, in the final analysis, British opposition would be restrained. Mussolini was still ready to bargain, although the options were narrowing and the opportunities for success were fast closing.

At the end of April and at the start of May, on instructions from Rome, Grandi met with Vansittart and Simon. To Vansittart, Grandi made it clear that the issue was no longer merely the settlement of the Walwal incident. Grandi also deplored Simon's proposal of 15 April as constituting a hostile attitude toward Italy. Vansittart rejected this interpretation, claiming that, on the contrary, the British government had acted during the past five months with one aim only: to avoid establishing the Ethiopian dispute within the framework of the League. The British proposal, Vansittart explained, was motivated only by a desire to hasten arbitration proceedings, thereby depriving the Ethiopians of the no-progress argument which they could use to insist that the council take cognizance of the entire dispute.[46]

Following Guariglia's instructions, Grandi pressed further. Italy, he said, foresaw in the near future a new conflict in Europe. It was there-

[44] Guariglia, *Ricordi*, 229–30. The first elements of the Gavinana division of the regular army landed at Massawa on 18 April. De Bono, *Anno XIIII*, 105.

[45] Villari, *Storia diplomatica del conflitto italo-étiopico*, 93.

[46] If, as Vansittart claimed, Simon's proposal was presented as a means of thwarting not Italy's but Ethiopia's diplomacy, it is difficult to understand why the British did not offset the Italians' anger by informing them of the plan.

fore necessary quickly to eliminate the danger Ethiopia presented to the Italian colonies, in order to end the threat before problems in Europe became acute.

> The same political and military arguments invoked by England to make Italy desist from its African undertaking, said Grandi, constituted exactly Italy's reasons for liquidating as swiftly as possible the African problem and should cause England to consider the opportunity not of creating obstacles but, on the contrary, of collaborating effectively with Italy so as to ensure that this undertaking was completed in the shortest period of time and with the smallest expenditure. If England wanted to have Italy militarily strong on the European continent, just as Italy wanted to see a strong British empire, England should collaborate with Italy to hasten as soon as possible the Ethiopian affair instead of encouraging, by its vacillating Genevan policy, the resistance of Ethiopia.[47]

Vansittart replied that Grandi was telling him nothing new. He realized that Italy intended to seize Ethiopia, and he recognized the merits of the Italian argument. But the British government could not act contrary to British popular opinion, especially when the government had to face a general election in November. British public opinion, Vansittart warned, would be decisively against Italy in the case of an Italian-Ethiopian war. The League of Nations, which Grandi characterized as a "myth," a "fetish," was in fact the only instrument through which the British people would accept military obligations on the continent. For this reason, its interest in Europe, the British government would do all it could, in the case of an Italian-Ethiopian war, to prove to an uncertain populace the efficacy of the League. In answer to Grandi's suggestion, Vansittart said that British and Italian interests in the colonial sphere were not irreconcilable, but London could not at this time enter into treaty negotiations because the British people were hostile to such dealings. To embark on negotiations now, he contended, would damage, rather than help, British-Italian relations. Vansittart said too that MacDonald and Simon were relieved not to have been faced with this issue at Stresa.

Grandi talked to Simon next. Simon opened the discussion with an exaggerated eulogy of Mussolini. He said he considered it a crime that Mussolini had not brought up the Ethiopian issue at Stresa. Grandi repeated the comments and proposals he had made to Vansittart. Simon gave back a few of the British objections, but in an incoherent and

[47] Guariglia, *Ricordi*, 231–2.

rather pitiful fashion. He begged Italy to consider the embarrassing position in which the conflict placed the British government, causing it to make a difficult choice between a friend and the principles of the League. He tried to convince Grandi of the convenience *for Italy* of not insisting on the opening of conversations to reach an accord over Ethiopia.[48]

This performance is a glaring example of Simon's incompetence as a diplomat. The strongest warning he presented to Grandi was the danger of weakening the Stresa front by prolonged Italian military operations in Africa. It was Britain, not Italy, however, which scuttled the Stresa front, and the damage was done by Simon himself first at Stresa, then at the League, and later with the British-German naval treaty. Vansittart, and on 11 May Austen Chamberlain, gave Grandi accurate warnings for the future,[49] but the conversation with Simon, the foreign secretary, could only confirm in Italian minds the infirmity of Britain's policy and the confusion of its diplomacy. Eden wrote:

> I had no confidence that the Foreign Secretary's rather oblique warning would produce a change of heart in Rome. Once again we were resting our case on the effect of Italian action on British opinion . . . Grandi was the most astute and experienced of ambassadors . . . but the only conclusion he could draw from his exchange with the Foreign Secretary was that we were troubled and uncertain in our course. I wrote of Simon's interview in my diary that night: "Even from his own account nothing like stiff enough. Italy's request was a diplomatically phrased demand for a free hand in Abyssinia. This should have been strenuously resisted, emphasis laid on our support of the League, etc. It is useless to ask Musso[lini] how he thinks that Simon can answer questions on the subject in the House."[50]

Italy's response to these conversations is not surprising. After all their concern, the Italians no longer needed to consider Britain as a potentially serious obstacle to their plans.[51] Grandi had outlined Italy's general intentions as frankly and fully as diplomatic phraseology required in the face of the unconcealed military preparations. The

---

[48] Guariglia, *Ricordi*, 232–4; Avon, *Facing the Dictators*, 202–4.

[49] Chamberlain warned Grandi of the dangers to Europe if the Italian army were tied up in Africa. Grandi said that Mussolini could not be deflected from his purpose. C. Petrie, *The Life and Letters of the Right Hon. Sir Austen Chamberlain* (London, 1940), II, 403.

[50] Avon, *Facing the Dictators*, 204.

[51] So Ciano told Flandin at a meeting in Paris early in May. See Flandin, *Politique française*, 177–8.

British could never claim they were deceived. To underscore the point, Mussolini called in Drummond on 4 May and told him that "it is necessary for Italy to resolve the Ethiopian problem by any means in order to have freedom of action in Europe." [52] From London came no strong warning, no strong protests. Indeed, on the 4th, Drummond had scouted the unlikely possibility of evading the issue by finding some way to expel Ethiopia from the League.[53] The British government was clearly uncertain and unprepared to act. Mussolini, as one might expect, took no notice of the warnings about the significance of British popular opinion.

At last the British enigma seemed solved. The puzzle of the government's policy had been confronted, and it turned out that there was no Ethiopian policy. The much discussed choice between Italy and Ethiopia within the League of Nations seemed to present no danger. Grandi noted also that the spirit of British diplomacy had led to conciliation with the two outstanding violators of the principles of the Covenant, Japan and Germany. Italy could take a firm and uncompromising stand at Geneva.[54]

The British weakness and confusion, witnessed consistently for three months, was what encouraged Mussolini to adopt a harder line in the Italian-Ethiopian conflict. He saw that now he could act alone. There was no longer a need to come to an understanding with the British, for England was no longer diplomatically necessary to Italy in east Africa. To win Ethiopia, *Italia farà da sè* — Italy would do it by itself, regardless of London or Geneva. At the beginning of May, Mussolini reached his point of no return. From then on, he moved toward invasion as swiftly as he was able, believing that nothing in Europe would stand in his way. All efforts could be concentrated on the final objective — a war against Ethiopia and the military conquest of the country.

[52] Guariglia, *Ricordi*, 235.
[53] Aloisi, *Journal*, 269.
[54] Guariglia, *Ricordi*, 234.

Chapter 7

May: Italia Farà da sè

During the first three weeks of May, before the meeting of the League scheduled now for the 20th, Mussolini's confidence was expressed in a series of assertively independent acts and speeches. On 7 May, more mobilizations were decreed. The Sabauda division of the regular army and two Blackshirt divisions of the Fascist militia, the XXIII March and the XXVIII October, were called up. In addition it was announced that all metropolitan units of the militia were being placed on a war footing, that a new army division was being formed, and that all men registered in the 1911, 1913, and 1914 classes had been called into service.[1]

While military preparations were being increased, Mussolini added another dimension to his mode of imperialism. In the first months of 1935, when the future course of British policy was uncertain, Mussolini refrained from identifying the Ethiopian campaign too closely with Italy's national interest and prestige. But the British silences of April seemed to remove the threat of British resistance, and the chance of success in Africa was greatly improved. So now the Fascist government sought to involve the entire Italian nation in its venture.

The connection between the interests of the government and those of the Italian people in this affair was contrived entirely by the government for its own purposes. Mussolini decided upon imperial conquest as a means of strengthening his regime. War and adventure abroad, not

[1] Mussolini, *Opera omnia*, XXVII, 343; *The Times* (London), 8 May 1935. The number of men pressed into action on 7 May was 143,000, not including the classes of 1911 and 1914. Divisions of the Fascist militia were named to commemorate important Fascist anniversaries. 23 March 1919 was the date of the founding of the first *fascio* in Milan; 28 October 1922 was the day of the march on Rome, and it also marked the end of the Fascist year. Thus 28 October 1935 was the last day of the year XIII of the Fascist era, and 29 October was the first day of the year XIV.

peaceful social development at home, were Mussolini's answer to the problems he faced within Italy. The Ethiopian enterprise was to be the outlet for the unemployed energies of the people. If his conquest succeeded, then, at least for the next few years Mussolini's reputation and authority would be unchallenged.

The degree of benefit to the Fascist regime in the coming conflict was directly related to the extent of the nation's commitment. Only with full popular support, only as a national and common cause, would the campaign against Ethiopia make Mussolini the majestic Italian leader without a modern parallel, bring him and the state to new heights of power and influence at home and abroad, and quiet all criticism of the regime. Only as the head of a national crusade could Mussolini hope to ride out any storm that might blow up on international seas. This new emphasis had profound consequences for international diplomacy. As long as Mussolini's ambitions had been relatively personal, there was a chance that he could be restrained. Once the whole Italian nation became involved, once Fascism committed the full interests of the nation to the conflict, Mussolini could not turn back without admitting a defeat he feared he could not survive. His commitment to a war of conquest thus became irrevocable, and the chance for compromise or mediation became almost impossible.

On 7 May, acting on the direct order of Mussolini, Alessandro Lessona, the undersecretary for the colonies, undertook to provide justifications for the coming action in east Africa. Speaking before the Italian Chamber, Lessona claimed that the Ethiopian government was incapable of maintaining order in the country. The land was in anarchy, he said, and the threat to Italy's possessions was untenable. For the sake of Italian prestige and dignity, and for the safety of the Italian colonies, the Fascist government could delay no longer. The time had come for Italy "to resolve, once and for all, the problem of [its] relations with Ethiopia." [2] Reports to the Italian Senate and Chamber on 9 May spoke of Africa as "destined to be a great battlefield between the civilizations of west and east." By engaging in the fight for civilization there, the reports claimed, Italy would be defending not only its own rights but also protecting "ordered and productive civilization against a sterile and anarchical regime that tyrannizes over enslaved peoples

[2] Lessona, *Memorie*, 177; A. Lessona, *Verso l'impero* (Florence, 1939), 120; Toynbee, *Survey of International Affairs, 1935*, II, 151.

and creates dangerous disturbances on the borders of territories already won over for pacific and productive civilized labor." On 14 May, in a speech to the Senate, Lessona surveyed the historical and strategic reasons for Italian action in east Africa. He noted the "terrible responsibility" of the European powers for the "cause of civilization" in Ethiopia. Italy especially was "entrusted" with this responsibility and was, "as international treaties recognized, the principle power interested in Ethiopia." [3]

Lessona's speeches were designed to give reasons to the Italian people for the action in Ethiopia.[4] The task of dealing with other nations was Mussolini's. Since the British persistently refused to engage in any discussions with Italy over the Ethiopian question, it was no longer necessary, Mussolini felt, to continue his attempts to solicit prior approval from London. What remained was to make these decisions public and final in order to prevent any possibility of a future British or British-French about-face.[5] Britain and France had to be told that the time for discussion was passed, that there was no longer any opportunity for diplomatic mediation, that Italy would brook no interference in its design for conquest.

On 14 May, speaking to the Senate immediately after Lessona, Mussolini gave the clearest public announcement yet of Italy's position. He spoke directly to the British and to the French. Mussolini "formally and immediately" denied that there had been any British-French representation (passo) in Rome over Ethiopia. He did not expect any to come. Italy had presented its position frankly, Mussolini said, and there was no need, now or in the future, to resort to extraordinary means of diplomatic procedure. Britain and France were concerned that operations in east Africa would weaken the Italian stand in Europe, but this worry was baseless. Italy had under arms hundreds of thousands of men for the protection of its European frontier. On the other hand, at present the danger to the Italian nation lay not in Europe but in Africa, where the colonial frontiers were

[3] *The Times* (London), 10 and 15 May 1935. The Ethiopian government, in a note to Italy of 10 May, protested and rejected this "civilizing" argument. The note denied there was an "Ethiopian problem" and maintained that, even if there were, it was no business of Italy's. *The Times*, 11 May 1935.

[4] The Italian press now became filled with speculations on a general mobilization in Ethiopia. Stress was laid on the immediate need to rush large numbers of troops to east Africa to reinforce colonial garrisons. *Bulletin périodique de la press italienne*, 308:14–5.

[5] Aloisi, *Journal*, 270.

under the threat of an increasingly militant Ethiopia. This danger had to be met and resolved. In view of the distance and the need for Italy to be on guard in Europe, the faster the colonial matter was settled the better. Italy would not rest easily in Europe until its security in Africa was assured. To accomplish this, Italy was prepared to commit as many men as necessary. No one except an Italian was capable of judging the interests of Italy or the needs of Italian national security: the threat to this security in Africa was for Italy alone to resolve, and Italy would tolerate no interference. Italian relations with Britain and France were cordial. There was not the slightest reason for them to interest themselves henceforth in what was purely and simply an Italian matter.[6]

This was a clever speech. While warning against interference, Mussolini also tried to allay the British and French fears for European security. Indeed, he placed a premium on allowing Italy freedom to act in Ethiopia. To resist Italy would be to prolong and widen the conflict; to permit Italy to act swiftly and decisively would be in the best interests of Britain and France. This line of reasoning strongly appealed to many officials in both London and Paris. One thing was clear from the speeches of Lessona and Mussolini: the Ethiopian matter had advanced far beyond a mere dispute over the settlement of the Walwal incident. Both speakers dwelt, as increasingly the Italian press did, on the disorder within the country, the resort to arms by many Ethiopian chieftans, and the belligerent and recalcitrant spirit in Addis Ababa. "Italy in danger" was the Fascist government's rallying call to the Italian people, and while at the moment the only part of Italy that was, supposedly, in any immediate danger was a remote colonial frontier, this was a sufficient excuse for a national war of self-defense. Although Mussolini specifically stated that negotiations leading to arbitration of the Walwal incident would continue, and the Italian arbitrators were named the next day, it was now asserted that the whole situation had to be dealt with comprehensively by Italy, and that settlement of the Walwal incident was not sufficient to assure peace in view of the existing disorder and threatening hostility of Ethiopia.

Italy's public position did not yet exclude some possibility of a

---

[6] Mussolini, *Opera omnia*, XVII, 72–4. *Il Popolo d'Italia* called it "a solemn warning." The *Corriere della sera* viewed it as "one of the most important speeches of recent times."

peaceful settlement, but in private the commitment to war was final. On 18 May, before the League met, Mussolini wrote to De Bono that he had offset the possibility of a British-French démarche.

> I have made it understood that we shall not turn back at any price . . . In the meantime, with the nomination of the two arbitrators on the Italian side, we shall get the better of the next Council of the League of Nations, but in September [the time of the next scheduled League meeting after the May session] we shall have to begin all over again. It may be necessary to withdraw from Geneva. It is precisely in view of this eventuality that it is absolutely indispensable not to alter the date of October which we have established for the beginning of the eventual operations. Before this time you must have on the spot the whole ten divisions. You must make sure beforehand of victuals and munitions for at least three years, and also, however absurd it seems, because there are formal conventions in existence relating to the passage of the Suez Canal in peace and war, one must expect difficulties in respect to its passage. In the House of Commons there has even been talk of closing the Canal. One must always make ready for the most pessimistic and difficult eventuality.[7]

Mussolini's speech of 14 May deeply disturbed the British. Coming on the eve of the council meeting, it required of them some policy decision. There was a division of counsel within the Foreign Office. The "Leaguers," represented by Eden, were prepared to support the League in this dispute even to the point of a rupture with Italy, although not, probably, to the point of war. Vansittart, the permanent undersecretary, was sympathetic to the League but saw it as a losing bet. He "could never see the League's components tackling an aggressor of weight." The League, he believed, could not save Ethiopia without war, and no one in Britain wanted a war with Italy. Mere political support of the League, therefore, would be a futile exercise. Regardless of the justice of the Ethiopian position, expediency and political reality demanded that the danger of an aggressive Germany be given a higher priority. To support the League to no purpose would run the risk of alienating Italy, of losing a friend on the other side of Germany. With Italy committed to Africa, Germany would be likely to move to the south, to Austria, "the first point of Hitler's expansion which, once permitted, would be boundless." The choice

---

[7] De Bono, *Anno XIIII*, 161; Mussolini, *Opera omnia*, XXVII, 276.

Britain must make, Vansittart thought, was between the defense of Austria or of Ethiopia. The injustice of Italy's conquest must give way before the greater "justice" of Britain's true interest, the containment of Hitler, a necessary element of which was a friendly Italy.[8] "Fate," Keith Feiling writes, "could hardly have presented a worse ground for a test of principle" than the Italian-Ethiopian conflict.[9]

But the British government, unwilling as ever to pledge Britain to specific action on the continent, was not prepared to make this commitment to Austria. Simon called for a memorandum on the Italian-Ethiopian situation. The memorandum correctly reported the Italian military build-up and detailed the policy of diplomatic evasion that masked the Italian design. There was no doubt in British minds that a large-scale offensive was scheduled for the end of the rainy season, in late September or early October. The memorandum contained no recommendations for British action, and a Cabinet meeting was called for 15 May to discuss the problem of what Britain was to do. Mussolini's next move had been foreshadowed by the Italian nomination of members to the commission for arbitration and conciliation. This provided Italy an argument for once again bypassing the League. One decision resulted from the Cabinet meeting on the 15th. Eden, the British representative going to the League council, was given instructions to refuse "to agree to a procedure which would result in no action being taken to prevent hostilities before the next Council Meeting," scheduled for September.[10] This was the only guideline Eden had when he left on the 18th for Geneva.

Britain still had no policy, no positive proposals to put forward. A message was sent to Mussolini informing him that Britain thought the League could not neglect the dispute between May and September, and Drummond was called home for consultation, then sent back to Rome to call on Mussolini. For what it was worth, Britain no longer stood on the side of the obstructionists at Geneva. But this was in fact a debilitating, not even a neutral, position. If the League was to function at all, the British could not simply watch events — they would have to lead. Nonetheless, the new British position was a serious blow to

---

[8] Vansittart, *The Mist Procession*, 522. "Vansittart regarded the prevention of an Anschluss as the primary objective and his policy towards Italy and France followed from this." See Gehl, *Austria, Germany, and the Anschluss*, 63.
[9] Feiling, *Life of Neville Chamberlain*, 263.
[10] Avon, *Facing the Dictators*, 205.

Italy's diplomatic strategy, for if sincere it meant that London would no longer aid and abet the Italian effort to keep the conflict away from the League.

The Ethiopians viewed the events of the first three weeks of May with increasing disquiet. It will be recalled that the conflict had not been discussed at the extraordinary session of the council held in mid-April because the members had acceded to the Italian point that, since Italy on 14 April had agreed to a process of arbitration, the League had no need to interest itself in the dispute. In this note of 14 April the Italians raised an issue that was to plague all further Italian-Ethiopian negotiations: it became another vehicle for an Italian stall and made the Ethiopians rue their decision to press ahead with arbitration as a means of settling the conflict. The Italians declared that "the precise point at issue" was the immediate responsibility for the fighting which had taken place in the Ogaden, notably at Walwal. This meant only the determination of who had fired first on the spot. Not until this specific responsibility was fixed would Italy agree to undertake negotiations on the location of the frontier. The Italians were willing to consider as open the matter of responsibility for the fighting per se; they were not willing even to consider, until this particular question was cleared up, the matter of who was trespassing on the territory on which the incidents took place.

The Ethiopian government did not accept such a restrictive definition of the issue to be arbitrated. In a reply to Vinci dated 17 April, Foreign Minister Herouy stated that the question of responsibility for the fighting was intimately connected with the questions of the frontier, of who owned the land and who was in trespass. Because Ethiopia asserted that the establishment of the Italian garrisons in the Ogaden was illegal did not mean that it was attempting to evade the question of responsibility for the fighting. But the two matters were inseparable and had to be matters of simultaneous concern to any tribunal. The question of ownership, indeed, was the central one under the Ethiopian interpretation of the treaty of 1928. It was Italy's refusal to submit this question to arbitration that justified Ethiopia's appeal to the council under article 15 of the Covenant.[11] This presentation of the two opposing arguments made it clear that there would be great difficulty in

[11] Italian note of 14 April and the Ethiopian reply of 17 April in League, *Official Journal, 1935,* 749.

establishing the frame of reference, the sphere of competence, of any committee of arbitration, even if such a body could be finally brought into being.

The Ethiopians were alarmed by the acceleration of Italian military preparations and by the increase in the number of belligerent statements from Rome during the first weeks of May. On 11 May Tecle Hawariate again wrote to the secretary-general invoking article 15 of the Covenant.[12] Negotiations leading to arbitration had broken down, the Ethiopian note stated. In April, directly after the council meeting, Ethiopia had suggested to Italy that 10 May be agreed on as the date for the simultaneous designation of arbitrators. Italy gave no reply, took no action, except to put pressure on certain foreign governments not to allow their nationals to be nominated by Ethiopia.[13] Italy proposed that arbitrators from the Ethiopian side be of Ethiopian nationality. These deliberate efforts at delay could go on no longer, said the Ethiopians, especially in the face of military preparations and the clearly hostile intentions of Italy. For these reasons, "at this critical hour in its history," Ethiopia appealed to the League for protection against aggression.[14]

Prodded by this letter,[15] but even more by the forthcoming council meeting, Mussolini on 15 May announced the names of Italy's two arbitrators. Both were men closely associated with the Italian government. They were Count Luigi Aldrovandi-Marescotti, an ambassador

[12] On 10 May the emperor had taken another step which attracted much attention but which came to nothing. The matter of British-Egyptian-Sudanese cooperation in constructing a dam on Lake Tana, an on-and-off matter for many years, was revived. Spurred no doubt by a desire to have the British government establish a vested interest in Ethiopia under the aegis of his government, on 10 May Haile Selassie invited the three governments to send delegates to a conference at Addis Ababa. The British and Sudanese replied that they favored postponement of this conference in order not to "aggravate the present unfortunate controversy between Italy and Abyssinia," and it was not held. Nonetheless, the Egyptian government voted a large-scale irrigation plan on 22 May, £E 3 million of which were set aside for the Tana dam project. At the same time, negotiations were undertaken with the government of the Sudan to split this cost and to arrange a partition of the waters, so that later arrangements could be made with Ethiopia. See W. L. Langer, "The Struggle for the Nile," *Foreign Affairs*, 14:272 (January 1936); and Eden's comments in the House of Commons, 9 July 1935, *Parliamentary Debates*, 304 H.C. Deb. 5s., cols. 156–7.
[13] E.g., the Ethiopians wished to name Nicolas Politis, Greek ambassador to France, as their representative on the commission, but the Italian government protested to Athens and Politis' nomination was prohibited. U.S. *Diplomatic Papers, 1935*, I, 624.
[14] League, *Official Journal, 1935*, 720–1.
[15] See Cohen, *La Société des Nations*, 94n.

who had served on the Manchurian (Lytton) and Chaco commissions of the League, and Raffaele Montagna, a former member of the League secretariat. The Italian move came as a surprise. The next day Ethiopia named its nominees, a Frenchman, Albert de Geouffre de La Pradelle, professor of law at the University of Paris, and an American, Pitman B. Potter, then professor at the Graduate Institute of International Studies in Geneva.

At this point the Ethiopians were partial to the idea of taking one step backward in order to jump two steps forward. On 16 May they informed the Italian government that they would be willing to limit arbitral proceedings to the immediate circumstances of the Walwal incident, even though they would continue to press for a complete solution of the frontier question.[16] The Ethiopians did not pursue this line, nor did the Italians take it up, and nothing more was heard of the proposal.

Yet this mood of partial concession is reflected in the Ethiopian telegram to the secretary-general of 20 May, in which the emperor presented his case as the League council convened.[17] After noting Italian diplomatic procrastination and the threat to Ethiopia's frontiers presented by the growing Italian military force, Haile Selassie appealed to the League to secure the independence of Ethiopia. But the emperor did not directly invoke article 15 of the Covenant.[18] Rather, he returned to the request that article 15 be implemented if Italy failed to agree that the arbitrators should concern themselves with the question of ownership, of boundary lines, as well as with the question of immediate responsibility for the incidents. Ethiopia reverted to insisting that both matters be included in arbitration, but it held that arbitration took precedence over League involvement. It is not clear why the emperor still considered the success of arbitration more important than the invocation of the Covenant. Perhaps he felt that in arbitration, if it were tied to the question of ownership, Ethiopia had a strong and convincing case. Perhaps, and more likely, the Ethiopian government realized that it was above all important to finish the matter

[16] This note is found in the archives of the League and is printed in part in Cohen, *La Société des Nations*, 74–5. Cohen notes the Italian efforts to suppress publication and distribution of the Ethiopian concession.

[17] League, *Official Journal*, 1935, 721.

[18] On the other hand, according to the American chargé in Addis Ababa, on the 18th the Ethiopian government instructed Tecle Hawariate to invoke article 15 at the coming council meeting. *U.S. Diplomatic Papers*, 1935, I, 600.

of arbitration swiftly.[19] If arbitration succeeded, Ethiopia's case would be vindicated and Italy as a trespasser would be exposed. If it came to nothing, and failure seemed certain in view of Italian intransigence, then the responsibility for the failure would be Italy's. In any case, the danger to Ethiopian independence seemed certain to persist, and then, the matter of arbitration being over, Ethiopia could adopt an approach based solely on the League. By his telegram on 20 May, the emperor was holding the way open for the League to take up the dispute.

On 19 May, the day before the council meeting opened, representatives of the four most interested nations gathered at Geneva.[20] The Ethiopian issue was on the council's agenda. All diplomacy centered on this fact.

The French, unwilling to antagonize Mussolini, were still eager to find a way to keep the controversy from coming before the council.[21] The British were no longer as cooperative as they had been in April. Already the British government had given Mussolini formal warning that it wanted to see the dispute settled peacefully, that Britain would not countenance a prolonged neglect of the conflict by the council, and that it was resolved, in the interests of collective security, to see the dispute considered by the League sometime before the sitting of the council scheduled for September.[22] The British were prepared to postpone discussion for the moment if bilateral arbitration appeared to be under way, but they wanted the proceedings placed under the auspices of the League. Such a connection would serve as a warning to Italy to behave peacefully, an inducement to make the arbitral proceedings succeed, and an insurance that the conflict could be brought to the League if the bilateral negotiations resulted in a stalemate.

Beginning at this time there was a noteworthy change of roles between Britain and France in their relations with the League. For years France had been the champion of the position that the provisions for collective security of the Covenant should be rigorously followed and

[19] See Cohen, La Société des Nations, 76.
[20] Although these four determined the course of events, henceforth all nations took an active interest in the Italian-Ethiopian conflict. For example, on 10–11 May the foreign ministers of the Little Entente countries, and Greece, met in Bucharest to discuss how seriously the idea of a Danubian pact was jeopardized by Mussolini's African policy. See F. Vondracek, The Foreign Policy of Czechoslovakia, 1918–1935 (New York, 1937), 406–7.
[21] Toynbee, Survey of International Affairs, 1935, II, 152–3.
[22] Avon, Facing the Dictators, 206.

applied regardless of the specific case. This would guarantee the application of the Covenant to any disturbance which might threaten France's interests in Europe. Now, seeking this security outside the League, the French seemed more willing to condone a violation of the Covenant in Africa and less ready to take their stand on principle. The British government had long been a defender of its freedom to examine each international problem separately and to make *ad hoc* decisions. Now, out of political concern for the apparent sensibilities of public opinion, the British began gradually to adopt the position that whereas the consequences of alienating Italy were serious, and should be avoided if possible, even more serious, although no one seemed certain why, would be a failure of the government to offer some degree of support to the League in its hour of crisis.

The Italian delegates to the council session had as their guide Mussolini's speech of 14 May. They took an uncompromising position, based on the finality of Italy's decision to settle the Ethiopian question once and for all in its own manner, regardless of the opinions or actions of its erstwhile friends in the League.[23] Ethiopia, now more than ever a "pawn" in European diplomacy (this phrase is Ernest Work's), sent its delegates to Geneva completely uncertain of what the future held.

The first move came from the British and French delegations. They hoped, before the council came to the Ethiopian item on its agenda, that informal negotiations could induce the two disputants to agree to arbitration without delay. They wanted to create a means by which the council, while maintaining an official contact with the procedure, would not itself have to take formal responsibility for a successful and peaceful solution. Eden took the lead. On 20 May he met with the Ethiopian delegation, which now included, in addition to Tecle Hawariate, the Frenchman Gaston Jèze, professor of law at the University of Paris.[24] In line with the position taken in the Ethiopian letter

[23] Aloisi, *Journal*, 270–1; Avon, *Facing the Dictators*, 208.

[24] The Ethiopian delegation was at a relative disadvantage owing to the inexperience of its delegates. "Jèze was a brave and honest man, but he was no match for Aloisi, with his familiar knowledge of a Council to which he had rendered great service in the past. The one argued as a lawyer, the other spoke with the confident authority of an experienced delegate." Walters, *History of the League*, II, 634. Jèze was a well-known radical lawyer, associated with the popular-front movement. His espousal of the Ethiopian cause aroused considerable anger against him among rightist elements in France. Students protested by boycotting and demonstrating at his lectures, causing a great disturbance. For two views of the notorious "Jèze affair," see S. de Beauvoir, *The Prime of Life*, P. Green, trans. (Cleveland, 1962), 210–1; D. W. Brogan, *The Development of Modern France, 1870–1939* (London, 1940), 695.

of 16 May, the Ethiopian delegates agreed to make no difficulties concerning the details or time limits of the arbitration procedure, on one condition: that Italy would enter into a pact of nonagression in front of the League council. That night, 20 May, Eden dined with Aloisi. Aloisi repeated arguments he had made earlier that day to the French official René Massigli. First, the Italian decision to end the Ethiopian question was now irrevocable and beyond compromise. Second, although the Italian decision was based in part on the long-standing resentment that Italy never had been given colonies or mandated territories sufficient to place the country among the great powers, more than winning an empire was at stake in the present enterprise. What was at stake was no less than the prestige of Mussolini's regime. Mussolini already had spent over 600 million lire,[25] and he could not, Aloisi said, be expected to give all this up merely at the request of the League of Nations. Nor could Mussolini back down in the face of protests stemming from the British public. Third, Aloisi recognized the dangers for Italy in making itself an outcast among the nations of the League. He was striving to find a way to mitigate the international effects of the Italian action, and for this he sought the help of Britain and France within the League. These two countries, and the League as a whole, had put up with Japan's conquests in Manchuria. Why could not this precedent be followed with regard to Italy's conquest of Ethiopia? Fourth, Aloisi emphasized that nothing could be achieved by threatening Mussolini. The meeting between Eden and Aloisi ended and nothing was accomplished. Each man was depressed by the grave prospect ahead.[26]

On 21 May Eden, Aloisi, and Massigli met again, again to no result. Eden stated the alternatives as the British viewed them: "Either we must work out a procedure which would enable the Council to remain in close contact and do its work of removing the threat of war, or inevitably we should have a debate at the Council table this week about the merits of the dispute, which would be prolonged and acrimonious." But no means were found by which the council could maintain contact, and no decision was taken about further arbitration. Aloisi would not admit the League as a party to the dispute, and stressed again the

[25] On 19 May the Italian minister of finance announced that the cost of extraordinary "exigencies" in east Africa amounted to 620 million lire by the end of April 1935. *The Times* (London), 20 May 1935. Military expenditures in both Eritrea and Somalia for fiscal year 1934–35 were originally projected, in the summer of 1934, for only 22,144,300 lire. Lessona, *Verso l'impero*, 61.

[26] Aloisi, *Journal*, 271–2; Avon, *Facing the Dictators*, 206–8.

fact that Mussolini's regime was now at stake. The matter rested on this ominous note, with the British and Italian delegates holding off until the next day when, on the basis of information received following Ambassador Drummond's much anticipated interview with Mussolini, they would have a clearer definition of their governments' policies.

The news arriving from Rome on that afternoon of the 21st was grim. Instructed by London, Drummond had presented the British situation to Mussolini. If Mussolini forced the British to choose between its long-time friendship with Italy and its support of the League, British public opinion and the government's new determination might well force Britain to choose against Italy. Drummond wondered if something could be done to save the face of the League, if not its principles. Could not, for example, a member of the council follow the arbitral proceedings as, say, a rapporteur? Mussolini rejected this alternative. The League, he said, had no reason to take cognizance of the dispute while bilateral negotiations under the treaty of 1928 were in progress. More than this, the Italian-Ethiopian conflict was, for Italy, a purely colonial venture. The situation between the two countries was intolerable and had to be resolved. Mussolini said he had not spent vast sums of money and made great military preparations just to settle the Walwal incident. He brushed aside impatiently Drummond's suggestion that, if Italy was worried about the Ethiopian army, perhaps Britain might influence the emperor to reduce the number of his troops. Italy, Mussolini said, was going to secure its colonies by any means it needed, including war. He noted that France, and Britain in Egypt, had resorted to force in gaining colonies. Drummond warned that Italian action might lead to the destruction of the existing security systems created since Locarno. Mussolini replied that his mind was made up. Collective security, he said, should be confined to Europe, as the Stresa conference emphasized. If the League supported Ethiopia against Italy, Mussolini would leave the League, never to return.[27]

The Drummond conversation should have banished any remaining doubts about Mussolini's intentions to go to war. The Italian position seemed now to admit no possibility of compromise. On the afternoon of the 21st, following the Mussolini-Drummond meeting, Aloisi received instructions from Rome to take a stand of absolute intransigence in the face of all efforts to involve the League formally in the dispute.

On the morning of 22 May, the French foreign minister arrived in

[27] Avon, *Facing the Dictators*, 209–10; Guariglia, *Ricordi*, 236–7.

Geneva. Meeting with Eden, Laval was at pains to disclaim the rumor that he had given Mussolini a free hand in Ethiopia or any encouragement for military action. Laval was perturbed by the growing seriousness of the affair. He and Eden agreed that Britain and France must maintain continuous contact and must act together. Eden rightly saw that, if any pressure were to be brought to bear on Mussolini, it would have to be the product of strong British-French unity. That evening Eden and Laval met again. Distressed by Italian obduracy, they agreed it was no longer useful to wait upon events. They agreed to take a limited initiative and draft a resolution to submit to the council, based on the emperor's request that the arbitration procedure should deal with *all* the incidents in the Ogaden (excepting territorial rights), and that if no decision was reached within a limited time the council would meet to examine the problem. A draft proposal was drawn up by the French delegation, and later that evening, on 22 May, Eden, Laval, and Aloisi, joined by their advisers William Strang, Massigli, and Guarnaschelli, met to discuss it. Aloisi was prevailed upon to submit the text of the proposal to Mussolini, although he gave solemn warning that the chances of acceptance in Rome were negligible.[28]

Much to everyone's astonishment, on 23 May Mussolini accepted the text, subject to the removal of the condition that no force was to be used by either party. With this turn of events, the following day, 24 May, was completely devoted to negotiation, made harrowing by the ever present possibility that the Duce would withdraw his approval. Laval, working hard and effectively to conclude the matter before leaving for Paris to attend to political problems brought about by France's serious financial crisis, acted to moderate the proposals so that Italy would not change its mind later. London backed up Eden's demands that Italy reaffirm its obligations under the treaty of 1928. The day was long and trying, and not until late that night were the compromise proposals, expanded on Italian demand, satisfactorily completed. The Ethiopians, rarely if ever consulted, showed great restraint and bowed to the wishes of Britain and France. At last a hastily called meeting of the council was arranged for 12:30 A.M. on the 25th, and the two proposals were submitted for approval.

The first resolution stated that both countries, in compliance with article 5 of the treaty of 1928, agreed to arbitrate all incidents that had broken out along the frontier and agreed to fix 25 August 1935 as

---

[28] Avon, *Facing the Dictators*, 211–2; *Journal*, 272–3.

the date on which this procedure of "conciliation and arbitration" was to be concluded. Italy withdrew its objection to non-Ethiopian arbitrators. The second resolution stated that the council granted the two parties "full liberty" to settle the dispute in accordance with article 5. The council resolved to meet if the four arbitrators could not agree and if they failed to appoint a fifth arbitrator by 25 July, or that it would meet if by 25 August settlement under these conditions had not yet been reached. The first resolution was passed unanimously, the second by a technical unanimity — the Italian delegate abstained from voting.[29]

Jèze, for Ethiopia, stated that the frontier question, the question of ownership, would have to be discussed simultaneously with the question of responsibility. He tried diligently to base the issue on article 2 of the treaty of 1928, which forbade any action calculated by either power to injure the other, and noted his expectation that the Italian government would stop transporting troops to east Africa. He pointed out that the council had undertaken an obligation of interest in the conflict. Aloisi, referring to Mussolini's speech of 14 May, claimed that Italy would maintain full sovereign freedom in any action it might take with regard to what it interpreted as its own security, and would not brook discussion of limitations on troop movements or other military activities. He avoided committing Italy to an observance of article 2. Italy further refused to have the arbitrators deal with the frontier question. No one tried to force an agreement between Italy and Ethiopia over the scope of competence of the arbitrators or over the precise definition of their functions. These matters remained undecided, and later led to trouble. Eden in his turn noted that the council "will remain in close contact with the situation and will meet again to deal with the matter should circumstances render that course necessary." [30]

[29] The condition concerning the fifth arbitrator referred to a supplement to the 1928 treaty, established on Ethiopian initiative in letters between Tafari and Cora on 3 and 4 August 1928. These notes set the manner in which arbitrators were to be appointed and concluded: "If [the four original arbitrators] do not succeed in arriving at an agreement, they will choose by common agreement a fifth arbitrator and the controversy will be resolved by a majority of votes." For the text, see Potter, *Wal Wal Arbitration*, 35–6. One reason, important for propaganda purposes, for the Italian abstention from the voting was that Italy could, in informing the press, concentrate attention on the first and less constraining proposal. *U.S. Diplomatic Papers, 1935*, I, 605. The diplomatic value of abstention was, of course, that Italy could claim to be disassociated from the resolution, which brought the League closer than ever to the conflict.

[30] League, *Official Journal, 1935*, 640–2.

With the adoption of the proposals of 25 May, there was another sigh of relief. Once again, for the third time, the Ethiopian request that the council concern itself with the real issues of the conflict was turned aside. Britain and France, eager to localize and minimize the dispute, pretended that the issue was merely one of the arbitration of a minor incident. They hoped to gain time in which to explore the possibilities for a negotiated settlement outside the League and did not want either to affront Italy or to compromise the League. Whatever may be said in favor of the plan, the fact is that such a maneuver did serve to weaken the moral stature and political authority of the League. No notice was taken of the mortal threat to Ethiopia or the potential challenge to the Covenant posed by Italian military preparations. No guarantee was given Ethiopia that its national security and independence would be protected.

These evasions were politically motivated, but it is also a fact that the machinery of the League was not geared to dealing with cases of premeditated aggression. This was the greatest structural weakness of the Covenant. The founders of the League should have paid some attention to Hobbes's definition of the state of war as being "not in battle only, or in the act of fighting; but in a tract of time, wherein the will to contend by battle is sufficiently known and therefore the notion of time is to be considered." Instead, generalizing from the way the First World War broke out, the League's founders thought only in terms of a sudden, unexpected incident which might lead to war in an otherwise pacific atmosphere. The Covenant provided a series of procedures meant to remove the settlement of any resulting controversy from the battlefield to the courtroom. The Walwal incident per se was such an event. But to isolate it from the broader context of Italy's preparations for war was to give Walwal a false significance. Italy was now using the process of pacification relative to this minor incident to divert formal attention from its military preparations. That Britain and France went along with this policy suited the Italians, who did not mind their work of camouflage being done for them by the very leaders of the League.

Italy did not fear the League as an organization: its punitive powers posed no immediate threat. Article 16, which directed all members to a policy of sanctions and concerted action against a violator of the Covenant, could not take effect until there was "resort to war." Until that time, when a state actually began military action, a potential aggressor, no matter how plain its intentions, was immune from any kind of forcible League interference. No one, it seemed, was willing to ascertain whether or not the council was so bankrupt in resources that it could not "have devised a procedure to form themselves into a Committee to face the question of Abyssinia even if it meant excluding the Italian representative." [31]

There was another way of stopping Italy. Article 15, which the Ethiopians were trying so hard to invoke, contained in its paragraph 7 the famous "gap" of the Covenant. According to this paragraph: "If the Council fails to reach a report which is unanimously agreed to by the members thereof, other than the Representatives of one or more of the parties to the dispute, the Members of the League reserve to themselves the right to take such action as they shall consider necessary for the maintenance of right and justice." On this basis it was theoretically permissible, in the event of prolonged Italian obstructionism, for Britain, say, to act alone to preserve Ethiopia's security. This eventuality did not worry Mussolini. The British people, and the British government, supported the League specifically because it offered an institutional alternative to independent action. Italian policy was calculated on the unlikelihood that any country would intervene alone.

As it was, the proposals of 25 May gave the League an option to become a party to the dispute at the end of August if the bilateral arbitration failed. This in itself was enough to forestall any independent moves by Britain or France. With a little astute diplomacy, Italy could probably prevent the council from taking up the issue until September. By then it would be too late to affect the Italian momentum, for September marked the end of the rainy season in the Ethiopian highlands and the launching of the invasion.

The Italian delegates were well satisfied with the events of 25 May. "Basically, we have safeguarded all our positions," wrote Aloisi in his diary.[32] Once again, with the cooperation of France and Britain, Italy had succeeded in preventing Ethiopia's plea from being heard by the League of Nations. Of much greater significance for the future than this, however, were three new changes in Italian attitudes and policy.

One stemmed from Aloisi's assertion, echoing Mussolini's speech of 14 May, that Italy would allow no restraints, would accept no comment, on its military preparations. This was "Italy's first defiance of the

[31] Temperley, *Whispering Gallery of Europe*, 334.
[32] Aloisi, *Journal*, 275.

Council in open session." [33] No one picked up the challenge. Henceforth Italy treated the League with contempt.

Second, Britain's apparent opposition to Mussolini's military ambitions and the British determination to involve the League in the dispute ushered in a new era in Italian-British relations. "The duel," wrote Aloisi on 24 May, had become "not Italo-Ethiopian but Anglo-Italian." [34] It was unimportant, or only an example of British feebleness, that British opposition at this time was marked by great caution and brought only minor practical results. What was relevant, to Mussolini, was that Britain now appeared aligned against him. In the middle of May, Mussolini had a simple rule to gauge his friends: friends supported Italy in the Ethiopian conflict; those who opposed were enemies.[35] The extent to which the Ethiopian affair had become the major preoccupation of the Duce can be judged from the way it became his touchstone for all relations with other countries. Britain's attitude, its disfavor was resented more than any other. It was the most unexpected to the country at large, and the most potentially dangerous to the Italian government. Up to this time Mussolini thought that at worst Britain would be neutral in the conflict. He feared the British less than his subordinates did, but now even he could not be certain of the future course of British policy. New influences were working on the government. The old British permissiveness over Ethiopia, agreement with men like Austen Chamberlain and Simon's silence at Stresa, central factors in the development of Mussolini's ambitions, seemed to be fading. New men, Eden the prime example, were bringing to the Foreign Office an idealism that threatened to upset the balance of British-Italian relations. These men appeared not to care if, in the course of their League policy, they toppled the very throne on which the Duce sat. Even the present methods of cooperation in Europe appeared to count for nothing, although a discerning eye could realize that it was the hope of retaining some measure of this cooperation which restrained the British from moving to prohibit Italian imperialism. This qualification did not matter to Mussolini. The damage to British-Italian friendship — the first really serious divergence of policy between the two countries since Italy was unified — was done

---

[33] Walters, *History of the League*, II, 634.
[34] Aloisi, *Journal*, 275.
[35] See J. Szembek, *Journal, 1933–1939*, J. Rzewuska and T. Zaleski, trans. (Paris, 1956), 91, 93.

when Britain chose, even hesitantly and partially, the League above Italy.

Yet for all its possible dangers British opposition, as it later developed, was turned by the Fascist government into a source of strength. It was the principal means by which Mussolini was able to convert the Ethiopian campaign into a popular and patriotic crusade. Until June there was no mass enthusiasm for the campaign. Fascist propaganda had to make do with weak devices to solicit support. Revenge for Aduwa was a rallying call, but it was not strong enough to unite the nation in the face of the risks and sacrifices involved or to overcome the suspicions of the people that there were other, political, reasons behind the government's actions. The alarms sounded by Lessona and Mussolini, that the security of Italy was threatened on a remote colonial frontier, were hollow and fell on deaf ears. No one believed that Italy itself was in danger. Few were willing to risk their lives in a civilizing mission in distant Ethiopia.

Now, however, a foe appeared capable of arousing the anger and fear of the Italian people and, with some clever manipulation, to unite them behind the Ethiopian campaign. Skillfully if crudely interpreted by Fascist propaganda, British opposition was presented to the people as a direct challenge to Italian national security, national independence, national interests, and national pride. Britain was portrayed as a selfish, satiated, retired imperialist, now intent, for reasons as petty as the dog's in the manger, on denying Italy its rightful share of colonial riches and international greatness, intent on interfering with the exercise of Italy's sovereignty. Later, after sanctions, the British were seen as a direct threat to the existence of the Italian state and to the very lives of the people.

This Fascist propaganda convinced many if not most Italians. If Britain, the oldest friend, had become such an enemy, anything was believable. According to responsible observers, nothing did more to win wide popular approval for the Ethiopian conflict than this. British opposition was the factor that turned the Italian people from apathy or disapproval of Mussolini's private adventure toward vigorous and patriotic support of Italian imperialism and Italy's right to independent action.[36] Although this propaganda did not attain its full effect until

---

[36] See Chabod, *History of Italian Fascism*, 77–8; Lessona, *Memorie*, 179; Starhemberg, *Between Hitler and Mussolini*, 216–7; *Le Temps*, 5 August 1935; Macartney and Cremona, *Italy's Foreign and Colonial Policy*, 177. Military men and indus-

after sanctions had been applied, it was now that the Fascist government began its anti-British campaign. From June 1935 onward, Great Britain was an official foe.

This anti-British policy was Mussolini's greatest gamble during the conflict with Ethiopia. It brought about the possibility of war with Britain and, with a nation uniting behind him, it required Mussolini to gain success not only over Ethiopia but over Great Britain as well. His political future depended on its outcome.

The third great change that occurred at this time was a shift in Italy's relations with Nazi Germany. At the beginning of May, Mussolini's antipathy toward Nazism was at its height.[37] The Stresa front, the good relations with France and Britain, augured a Western orientation for Italy. Then came Britain's objections to the Ethiopian campaign, and the Stresa front began to disintegrate. If Mussolini could not count on his Western associates, why should he not revert in some degree to his old policy of balancing off the West and Germany? There were two conditional factors: Germany's attitude toward the Ethiopian conflict and Germany's attitude toward Austria.

On 14 May Mussolini told the German ambassador that he would remember precisely what attitude individual countries took toward Ethiopia, whether friendly, neutral, or hostile.[38] The Germans at this stage were not ready to take a positively friendly stance toward Italy, let alone cooperate in Italy's imperialist designs. Indeed, during the spring of 1935, smarting over the French-Italian rapprochement and the Stresa conference, the German government encouraged a film called *Abyssinia Today*, which was notably sympathetic to the emperor, to be shown throughout Germany.[39] On the other hand, mid-1935 was a time of such shifts in European international relations that there was no telling what the future might hold for Germany. As one very substantial result, thought the Germans, Italy's deep involvement in east Africa would take Italian attention away from Austria and open the way to increased German influence in that country. Italy's African

trialists, who were at first disconcerted by Mussolini's plans and thought a colonial war unwise and expensive, had by June realized personal profit and advantage from the new situation, and now also responded favorably to Mussolini's warmongering. U.S. Diplomatic Correspondence, 765.84/425, dispatch from Rome of 1 July 1935.

[37] Aloisi, *Journal*, 269.
[38] *Documents on German Foreign Policy*, IV, 152.
[39] E. Wiskemann, *The Rome-Berlin Axis* (London, 1949), 47; Magistrati, "La Germania e l'impresa italiana di Etiopia," 571–3, 584–5.

complications would result in greater peace in the Balkans.[40] Further, the more Italy became committed to the conquest of Ethiopia, the greater would be its conflict with the League. This could only redound to Germany's benefit, for it could mean the destruction of the Western alliance against Germany and even the collapse of the League. There was everything to gain and nothing to lose by the tensions in the collective-security system which the Ethiopian affair appeared likely to bring in its train. So, for the moment, Germany adopted a wait-and-see attitude. Germany neither helped Italy nor hindered Italian preparations by any official disapproval or unsettling action in the Alps. Germany took an attitude of strict neutrality toward the conflict, watching to see how events developed.[41]

Mussolini also wanted to know Germany's attitude toward Austria. The search for support in guaranteeing Austrian independence had led Italy to associate itself with the Western democracies during the first part of 1935.[42] But the British government had not taken Vansittart's advice to contain Germany by defending Austria, and France's support there was uncertain. The Stresa front was now crumbling over the Ethiopian conflict. If Italy had to assume primary responsibility for Austrian independence, if it had to worry constantly about keeping a guard on the Brenner Pass, Italy might never be free to move its armies to Africa. For these reasons Mussolini welcomed Hitler's speech before the Reichstag on 21 May 1935. Hitler said: "Germany neither intends nor wishes to interfere in the internal affairs of Austria, to annex Austria, or to conclude an 'Anschluss' . . . The German Government regret the tension which has arisen from the conflict with Austria all

[40] Dispatch of the American ambassador in Germany, 15 May 1935. U.S. Diplomatic Correspondence, 765.84/315 and 751.62/299.

[41] An order for strict neutrality had already gone out on 26 March. *Documents on German Foreign Policy*, III, 1083. See the message of Foreign Minister Neurath to the German ambassador in Rome, Ulrich von Hassell, of 24 June 1935. *Ibid.*, IV, 347–8. On 3 April, 15 May, and 5 June 1935 Germany assured Italy that it was not exporting arms to Ethiopia. On 1 June, 28 June, and 3 July the German government denied that it was allowing recruitment for Ethiopia's army in Germany. The Italian government realized that German interests were being served by Italian involvement in Africa, but were grateful for Germany's noninterference and friendly attitude — such as when Italy abandoned its 40 percent gold base in July. Ministero degli Affari Esteri, *Germania: Situazione political nel 1935* (Rome, 1935), 9–10. This document was a secret position paper of the Italian foreign office.

[42] The major documents in the Austrian situation were the French-Italian protocol of 7 January, its sequel in the British-French declaration of 3 February, the Stresa resolution of 14 April, and the French-Italian military agreements.

the more because it has resulted in disturbing our former good relations with Italy, a State with whom we otherwise have no conflict of
interests." [43]

Mussolini responded at once to the conciliatory tone of these words
and moved to reopen his contacts with Germany. He still hoped to
freeze the Austrian problem long enough to complete his colonial
dream, but now he was not going to be distracted from Ethiopia for
any reason.[44] According to Grandi, at the Stresa conference Mussolini
finally realized that, if he was to go ahead with his plans for Ethiopia,
he would have to give up or postpone his ambitions in Austria.[45] Time
was all-important to Italy: the matter had to be resolved as advantageously as possible in the short time available before the autumn
campaign. So Mussolini expressed his appreciation for Hitler's speech,
which he considered a decided step toward an understanding between
Germany and Italy. He viewed it as having a considerable effect in
Rome in easing the way for friendlier consultations. On 25 May
Mussolini spoke to the departing German military attaché of a "basic
reorientation" of Italian policy, and expressed the hope that "a gradual
and systematic rapprochement between Germany and Italy would
come about within the framework of this reorientation." [46]

This was Italy's first step on the road leading to the Axis. Mussolini,
in the space of a few days, turned away from reliance on the West and
toward Germany.[47] The new turn was confirmed by later developments in the Italian-Ethiopian conflict, and it became more definite in
direct ratio to the alienation Mussolini felt from Britain and France.

[43] Wheeler-Bennett and Heald, eds., *Documents on International Affairs, 1935,*
I, 171.

[44] The Austrians were well aware of the significance of the Ethiopian campaign
for their own future and, it was said, watched its progress even more closely
than the Italians did. Starhemberg, *Between Hitler and Mussolini,* 214.

[45] D. Grandi, in *Oggi,* 15:12 (28 May 1959), cited in Gehl, *Austria, Germany,
and the Anschluss,* 116n.

[46] *Documents on German Foreign Policy,* IV, 209, 231, 232.

[47] On 30 May Hassell wrote Neurath: "The tendency here towards improving
relations with Germany has become more marked and during the last few
days has increased so much that one might almost speak of a reversal of the
Italian attitude towards Germany." *Ibid.,* 230. Hitler remained sympathetic to
Mussolini for ideological reasons as well as for reasons of political interest — he
never accepted the breach that Mussolini caused in 1934. Certain people in Berlin, notably Baron von Stumm of the press department of the German foreign
office, his Italian wife, and Countess Magistrati, Ciano's sister, tried to counteract
any signs that indicated a split between the two countries. Wiskemann, *Rome-
Berlin Axis,* 48.

When that alienation became complete, the Axis was complete. After Ethiopia, the only acceptable friend remaining to Mussolini was the Nazi dictator.

On 25 May Mussolini spoke before the Italian Chamber of Deputies, giving a sketchy *tour de horizon* of Italian foreign policy.[48] The keynote of the speech was that changes were taking place in European relations. As new events occurred (and the Ethiopian affair was at the front of everyone's mind), each state would react according to its own interests and new positions would be taken. Italy would take note of these "inevitable transformations" of policy and opinion, and act in its own best interests as the various shifts became evident. Mussolini barely mentioned Britain. Toward France he spoke with some warmth: the "state of feeling" between Italy and France had "much improved."

This was true, despite some cooling of the enthusiasm of January. Cultural exchanges and military and commercial accords took place regularly during the spring of 1935, in the amicable aftermath of the Laval-Mussolini talks.[49] Mussolini had every wish to maintain good relations with France and, despite his overtures to Hitler, still counted on France and the French fear of Germany as his best security with regard to Austria. Now in preparation were agreements whereby the French army would intervene with Italy if Austria were menaced. There was a constant interchange of information about the security of Europe between Gamelin and Badoglio and between other commanders. Reciprocal tours of inspection of military establishments and visits of friendship by French military units took place during this period. Despite the seriousness of the financial crisis in France, and the fear that the government might fall,[50] so long as Laval remained at the helm

[48] Mussolini's speech of 25 May in *Opera omnia*, XXVIII, 76–80.

[49] See, e.g., Salvemini, *Prelude*, 207, and Mallet, *Laval*, I, 71n, 94–5. Military talks between the general staffs took place on, e.g., 25 January, 20 February, 7 March, and 6 April. See Assemblée Nationale, 1947 session, *Rapport fait . . . sur les événements . . . de 1933 à 1945*, IX, 2571–3. The aeronautical convention of 13 May and the secret agreements of 19 and 28 June were especially important to Italy. The military accords "were only denounced in December 1938. Until then they were an avowed preoccupation of the Italian government. Mussolini demanded confirmation of them at perilous moments of the Ethiopian affair." Lagardelle, *Mission à Rome*, 118. Sources for the dates on which the secret "papers" were signed in June are: Aloisi, *Journal*, 284; Gamelin, *Servir*, II, 167–9; Salvemini, *Prelude*, 223; *Bulletin périodique de la press italienne*, 308:17–18.

[50] For a good discussion of these difficult days in May, when Flandin's government teetered and fell on the question of how to respond to the monetary crisis (the outward gold flow reached the astronomical proportions of 3,915 million francs worth between 17 and 25 May), see Herriot, *Jadis*, II, 542–50.

of French foreign policy Mussolini correctly believed that there was substantial benefit for Italy in maintaining the French connection. Mussolini did not allow any public manifestation of mistrust or hostility toward the French. He wanted to create the impression that Britain was isolated in its opposition to Italy and that Italy was receiving the loyal support of her Latin sister.[51]

Nonetheless, it was evident that the future of French-Italian relations depended on how the French government acted in the Ethiopian matter. In his speech of 25 May, Mussolini gave a warning to France: "Let us hope that nothing in the future will happen to trouble again" the good relations between the two countries.[52]

Toward Germany Mussolini was moderate. He seconded Hitler's statement of the 21st that only Austria stood as a barrier between Italy and Germany. Mussolini took the opportunity, in his speech of the 25th, to revaluate Italy's position toward Austria and to indicate its significance for the Ethiopian campaign. He addressed himself to "those who would like to fossilize us on the Brenner to prevent us from moving in any other part of the world." To lively applause Mussolini asserted that the Austrian problem was a European, not exclusively Italian, problem.

> Fascist Italy does not mean to limit its historic mission to a single political problem [*approvazioni*] or to a single military sector [*approvazioni*], such as the defense of a frontier, even such an important one as the Brenner, because all our frontiers, at home and in the colonies, are indistinguishably sacred and must be vigilantly defended against any threat whatsoever, even if it is only a potential one [*nuove, vivissime, reiterate acclamazioni*].

Mussolini now reached the crucial point in his speech. All the problems he had detailed in Europe, he said, had specific reference "to what may happen in east Africa and in relation to the attitudes which individual states may take up when the time comes for them to show us real friendship, not a superficial one based on words alone." Italy must rely on itself, but its future policy in Europe would be based on the reaction of the European states to Italy's campaign in Ethiopia. Musso-

---

[51] *Documents on German Foreign Policy*, IV, 337. Laval had indeed done his best at the recent League meeting to temper the Ethiopian demands and to cause the British to respond moderately. He acted in the interests of Italy, not of the League, and as frankly and straightforwardly as could be expected.

[52] Mussolini's references to good relations with France and the hope for their continuance were greeted with applause by the puppet deputies in the Chamber.

lini left no doubt that the Ethiopian matter was at a stage of crisis, assuming "greater proportions every day." Speaking, it seems, impromptu, Mussolini made it clear that Italy was headed for war. No one could feign surprise at the "military measures which we have already taken or are about to take." The outcome of this conflict, stated the Duce, was obvious. Italy by itself was "ready to accept all responsibilities, even the greatest of all" — war.

The nations of Europe were thus warned. "Let no one hope to make Abyssinia into yet another pistol to be aimed at us forever and which, in the event of troubles in Europe, would make our position in east Africa untenable." To Britain and France the warning was plain: they could have Italy as an ally only by virtue of noninterference in Italian imperialism. To Germany the speech was an overture for better relations, on the condition of German benevolence during the coming campaign. Mussolini involved all of Europe in the outcome of his African plan. In his speech of 25 May, he gave public notice that the game was under way and that Italy placed as the stake of the Italian-Ethiopian conflict the balance of power in Europe.

At the end of May, Mussolini was in a disagreeable temper. The trouble raised at the League council meeting, the disillusionment with Britain, the seeming dissolution of the Stresa front, the course of events in Europe beyond his control, the new and problematic alternative of a rapprochement with Germany, the realization that Italy would have to run the risks of acting by itself in Ethiopia and that it might face significant opposition from the League, the feeling that he was being pressed on all sides — these factors made Mussolini belligerent and truculent. His anger and exasperation burst out in his conversations of 27 and 28 May. If Italy had to go it alone, Italy would do so with a vengeance. Mussolini wanted to denounce the Italian-Ethiopian treaty of friendship of 1928. He wanted to break with the League. He mocked world public opinion. He was, he said, prepared to go to the extreme in Ethiopia and would not hesitate to set Europe on fire. He wanted to mobilize three more divisions, to bring the number mobilized to eleven.[53]

To the cooler heads among the Italian planners, these proposals seemed unnecessary and dangerous. They contradicted the whole

---

[53] By 28 May Mussolini regretted his concessions of the 23rd, especially after they were blown up in the foreign press as a British victory. Aloisi, *Journal*, 275-7.

course of Italian diplomacy followed in this dispute. To denounce the treaty of 1928 would end any hope of using the arbitration process as a delaying tactic. If the treaty of arbitration were denounced, the resolution that the council accepted on 25 May would become a dead letter. That eventuality, or a break with the League, would give the council a reason for meeting at once to consider the conflict and to label Italy a disturber of the peace. The League could not ignore an officially declared preparation for aggressive war. The announcement of the mobilization of three more divisions, which could easily be construed as a violation of article 2 of the treaty of 1928, might have similar consequences. Italian diplomats wanted to avoid such provocations. In their opinion Italy could still work within the Covenant, not only without detriment but indeed to gain advantages through the use of technical delays. Best of all, through this means of formalist camouflage, Italy could keep some degree of friendship with France and some degree of influence in Europe. By playing the provisions of the 1928 treaty off against the Covenant, Italy already had gained five months for unencumbered preparations for war. This device was too helpful to drop in a fit of picque.

Arguments along these lines were presented to Mussolini by his advisers. From Africa De Bono and Graziani, whose opinions were solicited by the Duce, argued against denouncing the treaty. The issue was in doubt until 31 May — this was the length of Mussolini's spell of anger.[54] On that day announcement was made of the mobilization of three more divisions, the Gran Sasso division of the regular army, and the XXI April and the III January divisions of the Blackshirt militia, another 42,000 men.[55] New reserve units were also created. To the relief of the Italian diplomats, there was no mention of denunciation of the 1928 treaty or of withdrawing from the League. That this matter was undecided until the very last moment is an example of the authoritarianism of Mussolini. The same day, the Duce telegraphed De Bono that the mobilization order was necessary, in view of what

[54] De Bono, *Anno XIIII*, 162; Aloisi, *Journal*, 278.

[55] Mussolini, *Opera omnia*, XXVII, 346. 21 April was the supposed anniversary of the founding of Rome by Romulus and Remus. Since ancient Rome was noted for its public works, this was one of the two days of the year (the other being 28 October) when new public works were dedicated. After 1922, 21 April was also celebrated as Labor Day in Italy. 3 January commerated the momentous day in 1925 when Mussolini decreed the "definitive abandonment of a constitutional, liberal, and parliamentary state" and a Fascist dictatorship was finally imposed on Italy.

had happened at the council meeting in Geneva, to show that Italy's purpose in the Ethiopian conflict was determined.[56]

At the end of May 1935, Italy had an estimated 900,000 men under arms.[57] These troops were not yet prepared for combat, but they constituted the largest army in Europe, over three times the size of the French metropolitan force. This call to the colors and the other activities associated with the preparation for war, such as the transportation of Italian laborers for construction work in east Africa, had the result of decreasing the number of unemployed in Italy from a January 1935 total of 1,011,711 to 638,100 in June.[58] The Italian-Ethiopian conflict was succeeding as outlet for the discontents within Fascist Italy.

The demographic and economic arguments presented by Fascist propagandists to justify the coming war were largely smokescreens. The main claim was that colonial expansion was caused by the pressures of a surplus population. Certainly at the beginning of 1935 there was a social problem in Italy: there were more people than there were jobs. In earlier times emigration was the answer for many to this chronic problem of domestic poverty. But there were now new restrictions on emigration. Since the 1920s some nations, notably the United States, had closed their doors to Italian immigrants. Still, other countries remained open and opportunities for employment were to be found outside Italy. During this period, however, Mussolini raised his own domestic obstacles to emigration, making it a crime to leave the country for long periods, punishable by imprisonment and loss of citizenship.[59] Emigration was represented as a battle lost every year by Italy. Furthermore, Mussolini did nothing to limit Italy's population growth at home. On the contrary, the Duce was determined to increase Italy's birth rate, despite what this did to aggravate the persistent imbalance between the men and resources in Italy. Large families were officially encouraged, with Mussolini himself setting an example; birth control

[56] Mussolini, *Opera omnia*, XXVII, 293.

[57] E. Polson Newman, *Italy's Conquest of Abyssinia* (London, 1937), 63.

[58] League, *Statistical Year-Book, 1935–36*, 60.

[59] Emigration did fall off compared to pre-Fascist levels. See D. Kirk, *Europe's Population in the Interwar Years* (Princeton, 1946), 284–5. Charles Delzell also gives statistics that show a spurt of emigration soon after the Fascists came to power, a tapering off when Mussolini imposed his retrictions, another spurt when the depression hit. The Ethiopian war soaked up remaining dissidents and the unemployed. Here are emigration figures for selected years: 1921, 201,000; 1923, 390,000; 1929, 150,000; 1930, 280,000; 1936, 42,000. C. Delzell, *Mussolini's Enemies: The Italian Anti-Fascist Resistance* (Princeton, 1961), 44. Emigrants from Fascist Italy were called *fuorusciti* by the Fascists.

became a crime; and penalties were leveled against celibacy.[60] In these circumstances it is not surprising that "population pressure" should develop to plague the Fascist regime. The interesting fact for our story is that, as a means of absorbing the unemployed who sought to emigrate, Mussolini decided not to work for the widespread internal expansion of the economy, but rather chose to solve Italy's problems through militant imperialism. Military action abroad and a supporting war economy at home would, it was expected, use up the unemployed energies of the nation. A warrior state and a war overseas would discipline and unite Italians in a patriotic cause, under the leadership of the Duce. And, the claim was put forward, new land for settlement would solve the problem of wasteful Italian emigration.

A Fascist argument for colonies was that Italians could seek land and fortunes on Italian territory, under their own flag, and thus prevent the annual national loss from emigration. Mussolini, with his romantic notion of a nation of small farmers, hoped that the colonization of Ethiopia would provide an outlet for the land-hungry Italian peasantry. There was no valid basis for this hope, the very idea of which was economically unsound. Colonialism has rarely solved the demographic problems of a nation, and African colonialism was no better economic alternative than domestic reform. Certainly Italy's own experience in modern times lent no support to the arguments for colonialism in east Africa.

Italian expansion into its possessions of Libya, Eritrea, and Somalia had been entirely artificial and unprofitable. The government lacked the experience and the capital necessary to build up an undeveloped area. Nor did the people of Italy have sufficient funds to set up farms in remote Africa. Italian emigrants did not desire to go overseas to become farmers in backward and inhospitable countries. They went to wealthy nations where wages for manual labor were high. Prior Italian efforts to settle the Eritrean plateau with farmers from the peninsula were complete failures.[61] In 1931 there were only 84 Italians living on the Asmara plateau who were engaged in agriculture. Before

---

[60] Mussolini once told Aloisi that he intended to dismiss any unmarried diplomat over the age of 35 years, unless the man married at once. Aloisi, *Journal*, 5–6. Bachelors were heavily taxed. For an important discussion of Italy's population, see G. Salvemini, "Can Italy Live at Home?" *Foreign Affairs*, 14:243–58 (January 1936).

[61] For a detailed account of this, see the report of Corrado Zoli, a governor of Eritrea: "L'Avvaloramento agraria dell'Eritrea," *Rassegna italiana*, 26:203–17 (May–June 1930).

the conflict with Ethiopia, there were in all Eritrea only 4,500 Italian civilians, of whom only about 400 were adult settlers. Italian Somaliland, which after thirty years of direct rule still faced a large annual deficit, had less than 2,000 Italian residents. Before 1935 the Italian government ignored these overseas nationals and abandoned them "to their own devices," in De Bono's delicate phrase. The some 10,000 soldiers present in Eritrea and the 6,000 troops in Somalia before the war, sufficient only to maintain local order, wc¬e a financial drain.[62] The assertion that the Italian colonies were "developed to full capacity," and that new lands had to be found, is entirely false.[63] Without massive governmental support, more than Italy could reasonably afford, would Italians who avoided Eritrea be any more inclined to go to Ethiopia?

There was no assurance that Ethiopia, if colonized, would become a profitable venture. The cost of developing the country, let alone the cost of conquering it and maintaining order, would be so high that no return on the investment would be forthcoming for years, regardless of the wealth expected to be found there.[64] And there was no certainty that many of the anticipated riches, such as oil, actually existed. To furnish the capital necessary for large-scale development of any of Ethiopia's natural resources would bleed Italy severely, at a time when the home country could ill afford to pay the price. In Salvemini's words, "the conquest of Ethiopia, far from remedying the lack of balance between population and resources, would aggravate it." [65]

In any case, economics was not the primary causal factor in the conquest of Ethiopia, nor was the matter of population.[66] Mussolini

[62] Lord Lugard, "The Basis of the Claim for Colonies," *International Affairs*, 15.1:5 (January–February 1936); Salvemini, "Can Italy Live at Home?" 247; Jacini, *Il Regime fascista*, 154; I. Lewis, *The Modern History of Somaliland* (London, 1965), 100–1; De Bono, *Anno XIIII*, 32; A. Tosti, *Storia dell'esercito italiano, 1861–1936* (Milan, 1942), 294. Zoli in *La Tribuna* of 10 May 1935 gave figures of 5,000 troops in each colony.

[63] The assertion is made by L. Villari, "Abyssinia and Italy — The Italian Case," *Journal of the (Royal) African Society*, 34:372 (October 1935).

[64] In the four years Italy did have control of Ethiopia the Italian government spent some 5 billion lire in non-military, non-constabulary expenditures alone. Most of this money went for road construction. L. Pignatelli, *Le Guerra dei sette mesi* (Naples, 1961), 8.

[65] Salvemini, "Can Italy Live at Home?" 246.

[66] This was admitted by Edmondo Rossoni, minister of agriculture and forests, and a member of the Fascist Grand Council. "The Abyssinian war perhaps has economic reasons. But chiefly the reasons are moral and political. France did not acquire colonies because she was overpopulated. Nor did England . . . Italy can make new contributions to civilization. It must carry civilization to the world." L. Fischer, *Men and Politics* (New York, 1941), 276–7.

undertook the Ethiopian campaign as a means of glorifying the Fascist regime. Only in this context can the enterprise be properly understood.[67] Only by realizing that this campaign was a vital political matter can one understand why Mussolini took the risks he did in international affairs.

The month of June opened with a meeting of the Italian-Ethiopian arbitral commission. Contrary to the usual practice of meeting on neutral soil, and lacking directions on the meeting site, at the end of May the four members of the commission agreed among themselves that the first meeting would take place in Milan on 6 June.

Several obstacles stood in the way of swift action. The treaty of 1928 and the council's resolutions of 25 May contained ambiguities that gave rise to confusion over the procedure to be followed and the committee's sphere of competence. Article 5 of the treaty of 1928 spoke of resort to "a procedure of conciliation or arbitration" — "conciliazione o arbitrato" in the original text. The two processes are different, of course, and it was not clear from the enabling agreements which was to be conducted first or if both were to be undertaken simultaneously. The most expedient method is to use the two procedures successively, conciliation first followed by arbitration if necessary. But from the Ethiopian standpoint conciliation, which presupposed a minor incident, limited territorial ambitions, and basic friendship, was out of the question. The present dispute was too serious, and for the Ethiopians only arbitration was possible.[68] This clashed with the Italians' position that conciliatory negotiations should be undertaken first, in the hope that the proceedings could be stretched out to the limit of diplomatic tolerance. The confusion was not lessened by the fact that, though the League often and the Ethiopian government always referred to the commission as one of arbitration and to its members as arbitrators, the League, to describe the commission formally, also continued to use the puzzling designation that joined the two different procedures together.

Potter and La Pradelle, the Ethiopian nominees, did their best to

---

[67] Practical Americans failed to understand this dimension. Secretary of State Cordell Hull asked the Italian ambassador in November 1935 why Italy had not taken $100 million to Ethiopia and brought back the key to the entire empire instead of spending several hundred millions in a military conquest "with all of the worry and threat of danger to the balance of the world." *U.S. Diplomatic Papers, 1935*, I, 832.

[68] La Pradelle, *Le Conflit italo-éthiopien*, 171.

clarify the matter. They pointed out that they did not regard themselves, nor were they so appointed or instructed, as the diplomatic
representatives of Ethiopia. Hence they were not qualified to undertake the process of conciliation. They made an explicit effort, beginning in Milan, to have the proceedings regarded entirely as arbitration.[69] But the confusion remained, and it was to the Italians' advantage to delay settlement of the question for as long as possible. It
is to be remembered that the Italian members of the commission were
not neutral free agents, but employees carrying out the instructions
of their government.

Also missing was a formal *compromis* governing the process of arbitration.[70] There was no definition of the jurisdiction of the commission, no decision on a place of meeting, the means of proceeding, the
language to be used, the methods of pleading. The issue before the
commission was never authoritatively defined. The commission was
to determine the responsibility for the outbreak of the fighting at
Walwal, but it was not decided whether this also meant that it could
render a decision or hand down an award. Most important of all was
the question of whether or not the commission could take into account the juridical status of the territory in which Walwal was
located. This might or might not be decisive in a determination of
responsibility.[71] The Italian government, we have seen, was determined to keep this matter of ownership out of the discussion. Potter
hoped there could be some general determination of the boundary
as it affected the political status of Walwal, but this central issue
remained in doubt.

These matters were not settled at the meetings in Milan on 6 and
7 June. The commission now requested the governments concerned
to submit documents and statements in support of their positions. A

[69] Potter, *Wal Wal Arbitration*, 22.

[70] La Pradelle in retrospect felt that an authentic peaceful solution of the dispute could have come about only through direct negotiation with Italy by
the governments of Britain and France. "The simplest way to understand the
role of the commission of conciliation or arbitration, to which the League of
Nations had given its trust, was that it should assure a continuity from point
to point, from 25 May to 25 July, then to 25 August, so that, parallelly, mediation by the signatories of the 1906 agreement would be able to exercise itself."
The commission's job was to provide a regulated period of delay, to "gain
the time which would enable the *true conciliators* to conclude their task." La
Pradelle, *Le Conflit italo-éthiopien*, 170–2.

[71] Potter, *Wal Wal Arbitration*, 24–6; *U.S. Diplomatic Papers, 1935*, I, 606–7.
For a fascinating study of the question of possession, see La Pradelle, *Le Conflit
italo-éthiopien*, 550–60.

secretariat for the commission was created, consisting of Raymond de G. de La Pradelle, son of the senior Ethiopian-appointed arbitrator, and three officials of the Italian government. The composition of the Italian group gave further proof that the commission's proceedings would be treated merely as a branch of Italy's general diplomacy in regard to Ethiopia. It included Giovanni B. Guarnaschelli, director of African affairs at the Italian foreign ministry and a party to all policy decisions in Rome; Enrico Cerulli, adviser to the minister of colonies and a well-known student of Ethiopia; and Captain A. Zanchi of the Italian army. After creating the secretariat, the commission agreed to meet again on 25 June at Scheveningen, a suburb of The Hague. The meeting adjourned, and the members separated on the evening of 7 June.

Chapter 8

June: British Vacillations

In the first week of June, new governments were constituted in Britain and France. In London MacDonald stepped down and Stanley Baldwin, long the power within the National government, took office as prime minister now in name as well as in fact. Simon, who had found it so difficult to devise a foreign policy, was shifted to the Home Office. The successor to the "damnosa hereditas" [1] at the Foreign Office was Sir Samuel Hoare. It had been generally assumed that the post would go to Anthony Eden, the rising young politician who had made a public name for himself as an advocate of the principles of collective security through the League of Nations. But at the last moment before the reconstruction of the Cabinet, Hoare's nomination had been pressed on Baldwin by men of influence: Geoffrey Dawson (editor of *The Times*), Lord Lothian, and Neville Chamberlain. They respected Hoare's ability at reconciliation and mediation and knew his sympathies to be close to theirs and to Baldwin's. They contended too that Hoare had prior claim to the post. He had just completed the long and burdensome task of creating and shepherding through Commons the Government of India bill, and the Foreign Office was the reward he should get for his labors. [2]

The choice of Hoare at this time was unfortunate. His health was

[1] So Walford Selby described it, in *Diplomatic Twilight*, 48.
[2] Avon, *Facing the Dictators*, 219; Templewood, *Nine Troubled Years*, 108. Hoare's work on the bill was Herculean. The bill took years to formulate, and a measure of its size can be gauged from Hoare's description of his efforts in the House of Commons. He had, Hoare said, seen its "473 clauses and 16 Schedules through all the critical stages, and I made the greater part of the 1951 speeches that, with their fifteen and a half million words, had filled four thousand pages of Hansard." Templewood, *Nine Troubled Years*, 100, 109. Baldwin's great interest in the India bill is noted in Young, *Stanley Baldwin*, 186–9.

not good, and he was greatly in need of a rest. His efforts had left him "physically weak and mentally tired." [3] And there was another, personal, dimension to Hoare that was to prove of great importance. In a significant piece of self-analysis, written, interestingly enough, in the third person, Hoare speaks of himself as

> someone who is very sensitive, perhaps over sensitive, to his environment . . . One of his most persistent failings has been the habit of retiring into his shell in unsympathetic atmospheres and leaving his opponents to their own devices. This sensibility had another bad effect. It has often made him tire of an enterprise before it was fully completed . . . someone of quiet and conventional habits, who hates extremes and, true to the tradition of all bankers who never go to law, prefers to agree with his adversary whilst he is in the way with him . . . this cautious and unaggressive mentality . . . In all these activities he was anxious to see quick and concrete results, and to achieve even a part of his objective he was usually ready to accept a compromise. This very English habit of compromise has sometimes landed him in trouble, and it may be that excessive sensibility has exaggerated the dangers of more resolute action. [4]

Most important, Hoare was inexperienced in the broader reaches of foreign affairs. The four years spent with the India bill, in the "almost Trappist seclusion of the India Office," left him woefully ill-informed on the political situation elsewhere. He often had failed to attend the meetings of the Cabinet. When the permanent undersecretary at the Foreign Office, Robert Vansittart, undertook to lecture him on the German danger, this was Hoare's reaction: "Coming as I did from the distant world of India, the fervid recitation of [Vansittart's] faith at first shocked me. I had not before realized the imminence of the German menace, and the slowness of our rearmament programme." Impresssionable as always, Hoare learned and accepted Vansittart's argument: "We are terribly weak. We must gain time for becoming stronger. Only military strength will stop Hitler, and at present we do not possess it." [5]

This weakness of Britain's armed forces greatly influenced the

[3] Templewood, *Nine Troubled Years*, 109.

[4] Viscount Templewood, *Ambassador on Special Mission* (London, 1946), 10. Even Hoare's new surroundings at the Foreign Office, with its huge and uncozy salon for the minister, depressed him. Templewood, *Nine Troubled Years*, 137.

[5] The extent of Hoare's ignorance in things Ethiopian may perhaps be judged from the fact that, writing in the mid-1950s, Hoare still held that Walwal was "situated in what had been recognized in fact as part of the Italian colony." Templewood, *Nine Troubled Years*, 108, 138, 150.

makers of British foreign policy during the 1930s. By 1935 British hopes for a stable and peaceable postwar world had been undermined by the rise in power of two ambitious nations, Japan and Germany. In the face of these potentially dangerous conditions, the British armed services, the army and air force much reduced since the war and the navy limited in its size by international agreements, were simply not strong enough to meet Britain's large responsibilities for defense at home and overseas. In February 1933 the British chiefs of staff submitted a memorandum to the Cabinet which stated: "The whole of our territory in the Far East as well as the coast-line of India and the Dominions and our vast trade and shipping is open to attack." [6] There was a fear that Japan might take advantage of Britain's weakness to move in on these vital interests. Until the naval base at Singapore was better fortified, and this would not be completed until 1936 or 1937, protection for the British fleet in the Far East could not be assured.[7] As a matter of imperial defense, it was essential to keep open and secure the main route to the east, so that the British navy could be moved there with the greatest rapidity if the need arose. Lord Chatfield, then First Sea Lord, wrote:

> our naval limitations, resulting from the London Naval Treaty of 1930, were such as to make it quite impossible to fight successfully in Europe and in the Far East simultaneously, unless a friendly (or neutral) Italy was assured. The Mediterranean was our main line of communications with India, Australia and New Zealand. Any act therefore which was likely to create for us a hostile nation in the Mediterranean . . . was directly opposed to naval strategic interests.[8]

And there was now a new danger closer to home to add to the strain on Britain's limited armed force. A rearming Germany presented a threat to the political settlement of Europe and to the security of the United Kingdom itself. Early in 1934 a report issued by a special subcommittee of the Committee of Imperial Defence concluded that the "ultimate potential enemy" of Britain was not Japan but Germany. Just as the Admiralty wanted an expanded navy to deal

---

[6] Cited in D. C. Watt, *Personalities and Policies: Studies in the Formulation of British Foreign Policy in the Twentieth Century* (South Bend, 1965), 84.

[7] S. W. Kirby, *The War Against Japan* (London, 1957), I, 10–13.

[8] Lord Ernle Chatfield, *The Navy and Defence*, II: *It Might Happen Again* (London, 1947), 89.

with imperial security, so air rearmament at home was considered imperative to put Britain in a defensible condition relative to Germany. Against Germany, the report said, "we have time, but not too much time, to make preparations." [9]

The extent and pace of rearmament was a matter for political decision, the responsibility of the Cabinet. Given the unpopularity of rearmament among the electorate of Britain, and the reluctance of the Cabinet then to undertake a large-scale program, it would be several years at best before Britain's military weakness could be overcome. The job of the Foreign Secretary, taking the limitations of Britain's strength into account, was to conduct a foreign policy for the protection of Britain's interests through diplomatic means. Samuel Hoare, when he came into office in June 1935, considered it his task to "gain time for becoming strong." This was not a bad policy; indeed, it was a sensible one. But it led, as Vansittart saw, toward appeasement of Italy. The proponents of the effort to gain time did not want to take a firm stand against Mussolini over Ethiopia. In almost any calculation of Britain's strategic interests, Italian friendship was valuable. A friendly, or at least a neutral, Italy would assure a stable Mediterranean, which meant that extra units of the British fleet would not have to be tied up there. On the continent, an Italian ally, maintained in the spirit of the Stresa front, might provide an opposing force to Germany in the south.

The problem with the Italian-Ethiopian affair was that it involved the League of Nations. The Covenant required the League's members to take action against an aggressor state and so imposed the obligation to apply sanctions against Italy if Italy attacked Ethiopia. It was now clear that Britain would soon be faced with the choice either of fulfilling its obligations to the League or of appeasing Italy. The effect of either decision would be to cause serious, if not irreparable, damage to European efforts to contain Germany. The League would be doomed if Italy were not punished; Italy would be lost to the democracies if the required sanctions were imposed.

In London, Vansittart and the proponents of gaining time for Britain's rearmament were prepared to scuttle the League, if nec-

---

[9] There was a fear that at the outbreak of a war Germany would deal a "knock-out blow" to Britain from the air. The Cabinet was urged to strengthen the air force. B. Collier, *The Defence of the United Kingdom* (London, 1957), 25–6; W. Hancock and M. Gowing, *British War Economy* (London, 1949), 64.

essary, in order to avoid a conflict with Italy.[10] Vansittart, obsessed by the German menace, argued that Britain's choice was "between Austria and Abyssinia," between Italy and the League, and he opted for Austria and Italy.[11] But there were other counsels at the Foreign Office, pressing different arguments on the new secretary. Opposing Vansittart's view were supporters of the League, and they had, it appeared, a friend in power. An extraordinary situation existed at the Foreign Office. While making Hoare foreign minister, Baldwin had at the same time contrived a special post for Eden. He created a new ministry, "for League of Nations Affairs," and put Eden at its head. This gave Eden membership in the Cabinet and made him, at least in the public eye, almost coequal to the foreign secretary. League affairs were after all foreign affairs, and the two could not be separated.[12]

Too much should not be made of this apparent duality in the Foreign Office. Eden could not contrive or follow a foreign policy different from Hoare's. Eden worked within the Foreign Office; he did not have a separate ministerial bureaucracy. And although in the system of cabinet government it is the Cabinet that must assume the final responsibility, in Baldwin's Cabinet of the last half of 1935 Samuel Hoare was left largely on his own to create and carry out foreign policy. As we shall see, it was primarily Hoare who set Britain's course in League of Nations affairs, with Eden acting as the government's agent.

But Baldwin's decision to include Eden in the Cabinet had one important consequence. Eden's office by its very nature caused him to concentrate most of his attention on the Italian-Ethiopian conflict, and thus this matter was given a public prominance that caused it and League affairs to weigh more heavily in political considerations than many members of the government would have liked. Certainly, in the

---

[10] The British politician Leopold S. Amery wrote in his diary at the time: "The best feature in the new arrangement is putting Sam [Hoare] at the F. O. where he will have all his work cut out clearing up the mess into which Eden has got us over Abyssinia. I shall look forward to September when Eden will be sent to Geneva with orders to unsay all his high talk of last month about coercing Italy to respect the 'collective system.' That is, if Sam wins, as I expect he will, though Eden will have strong Cabinet backing." Amery told Hoare, a few days later, "that his one task was to pull back Eden by his coat tails, and thought that he [Hoare] fully understood the danger to Stresa and to European peace." Amery, *My Political Life*, III, 168.

[11] Vansittart, *The Mist Procession*, 522.

[12] See Avon, *Facing the Dictators*, 218.

public's opinion, Eden's appointment, coming at a time when the League was facing its greatest trial, made the government appear to be standing four-square behind the Covenant.

Such a policy seemed to appeal to the majority of the British electorate, and the government, with an election not far off, was well aware of the political advantage to be gained by having the young and popular Eden at his new post.[13] On the other hand, the British electorate was unenlightened about what a pro-League policy would mean in practice. They saw in the League a means to certain peace. Although Baldwin had stated in the House of Commons in May 1934 that "there is no such thing as a sanction that will work that does not mean war, or, in other words, if you are going to adopt a sanction you must be prepared for war," [14] the people at large did not see collective security in this light. The government never sufficiently instructed them by explaining that a pro-League policy might lead to the use of force and that this might have serious consequences for British national security.

Sanctions against Italy would have to be imposed primarily by the British fleet. Sanctions might lead to a conflict with Italy that would endanger the route to the east, the stability of the Mediterranean, and possibly bring about Italian attacks on British bases and British ships. The fleet would be tied up in blockading Italy and fighting the Italian navy. The Admiralty had no ships to spare for such an enterprise far from the scenes of other, more pressing dangers and dreaded the losses that might ensue.

There were other difficulties to be considered. Would Japan take advantage of Britain's involvement in the Mediterranean to act aggressively in the east? Would the security of Australia or India be jeopardized by a further weakening of Britain's defensive capability? What would be the reaction of the United States, with whom Britain sought to be on good terms? The United States insisted on free trade and free movement on the seas, and American ships might become involved in any blockade of Italy. Baldwin had this worry in mind when he said on 23 November 1934: "Never so long as I have any responsibility in governing this country, will I sanction the British Navy being used for an armed blockade of any country in the world

[13] In Randolph Churchill's opinion, Baldwin intended to keep Eden in "tutelage" and not give him much power in the shaping of policy. R. Churchill, *The Rise and Fall of Sir Anthony Eden* (London, 1959), 88.

[14] *Parliamentary Debates*, 289 H. C. Deb. 5s., col. 2139.

until I know what the United States of America is going to do." [15]
And what about the Dominions? Would Canada, drawing increasingly
into isolationism, come to Britain's aid in a conflict so far from Canadian shores? Would the other Dominions support a League action in
Europe that weakened Britain's position in the east? These were some
of the questions posed by the Italian-Ethiopian conflict that the British government, if not the uninstructed British electorate, had to face.

In any event, Eden's appointment as minister of League of Nations
affairs did not mean that the British Cabinet was prepared to take the
lead in upholding the Covenant against an Italian violation. Baldwin,
the prime minister, "never whole-heartedly believed in the League
of Nations as an effective force in the affairs of the world. Though
he could speak beautifully about the Assembly . . . he would never
take the few miles' journey from Aix to Geneva to see it in action.
But to acknowledge his disbelief was to invite political extinction." [16]
Hoare, like Simon before him, quailed before the thought that Britain
might get involved in a conflict with Italy. If the makers of British
policy had been more imaginative, they might have created, as Vansittart hoped, a policy concentrating on Germany and based on national
self-interest apart from the League. There was still an outside chance,
at the beginning of June 1935, that appeasement would work with
Mussolini, if Hoare could make the issue clear to himself and followed through the anti-German line. But the British government was
now constrained by political considerations and ministerial commitment, as well as by principle, at least to pay lip service to the Covenant.

Here was Hoare's dilemma. Newly arrived at the Foreign Office,
puzzled, indecisive, he found to his dismay two "diametrically opposed views" being pressed upon him.[17] The two policies he wanted
to follow, avoidance of a conflict with Italy and support of the
League, appeared incompatible. Unable to choose between them,

---

[15] Quoted in A. W. Baldwin, *My Father: The True Story* (London, 1955), 207.

[16] Young, *Baldwin*, 173. There is an insightful portrait of Baldwin's pacifism
and his disinterest in foreign affairs in F. Williams, *A Pattern of Rulers* (London, 1965), 5–59.

[17] Templewood, *Nine Troubled Years*, 137. It was later written of Hoare:
"There is no more forlorn spectacle in politics than that of a statesman strug-
gling with circumstances of adversity, perplexity and peril for which neither his
previous training and experience nor his temperament has prepared him."
J. Robertson (J. Connell, pseud.), *The 'Office', a Study of British Foreign Policy
and Its Makers, 1919–1951* (London, 1958), 178.

Hoare decided to follow both courses at once.[18] In the event, he acted ineptly. Hoare took a League line to the extent of alienating Mussolini, but not far enough to strengthen the League — not far enough either to prevent aggression in Ethiopia or to contain Germany — because he did not believe in the League's effectiveness and he was afraid of a conflict with Italy. He tried to appease Mussolini only part way, because appeasement conflicted with the stated principles of the League and above all with the opinion of the people of Britain.

On 7 June a significant exchange took place in the House of Commons. Clement Attlee spoke for the opposition.

> What has happened is that the procedure for the settlement of part of that dispute has been established, but military preparations on the part of Italy still go on . . . This matter gets worse the longer it is allowed to drag on. One has to face up to the position of Italy. We have there a country ruled by a dictator and a Government that is in urgent need of something to take off the tension from its internal situation and to reestablish its prestige. There is very serious unemployment in Italy, an almost desperate financial situation, rising prices, declining foreign trade, and a considerable volume of criticism of the existing regime. In such circumstances, it is not uncommon to find an attempt being made to divert attention from discontents at home by interests abroad.
>
> What was actually accomplished at Geneva was that some kind of breathing space was obtained, a time limit for conciliation and arbitration, but there were certain very important defects in that agreement . . . Italy has not renounced the use of force. Preparations go on and troops are constantly used to meet the situation . . . This incident, this tension between Italy and Abyssinia, is a test of the reality of the League and the sanctity of the Covenant of the League . . . There is today, I believe, a great opportunity in this incident for reestablishing the authority of the League and the rule of law in Europe. We require a clear statement by our Government. We want to tell Signor Mussolini that among the political realities of which he has to take account is that this Government, like other Governments, uphold the Covenant against an aggressor state, that it believes it is a matter that affects our honour and our vital interests, that the refusal to accept the League's authority constitutes a refusal by an aggressor . . .

[18] Harold Nicolson wrote: "There was much to be said for a League of Nations policy, even as there was much to be said for a rapid return to the Balance of Power. But the two policies were mutually exclusive; to seek to combine them was to court disaster." Nicolson, *George V*, 528.

The vital point in this matter is the question of the control of the Suez Canal. If Italy were to count on the fact that the League would not act if she intended to use force, she ought to be told frankly that in the event she would not have the use of the Suez Canal. This is really a vital matter, and it ought to be decided at once . . . The matter has already drifted on too far . . . The League will be destroyed altogether if, within the circle of the League, powers are enabled to carry out Imperialist, filibustering, enterprises.[19]

Eden made the government's reply. The gist of his speech was that there was no cause for alarm. Italy, by accepting article 5 of the treaty of 1928, had agreed not to resort to force. There was no reason to believe otherwise: afterall, it was a "cardinal principle of British law that a man is innocent until he is proven guilty." Britain wanted and was working for a "permanent settlement mutually satisfactory to Italy and Ethiopia." The government hoped, Eden said, that such a settlement would be achieved and that it would lie within the framework of the governing treaties, the Covenant, the Kellogg-Briand Pact, and the 1928 treaty. Eden made the point that the League was scheduled to meet if the arbitration commission should fail in its task.[20]

Eden's speech was markedly friendly to Italy. Attlee's warnings and demands went unheeded. Little emphasis was placed on the position of the League in the dispute, and there was no comment about the Suez Canal or the possibility of sanctions. Most of Eden's reply was taken up with denying that Britain had any interests in Ethiopia that would lead to the frustration of Italian ambitions there.[21]

Conciliatory words had no effect on Mussolini. He was angered by the reproaches he was receiving from Englishmen, and by the persistence with which they butted into his business. The day following the exchange in the House of Commons, Mussolini spoke at Cagliari to the Sabauda division of the army as it prepared to set sail for east Africa. His remarks were directed at the British.

We have both old and new accounts to settle: we shall settle them. We shall pay no heed to what may be said abroad, for we are the

[19] *Parliamentary Debates*, 302 H.C. Deb. 5s., cols. 2193–5. This talk about closing the Suez Canal aroused considerable concern in Rome, and members of the Italian government began to study ways of offsetting such a move — by arguments from international law. Guariglia, *Ricordi*, 238.

[20] *Parliamentary Debates*, 302 H.C. Deb. 5s., cols. 2208–10.

[21] Aloisi approved Eden's reply to Attlee, seeing it as "a visible effort to settle things." *Journal*, 279.

only judges of our interests and the only guarantors of our future, we ourselves alone, and no one else. We shall take a leaf out of the book of those who are lecturing us. They have shown that when an empire was to be created or defended they themselves paid no heed to world opinion.

On 10 June, retorting to a statement made by Baldwin on the 8th that there was no popular support in Italy for the Ethiopian campaign, Mussolini, reviewing troops at Sassari, stated: "public opinion abroad is only a ridiculous puppet which will be burnt with the ardor of the Blackshirts." He repeated Italy's claim to independent action and Italy's determination to act alone.[22]

These speeches represent a new bellicosity in Mussolini's public orations. Now that the council meeting of late May was past and there seemed no further danger of League action until the autumn, the Duce no longer restrained himself.[23] After June, fired by his own determination, by his anger at being underrated abroad, by the threats against Italy of the use of some sort of sanction, and above all by his need to arouse popular support, Mussolini's speeches became ever more uncompromising. There is no surer sign that Mussolini had passed the point of no return than that, from this period on, he increasingly committed himself publicly to a collision course. An example of Mussolini's confidence at this time is that he requested a study to determine, in accordance with Ethiopian custom and history, what would be the best way of proclaiming the king of Italy as emperor of Ethiopia.[24]

At the beginning of June, Italian diplomats carried on as usual, turning their attention to Geneva, concerned with finding ways to neutralize any hostility that might materialize there. Opinion in Rome favored Italy's remaining in the League. Such a position was not without its paradoxical aspect, as Aloisi noted in his diary on 7 June:

> We have always been hostile to [the League], and at this moment it is in our favor. It absorbs the blows we should receive and, in the last analysis, will permit us to go forward in our designs on Abyssinia without excessive embarrassment. The League is under the command

[22] Mussolini, *Opera omnia*, XXVII, 84–6; Lessona, *Verso l'impero*, 127.
[23] Reale, *La Politique étrangère du fascisme*, 32.
[24] Guariglia, *Ricordi*, 239. Before Aduwa, Crispi had informed the *Almanach de Gotha* that the name Ethiopia would soon disappear from the map; silver coins had been struck, showing the king of Italy wearing the imperial crown of Ethiopia. Mack Smith, *Italy*, 182, 185.

of Britain. No one there dares contradict the British will. All the nations remain calmly behind the windshield of Britain. Britain fears an actual Anglo-Italian conflict, which if it became too acute, would mean that Italy would leave the League and thus break the powerful instrument which Britain has in its hands.[25]

British domination was what Italy had always railed against at Geneva. Now this very factor was what, Aloisi thought, would keep the League from acting against Italy, as long as Italy remained a member. Rome did not understimate the value of the League for delay and distraction.

If there were good arguments for remaining at Geneva, could anything be done about actually bringing the League over to the Italian side? A lead here came from none other than Joseph Avenol, the secretary-general. In conversation with Alberto Theoldi, Avenol presented an intriguing proposal.

The problem Italy faced, said Avenol, was to work a change in British public opinion. The way to do this was to discredit Ethiopia in the eyes of the British and before the League. Assuming the verdict of the commission investigating the Walwal incident would be favorable to Italy, Italy should then go immediately before the League and denounce Ethiopia as a bad and troublesome neighbor, accuse the emperor's government of being unable to maintain internal order, condemn it for allowing slaveholding, and repressing subject peoples, and prove the country deficient in the knowledge and practice of civilization. By this tactic the position of Ethiopia as a worthy member of the League would be cast in doubt; even expulsion might follow. The people of Britain and France would come to see Ethiopia, and Italy's civilizing mission, in a new light. They would no longer demand of their governments support for the Covenant, for Ethiopia would be viewed as a barbarous state beyond the pale of civilized peoples. The governments of Britain and France would then be able to maintain a commitment to the League, for use in Europe, without feeling compelled to protest or impede Italy's imperial conquest.

This idea was given serious consideration in Rome. Although the Italians did not share Avenol's optimism, the tactic recommended itself as a means of propaganda. Avenol's proposal was the source of the Italian argument of "continual aggression" used against Ethiopia and contained in the voluminous memorandum presented to the League

[25] Aloisi, *Journal,* 279.

on 4 September 1935 — the major propaganda statement of the Italian government in the course of the conflict.[26]

On 18 June 1935, to the astonishment of the world, there was announced in London the conclusion of a naval agreement between Great Britain and Germany. The British government gave its formal approval to the construction of a German warship fleet of a weight up to 35 percent of the total tonnage of the British navy and approved a German submarine force equal to the tonnage of the forces of the Commonwealth nations. The argument for this accord was that, if Germany was going to rearm, it would be better to put a limit on the quantity of arms it would be allowed. In this way another expensive, escalating arms race, such as had preceded the world war, would be avoided. The notion of allowing Germany arms was part of the general British opinion that Germany had a right to great-power status and could no longer be kept shackled by the chains of Versailles. It was felt that the surest way to guarantee some control over German rearmament was to give it a clearly defined limit from the beginning so that, even when rearmament came to pass, the Western countries would still be assured of military superiority. Whether one thought, as did those who agreed with Dawson and *The Times*, that the time had come to end old enmities, to stop treating Germany as a beaten foe, and to bring the country back into the community of nations, or believed, as did Vansittart and the British naval command, that in the absence of any determination by the Western powers to stop German rearmament it would be best to contain it under favorable terms by treaty, the naval agreement was supported by the British government and the British people.[27]

The proposal for the agreement had come from Germany and was accepted by Simon. When Hoare took over the Foreign Office on 7 June, the first document he found on his desk was the completed agreement, waiting to be signed. Joachim von Ribbentrop, the German sponsor, was already in town for the ceremony. Hoare, who accepted Vansittart's viewpoint in favor of the agreement, wanted first to solicit opinions from the world's other naval powers. The

[26] Guariglia, *Ricordi*, 241–3.
[27] For the Navy's defense of the treaty, see Chatfield, *The Navy and Defence*, II, 73–6; Kirby, *The War Against Japan*, 13.

United States replied that the matter was up to the British; Japan had no objections. No direct answer came from Italy and France. Ribbentrop became restless with the delay and threatened to go home. Thinking that he was acting in the best interests of France and Italy, and hurried on by the "black cloud that overhung Abyssinia," Hoare agreed, not unwillingly, to sign.[28]

For Germany the agreement was a brilliant success. The German naval staff was entirely satisfied with its terms. They did not believe that Germany could achieve a larger tonnage than that permitted before ten years were out. But the real success for Germany lay in the political sphere. A memorandum prepared for the commander of the German navy read: "As a result of the Agreement the most powerful of our former enemies and of the signatories of the Versailles Treaty has formally invalidated an important part of this Treaty and formally recognized Germany's equality of rights. The danger of Germany's being isolated, which definitely threatened in March and April of this year, has been eliminated."[29] Hitler had been frightened by the Stresa front. Now this grouping against him was destroyed. It was "Hitler's greatest victory to date," and he called the day the agreement was signed the happiest day of his life.[30]

Italy had only a secondary interest in the military aspect of this pact, since the spheres of action of the German and Italian fleets lay far apart. The Italians were interested most of all in the political repercussions of the agreement.[31] The Italians did think they should have been more thoroughly consulted, and to this extent the British departure from the Stresa front annoyed them.[32] But Italy's response was not shot through with fear as France's was. Mussolini had given

[28] Templewood, *Nine Troubled Years*, 141–2, 149; Eden's explanation recorded in Aloisi, *Journal*, 281; J. von Ribbentrop, *The Ribbentrop Memoirs*, G. Watson, trans. (London, 1954), 40–1.

[29] *Documents on German Foreign Policy*, IV, 587–8.

[30] G. Craig, "The German Foreign Office from Neurath to Ribbentrop," in Craig and Gilbert, eds., *The Diplomats, 1919–1939*, 424; Ribbentrop, *Memoirs*, 41; Mallet, *Laval*, I, 79; Gamelin, *Servir*, II, 171.

[31] See Suvich's comments to Hassel of 21 June, *Documents on German Foreign Policy*, IV, 335.

[32] Templewood, *Nine Troubled Years*, 145. A press dispatch was prepared by Mussolini for release on 20 June in which the Italians took Britain to task for acting alone in this delicate matter: "Italy was not informed of this in advance." The unilateral action was scornfully contrasted with Britain's recent espousal of "the so-called collective security system." This Italian dispatch was never released in deference to Eden's forthcoming visit to Rome. M. Toscano, "Eden a Roma alla vigilia del conflitto italo-etiopico," *Nuova antologia*, 478:25n (January 1960).

up hope for a solid Western stand against Hitler Germany. The naval agreement only confirmed the suspicion and resentment he felt toward Britain. If the agreement gave the final blow to the Stresa front, it was because the front was already crumbling because of Mussolini's anger with Britain's pro-League policy in the Ethiopian dispute and because of Britain's unwillingness to guarantee Austria's independence. As a matter of fact, considerable advantage might accrue to Italy from this agreement. If British, and French, attention was now to be focused on a growing German navy in the North Sea, their concentration on the Mediterranean would decrease. This meant a greater chance to realize Italy's naval dream: predominance in the inland sea. Mussolini decided at once to build ten new submarines.[33] What interested the Italians most at the moment, however, was the reaction of France to the British-German naval agreement.

The French were astonished and furious. The intrinsic seriousness of the agreement was bad enough. Did not the British realize that to give Germany rights to a strength equal to 35 percent of the entire British navy would, just on the basis of tonnage, give the new German fleet a proportion of 70 percent to the British force in European waters? And this German fleet, newly commissioned and of modern construction, would on a ton-for-ton basis be a better fighting force than either Britain's or France's.[34] The British fleet was the shield of the West on the water, the way the Maginot Line was on the land, and now the naval shield was lowered. What disturbed the French most was the way in which the agreement was reached; they felt betrayed. By its action Britain unilaterally recognized Germany's violation of the naval and armament clauses of the Treaty of Versailles, ignored the condemnation pronounced by the League against Germany on 16 April, and violated the agreements of 3 February and Stresa not to negotiate separately with the Germans. The negotiations smacked of conscious deception, for France had been warned only at the last moment. Laval first learned of the negotiations in a British aide-mémoire of 7 June. He did not rush a reply because, first, on that very day he was in the midst of forming a new government to "defend the franc" and, second, because he and the French diplomats considered the conversations in London to be only exploratory.[35]

[33] Lagardelle, *Mission à Rome*, 138.
[34] A. Géraud, "France and the Anglo-German Naval Treaty," *Foreign Affairs*, 14:53 (October 1935).
[35] Mallet, *Laval*, I, 80; *U.S. Diplomatic Papers, 1935*, I, 163–5.

When France learned differently, a chill of fear ran through the country. Might not this agreement merely be the first step to a profound reversal of British policy, which would end with Britain's abandoning the allied front and accepting full-scale German rearmament? Might not the British find it necessary to sign an air pact with Germany under this new pretext of "political realism"? [36] An awful suspicion seemed realized: Britain was not in fact able to resist the siren call of Nazi Germany. It was noted in France that the agreement was signed on the 120th anniversary of Waterloo. Was a new "Belle Alliance" in the making at the expense of France?

There was a crisis in the *entente cordiale:* the old idea of solidarity and France's confidence in Britain were badly shaken.[37] "One cannot exaggerate the gravity of the consequences" of the treaty, wrote Herriot.[38] Laval, since 7 June premier as well as foreign minister, was initially seized by "a most lively desire for independence, for autonomy." [39] When the shock of anger wore off, however, Laval realized that the friendship of Britain, and British-French cooperation, was still the basis of France's security. In this spirit he accepted Eden's mission later in June. As Eden described it, Laval, was "not unduly disposed to cry over spilt milk. He is . . . determined to preserve what is left in the can of February 3rd." [40] There were conditions, however. Laval insisted to Eden that the two countries henceforth must never act

[36] Géraud, "France and the Anglo-German Naval Treaty," 60. This suspicion was completely justified. See Avon, *Facing the Dictators,* 234–5.

[37] One common French explanation of Britain's action was that the British were nursing a year-old grudge. On 17 April 1934 France had turned down a German offer to return to the League and to cooperate in Europe if rearmament was allowed. France's rejection ended any hope for success in the Disarmament Conference, made France increasingly dependent on her allies for protection, and angered the British. "At bottom England always reproached us for the note of 17 April," wrote Herriot at this time. Herriot, *Jadis,* II, 561. For a similar thought, see P. Vaucher and P.-H. Siriex, *L'Opinion britannique, la Société des Nations et la guerre italo-éthiopienne* (Paris, 1936), 12–14. Britain's anger is confirmed in Avon, *Facing the Dictators,* 89.

[38] Herriot, *Jadis,* II, 560–2. The blow to Britain's international standing was severe. The Austrians came to fear that Britain would use them as a pawn. Russia and almost everyone else thought that the construction of a new German fleet would cause the British to keep the greater part of its force in the North Sea, and so Britain would have to reduce not only its fleet in the Mediterranean but also in the Far East. This, it was thought, meant the end of the base at Singapore and an opening for the Japanese. Selby, *Diplomatic Twilight,* 49–50; *U.S. Diplomatic Papers, 1935,* I, 168–9. Kirby, *The War Against Japan,* 13, claims that the treaty "completely altered the strategic position in the Far East."

[39] Mallet, *Laval,* I, 81.

[40] Avon, *Facing the Dictators,* 231.

independently toward Germany and that further undermining of France's confidence in Britain must be avoided.

For all this determination to reconstitute the Anglo-French front, relations between France and Britain could never be the same. Both Laval and the French people carried the scars of Britain's unfaithful action. One popular reaction took the form of a stronger attachment to Italy,[41] and the French government felt a similar tendency. If Britain could allow itself to be seduced by Germany, if it could permit Germany so easily to drive a wedge between the allies of the past February, then France must depend all the more on Italy for security in Europe. On 19 June, the day after the signing of the naval agreement, Generals Gamelin and Badoglio signed the secret military convention by which French and Italian troops would march together against Germany in the event that Austria was attacked.

From the time of the naval agreement, Laval and the French were no longer so willing to follow the British. Nowhere was this more clearly indicated than in regard to the British effort to bring pressure to bear on Mussolini. It was widely felt that Britain's moral position vis-à-vis the Italian-Ethiopian conflict was seriously weakened by Britain's own massive disregard of its legal and moral commitments in benefiting Germany while wounding a friend. France would not break its ties with Britain, but it would no longer go out of its way to help the British restrain Mussolini. Eden found when he visited Paris that the "firm convictions" Laval had expressed at Geneva in May over the importance of collective security, the need to bring the League into play in the Italian-Ethiopian conflict, had "evaporated." [42]

On 18 June, perhaps in an effort to shore up Laval's reluctance to take action against Italy, the Italian government announced to Laval that its precise intention in Ethiopia was to obtain the direct control specifically over the "peripheral" zone of the empire, placing the central, Amharic, plateau under an Italian protectorate which, presumably, would leave that part of the realm its titular independence. Laval raised no objections to this plan, limiting himself to pointing out difficulties in its realization.[43]

Immediately after concluding the naval agreement with Germany, the new British government confronted the Italian-Ethiopian question.

[41] Pro-Fascist groups, such as the Croix de Feu, encouraged pro-Italian sentiment among the French people during the months of June and July, 1935.
[42] Avon, *Facing the Dictators*, 234.
[43] Askew, "The Secret Agreement," 48.

On 18 June the Foreign Office received the secret report of the interdepartmental commission which had been established three months before, in the wake of Vitetti's conversations at the Foreign Office on 29 January, and which, under the chairmanship of Sir John Maffey, had been instructed to consider the extent of British interests in Ethiopia. No official reply had ever been given in Rome in answer to the Italian overture of January. The British government was awaiting the Maffey report, which now finally arrived.[44] The report was composed of three sections, one dealing with data on Ethiopia, the second listing Italian complaints, and the third considering British interests in east Africa.

The comments on Ethiopia were harsh, reflecting troubles that British colonial administrators had long experienced on the frontiers. The instability of the country was traced to ineffective governmental control in the outlying regions and the "striking absence of homogeneity" in the people of the country, aggravated by "the discordant ambitions of the various races, made acute in some cases by the harsh treatments of others by the Amharic dominators." Similar observations, of internal disharmony and uncivilized behavior, were basic Italian propaganda themes. The Maffey report noted Italian ambitions in Ethiopia and referred to the agreement of 1906 by which, it stated, "His Majesty's Government recognized almost the whole of Ethiopia as pertaining to the Italian sphere of influence." The report ended with eight conclusions and recommendations.

(1) Italy's intention was to gain full control of Ethiopia in the next few years.

(2) "No vital British interests exist in Ethiopia or adjoining countries sufficient to oblige His Majesty's Government to resist a conquest of Ethiopia by Italy." Italian control would even be advantageous for Britain, in terms, for instance, of the safety of frontier zones. In other ways, trade for instance, it would not be. Generally, "it is a matter of indifference whether Ethiopia remains independent or is absorbed by Italy."

(3) Although an independent Ethiopia would be preferable to an

---

[44] For the content of the report, see *New York Times*, 20 February 1936. A copy of the Maffey report was sent to the British embassy in Rome where, unbeknownst to the British, it was photographed by the head chancery messenger, a "grave and dignified Italian," who was in the employ of the Servizio di Informazioni Militari — the military secret service. It was first published by the *Giornale d'Italia* on 19 February 1936, at Mussolini's orders, to confute British assertions of 24 October 1935 that Maffey's commission had not finished its work.

Italian Ethiopia, the threat to British interests "seems very remote and would become real only in the event of war between Britain and Italy" — an "improbable" prospect.

(4) The chief British interests in Ethiopia were Lake Tana and the Nile basin, which were also the interests of Egypt. "In the event that Ethiopia should disappear as an independent State, His Majesty's Government should seek to secure territorial control over Lake Tana and an adequate corridor joining this lake to the Sudan." Similar precautions should be taken for the other Nile tributaries, and an understanding should be made with Italy, in the event it established itself in Ethiopia, not to impede the flow of the tributary rivers.

(5) If territorial control over Lake Tana was impossible, British and Egyptian hydrolic interests would have to be safeguarded by concessionary stipulations.

(6) Assuming the success of an Italian conquest, "every effort" should be made to assure pasturage rights beyond the Somali frontier for the tribes protected by Great Britain.

(7) In the event Italy absorbed Ethiopia, efforts should be made to ensure British subjects equal rights in commercial ventures, even though at present such interests were "negligible."

(8) "It would be well to seize the occasion" of an Italian conquest to obtain rectifications of the frontiers of British Somaliland, Kenya, and the Sudan (to achieve better economic and ethnic unity in these areas).

One conclusion of the Maffey report was clear. Britain had interests in Ethiopia, but the protection of these interests was compatible with Italian domination of the country. The function of the Maffey commission was only to ascertain and appraise particular facts. It was not its task to formulate British policy toward the Italian-Ethiopian conflict. The creation of such a policy had to be based on wider considerations, on factors beyond the commission's ken, and this job belonged to the Foreign Office.

Britain's need for cordial relations with Italy was more acute when to the danger in Europe from a rearmed Germany was added the threat of war in the Far East with Japan. "It was essential to British security to have a friendly Italy in the Mediterranean that would both guarantee our lines of communication to the Far East and make it unnecessary for the French to keep an army on the Italian frontier." [45] Only with Italy friendly could Britain move freely in both its theaters of interest. With the British fleet now predominantly occupied near home, a hostile Italy at the wasp waist of the Mediterranean would make more difficult any powerful and sustained action beyond Suez. On the other hand, the British government could not afford to ignore the consequences of its obligations to the League. Only by averting a war of aggression in Ethiopia could Britain avoid the climactic choice between Rome and Geneva. Hoare never considered warning Mussolini directly against war in Ethiopia or threatening British intervention. Rather, the makers of British policy in June 1935 allowed their steps to be guided by anachronistic memories of the past, misinterpretations of the present, and wishful thinking about the future.

In the first place, the British counted too much on the tradition of British-Italian friendship. Hoare believed that this old friendship was in itself strong enough to enable Britain "to influence Italian opinion and bring pressure on Mussolini." [46] He failed to understand the anger in Rome brought about by British resistance at Geneva. So certain were the British of the efficacy of the old tie that they thought they could act alone. The British made no effort in June 1935 to associate the French in their plans.

The second mistaken assumption was the belief that Mussolini was "at the time on very bad terms with Hitler." [47] Hoare relates in his memoirs that he had in mind at this point Mussolini's action on the Brenner following the assassination of Dollfuss. The reserve of credit this action gave Mussolini in Britain seemed unlimited, and Hoare did not seem to realize the significance of the ensuing events. In his memoirs Hoare uses this example of Mussolini's anti-German action as proof that the Stresa front still held — a curious bit of reasoning, for the events of July 1934 had preceded the Stresa meeting by some ten months. There seemed to be no realization in Britain, despite the signs, that the Stresa front was cracking under the pressures of the Ethiopian affair, that Mussolini was drawing away from Britain in contempt and reversing his attitude toward Germany.

A third assumption made by the new British foreign minister was that his "past associations with the Duce might still have some effect on him." During the world war, Hoare, then a young lieutenant-

[45] Templewood, *Nine Troubled Years*, 153.
[46] Templewood, *Nine Troubled Years*, 152.
[47] Templewood, *Nine Troubled Years*, 153.

colonel on the Italian front, once made a secondhand contact with the young socialist editor of *Avanti!* After the rout of Caporetto, Hoare requested Mussolini to activate a resistance movement in Milan. Hoare now sent personal appeals to Mussolini, hoping to convince the Duce of Britain's good will by recalling their former association. "Almost anything was worth trying," said Samuel Hoare. Of course this effort came to nothing. The incident is illustrative of the naiveté, the amateurishness, of Hoare in his new job. "Perhaps," wrote Hoare in his memoirs, "we were too optimistic. Perhaps we did not sufficiently realize the contrast between Mussolini's outlook and ours."[48] It was this failure to understand the extent of the issues involved in the Italian-Ethiopian conflict that led to the formulation of the British plan of June 1935.

Hoare's personal messages of friendship were rebuffed by Mussolini. The Foreign Office needed a better means to approach Mussolini. On the weekend of 15–16 June, Hoare, Eden, and Vansittart worked out a plan contrived to induce Mussolini to give up his intention of making war on Ethiopia. Britain would cede to Ethiopia the port of Zeila and a corridor to it through British Somaliland.[49] This would give Ethiopia free access to the sea on its own territory. Britain would then be in some position to put pressure on Ethiopia to make major concessions to Italy. These might include the cession of the province of Ogaden, economic concessions within the empire, and other advantages for Italy to be determined later. The British hoped this offer would satisfy what they persisted in considering the primary Italian ambition — an expansion of economic influence in Ethiopia — and at the same time maintain the political independence of the Ethiopian state. The offer would also show Britain's good faith and its desire for a negotiated settlement. The Ethiopian government was not consulted. Nor was France.[50]

[48] Templewood, *Nine Troubled Years*, 153–4. For a curious note on this matter, see E. Serra, "Mussolini, l'Etiopia e un segreto di Sir Samuel Hoare," *Nuova antologia*, 476:481–8 (April 1960).

[49] Details of the proposed cession were given in the House of Commons in July 1935. *Parliamentary Debates*, 303 H.C. Deb. 5s., cols. 1520–22, 2004–9; 304 H.C. Deb. 5s., cols. 5–8.

[50] Toscano, "Eden a Roma," 29, quotes from the Italian verbatim account of the Eden-Mussolini conversation of 24 June. Cession of the Ogaden to Italy was to be a "prestige solution" for Mussolini. Avon, *Facing the Dictators*, 221. The Maffey report stated that Italy's present intention might be "to limit her action to the conquest of the lowlands bordering on Italian Somaliland." Haile Selassie was not informed of the British proposals until 3 July. *U.S. Diplomatic Papers, 1935*, I, 612.

To anyone following events with care, it was obvious that this proposal would not satisfy the Italians. At this point they could not be content to receive only another semiarid plain. The plan provided no certainty they would get even that, for the cession of the Ogaden depended on Ethiopian approval. Of mere promises for support at Addis Ababa the Italians had had their fill, remembering that such promises had consistently been honored in the breach. Geoffrey Thompson was called in. Astonished at the plan he blurted out: "But Mussolini will never accept." Eden and his aide, William Strang, both appeared "rather pained" at this, but Strang replied, "Well, we've got to put it to him, anyway." [51]

Eden was chosen to go to Rome. The next step was to consult Ambassador Drummond, whose response was favorable. The attempt to enter into negotiations, to make a sacrifice even, would end the feeling in Rome that Britain was shirking conversations with the Italian government. After all, there had never been a British response to the Italian overture of 29 January, and only on 18 June did the Maffey report come formally to the Foreign Office. Drummond was instructed to request Italian approval for Eden's visit. The British cabinet, "although somewhat taken aback by the suddenness of the move," gave its approval.[52]

Mussolini was out of town on 19 June when Drummond approached the Italian foreign ministry. Suvich received the ambassador. Drummond said that the British government was trying to avoid a war and wanted to bring about a solution of the dispute that was satisfactory to both Italy and Britain and consistent with the principles of the Covenant. Suvich replied that the Ethiopian matter was no longer merely one of the settlement of the Walwal incident or the procurement by Italy of a railroad between its two colonies.[53] The affair was now more involved and only one solution would be satisfactory to Italy: "the definitive liquidation of the Ethiopian question." The only value of a visit by Eden would be to convince the British that Italy could not agree to a negotiated settlement. Britain must understand, said Suvich, the "immovable determination" of Mussolini.

Drummond did not, and could not, discuss the terms of the British

---

[51] Thompson, *Front-Line Diplomat*, 103.

[52] Templewood, *Nine Troubled Years*, 155; Avon, *Facing the Dictators*, 221.

[53] The railroad question under the tripartite agreement of 1906 had never been settled.

proposal. But, like Chambrun in January and Grandi at Stresa, Drummond was eager to bring the matter into negotiation and did not want to see the Italian government reject this chance for discussion. For this reason he painted an exaggeratedly favorable picture of what the British were prepared to offer. One of the worst sins an ambassador can commit is to falsify the intentions of his government and thereby raise the hopes of another country. This is what Drummond did. He told Suvich that this time the British were taking a new approach to the problem and that what Britain had to offer Italy would satisfy, in his opinion, half of the Italian demands and create conditions which could be developed further in Italy's favor.[54] The Italians were impressed. If the British had read Mussolini's speeches and listened with care to Grandi, the concession of half of Italy's demands would be a major and important step forward. If more, say 75 percent, could be gained later, before even a shot was fired, the British proposal would certainly be worth the most serious consideration. Therefore, Eden's visit was approved and set for 24 June. Care was taken to disguise it as a meeting concerned solely with a discussion of a proposed air pact and the question of naval armaments.[55]

Eden went first to Paris, with the uncomfortable mission of trying to alleviate the tension between France and Britain brought about by the British-German naval agreement. He made no mention to Laval of the proposal he was going to put to Mussolini. This silence was a most serious and deplorable diplomatic error — a deliberate concealment of an important policy decision from an intensely interested ally whose help in any further developments would be needed and who had every right to be informed of Britain's moves toward Italy. During Eden's visit Laval warned him that the British "must not give Anglo-French confidence another sharp jolt." [56] Yet this was just what would happen if the Zeila plan were kept hidden. The French had strong political and economic interests in Djibouti and the Djibouti–Addis Ababa railroad. The British proposal gave Ethiopia a private bypass only a few miles south of the French port, and such a threat to their vested interests naturally concerned the French. Eden claimed that he did not bring the matter up because he wanted to be free in his conversation with the Italians without having to worry about or anticipate

[54] For the Drummond-Suvich exchange, see Guariglia, *Ricordi*, 243–5.
[55] Aloisi, *Journal*, 280; Toscano, "Eden a Roma," 25n.
[56] Avon, *Facing the Dictators*, 231.

French reactions.[57] But if the French had objections later, they would have them then, and in either case they could make their objections felt. To conceal the offer served no purpose. It could only anger the French and give them yet another example of the double-dealing of perfidious Albion. Moreover, the French already had some information from Ethiopia which might have influenced negotiations. The French government had made some cautious soundings in Addis Ababa to find out whether Haile Selassie would accept an Italian protectorate. The emperor replied negatively, saying that the rases would rebel if he gave in to any Italian pressure. This information was also known to the Italians.[58] Furthermore, on 18 June the Italian government had stated to Laval certain specific claims in Ethiopia, and these too might have been conveyed to the British.

Laval must have realized that something was afoot. On the 22nd, Eden's last day in Paris, he instructed Chambrun to tell Mussolini that France intended to remain faithful to the political line established on 7 January. Neither Britain nor any other country, said Laval, would be able to disturb the French-Italian friendship. Suvich, to whom Chambrun reported on the 23rd, asked whether France's commitment to the League might not cause this disturbance. Chambrun replied that, though France could not oppose the League, it would do everything in its power to meet Italian demands and to help Italy obtain the results it wanted in a peaceful way.[59] Laval wanted to be certain that Mussolini knew he had France's support before Eden arrived in Rome. Laval did not go into the Ethiopian matter with Eden: if there was to be a secret British démarche, it was better that the French stay out of it.

Eden left Paris on the morning of the 23rd. Up to this time the Italian government had no idea of the specific proposal the British minister carried with him. They knew something was coming and, on the basis of Drummond's enthusiastic comments, waited with keen interest and

---

[57] Toscano, "Eden a Roma," 25–6. Italian diplomatic reports sent to Rome on 21 and 22 June emphasized that Eden did not mention Ethiopia to the French, and, it might be noted, the French were quiet too.

[58] Toscano, "Eden a Roma," 27. From the available evidence it does appear that at this time the emperor wanted a peaceful settlement, even if it meant conceding to Italy territory in the southern lowlands. He was unable to pursue this, however, because the strength and confidence of the rases were such that they would act to prevent any pro-Italian settlement. If the emperor did not stand up to Italy, he was in danger of losing his throne. See Avon, *Facing the Dictators*, 228, 233; Aloisi, *Journal*, 287.

[59] Toscano, "Eden a Roma," 28; Aloisi, *Journal*, 280.

expectations. We do not know whether Mussolini already had seen a copy of the Maffey report. But if he had, Mussolini was aware that Britain had no interests in Ethiopia deemed incompatible with Italian control. When Eden arrived in Rome the night of the 23rd, he learned to his dismay that a leak had occurred in London and an account of the British proposal had been published. The Italians now knew of the pathetic inadequacy of the British offer. This must have been particularly galling to the Italians when they reflected that, as far as a negotiating position went, the British could give no acceptable reasons for wanting to hold Italy to such a petty position in Ethiopia. Britain seemed to be playing a double game with Italy, as well as with France. Eden's offer, even before it was tendered, was the object of great anger and contempt in Rome.

On the morning of 24 June, Eden and Mussolini met. Eden began by asserting Britain's commitment to the League and its anxiety that the Italian-Ethiopian conflict might force the British to act against Italy at Geneva. To prevent this, and in the hope of finding a satisfactory solution, the British government had contrived the Zeila proposal. Mussolini at once rejected the proposal. First, to give Ethiopia access to the sea would make the country a maritime power, augment its strength and prestige, and provide a free opening for the import of arms.[60] Second, the implications of the proposal would give Ethiopia reason for claiming a diplomatic victory over Italy. If Ethiopia made any concessions to Italy, it could claim that the step was taken out of friendship for Britain, not as a tribute to Italy. This would be an intolerable affront, and Italy could not accept concessions won through the intermediary of a third power. Third, Britain would emerge as Ethiopia's protector and benefactor, and, despite Britain's disclaimers of interest, this could not be to Italy's benefit. Fourth, the terms of the offer did not come close to satisfying Italy's claims on Ethiopia.

Since Eden had come to Rome, Mussolini continued, and since Italy appreciated the good efforts of London, it was only fair to state the Italian position in full, so that there would no longer be any misunderstanding of aims. Italy wanted control of all the territories surrounding the region of the old Amharic kingdom. The central plateau

---

[60] No one at this time noted that in 1931 Haile Selassie offered to give Italy part of the Ogaden in exchange for an outlet to the sea. Italy had rejected this proposal as tending to increase Ethiopia's strength. Italy considered the Ogaden economically worthless. Villari, *Storia diplomatica*, 99.

could remain under titular Ethiopian sovereignty on the condition that it be kept under effective Italian control. These goals Mussolini hoped to gain by peaceful means. If Ethiopia did not agree to the terms, Italy would fight to get them and, accordingly, Italian demands would increase. Italy had already spent a billion lire in preparation, and 150,000 men were already in east Africa. Mussolini said he was prepared to increase the number of men to 500,000 if necessary. Italy intended to resolve the Ethiopian question, fully and immediately.

Eden reverted to the point that Ethiopia was a member of the League. Britain must support the conditions of the Covenant. If Italy continued with its plans for conquest and the matter came before the League, the result would be a rupture between Britain and Italy. Mussolini recognized this danger and hoped that such a break could be avoided. If worse came to worst, however, he was prepared to leave the League. Mussolini said there were only two alternatives for a solution, one through peace or one through war. The first would mean Ethiopia's outright cession to Italy of all regions conquered by Menelik and since his time, plus Italian control over the nucleus of the empire. War would mean the eventual disappearance of all of Ethiopia from the map.

Eden now noted France's concern with the growing seriousness of the conflict. Mussolini explained that Laval, at the meetings in January, had given him a free hand in Ethiopia. The notion of a purely economic interpretation of Italian actions was only a ruse adopted for public appearance. He and Laval understood perfectly that the implication was that Italy should have freedom in all matters. Eden repeated Laval's assertion that there could only be an economic application. After all, Laval had told Mussolini in January: "You have strong hands. Take care." "At this," Eden records, "Signor Mussolini flung himself back in his chair with a gesture of incredulous astonishment." [61]

The meeting broke up, to be resumed on the following day. Contrary to most later reports and to then current rumors, the conversation was conducted in a calm and orderly fashion. There were no outbursts of temper, no displays of rudeness or hostility. The Italian com-

[61] The three main reports of the Eden-Mussolini conversation of 24 June are found in Avon, *Facing the Dictators*, 221–5; Toscano, "Eden a Roma," 28–30; Villari, *Storia diplomatica*, 96–7. It is important to record that during these British-Italian conversations, the French government did its best to assure Mussolini of French sympathy. There was, we have seen, Laval's message of the 23rd. On the 24th Chambrun announced that Gamelin, at Badoglio's invitation, would arrive soon in Rome for military conversations. Aloisi, *Journal*, 282.

muniqué, which did not mention that Ethiopia was discussed, used the term "cordiale" to describe the atmosphere of the talk.[62] But, nonetheless, the meeting on the 24th put an end to any hope that the British proposals would be accepted. The Duce's objections were conclusive, and there was no further British effort to get Mussolini to re-examine the terms of the offer. In this sense, Eden's visit was "a complete failure." [63] It was not the premature press release of the 23rd but the content of the British offer itself that caused Italy to reject it. The British simply came too late with too little. Instead of conciliating the Italians, the British proposal made them suspicious and indignant. They saw in the British move only a screened attempt to deny Italy its colonial ambition and to establish Britain as the predominant influence at the Ethiopian court.[64] The most generous opinion Guariglia could offer was that the proposal was the work of bureaucratic underlings in London, and not a really serious statement of governmental policy. Aloisi called the proposal a "trap" and Eden's visit a "most maladroit gesture." [65]

If any constructive result at all came from this meeting, it was that the new British government was now put in formal notice of the true seriousness of the affair. Mussolini's warnings could not have been clearer. There could be no more wishful thinking or half-measures in London. Realization of this is why the Zeila offer was not pushed further, and it explains Eden's low spirits during the remainder of his stay in Rome. It also provided an opportunity for Italy to persuade the British to take another course at Geneva. Aloisi spoke to Eden at lunch on the 25th. He proposed a plan which, he said, would safeguard the prestige of the League and still allow Italy to fulfill its aspirations in Ethiopia. The scheme was the one Avenol had suggested. "At the right moment," Aloisi proposed, Italy would denounce Ethiopia as being unfit for membership in the League. This charge was currently being documented in Rome. Then, with the concurrence of Britain and France, an effort would be made to apply the precedent of the Chaco dispute and have the matter referred to certain interested powers, namely Britain and France, who would attempt to resolve

[62] Mussolini, *Opera omnia*, XXVII, 348.
[63] Aloisi, *Journal*, 282.
[64] Toscano, "Eden a Roma," 31; Lagardelle, *Mission à Rome*, 139.
[65] Guariglia, *Ricordi*, 247; Aloisi, *Journal*, 282, 284. "Romulus" in the *Nuova antologia*, 380:288 (16 July 1935), stated that the offer demonstrated "a total incomprehension of the Italian attitudes toward Ethiopia." This was a fair assessment.

the question. In these circumstances, Aloisi told Eden, public opinion would not consider that the League was being humiliated, it would heed Italy's indictment, and Italy's aims would be achieved through arrangement with the other two interested European powers. Eden listened with interest to this proposal and told Aloisi that William Strang would consult with him on the next day.[66] Strang also listened "with interest." Aloisi was using the plan as a trial balloon to see whether Britain's real opposition stemmed from its concern with the League. For if it did, the Italians believed, this new scheme offered "a way out."[67]

On the evening of the 25th, Eden met again with Mussolini. He noted that the British proposal would not be pursued further, and asked Mussolini to indicate on a map the extent of Italy's territorial demands. They amounted to a dismemberment of the Ethiopian empire. The Italian claims included the region bordering southeastern Eritrea, the Aussa country, the province of Harar, the Ogaden, the two sultanates to the south that bordered on Kenya, and a strip reaching from the frontier of the Sudan to the most southwestern point of Eritrea. In this area, which surrounded the central plateau, Italy wanted complete domination. The central region, the classical lands of Abyssinia proper, including Addis Ababa and the provinces of Tigre, Amhara, Gojam, and Shoa, Mussolini wanted under Italian control. Ethiopia would then have a status similar to Iraq, Egypt, or Morocco, as Drummond had suggested on 21 May. Eden quibbled over the distinctions of this last point, but Mussolini would not be put off. He advanced the strategic, economic, demographic, and colonial arguments used to justify the Italian case. The alternative to a peaceful settlement on these terms, he said, was war, and if there was war Ethiopia as a state would disappear. To Eden's assertion that Britain must stand by the Covenant, Mussolini replied that nonetheless the Italian government, possessed of "immense military, political, and moral strength," was determined to settle things once and for all. Eden must take home a clear idea of this determination and a realization

[66] Aloisi, *Journal*, 282. It is interesting to note that on 18 May 1934 Eden, speaking for the British government, had proposed the expulsion of Liberia from the League on the grounds that the Liberian government was conducting or condoning border raids, that it misgoverned the native population, and that it had not suppressed "practices analogous to slavery." League, *Official Journal, 1934,* 509–11. Recall also Britain's arguments in opposition to Ethiopia's original application for admission to the League.

[67] Aloisi, *Journal*, 283–4.

that the Italian people had never been "so quiet and so satisfied as at present." [68]

The conversations between Eden and Mussolini were over, and there had been no agreement. The new British government's effort to create a compromise settlement, to bring about a British-Italian détente, had failed.[69] On the other hand, British-Italian relations were not yet at the breaking point. Eden listened to suggestions that new ways might be found to satisfy Italian demands, and he was not intransigent in his opposition. It is obvious that the British were still not certain of their future policy. Eden left Rome with an expression of some good will and hope from Suvich, and the Italian press refrained from Anglophobic polemics.[70] The Italians were waiting, no doubt, to learn what effect their warnings and suggestions would have on London.

Eden left Rome on 26 June and went directly to Paris, where he met a hostile reception. The French were now well aware of the proposal that Eden had hidden from them. The Italians did not neglect to nurture the seeds of suspicion which this new British deception, following so closely after the British-German naval agreement, emplanted in French minds. Encouraged by a talk with Chambrun, on the 26th Suvich instructed the Italian ambassador in Paris to inform Laval personally, before Eden's arrival, of the Rome conversations. Suvich ordered Pignatti to make it clear that Eden's proposal acted against the spirit, and perhaps the letter, of the treaty of 1906, to which the French were a party. More than that, the Zeila offer held adverse

[68] This was a reference to the widespread opinion abroad that the Italian people were not behind Mussolini in the Ethiopian affair. The fullest account of the conversation of the 25th is found in Avon, *Facing the Dictators*, 225–8. Mussolini's comment to his son Vittorio is revealing: "I tried to make Eden understand that Africa does not begin any longer at Calais." V. Mussolini, *Vita con mio padre*, 62.

[69] Before he left Rome, Eden talked with Chambrun and Drummond, expressing his displeasure at the outcome of the talks. Chambrun told him that Italy could not accept the British proposals, and both he and Drummond stated that a further effort to pacify Italy had to be made. Toscano, "Eden a Roma," 37. This is an interesting example of the two ambassadors' strong inclination toward appeasement, which had its effects in muddling the diplomacy of the period. Chambrun even tried to enlist American support in convincing the British to make another attempt to avert war by offering Mussolini greater concessions. *U.S. Diplomatic Papers, 1935*, I, 610–11. Chambrun himself was said to have concocted a proposal that involved a cession to Italy of Ethiopian territory and an Italian guarantee of the integrity of Haile Selassie's dynasty until the year 2000. Report of the American chargé in Rome, 27 June 1935, U.S. Diplomatic Correspondence, 765.84/472.

[70] Toscano, "Eden a Roma," 36, 40n. On the other hand, the word "cordiale" was missing from the Italian communiqué describing the talk of the 25th. Mussolini, *Opera omnia*, XXVII, 348.

economic and political consequences for France. If Ethiopia had its own outlet to the sea, it would naturally try to bypass the French port of Djibouti. Suvich shrewdly made a distinction between Italy's troubles with Britain and its conflict with the League. Knowing the French concern, he stated that Italy would not withdraw from the League, regardless of the quarrel with Britain, unless it was forced to.[71]

It was along these lines that Laval formed his attack when Eden arrived. Indignantly the French described the British proposal as "monstrous." Laval complained that Eden very nearly played a trick on France that would have forced the French to declare Djibouti a free port. The consequences would have been serious, for the Djibouti railroad provided for nine tenths of the budget of the colonial government of French Somaliland. Léger told Eden that the British offer, made unilaterally, was contrary to the treaty of 1906. Both men complained bitterly that France was not consulted in advance. Eden had no defense. Nor could he give the French any indication of Britain's next move. Admitting the bankruptcy of British policy, he said his government had done all it could toward compromise — "it was now the French Government's turn." If Mussolini could be convinced that France was greatly disturbed, Eden said, perhaps the Duce might come to terms.[72]

The French were wary. In France as well as Italy it was believed that the British would take advantage of the confusion in east Africa to move troops into Ethiopia. This suspicion of British motives was not unrealistic. The Maffey report had referred to the possible need of Britain to "seek to secure territorial control over Lake Tana" and other regions in which tributaries of the Nile flowed, noting that it might be desirable to occupy Ethiopian territory adjacent to the British colonies. The Quai d'Orsay, indeed, thought that preparations were already under way for a British move into the highlands. If this was Britain's true intent, France could not take seriously its appeal that some way must be found to keep Italy satisfied with a limited share of the Ethiopian spoils. The mood of the French government was quite different from what it was a month before at Geneva. The more suspicious the French became of the British, the more unwilling they were to antagonize Italy. As for Britain's pro-League policy, this

[71] Toscano, "Eden a Roma," 37; Villari, Storia diplomatica, 99.
[72] Avon, Facing the Dictators, 233–4.

was viewed in Paris as simply a matter of domestic British politics, whereby the Conservative Party sought support in the country.[73]

For these reasons Laval refused Eden's appeal to pull the British chestnut out of the fire. France would not assume the role of mediator. The French did not have a much clearer notion of what their policy would be than the British did, but they were not going to take the risk of angering Mussolini. Laval and Léger proposed a plan to Eden in line with Mussolini's expressed demands. France was willing to agree to a "Morocconization" of Ethiopia, to an Italian protectorate over the country. Under the French scheme Italy would be given suzerainty in Ethiopia sufficient to allow Italy to fulfill its desire to exploit the land economically and to use the country for colonization. Haile Selassie would retain his titular sovereignty and the empire would not be broken up. Laval said that the emperor might accept some peaceful arrangement if Britain and France endorsed the scheme.[74]

Eden listened without objection to the French comments. If a peaceful settlement was reached between Italy and Ethiopia, the British government might accommodate itself to its terms. However, the French did not seem ready to speak up in Rome to gain Italy's acceptance of such a plan, and it was unlikely that France would use its influence to restrain Mussolini from military action. The French were too interested in keeping on the good side of Italy to pit themselves against the Duce in this dispute.[75] June 1935 saw the "solstice" of French foreign policy when, as one writer has said, the foreign situation "was the best France had known since 1918." [76] Great changes were coming; storms were gathering in the east and to the south. For the moment, regarding the Italian-Ethiopian conflict, the French steered a cautious and noncommittal course, hoping to avoid a choice between extremes and waiting to see what the future would bring.

It was obvious that Britain held the key to the outcome of the Italian-Ethiopian conflict. But it was just as clear, as Eden left Paris for London, that the British government had no idea of what to do. Eden arrived in London on 27 June. On the same day Lord Robert

---

[73] Toscano, "Eden a Roma," 38, 40; Villari, *Storia diplomatica*, 99–100.

[74] The fullest account of this conversation is found in Avon, *Facing the Dictators*, 231–4.

[75] General Gamelin departed for Rome on 25 June. On the 28th, he and Badoglio signed a secret agreement for French-Italian military collaboration. For details, see Gamelin, *Servir*, II, 167–9.

[76] Mallet, *Laval*, I, 94–6.

Cecil announced the results of "The National Declaration on the League of Nations and Armaments," popularly known as the Peace Ballot.

The origin of the Peace Ballot went back to a questionnaire circulated in the Ilford area by a local newspaper in January 1934. In this test of public opinion, responding to the question "Should Great Britain remain in the League of Nations?" 21,532 persons answered yes, and 3,954 answered no. To the question "Do you agree with that part of the Locarno Treaty which binds Great Britain to go to the help of France or Germany if one is attacked by the other?" 5,898 answered yes and 18,498 answered no. Inspired by this enterprise, the League of Nations Union, a nonparty organization, decided to make the questionnaire into a national plebiscite in favor of the League. To increase the chance of success, the pollsters of the Union decided to eliminate troublesome references to specific treaty obligations and to appeal in simplified and general terms to the idea of peace through collective security. In this way the large negative majority, which had clearly seen that Britain's specific treaty obligations could lead to war, would be converted to a large affirmative majority in favor of the idea of collective security and the League, by which Britain would act only in conjunction with "other nations." [77]

For our purpose the three significant questions on the Peace Ballot were:

(1) Should Great Britain remain a Member of the League of Nations?
(5) Do you consider that, if a nation insists on attacking another, the other nations should combine to compel it to stop by
  (a) economic and non-military measures?
  (b) if necessary, military measures?

Polling began in November 1934 and continued until June 1935.

The National (that is, Conservative) government was embarrassed by the Ballot, and at the beginning the members of the government were strongly opposed to the poll. Baldwin called it misleading. To Vansittart it was a "misfortune," a "free excursion into the inane." He saw "the very name of the movement" as a "trap" and the Peace Ballot's formulas as "idealistic frauds." The title and the presentation implied that an affirmative vote was for peace and a negative vote was presumably for war. Sir John Simon also deplored the poll: "The question of

[77] A. Livingstone, *The Peace Ballot: The Official History* (London, 1935), 7, 10.

war and peace is not one on which the opinion of the uninstructed should be invited." Neville Chamberlain called the movement "terribly mischievous" and wrote contemptuously of the "League of Nations cranks." *The Times* called the "whole business . . . a deplorable waste of time and effort" and denied its importance. Eden never gave the Ballot the "slightest encouragement" and until a very late stage was actively opposed to it.[78]

There were many possible objections to the Ballot. Question 5 made it appear that sanctions of an economic and nonmilitary nature were real and effective alternatives to the use of force. Under the international economic systems of the day, however, tied as they were to national security and prosperity, the imposition of an economic sanction might itself lead to war. This was not recognized or even suggested in the words of the Ballot. The oversimplified phraseology also abetted a general misunderstanding of the nature of collective security. The Ballot seemed to encourage the idea "that collective security was something that could exist independently of the policies and armaments of the great powers who were members of the League.[79] To make the League work effectively, Britain itself would have to take the active lead; to deter aggression might well necessitate the use of armed force; and the major responsibility for any military sanctions would fall to Britain. But the tenor of the Ballot and the notions of the times seemed to assume that, somehow, any action taken by Britain in the name of collective security would be undertaken within the framework of an already existing mechanism in which the burdens would be equally shared with the "other nations." Neither the League of Nations Union nor the British government tried to make the public understand that no such mechanism existed, that spontaneous cooperation in international affairs is a very rare phenomenon, despite the provisions of the Covenant, that other nations would act *only* if Britain led the way, that with the responsibility of leadership came the need to accept a greater than average share of the burden, and that collective security under the League might require war against aggressors.

Despite these objections, the opposition of members of the govern-

---

[78] A. Baldwin, *My Father*, 207, 219; Vansittart, *The Mist Procession*, 503; Salvemini, *Prelude*, 209; Feiling, *Neville Chamberlain*, 262; I. Macleod, *Neville Chamberlain* (London, 1961), 181; *The Times* (London), 27 July 1934; *History of "The Times,"* IV, part 2, 896; A. Johnson, *Anthony Eden* (New York, 1939), 112.
[79] Macleod, *Chamberlain*, 181.

ment abated as it became evident that the Peace Ballot was capturing the imaginations of the people on an unparalleled scale. After all, the government led a political party that during elections put to this very same electorate questions of comparable complexity. And the government had to go to the people at a time not far off. If politicians wanted a straw to see which way the wind of public opinion was blowing, they had a good indicator in the Peace Ballot.

The results announced in June 1935 revealed that over eleven and a half million persons over the age of eighteen had voted. It was a spectacular success.[80] What was even more interesting was the one-sided nature of the returns. To question 1, asking whether Britain should remain a member of the League, 11,090,387 persons voted yes and only 335,883 voted no, an affirmative majority of 97 percent; 102,425 voters abstained. To question 5a, asking whether economic and nonmilitary measures should be imposed on an aggressor, a total of 10,027,608 voters recorded yes and 635,074 no, an affirmative majority of 94 percent; 855,107 voters abstained. In each of these totals the number of voters registering yes was higher than the record vote secured by any political party in any general election, apart from the "abnormal" election of 1931. To question 5b, whether "if necessary" military measures should be taken against an aggressor, 6,784,368 British voters said yes and 2,351,981 no, an affirmative majority of 74 percent. 2,364,411 persons abstained from voting on this question, but the percentage of all responses on this question was still 58.6 percent affirmative.[81] Though the size of the total vote impressed the government, the size of the majorities in favor of the League and against aggression struck observers all the more forcefully for being unexpected.

In no country did public opinion exercise a greater influence on governmental policy than in Britain. Few British governments were more responsive to public opinion than Stanley Baldwin's. Baldwin now found himself confronted with a dilemma. The prime minister was a pacifist and feared that another war would do irreparable damage to England and to the civilization of Europe. He dreaded the prospect of leading Britain into a new era of military preparation. And yet, in 1935, a program of rearmament was urgently needed to assure Britain's security and the protection of its interests abroad. In

[80] Cecil had hoped for maybe 5 million votes. Cecil, *A Great Experiment*, 259.
[81] Livingstone, *Peace Ballot*, 48–51.

the past, Baldwin had accepted what appeared to be an increasingly articulate pacifist trend among the British electorate. In October 1933, the same month Hitler left the disarmament conference, a by-election was held in East Fulham, and the Conservative Party candidate lost a safe seat to the Labour Party man who, it was thought by the government, won his victory by appealing to pacifism. This assessment was inaccurate. The election in East Fulham, a depression-ridden London suburb, turned as much on personality, on local economic and social issues, as on the call for disarmament and collective security. But the prevailing interpretation of the event was that pacifism had been the decisive force behind the victory. After the election, Baldwin, as well as the Tory press and the Labour Party, accepted this view.[82] Eager to disprove the opposition's contention that "the Tories meant war," Baldwin could not bring himself to launch a program of vigorous rearmament. The power of public opinion, henceforth considered "so thoroughly pacific," became an important reinforcement for a government itself terrified of war, itself pacific, and tied the government's hands during these critical years.[83] "It was this 'opinion' that became the one authority on foreign policy respected by the Government and *The Times* after East Fulham," writes *The Times*'s official historian.[84]

But the tide of pacifism reached its peak in 1934, and the Peace Ballot of 1935 appeared to disclose "an extraordinary reshaping of opinion." [85] The Ballot seemed to show that the people, although they still desired disarmament above all and were reluctant to go again to war, were nonetheless prepared to see their government stand up to aggression within the framework of the League. Until this time official British support for the League had been, on the whole, sporadic and lukewarm. The idea of the openly principled new diplomacy of Geneva was not attractive to the makers of British foreign policy. They

---

[82] Dalton, *The Fateful Years*, 47; Amery, *My Political Life*, III, 151; Williams, *A Pattern of Rulers*, 52–4.

[83] S. Baldwin, *This Torch of Freedom* (London, 1935), 319; A. Baldwin, *My Father*, 189, 317. G. M. Young writes: "I always felt the nerve, injured in October 1933, the East Fulham nerve, never quite healed: [Baldwin] was afraid of pacifists: he could not bring himself quite to say, perhaps not quite to think, 'Germany is arming and we must arm too.'" Young, *Baldwin*, 200.

[84] *History of "The Times,"* IV, part 2, 887n.

[85] Robertson, *The Office*, 144; Young, *Baldwin*, 210. For an argument that the Peace Ballot was "an expression of ill-considered national desires" in that the British would not support the League "once it became clear that the defense of the Covenant might lead to war," see H. Nicolson, "British Public Opinion and Foreign Policy," *Public Opinion Quarterly*, 1:53–63 (January 1937).

did not want to become involved in matters that did not appear to concern Britain's vital interests or to antagonize states with which they sought good relations. They were not convinced the League was an effective instrument because its idealized statutes did not seem to correspond with political realities and did not take account of the blunt fact that powerful nations, the United States, Germany, Japan, were not included in its membership. For these reasons the British government had never taken a strong political lead at Geneva, and they were all the more unwilling to involve the country in punitive action where Britain would have to assume the primary burden, carry along the weaker member states, and absorb the major cost and responsibility. The majority of the British cabinet "never whole-heartedly believed in the League of Nations as an effective force in the affairs of the world," although to acknowledge this skepticism, as Baldwin's biographer wrote of the prime minister, would be "to invite political extinction." [86]

In the Italian-Ethiopian conflict, the British government had tried on every major occasion to circumvent the League. Both its regard for British-Italian relations and its unwillingness to consider using force on behalf of the Covenant restrained the government from strongly opposing Italy's preparations for aggressive war. The long tradition of agreement in Ethiopian matters on terms favorable to Italy was still strong in London. But in June the British policy of partial appeasement reached an impasse. Eden in Rome had learned of Mussolini's unquestioned intention to invade Ethiopia. The Zeila proposal and the offer of British mediation failed to satisfy the Duce and aroused criticism in Britain. When Eden arrived in London on 27 June, the British still had no policy, and on that same day the results of the Peace Ballot were announced. Despite the confusion of its terms and the possible failure of the public to understand the full implications, the fact remained that the vast majority of those voting had supported a policy of the punishment of aggression through the medium of the League of Nations. It was probably not lost upon the government that this high rate of voting favorable to sanctions came at a time when

---

[86] Young, *Baldwin*, 173. Young adds: "Though [Baldwin] could speak beautifully about the Assembly . . . he would never take the few miles' journey from Aix to Geneva to see it in action." Lord Arthur Salter attributes this fact not to an unfriendly attitude but merely to Baldwin's laziness — he did not want to interrupt his holiday. Lord Salter, *Memoirs of a Public Servant* (London, 1961), 205. Amery discusses various views of the effectiveness of the League in *My Political Life*, III, 141-2, 153.

the world was becoming conscious of the seriousness of the Italian-Ethiopian conflict.[87] To the government, drifting and uncertain in the spring months of 1935, the results of the Ballot were an apparent mandate for support of the League.[88]

The Ballot did not cause the government to become the League's champion, for the private skepticism of officials remained as strong as ever. But appeasement of Mussolini now became more difficult for the government to justify at home, and some increased measure of support for the League was politically expedient. The government's turn toward the League in the Italian-Ethiopian conflict was insincere and incomplete, then. Because the government did not intend to follow the course to its logical end, it did not educate the people of Britain in what the road to resistance involved. Winston Churchill wrote later: "Half-measures were useless for the League and pernicious to Britain if she assumed its leadership. If we thought it right and necessary for the law and welfare of Europe to quarrel mortally with Mussolini's Italy, we must also strike [Mussolini] down." [89] Lacking such a conviction, half measures are what the government took: far more than they cared to serve the League, they feared a war with Italy.

On 23 July, Baldwin told a deputation which formally presented him with the results of the Peace Ballot that the League of Nations was the "sheet-anchor of British policy." [90] What the prime minister did not say was that the government intended to fasten this anchor in the tangled weeds of evasive legalism, in the strict interpretation of the letter of the League's system of collective security. In this way the government could reap the political benefits of appearing faithful to its obligations while avoiding all the real responsibilities — for if the British did not lead, but only waited for the independent development of a collective system, such a system would never materialize and the

[87] During the spring of 1935 the weekly graph of the Ballot's progress shows a steady increase in votes for military sanctions and a corresponding decrease in votes for the abolition of naval and military aircraft. Livingstone, *Peace Ballot*, 44–5.

[88] This was the intention of its supporters: "We thought that some of the Ministers at any rate were inclined to agree [to a strong League policy] but afraid that such a policy would not have the support of the electorate. We hoped that the ballot would have convinced them that their fears were unjustified." Cecil, *Great Experiment*, 259.

[89] W. S. Churchill, *The Second World War: The Gathering Storm*. (Boston, 1948), 167. (Permission to quote granted by Houghton Mifflin Company and Cassell and Company Ltd.)

[90] Toynbee, *Survey of International Affairs, 1935*, II, 53.

British government would never have to face an unwanted, difficult, and probably dangerous duty.

While the British government at the end of June "paddled in a purée of words and hoped to catch a formula," [91] the diplomacy of the Italian-Ethiopian conflict drifted on as before. On 19 June Ethiopia wrote the secretary-general, protesting continued Italian military preparations in east Africa despite the May agreement to arbitrate. Trying to bolster its position before the League, the Ethiopian government requested the council to send a team of neutral observers to patrol the Ethiopian frontiers and investigate the incidents that had taken place between Italy and Ethiopia. This was a sensible proposal and would have served the interests both of Ethiopia and of international justice, but the League took no action.[92] Notwithstanding the warning by Ethiopia that aggression seemed "imminent," the League preferred to await the report of the arbitral commission rather than take the matter into its own hands. The members of the League ignored the Ethiopian reference to articles 10 and 15 of the Covenant; the Ethiopian letter of 19 June was vague about whether these were being invoked.[93]

On 25 June, as it had been agreed two weeks earlier in Milan, the commission of "conciliation or arbitration" met again, this time at Scheveningen in the Netherlands. During the interval the two contending governments had been requested to provide the commission with documentary evidence in support of their positions. The Ethiopians contented themselves, in a letter of 18 June, with referring the commission to the memoranda already presented to the League.[94] Italy did not provide its documentary support until the very last moment; since this was not received by Ethiopia's appointed arbitrators until 25 June, several days had to be devoted to its study.[95] As a result, and allowing time for preliminary discussion, the commission did not meet in formal session until 4 July. Each government had also appointed a representative to present the arguments in person. Jèze

[91] Vansittart, *The Mist Procession*, 487.

[92] The Italians considered this suggestion "absurd." *Le Temps*, 22 June 1935.

[93] League, *Official Journal*, 1935, 972–3.

[94] The two most comprehensive memoranda submitted by Ethiopia to the League concerning the Walwal dispute were those of 15 January and 22 May 1935. League, *Official Journal*, 1935, 252–74, 721–59.

[95] The Italian memorandum of 22 June is in League, *Official Journal*, 1935, 1534–84.

spoke for Ethiopia. The Italian agent was Silvio Lessona, professor of law at the University of Florence and elder brother of the Italian colonial undersecretary. The Italian arbitrators, Aldrovandi and Montagna, came armed with "definitive instructions" from the Italian government on the policy they were to follow.[96]

The Italian members could not be neutral; they were acting on Rome's orders. But at the beginning of the meetings it appeared that Italy might be flexible. Potter, an Ethiopian-appointed arbitrator, thought on the 27th that on the basis of the Italian memorandum, which he saw as "reasonable and conciliatory in tone," some agreement might be reached.[97] Such hope was quickly banished. On the second day of the formal meetings, 5 July, the discussion reached an impasse. Jèze, in a summary of his case, asserted that Walwal was located in Ethiopian territory. Silvio Lessona immediately objected, insisting that the question of ownership was not within the purview of the commission. Jèze retorted that he was not trying to determine a demarcation of the frontier. However, he said, the question of ownership was relevant to the question of responsibility for the fighting and thus must be considered. Here was a matter of great importance to Ethiopia's position. If the factor of territorial sovereignty over Walwal were admitted as relevant, Ethiopia could charge Italy with illegal occupation, with trespass, and thus with provocation. Jèze put the matter to the commission to decide. La Pradelle and Potter maintained that the commission had every right, indeed the duty, to decide whether the question of the ownership of Walwal was germane to the question of responsibility. It would be, they said, "on the part of the Commission, an abdication and at the same time a hindrance to the liberty of the defense to forbid the Agent of the Ethiopian Government to develop the reasons for which he believes that the Commission, free to judge all circumstances of the incident, may include therein that of the appurtenance of Wal Wal." [98] Silvio Lessona, seconded by the Italian members, rejected this interpretation. He declared that Italy would withdraw from the proceedings if the commission allowed Jèze to persist in this question of ownership. The two Italian members affirmed that the commission did not possess the authority to make

[96] On 22 June a briefing session was held in Rome, and the instructions were given to the arbitrators by Suvich and "all interested officials." Silvio Lessona also attended. Aloisi, *Journal*, 280.

[97] *U.S. Diplomatic Papers, 1935*, I, 609–10.

[98] Potter, *Wal Wal Arbitration*, 67.

a decision on this point. Aldrovandi and Montagna then insisted that the question be returned to the Italian and Ethiopian governments for settlement through the normal channels of bilateral diplomacy. Until then, the Italians said, the commission could act no further in the dispute.

With the commission members equally divided and opposed, the result was stalemate. There remained nothing to do but to adjourn and report the situation to the two governments. Potter and La Pradelle requested the appointment of a fifth arbitrator to break the deadlock, as provided for in the treaty of 1928. But the Italians refused, claiming that what was at issue was not a difference of opinion between the arbitrators but a difference of opinion between the governments. So on 9 July the commission adjourned *sine die*. The problem was referred to the two governments, and separate opinions were issued by the two sides of the board.[99]

[99] The transcript of the Scheveningen proceedings and the commission's documents are presented in Potter, *Wal Wal Arbitration*, 39–68, and in La Pradelle, *Le Conflit italo-éthiopien*, 373–437. On pp. 438–43, La Pradelle gives an important evaluation of this controversy and its relation to international law.

Chapter 9

July: No Help for Ethiopia

The British nation in 1935 feared war. The king no less than the people was frightened by this "constant nightmare." Samuel Hoare met with George V many times during June and July 1935. The gist of the ill monarch's anxious entreaties, as Hoare discerned it, was: "I am an old man. I have been through one world war. How can I go through another? If I am to go on, you must keep us out of one." [1] In the aftermath of the silver jubilee the cabinet ministers were not insensitive to the king's wishes, especially since his antiwar sentiments coincided with their own. They were faced with the fact that effective opposition to Italian aggression, alone or through the League, might lead to war. They were concerned that the Dominions would not follow Britain into a war with Italy over Ethiopia. They worried about what Germany and Japan might do if Britain's armed forces were engaged in the Mediterranean. They did not want to antagonize the United States by restricting trade to Italy in the course of imposing sanctions. The British government therefore moved with caution.

The government's "double policy," as defined by its inventor and executor, Hoare, was to maintain simultaneously Britain's "collective obligations under the Covenant, based on Anglo-French cooperation," while making every effort to prevent the outbreak of war by "negotiation with Italy." [2] The first half of this policy was composed of two complementary but dissimilar factors. One was the notion of "collective obligation"; the other was the conviction of the government that Britain must not act alone in opposing Italy.

The British government, soon up for re-election, could not afford

[1] Templewood, *Nine Troubled Years*, 159.
[2] Templewood, *Nine Troubled Years*, 161.

to ignore the strong current of public opinion, revealed by the Peace Ballot, that endorsed British participation in the League of Nations and the punishment of aggression by the use of sanctions in the company of "other nations." Britain was bound by treaty to support the League and the League was the proclaimed basis, the "sheet-anchor," of British foreign policy. The government could not disown the League. Indeed, there was an argument for the position that, in Winston Churchill's words, "more could perhaps be got out of the vindicated majesty of the League than Italy could ever give, withhold, or transfer." [3] But for the League to achieve a state of vindicated majesty it was necessary that Britain, the League's strongest and most respected member, take the active leadership, and this the British government was unwilling to do. The government's problem was to find a way to satisfy the pro-League opinion in the country and still avoid the consequences of standing behind the Covenant.

The problem was resolved by a piece of legerdemain. The British government decided to fortify the popular assumption that the League as an organization had weight and effectiveness in and of itself. The notion of collective security was elaborated *ad absurdum*. The government insisted that Britain's obligations to the Covenant lay only within and as a part of a collective responsibility. Britain would act in support of the League, but not alone, not first, not as a leader. Ignoring the true requirements of the situation, the British government announced that it would act *only when* the other nations of the League had acted. The government sought to evade its responsibility by attributing to the League a power that the organization did not have and was never meant to have. The League's security system was only as strong as its members made it and could become effective only by their actions. Britain's insistence on carrying out its obligations to the Covenant only if other nations were already engaged in carrying out theirs was an instance of willful distortion of the realities of international politics. Regardless of the validity of the reasons that led the government to take this course, there was a glaring disparity between what the British government might have done if it were truly prepared to support the League, as it proclaimed, and its actual unwillingness to take the initiative.

Nonetheless, this portion of Britain's double policy represented the strongest position to date that Britain had taken in support of the League in the Italian-Ethiopian conflict. If it did not encourage League

[3] Churchill, *The Gathering Storm*, 167.

action, at least it did not close the door against it. Despite their careful ambiguities and their renunciation of independent responsibility, the British might still be led toward action by the French. So, determined not to act alone, afraid of being isolated, the government passed the responsibility to France. The British Cabinet on 3 July concluded that, whatever further steps were taken, "everything depended on the attitude of France." [4] Neville Chamberlain, reflecting the thought of the Cabinet, wrote in his diary on 5 July:

> It is clear after Eden's visit to Rome that Mussolini has made up his mind to eat up Abyssinia, regardless of treaties, covenants, and pacts . . . The ideal way out is to persuade Mussolini to abandon the idea of force. The only way to do this is to convince him that he has no choice. If we and France together determined that we would take any measures necessary to stop him, we could do so, and quite easily. We could, e.g., stop the passage of his supplies through the Suez Canal. If the French would agree to play their part, the best way would be to go privately to Mussolini and warn him of our views and intentions, at the same time assuring him of our desire to save his face and get him some compensation from the Abyssinians. If the French would not play, we would have no individual (as opposed to collective) obligations, and we should not attempt to take on our shoulders the whole burden of keeping the peace. But if in the end the League were demonstrated to be incapable of effective intervention to stop this war, it would be practically impossible to maintain the fiction that its existence was justified at all.[5]

And yet the month of July passed with no serious overtures from Britain. The French in their turn were not willing to initiate the discussion. If the British would not act, they were prepared to let things drift. Exasperated with Britain, unwilling to antagonize Mussolini, and busy with the domestic economic and political crises, in the first weeks of July the French were in no mood to create a proposal for the effective restraint of Mussolini. The British approached Laval on 4 July and asked if he intended to take definite action of any kind. Laval replied he was too busy trying to save the franc to think about the matter, but that he would do nothing to force Italy out of the League or to impair French-Italian harmony.[6]

For a month the British government contented itself with waiting for a French move, which never came. For all its talk about acting

[4] Avon, *Facing the Dictators*, 238.
[5] Feiling, *Neville Chamberlain*, 265.
[6] Avon, *Facing the Dictators*, 237.

only in concert with the French, the British government feared that if the French *should* decide to act, to force League sanctions against Italy, the result would be war and confusion in Europe. Therefore, ignorance of France's intentions was Britain's bliss. The safest path, it seemed, was to avoid an inquiry that might give rise to troublesome answers, that might lead Britain into a course it was not prepared to take. The important question of whether the two countries would act to impose even minimum sanctions on Italy was never raised. Eden said in the House of Commons on 11 July:

> I state definitely that at no time in the conversations which we have been having with the French Government on this vexed affair has there been any foundation for any suggestion on our part that the French Government should join with us in economic action [against Italy].[7]

The second part of Hoare's double policy was negotiation with Italy to prevent war. The benefits to Britain were obvious. There would be no embarrassing conflict between principle and interest at Geneva; there would be no danger of coming into a war with Italy over sanctions; there would still be the chance, perhaps, that an appeased Italy would be a friendly Italy.

But to conclude a negotiated settlement was difficult, as Eden's trip to Rome revealed. Italy's demands were too great for Ethiopia to concede. The only way to reach a settlement would be by the use of pressure to compel one or both parties to accept a compromise. Yet, until December, the British continued to hope unrealistically that they right win some success with negotiation alone. The French abetted this notion, seeing it as a welcome alternative to resistance.[8] And the Italians encouraged the hope of negotiation as a means of delay and as a way to circumvent the League. For the British government, the chase after a negotiated settlement was its excuse for not becoming finally committed to unconditional support of the League. In a speech to the House of Commons on 11 July 1935, Hoare admitted his belief that the League was not strong enough to handle the substantive problems of the Italian-Ethiopian conflict. The League had to be protected, by the use of "old" diplomacy, from this dangerous test of its political strength. Its purely moral influence should not be exposed to failure. The value of the League, in this analysis, was almost metaphysical; it

---

[7] *Parliamentary Debates,* 304 H.C. Deb. 5s., col. 630.
[8] *Le Temps,* 8 July 1935.

could be best preserved by being kept far above the harsh demands of political reality. Hoare said:

> We are all, therefore, in duty bound to do our utmost to prevent the development of any crisis that is likely to weaken or destroy the principles upon which the League was built and upon which its influence for peace depends. This is the reason for our grave interest in the Abyssinian controversy. This is the reason why, even at the risk of criticism, we have been prepared to make constructive proposals for the avoidance of a war that, however it ends, must have serious repercussions upon the whole League system. This is our sole reason for our efforts to find a basis for settlement.[9]

The French position, of similar direction, was expressed by *The Times*'s correspondent as "a preference for the League [that] does not exclude parallel conversations among the Powers most directly concerned." [10]

It was one thing to have inflated hopes for a negotiated settlement; it was another to effect it. The British were unwilling to take the sole responsibility of presenting Mussolini with another proposal. There had been criticism enough in Britain as well as in France over the rejected Zeila plan of June.[11] On 11 July Eden said: "Our endeavour has been to discover whether the French Government had any constructive suggestions they could make towards a settlement of the dispute. We felt that we had made our contribution, and that it was their turn to make theirs." [12]

These efforts had no effect, and the French did nothing. If France would not make a move, perhaps some way to negotiation might be found through the already existing framework of the tripartite treaty of 1906. This idea had been renewed by Sidney Barton, the British minister in Addis Ababa, immediately after Eden's failure in Rome, although Barton thought a tripartite conference could be better used to warn Mussolini against aggression than to formulate a policy of compromise.[13] On 28 June Drummond was instructed to sound out the Italians on the precise nature and extent of their claims. Suvich's

[9] *Parliamentary Debates*, 304 H.C. Deb. 5s., col. 518.
[10] *The Times* (London), 18 July 1935. See also *Le Temps*, 8 July 1935.
[11] See the exchanges in the House of Commons on 4 July 1935, *Parliamentary Debates*, 303 H.C. Deb. 5s., cols. 2004–9, and the trenchant comments of Arnold Toynbee, Lord Salter, Lord Lothian, and Arnold Wilson in Toynbee, "Peaceful Change or War?" *International Affairs*, 15: 25–56 (January–February 1936), and 15:322–4 (March–April 1936).
[12] *Parliamentary Debates*, 304 H.C. Deb. 5s., col. 630.
[13] Avon, *Facing the Dictators*, 236.

reply was not calculated to encourage the British. He told Drummond that in any public comments the British government should avoid a statement on the Italian demands, that it was Italy's own prerogative to make such claims in its own way.[14] The Italian government went even further. At the beginning of July it informed the British that, if they directed diplomatic steps against Italy, they would lose Italy's friendship, destroy the tranquillity of the Mediterranean, and upset the Locarno agreements. If Britain sought to bring France into League action, Europe would be split into two camps and Italy would be compelled, it was intimated, to seek military alliance with Germany. To this warning the British Foreign Office replied that the British government would act on the basis of public opinion which, in Britain, was hostile to Italian aggression in Ethiopia.[15] On 2 July, as we have seen, the British were told by Laval that France had no proposals to make and would do nothing to antagonize Italy. Like Mr. Micawber, the British ambassador reported, Laval was basing his hopes for peace on "something turning up." [16]

Dismayed by Italian coolness and by French disinterest, the British government became discouraged in its hope for a negotiated settlement. On 5 July Hoare handed Grandi a stiff warning, that Mussolini's attitude in summarily rejecting British efforts to "help with a peaceful settlement" might mean the end of the opportunity for further discussion. Since this would be to Italy's disadvantage, Grandi responded by inquiring if it would not be possible to hold a meeting of the signatories of the treaty of 1906. The suggestion was passed on to Paris where Sir George Clerk, the British ambassador, was instructed to seek Laval's opinion. Laval wanted first to consult with Mussolini. Mussolini replied on 10 July that he could see no reason for a meeting and that such a meeting would be "useless and harmful" unless preceded by diplomatic preparation. Laval agreed and was not willing to press the matter further.[17]

In the face of such discouragement, the British might have given up. But the adjournment of the arbitral commission at Scheveningen on 9 July had given the policy of negotiation a renewed life in London. The government felt that if something were not done before the League met at the end of July, Britain would be confronted at last with a

---

[14] Toscano, "Eden a Roma," 41–2.
[15] Villari, *Storia diplomatica*, 103.
[16] Avon, *Facing the Dictators*, 237–8.
[17] Avon, *Facing the Dictators*, 238–9; Aloisi, *Journal*, 288.

decision between the League and Italy. On 9 July Hoare told the American ambassador he was determined to make every possible effort to bring about a negotiated settlement.[18] He began with an attempt to reduce the tension between Britain and Italy and to construct an atmosphere in which conciliation would be possible. In his major foreign-policy speech to the House of Commons on 11 July, Hoare said:

> I should like also to make it clear that we have always understood and well understand Italy's desire for overseas expansion. Indeed, we have in the past done our best to show our sympathy with Italian aspirations in a practical way. In 1925 we ceded Jubaland to Italy, and in the present negotiations we showed our willingness to endeavour to ensure for Italy some territorial satisfaction by a reasonable and legitimate arrangement with Abyssinia . . . Let no one therefore in Italy, in view of these outward and visible signs of our sympathy, suggest that we are unsympathetic to Italian aspirations.
>   We admit the need for Italian expansion. We admit again the justice of some of the criticisms that have been made against the Abyssinian Government. But are the facts that Italy needs expansion and that complaints are made against the Abyssinian Government sufficient cause for plunging into a war? We have surely found in the past that it is possible to adjust demands and differences of this kind without recourse to war, and I am not prepared even now to abandon any chance that may present itself for averting what I believe to be a calamity, whether it be through the machinery of the

---

[18] *U.S. Diplomatic Papers, 1935*, I, 613. Hoare told the American ambassador, Robert Bingham, of a further reason for seeking a peaceful settlement: "Mussolini has now put the issue in the shape of a contest between the black and white races which had had already unfavorable effects in Egypt, in Great Britain's African colonies and in British Dominions where there is a population of blacks." On 31 July Mussolini specifically denied that Fascism was making the conflict an issue of race. Mussolini, *Opera omnia*, XXVII, 110–1. But his "civilizing" arguments had all the tone of nineteenth-century imperialism. The Italian-Ethiopian conflict had great significance to the non-white peoples of the world. If Italy won, despite the principles of the League which offered protection equally to all members, it would be proof that the spirit of imperialism, of the subjugation of races, was still condoned by Europe. If Italy lost, "the spell of Europe" would be broken. In either case, if war came European colonial positions would be jeopardized. See W. E. B. Du Bois, "Inter-Racial Implications of the Ethiopian Crisis: A Negro View," *Foreign Affairs*, 14:82–92 (October 1935). 82–92. With the war, nationalistic reactions did occur all the way from the Levant to Siam. The colonial implications of the dispute no doubt encourage Britain and France to seek a negotiated settlement, but in the last analysis their policies were determined by strictly European political considerations. Pope Pius XI, viewing the Italian-Ethiopian conflict at the end of July, regarded the danger to "our Catholic interests" in Africa in much the same way the British saw the danger to the old colonial world. F. Charles-Roux, *Huit ans au Vatican, 1932–1940* (Paris, 1947), 135. See also *Le Temps*, 12 July 1935. For some later, but related, comments by the pope, see *Documents diplomatiques français, 1932–1939*, 2nd ser., I, 154–6.

1906 Treaty, or whether it be through the machinery of the League, or whether it be through both . . . [Rumors] are altogether without foundation, that we have asked the French Government to join in a blockade of Italy and against the country which has been our friend since the Risorgimento. We stand for peace, and we will not abandon any reasonable chance that may offer itself for helping to prevent a disastrous war.[19]

Aloisi saw Hoare's speech as evidence of a "change of front." [20] It was not quite this, but Aloisi was correct in noting that now, in mid-July, it was the negotiation part of British policy that was being emphasized. The following incidents illustrate this point.

In Rome at the end of June, Eden had warned Mussolini of the dangers of his course, basing his argument on the contention that Italian aggression would bring Britain down on the side of the League. He told Mussolini that he would report the Italian position to the Cabinet, but that Britain could not be unfaithful to the Covenant. On 3 July the Cabinet endorsed Eden's views. But the government did not send this notification to Rome as on official warning to follow up Eden's. Rather, the "collective obligation" aspect of British policy — in the form of a formal warning to Mussolini of Britain's determination not to ignore its responsibilities under the Covenant — was pigeonholed for four weeks in the Foreign Office; in the meantime Hoare pursued the conciliatory line, hoping to get Mussolini to agree to a three-power meeting.[21] Here was a clear example of the danger and confusion caused by the double policy. By putting forward first one

[19] *Parliamentary Debates*, 304 H.C. Deb. 5s., cols. 509–24. Clement Attlee on the same day indicted this speech as representing not "the idealist view of foreign affairs based on the League and the kind of principles we have been trying to establish in the world since the war," but "imperialist realism," an "entire going back upon all the principles of the League." He insisted that the government face up to its responsibilities under the Covenant. *Ibid.*, cols. 534–40.

[20] Aloisi, *Journal*, 286. Those portions of Hoare's speech favorable to Italy were played up in the Fascist press, but the contradictions were noted. Hoare's rhetorical references to traditional friendship were not enough to win over the Italians, in the absence of some concrete proofs. Fine words, it was said, butter no parsnips. *The Times* (London), 13, 14, 15 July 1935; League of Nations, *Revue des commentaires de la presse sur la Société des Nations* (Geneva, 1935), 16 July 1935, 13–16; *Bulletin périodique de la presse italienne*, 309:10–13. Hoare's statements did convince many Italians that Britain would make no attempt to arraign Italy before the League, as Germany had been arraigned in April, and this corroded domestic opposition to Mussolini. Hoare's disclaimers also strengthened Mussolini's hand when, later, they were used as proofs of British hypocrisy.

[21] Avon, *Facing the Dictators*, 239–40.

and then the other of his standards, Hoare gave the impression that the British government simply did not know its own mind.[22]

The Italian government, of course, was pleased with this British uncertainty. There was no need, in the present confused situation, to straighten matters out. Mussolini was confirmed in his confidence that he would be allowed his success in Ethiopia, and Italian military preparations went forward. A report for the fiscal year 1934–35 showed, on 30 June, a budget deficit of 2.03 billion lire: 975 million lire were accounted for as expenditure in east Africa. Between January and June 1935, 102 Italian naval units passed through the Suez Canal, as compared with 3 in the corresponding months of 1934.[23] On 6 July Mussolini spoke at Eboli after reviewing four Blackshirt divisions about to embark for east Africa. Standing on a gun carriage, he exalted the heroism of Italian soldiers. He referred to the cowardice of Ethiopians who fled the battlefield at Aduwa, despite their successes, when faced with the determined resistance of the Italians. Aduwa, Mussolini said, was lost not by the Italian soldiers in the field but by the despicable maneuverings of the parliament in Rome. Such weakness was not found under Fascism, and the Fascist government was resolved to carry the present "decisive" campaign to a final conclusion. For the first time, Mussolini publicly suggested that the Italian government was now committed to a military enterprise from which there was no turning back.[24] The next day two of Mussolini's sons, Bruno and Vittorio,

[22] Speaking in 1935 of the period before World War I, Eden noted this persistent British failing. England, Eden said, "often appeared poised and hesitant. It is even possible that on one occasion at least war did break out just precisely on account of a miscalculation as to our own country's position." Eden, *Foreign Affairs* (London, 1939), 80. Duff Cooper wrote: "The besetting sin of British foreign policy is refusal to let other nations know beforehand what Great Britain will do in certain circumstances. This reticence is often taken for compliance." Cooper, *Old Men Forget* (London, 1953), 189.

[23] Toynbee, *Survey of International Affairs, 1935*, II, 528; Cohen, *La Société des Nations*, 19–20.

[24] Mussolini, *Opera omnia*, XXVII, 102–4. It appears that another speech was prepared, and perhaps given, at Eboli and that at the last moment its publication was forbidden. See E. Reale, *La Politique étrangère*, 32. The text of this suppressed speech of Mussolini's is reproduced by Salvemini: "Abyssinia, which you are going to conquer, we shall have totally. We shall not be content with partial concessions, and if she dares resist our formidable strength we shall put her to pillage and to fire. You will have formidable armaments that nobody in the world suspects. You will be strong and invincible, and soon you shall see the five Continents of the world bow down and tremble before Fascist power . . . To those who may hope to stop us with documents or words, we shall answer with the heroic motto of our first storm troops: '*Me ne frego*', 'I

enlisted in the air force for action in east Africa. On the 14th the Rome correspondent of *Le Temps* estimated that there was only a 10 percent chance that peace could be preserved. On the 15th Mussolini announced the mobilization of two more divisions, one of Blackshirts and one of the regular army. This brought to ten the total of divisions mobilized for service abroad. It was estimated that 200,000 men were now in Eritrea preparing for war. Some 15,000 Italian troops were reported to have passed through the Suez Canal in the first two weeks of July. On 15 July Italy announced the beginning of construction on ten new submarines, short-range vessels designed for use in the Mediterranean and Red seas. This was, as Gaetano Salvemini noted, "a reminder to the British." Submarines could not serve in the mountains of east Africa. On 16 July Mussolini published an article in *Il Popolo d'Italia* noting that the League was planning to move, at the turn of the year, into new quarters, the newly built Palace of Nations in Geneva. He warned the League that what it needed was not merely a change of location but also a change of attitude; otherwise it might find itself outpaced by events and arrive at its new home a dead organization. On the 16th he wrote to De Bono, saying he was very satisfied with the progress the general had made in the preparations "to put Eritrea into a position to face present and future tasks." A similar letter was sent on 26 July to Graziani in Somaliland. In Italy the Fascist press was allowed to become more bellicose than ever before.[25]

The Ethiopians were naturally worried by these events of late June and early July. The collapse of the proceedings of the arbitration commission at Scheveningen on 9 July called forth a letter from Gaston Jèze to the secretary-general of the League, asking Avenol to circulate the texts that contained the positions of the disagreeing arbitrators and to draw the council members' attention "to the extreme urgency of intervention by the Council." The appropriate documents

---

don't give a damn.' We shall snap our fingers in the face of the blond defenders of the black race. We shall advance against anyone — regardless of colour — who might try to bar the road. We are engaged in a fight of decisive importance and we have irrevocably decided to go through with it." Quoted in *Prelude* (copyright 1951 by Gaetano Salvemini), 237, 255. One should note that the official version of the speech at Eboli, cited in my text above, comes from an edited version not published until a month after Mussolini spoke. This "true" text was released on 4 August, said *Il Popolo d'Italia*, to contradict "the apocryphal and tendentious résumés" published earlier by foreign journalists.

[25] *U.S. Diplomatic Papers, 1935*, I, 615; *The Times* (London), 16 and 17 July 1935; Mussolini, *Opera omnia*, XXVII, 105–6, 294–5; Salvemini, *Prelude*, 242.

were circulated on the 11th. This step by Ethiopia was "informally" considered in Geneva as "tantamount to a request for an early extraordinary meeting of the Council." [26]

What more could the Ethiopians do? They could solicit the support of the United States. On 3 July Haile Selassie called in the American chargé and asked that the American government "examine means of securing Italy's observance of engagements as signatory of the Kellogg Pact." Italy was one of the original signers of the pact in 1928 and had then pledged itself "to renounce war as an instrument of national policy." The emperor hoped that if the United States, the world's greatest neutral power, could invoke the faded memory of this treaty (memories would have to do, since there was no means of enforcing it), Italy might be persuaded that aggression would lead to condemnation and isolation. Cordell Hull, the American secretary of state, canvassed the opinion of the French and British ambassadors in Washington. The British ambassador, eager to avoid war and angry at the "blackmail" Italy was exerting on Britain and France, readily approved any American action that might promote peace.[27]

The United States government, however, had no intention of jeopardizing its neutrality. It did not want to be mixed up in colonial disputes any more than it wanted to become involved in conflicts on the continent of Europe. In the historian Max Beloff's words, "the whole rationale of American isolation — in so far as it had a rationale — was based on the idea that a European equilibrium could be restored and preserved by the efforts of European nations themselves." [28] With the League involved in the present dispute, Hull thought there was no need for America to complicate the situation.[29]

On 5 July Hull replied to the emperor in a cool and careful message. Hull noted with gratification that the League was giving its attention to the conflict, and hoped that the arbitral proceedings would end satisfactorily. He said the American government "would be loath to believe" that either Italy or Ethiopia would allow a war to develop, which would be "inconsistent with the commitments of the Pact." This was no help to Ethiopia and was too weak to have any restraining effect on Italy. Hull's statement to the press on 12 July, that "the Pact

[26] League, *Official Journal, 1935*, 973; *U.S. Diplomatic Papers, 1935*, I, 613.

[27] *U.S. Diplomatic Papers, 1935*, I, 723-5.

[28] M. Beloff, *The Great Powers: Essays in Twentieth Century Politics* (New York, 1959), 42.

[29] C. Hull, *Memoirs* (New York, 1948), I, 419-20.

of Paris is no less binding now than when it was entered into," also avoided any intimation that America might use its great economic and moral power to prevent a breach of the peace in Africa.[30] No action was taken on Hoare's suggestion that the American ambassador in Rome approach Mussolini directly with Hull's statement of the 12th, to reassert the validity of the terms of the Kellogg Pact.[31] The United States government contented itself with these bland and noncommital words as an answer to a troubled Europe and a threatened country. In Ethiopia, it might be added, America looked after its own interests. On 26 June and 2 July, before the emperor made his fruitless appeal to Washington, the American chargé in Addis Ababa had been instructed to advise all American citizens in Ethiopia to leave the country at once for their own safety.[32]

In the summer of 1935 Ethiopia was faced with a critical military situation. The country could not provide for its own defense. Massing on Ethiopia's northern border was a highly organized European army of several hundred thousand men, well equipped with modern weapons and aircraft, waiting only for the end of the rainy season. The Ethiopian army could not effectively resist the invasion force. Ethiopia did not lack men. By the end of September 1935, from a general conscription called in the spring, the emperor was able to raise a force of some 250,000 men.[33] But numbers alone tell very little: the men were not trained, there was no time to train them, and so this Ethiopian army was completely unprepared to meet the Italian invaders. "The

[30] *U.S. Diplomatic Papers, 1935*, I, 725, 731; Hull, *Memoirs*, I, 420–1.

[31] *U.S. Diplomatic Papers, 1935*, I, 732. The confusion that surrounded Hull's statements of July on the Kellogg Pact, whether or not they constituted an invocation of the pact, is noted by Brice Harris, Jr., *The United States and the Italo-Ethiopian Crisis* (Stanford, 1964), 34–5, 45–6.

[32] *U.S. Diplomatic Papers, 1935*, I, 876–8.

[33] Steer, *Caesar in Abyssinia*, 55. George Steer, *The Times*'s correspondent on the scene, made a careful investigation of this question. Other thoughful estimates endorse this figure. Corrado Zoli, in his account of the Ethiopian army in 1930, estimated this as a maximum figure for a general levy. See Zoli, *Cronache etiopiche*, 57–95. Badoglio estimated slightly higher, and he could not be expected to underestimate the number he had to meet. P. Badoglio, *La Guerra d'Etiopia* (Milan, 1936), 10. In 1945, in its demand for damages, the Ethiopian government claimed pay for 365,000 men, but this was probably an excessive estimate. M. Perham, *The Government of Ethiopia* (London, 1948), 66. The Ethiopian government tried to spread the rumor that it could mobilize nearly 1.1 million men, but this was a fiction spread to leave Italy in ignorance of Ethiopia's vulnerability. Steer, *Caesar in Abyssinia*, 123. This propaganda ploy had an adverse effect, in that it gave credence to claims that Ethiopia was capable of resisting Italy and hence not in urgent need of foreign support.

Ethiopians are warriors, not soldiers," wrote one Italian.[34] Throughout their history Ethiopians went to battle in one way only. The great regional chiefs, the rases, would gather under their individual leadership as many men as they could support. Together they would march toward the foe and charge in a frontal assault. The day would be won by storm or not at all. This way of fighting had beaten the Italians at Aduwa. Success had given the average Ethiopian soldier an unquestioned confidence in his military superiority over any invader.

The confidence of the Ethiopian warrior remained unchanged, but the nature of the challenge was now radically different. The Italian army of 1935 was not the careless and harried army of 1896, but a knowledgeable, mobilized, armored force capable of breaking up frontal assaults and mass attacks with artillery fire, with machine guns, and above all with bombings and strafings from the air. The Ethiopian foot soldier did not understand this change. And the new methods necessary to combat such a foe were not easily learned or accepted by the old commanders who had fought the Italians with Menelik. For all their memories, however, the long period of peace had undermined the martial spirit of many of the old chiefs, and many in the intervening years had sought to economize by reducing the size of their contingents. This dwindling but extremely influential band of older men, best exemplified by the powerful seventy-year-old minister of war, Ras Mulugeta, were confused by the new ideas of warfare espoused by the younger officers and foreign advisers in Addis Ababa.[35] They did not understand the subtleties of European diplomacy or the tactics of delay and guerrilla warfare. The old military tradition had other serious drawbacks. In the field there was a lack of liaison and strategic control — the rases, often too proud to ask for help, fought separately. An adequate central command organization was not developed, and the emperor was neither by experience nor inclination capable of molding his disparate forces into something like a unified army.

All these weaknesses were well known to Haile Selassie. But he never hoped to beat the Italians in pitched battle and did not believe he could win the war alone. He placed his hopes entirely in the support of Britain and in the assistance of the League of Nations. Haile Selassie

[34] Africanus (pseud.), *Etiopia 1935: Panorama geo-politico* (Rome, 1935), 111.
[35] Perham, *Government of Ethiopia*, 166–7; Steer, *Caesar in Abyssinia*, 123, 162–6.

thought of his army only as a delaying force.[36] The best way to utilize what resources he had was in the development of guerrilla warfare. In June 1935 General Virgin distributed throughout the empire "general principles and instructions for waging ruthless guerrilla warfare." Nonetheless, too many factors militated against the success of such a strategy. For one thing, the Italian airforce prevented the necessary freedom of movement. Guerrilla warfare depends further "on the readiness of the civilian population to support, feed, hide, and encourage the guerrilla fighters." [37] In a country like Ethiopia, however, comprised of many and often highly antagonistic groups of people, a state of war served to loosen the already tenuous cohesion and to magnify the underlying differences. Racial or regional separatism, not national unity, was often the result of a foreign threat, and in such conditions guerrilla warfare could not succeed.

Above all, the most important weakness of the Ethiopian army, and a primary cause of the nation's ultimate defeat, was that the Ethiopians had no weapons. Haile Selassie had eleven slow and unarmed airplanes, three of which could not leave the ground and one of which was given to the Red Cross. Ethiopia had 371 bombs. There were eight antiaircraft guns in the north and five in the south, all inadequately supplied with ammunition. A third of the rifles carried by the army were useless — the Ethiopian believed ultimately in his spear, and the rifle was mostly for display. All in all, there were only 50–60,000 modern rifles in the country, and half of these were in the hands of local chiefs. Worst of all was the lack of ammunition. At the end of the rains, the Ethiopians had only about 15 million rounds of small-arms ammunition.[38]

Ethiopia itself produced no arms or ammunition. Its entire arsenal had to be purchased abroad and brought in through the territory of the European powers. On 21 August 1930, wishing "to give a further proof of their desire to assist what appeared to be the programme of the reigning Negus, by reserving to him alone the power to receive and control imports of arms," Britain, France, and Italy, and Ethiopia signed in Paris a treaty "regulating the importation into Ethiopia of

---

[36] Steer, *Caesar in Abyssinia*, 64–5. The Italians were aware of this. De Bono, *Anno XIIII*, 174, 185.

[37] Virgin, *Abyssinia*, 167; Steer, *Caesar in Abyssinia*, 62.

[38] Steer, *Caesar in Abyssinia*, 51–6. See also the account of the American chargé in Addis Ababa in *U.S. Diplomatic Papers, 1935*, I, 689–94.

arms, ammunition, and implements of war." The preamble stated that the signatories were

> desirous of ensuring an effective supervision over the trade in arms and munitions in Ethiopia and in the territories adjacent thereto, with the object on the one hand of enabling His Majesty the Emperor of Ethiopia to obtain all the arms and munitions necessary for the defense of his territories from external aggression and for the preservation of internal order therein and, on the other hand, of preventing the menace to the peace of Ethiopia and the adjacent territories of the other three Powers which is caused by the acquisition of arms and munitions by unauthorized persons.

Only the emperor could order, receive, and maintain arms, and he was required to publish records of exports and imports. A reservation in article 9 of the treaty gave the three powers that controlled the accesses to Ethiopia the right to refuse authorizations for transit "if the attitude or disturbed condition of Ethiopia constitutes a threat to peace or public order." This was the only ground for such a refusal in the treaty, the purpose of which was to strengthen Haile Selassie so that he could maintain order within his country and the independence of his state.[39]

The emperor did not seriously abuse this agreement.[40] Certainly his purchases abroad were not excessive. In 1934, a normal year, the emperor imported 3,000 rifles, 59 machine guns, and 48,000 rounds of ammunition.[41] As the danger of Italian aggression grew, at the end of 1934 Haile Selassie sought to increase his supply with further purchases in Europe. He approached the Germans and was turned down. But in the first months of 1935 he got mountain artillery and mortars from French firms, 4 million cartridges from a Czech company, some antitank guns from Switzerland, and machine guns from a Danish concern.[42] Some gold and a few guns, Haile Selassie claimed,

[39] The text of the treaty of 1930 is printed in A. Lessona, *Verso l'impero*, 249–60.

[40] The Italians, in their memorandum of 4 September 1935, accused the emperor of having violated the agreement by selling arms to unauthorized persons and by failing to keep strict records of all purchases. League, *Official Journal, 1935*, 1388, 1410–2. An official report by a committee of the League council, submitted on 5 October 1935, rejected this contention. "There is no reason to believe that the Ethiopian Government deliberately or systematically violated [the treaty's] essential provisions." *Ibid.*, 1618.

[41] Steer, *Caesar in Abyssinia*, 53.

[42] *Documents on German Foreign Policy*, III, 543, 759–60, 1083.

came also from the Iman of Yemen and from King Ibn Saud.[43] The greatest part of these materials was imported by way of the French-controlled port of Djibouti and from there by the Addis Ababa railroad. Between January and July 1935, the emperor was able to procure 16,000 rifles, 600 machine guns, and 5.5 million rounds of small arms ammunition. But this was not enough. The Ethiopian supply as of July was "in quantity hopelessly inadequate for a campaign of moderate length, and in quality incapable of carrying a campaign to a speedy victory." [44]

It was obvious in July that, if Ethiopia was to have a fighting chance, the emperor must have more arms at once. Two factors worked against this. One was that the Ethiopian treasury was almost exhausted by the purchases that had been made in the first half of the year. On 17 July the government made an effort to procure funds from the German government for the purchase of arms, but nothing came of it.[45] Dr. Martin was sent as minister to London at the end of July expressly to raise funds or to get credit from the English. He had no success. The emperor devoted his entire fortune to the paying of wages and the buying of arms for his men, but he was not vastly rich and his private funds were not enough to meet the great and growing need. All requests for munitions loans from Europe were turned down.[46] The nations of Europe refused to help Haile Selassie in the one substantive fashion that would have enabled him to offer real resistance to the mortal threat facing his country.

Furthermore, the nations of Europe bowed to Italian requests that

[43] Lessona, *Verso l'impero*, 106. Representations to the Iman and the King of Hejaz were made in the first half of 1935 by an Ethiopian mission seeking support. *Le Temps*, 19 June 1935.

[44] Steer, *Caesar in Abyssinia*, 53; Villari, *Storia diplomatica*, 82.

[45] The emperor tried to make his request attractive to the Germans. His representative told the German foreign office that the political interests of Germany and Ethiopia were identical in that a conflict with Italy over Austria would someday be inevitable. He requested that 3 million marks be placed at Ethiopia's disposal for arms and ammunition to be bought outside Germany from German subsidiaries abroad. The Germans toyed with the idea but did nothing at the time. After war broke out, they assigned a shipment of arms worth 1.2 million marks to Ethiopia via Norway and Belgium. *Documents on German Foreign Policy*, IV, 454–5, 793.

[46] *Le Temps*, 26 July 1935; Steer, *Caesar in Abyssinia*, 125–7. The emperor spent 2 million English pounds in the course of the conflict, completely exhausting his own resources. Steer estimates that, since the emperor was able to hold out until two months before the rains of 1936, another loan of 2 million pounds would have protracted the war until the June rains when all military operations would have to halt until the next October, during which time sanctions could have had their effect.

they stop selling arms to the emperor. As a result, even if Haile Selassie could have found the money, his sources of supply were being cut off. In the first days of April the Italian government sent a strong protest to Belgium, Switzerland, Czechoslovakia, and Denmark against the export of arms and ammunition to Ethiopia and requested that prohibitions be placed on further sales. President Edouard Beneš of Czechoslovakia and Prime Minister Paul Van Zeeland of Belgium promised to do their best to prevent this traffic.[47] The Swiss took a similar line. In the middle of April a protest went from Rome to Paris, objecting to the use of the French-controlled Djibouti railroad for the importation of war supplies to Addis Ababa. The Quai d'Orsay turned the objection down, replying that they had no reason to close the line for this purpose. In May the Italian protest was renewed, with Italy's claiming that the French action was not in accord with the French-Italian agreement of 7 January. Again the French replied that they were only being faithful to the letter of the law in their dealings with Ethiopia and their allowance of the transit of arms. On the other hand, Laval agreed to do all in his power to prevent the export of arms from France to Ethiopia.[48] The French could not ignore the probability that in case of war their railroad from Djibouti, if it were carrying arms into Ethiopia, would be a prime and vulnerable target for Italian bombings. The less provocation offered Italy, the safer the railroad would be. On 27 May, therefore, Léger told the Italian ambassador that France would apply "with maximum rigor" article 9 of the 1930 treaty and prohibit the importation through Djibouti of any German munitions. On 9 May the British government informed Italy that, since the Walwal incident, no shipments of arms had left Britain for Ethiopia and that the government had cautioned private manufacturing firms against furnishing Ethiopia with arms. The British added that, since licenses were required for the export of munitions, none could be sent without the government's approval. In the summer of 1935 two applications for export licenses were received, but by the middle of July they were still under consideration by the government and not yet granted. The Italians asked the British further to prohibit the transport of arms across British-controlled lands bordering Ethiopia.[49]

[47] Villari, *Storia diplomatica*, 81–2, 84–5. A full and final prohibition on exports from Belgium was issued by the Belgium government on 19 August 1935. J. Miller, *Belgian Foreign Policy Between Two Wars, 1919–1940* (New York, 1951), 213.
[48] Villari, *Storia diplomatica*, 82–3. In this he appears to have been successful.
[49] The British had issued one license in September 1934, before the Walwal

The emperor was greatly disheartened by all of this, and in particular by the reluctance of Britain and France to live up to the spirit of the 1930 treaty, which had been signed to help Haile Selassie "obtain all the arms and munitions necessary for the defense of his territories from external aggression." On 10 July he remonstrated with the British, French, and Belgians for even considering restrictions on the export of arms to Ethiopia. Such action, the emperor said, would place "Ethiopia in a difficult position as, unlike Italy she possesses no local manufactures. At the present time war does not exist; hence the refusal to supply arms cannot be explained by a simple desire to observe an attitude of neutrality and impartiality." [50]

On 17 July Haile Selassie gave an interview to George Steer of *The Times*. Ethiopia, he said, desired the League to discuss the dispute at its meeting scheduled for the end of July. Until the League's decisions were known, Ethiopia would take no further diplomatic action. The emperor acknowledged the value of the treaty of 1906 as an instrument of pacification, although in the face of Italy's military preparations and France's indifference it seemed to him unlikely that the treaty still had much value. Ethiopia's hope rested with Britain. The emperor expressed no criticism of Britain's efforts to seek a negotiated settlement, but no proposals by any country had been yet presented to the Ethiopian government. Concerning territorial concessions, the emperor said he would accept Britain's Zeila proposal of June. He regarded this matter of a seaport as vital, "much more important than loans or other financial assistance" for the improvement and civilization of the country. In exchange for Zeila he would cede to Italy that part of the Ogaden between Walwal and Dolo. He would cede no land in the north. The emperor expressed "surprise that the export of arms caused any hesitation" when the terms of the treaty of 1930 made his allowance in this matter so clear.

> If Italy is still allowed to send munitions and export licenses for arms for Ethiopia are withheld, Ethiopia will be unable to maintain her independence. I am particularly injured at the attitude of Czechoslovakia and Belgium, where Ethiopian agreements with private firms had previously received official consent.

---

incident, but evidently no arms had been sent. In May they apparently were giving a gratuitous assurance because the Italian government had not yet made any requests to Britain to prohibit or restrict the export of arms. *Parliamentary Debates*, 304 H.C. Deb. 5s., col. 2483; 302 H.C. Deb. 5s., cols. 735, 941; Villari, *Storia diplomatica*, 83, 86.

[50] *The Times* (London), 11 July 1935.

The Italian threat to peace appears to me to be flagrant. If Italy declares war, or her troops dare to cross the frontiers, Ethiopia will fight immediately and simultaneously appeal to the League.[51]

The following day, 18 July, Haile Selassie addressed an assembly of Ethiopian notables in Parliament House. His speech was a strong affirmation to his people and the chiefs that the government would defend the independence and integrity of Ethiopia against any invader. He rejected the idea of a mandate or a protectorate over Ethiopia. He lambasted Italy's belligerency and cited Mussolini's recent pronouncements as proof that Italy sought to conquer Ethiopia. Mussolini's talk about avenging Aduwa was curious, Haile Selassie said. "Ethiopia was not even the aggressor at Adowa, did not draw advantages from her victory, and had not enlarged its domain" after the battle was over. If Mussolini attacked Ethiopia, the emperor stated, he would find a country united against Italy. The emperor appealed for unity among Christians and Muslims in this hour of national danger. Every man must think of himself as first and foremost an Ethiopian, and all differences of religion, race, or region must be put aside: "I, your Emperor, who address you, will be in your midst, not hesitating to pour out my life-blood for the independence of Ethiopia." Haile Selassie ended his speech with a warning against the traditional weakness of the Ethiopian battle formation and with an exhortation to bravery. "Soldiers, when you have heard that in the battle-fire a loved chieftain has fallen, do not weep or despair. The man who dies for his country is happy. Blind death destroys in peace as well as in war. Better to die free than live as slaves. Remember your fathers who fell at Adowa!"[52]

In public as well as in private the emperor was brave. But he could neither cure Ethiopia's weaknesses nor assure the country's safety. Sometime during the summer months of 1935, in fact, acting entirely on his own and in the secrecy of the royal palace, Haile Selassie proposed to the British ambassador that Britain take on Ethiopia as a protectorate. The British turned this offer down. They naturally did not want to accept sole responsibility for Ethiopia on the eve of an Italian invasion.[53] The security of Ethiopia was now the com-

---

[51] *The Times* (London), 18 July 1935; Steer, *Caesar in Abyssinia*, 37–40.

[52] *The Times* (London), 19 July 1935; Steer, *Caesar in Abyssinia*, 43–7.

[53] This information comes to me from a private source. The only official comment on such a matter came from the British on 4 June 1935 when the government issued a denial to an Italian allegation that Colonel Clifford, leader of

plete responsibility of the democratic states of Europe and the League of Nations.

The second half of July found the French and British, as usual, blowing hot and cold. On 18 July, in instructions sent to Chambrun in Rome, Laval stated that the French government could find no reason to persuade the Ethiopians to back down from the position they had taken at Scheveningen. France would not encourage a renewal of the sittings of the arbitration commission until the problem of its jurisdiction was solved. If the Italians would not agree to the appointment of a fifth arbitrator, the deadlock would not be broken and the council would have to meet. The council, according to Avenol, did not have the competence to appoint a fifth member to the commission.[54] A council meeting might be able to define the commission's purview, but it would also be compelled to discuss the conflict in full, according to the Ethiopian appeal to article 15 of the Covenant. To prevent these complications, Laval warned, Italy should reconsider its intransigence.[55]

On the 19th Laval ordered Chambrun to inform Mussolini that France could not ignore a violation of the Covenant, for the League was the basis of France's security system in Europe and only within the League could France be assured of an entente with Britain. If Italy broke with the League, "the gravest difficulties" would follow in the relations between France and Italy. Although France would do all it could to help Italy in the negotiations, Chambrun reported, if it came to a showdown France would have to stand by the League. For this reason Laval urged Mussolini to modify his ambitions, come to a negotiated settlement to avoid war, and, as a first step, agree to the appointment of a fifth arbitrator so that the machinery of conciliation could still function.[56]

Laval shared these warnings with the British, who concurred in his approach. On 24 July the British government presented a similar

---

the British section of the British-Ethiopian boundary commission that played a part in the Walwal incident, had stated that Ethiopia had asked Britain to institute a twenty-five-year protectorate over Ethiopia. *The Times* (London), 5 June 1935.

[54] Avenol was in Paris from 14–17 July and spoke at length with Laval on the 17th.

[55] Herriot, *Jadis*, II, 572.

[56] Herriot, *Jadis*, II, 572–3; Laval's speech before the Chamber of Deputies on 28 December 1935, *Journal officiel, débats parlementaires*, 29 December 1935, 2865.

statement of caution to Italy. Britain based its foreign policy on the League, Drummond told Mussolini. In this it had the unanimous support of the British public. It was only through the League that Britain was able to maintain a policy in Europe. Britain was eager to find a solution to the present dispute and still held to its efforts to find concessions for Italy in the Ogaden. Britain was gravely concerned by Mussolini's rebuff of the June proposals and by his greater demands and the threat of war. Drummond pointed out that Italian aggression would violate the Kellogg Pact, articles 10 and 12 of the Covenant, the Italian-Ethiopian treaty of 1928, and the tripartite accord of 1906.[57]

But beyond these general warnings, Britain and France were not willing to go. There was no attempt to threaten Mussolini with punitive action, no statement that Ethiopia would be supported and defended. France did not want to go to war against Italy. As always, any initiative for resistance would have to come from Britain. Yet the British, in mid-July, still imagined that negotiated settlement of the dispute was possible. Against a "dark horizon" Hoare thought he discerned "a faint ray of hope."[58] On 22 October Hoare described the British position of July: "I maintain that the League, being an organ for the preservation of the peace, had upon it this incumbent duty — so long as there was a chance of conciliation it was the duty of the League to maintain the path of conciliation. Until the month of August the door of conciliation was still open, and that, that being so, it would have been contrary to the principles of the League to bolt it and bar it by an ultimatum or abrupt action."[59]

For conciliation there would have to be a climate of opinion appropriate and conducive to a settlement. To this end Hoare, in his speech of 11 July, reasserted Britain's friendship and good will to Italy and, in conjunction with a similar French action, imposed a formal prohibition on the export of arms to Ethiopia.[60] The two countries were still allowing transit of arms through their protected territories, but this was of little benefit to Ethiopia since its main

[57] Villari, *Storia diplomatica*, 105–6.

[58] Templewood, *Nine Troubled Years*, 161. On the other hand, on 25 July the American embassy in London sent a report to Washington saying that the British Foreign Office believed that nothing short of a miracle could now stop a war. U.S. Diplomatic Correspondence, 765.84/730, 384.11/22.

[59] *Parliamentary Debates*, 305 H.C. Deb. 5s., col. 26.

[60] The embargo on arms to Ethiopia was placed over the protests of Eden and of Sidney Barton in Addis Ababa. Avon, *Facing the Dictators*, 288–9. It is to be noted that the prohibition extended to Italy as well.

sources of arms were now cut off. These prohibitions were clear violations of the spirit of the treaty of 1930 and had very serious effects in Ethiopia. They meant that Haile Selassie would face the end of the rainy season with only those weapons in his possession in July. This was a crippling blow to the emperor's defensive preparations. As the emperor said on 28 July: "While the embargo in its terms is impartial . . . the obvious result is the very opposite of impartiality. The other party has abundant domestic facilities for the production of war material; we have none." [61] The embargoes hurt only Ethiopia, for Italian military preparations continued unabated.

On 22 July the Italian government suspended its decree of 21 December 1927, which had required a 40 percent gold base for all readily negotiable liabilities of the Bank of Italy. This step was taken to find the money to pay for war matériel worth some 500 million lire, which had been purchased abroad.[62] Although Italy had substantial foreign credits, these could not be realized at once and the government found it necessary to raid the gold reserves[63] Popular support of the war effort grew. On 23 July it was announced that some 10,000 Italian men living abroad had volunteered for service in east Africa. The American chargé in Rome reported to Washington on 26 July that "as the period approaches which has been regarded as crucial it is clear that the Duce is able to point to a more enthusiastic demonstration of [popular] support for his policy than at any previous time." [64]

While Mussolini and the armed forces went their way, Italian diplomats were preoccupied with their customary problem — what to do about an upcoming meeting of the League council, this one scheduled for some time after 25 July. The Duce himself gave a new

---

[61] *The Times* (London), 29 July 1935.

[62] The decree of 1927, which inflated the lira and put Italy at a competitive disadvantage in the world market, was nonetheless a source of great pride to Mussolini. The inscription on the Lira Monument at Pesaro said that Fascism would defend the gold lira to the last drop of Italian blood. The "temporary suspension" of the gold coverage was therefore an embarrassment to Mussolini. During the first eight months of 1935, as compared to the first eight months of 1934, Italy's foreign purchases of coal were greater by 900,000 tons, its purchases of aviation gasoline up 21 percent, scrap iron up by 25 percent, and copper up by 47 percent. J. Leonard, "The Effect on Employment of Economic Sanctions on National and World Prosperity," *Proceedings of the Institute of World Affairs*, 13:223 (1936).

[63] The gold reserve fell, for example, by 226 million lire in the first ten days of August. *The Times* (London), 12 August 1935.

[64] *U.S. Diplomatic Papers, 1935*, I, 618.

interpretation to the significance of the League. The "moment of decision has come," and the question at hand was not one of law but one of civilization. It must be established, Mussolini said,

> whether Europe is still worthy of fulfilling the colonizing mission which for centuries has been a source of its greatness. If not, then the hour of Europe's decadence has irredeemably arrived. Has the League of Nations been created to give formal recognition to this condition? Is it to be the tribunal before which Negroes, backward peoples, and the savages of the world will drag the great nations which have revolutionized and transformed humanity? Will it be the parliament where Europe will succumb to the law of numbers and will see its decadence proclaimed?

Italy had fully prepared its course of action for the coming campaign and was certain of the outcome.[65]

The Italian diplomatic strategy was to avoid a general discussion of the conflict at the July meeting of the council. This would give Italy yet another free month before 25 August, the day on which the council was to meet if the arbitration commission had not settled the dispute. The simplest way to bypass the July meeting was to agree to the naming of a fifth arbitrator. It had been Italy's unwillingness to take this step that caused the July session to be called in accordance with the resolutions of 25 May. But despite all promptings, particularly from France, the Italian government took no action. Only after the strongest urging by Aloisi on 20 and 21 July did Mussolini take the coming council session seriously enough to consider formulating a policy to be followed there.[66]

There was no lack of interest in Italy's problems. Chambrun and Drummond hovered about the foreign ministry with suggestions. On 15 July both ambassadors requested that the Ethiopian matter be discussed by the three interested European powers on the basis of the 1906 agreement. Both ambassadors and their governments were still hopeful that this treaty could be used as the means to keep the Italian-Ethiopian problem under direct negotiation and away from the League. Directly in the middle of these proposals was Joseph Avenol, the secretary-general, acting on his own initiative. He prom-

[65] Interview with Henry de Kerillis of the *Echo de Paris,* given probably on 20 July. Mussolini, *Opera omnia,* XXVII, 106–110.

[66] For French promptings, see Laval's messages of 18 and 19 July, noted above, and Chambrun's urgings of 15 July in Aloisi, *Journal,* 286–8. Aloisi recognized that his task was made the more difficult at Geneva by Mussolini's "proclaiming *urbi et orbi* that Italy wanted to devour Abyssinia."

ised Grandi in London that he would do his utmost to postpone the coming council meeting in the hope that some compromise might be worked out under the aegis of the 1906 accord.[67] It was a return to the "old" diplomacy, with a European focus, and "such action was purely one-sided. Ethiopia possessed nothing that could be called a diplomatic service. The League as such was barred out, almost as completely as the general public, from all access to the diplomatic scene and from all influence upon whatever discussions might be going on behind the traditional curtain of secrecy." [68]

Mussolini was sufficiently interested by these overtures to receive Drummond on 17 July. This was the "faint ray of hope" that Hoare had seen. *The Times*'s Paris correspondent reported it on the 18th as "a small flower of potential agreement" which has "sprung up in the last few days from the arid soil of international controversy" and which "must be carefully tended and allowed to grow strong before it can bear the light of publicity." But it was a false hope, and the meeting of the 17th came to nothing. Mussolini at the time was already suggesting that study be made of the means of proclaiming the king of Italy emperor after the establishment of an Italian protectorate over Ethiopia. On the 18th Haile Selassie publicly refused to consider the idea of a protectorate.

New tacks were tried. On the 21st Aloisi got Mussolini's approval to ask the Ethiopians to agree to renew the arbitration proceedings under the condition that the frontier problem not be discussed. On the same day Chambrun asked Aloisi, in the name of the French government, to censure Ethiopia in the League, presumably referring to Avenol's idea that this would weaken Ethiopia's moral position.[69] Italian intransigence, we have seen, prompted the French and British notes of the 19th and 24th, warning Italy not to run afoul of the League by an uncompromising stand.

The Ethiopians were also getting impatient. On 19 July came their note to the League asking that a team of neutral observers under League auspices be sent to investigate the frontier incidents, and that articles 11 and 15 of the Covenant be considered relevant to the dis-

[67] Villari, *Storia diplomatica*, 119–20; Cohen, *La Société des Nations*, 90.
[68] Walters, *History of the League*, II, 638–9. The Ethiopian government, while viewing these negotiations without hostility, pointed out on 24 July that its knowledge of their existence came only through the press. League, *Official Journal, 1935*, 975.
[69] *Ibid*. Aloisi, *Journal*, 287–8.

pute. Nothing came of this move. On the 24th Ethiopia requested the secretary-general to alert the council to "the urgent necessity of their intervention" and, in accordance with the May resolutions, to call an immediate meeting.[70] The British now pressed for an early meeting as well and requested the president of the council, Maxim Litvinov, to convoke a session for 29 July. Avenol informed Italy on the 26th that 1 August would be the probable date of the extraordinary session. The French government wanted to postpone the meeting still more, but the pressures of the British and Litvinov allowed of no further delay.[71] In response to a poll of the council members by Avenol on the 26th, it was decided that the meeting should occur on 31 July.

Two questions arose as soon as it was decided that the council should meet. What was to be the scope of the discussion, and would the Italian delegation attend? The Ethiopians wanted to submit the entire conflict to the study and authority of the council. The French feared that such a step would result in an Italian boycott, and they were above all eager to keep Italy at the conference table. Italy insisted on limiting the discussion, as the resolutions of May implied, merely to finding a way out of the impasse that had halted the work of the arbitration commission. This would keep the League's attention focused only on the settlement of the Walwal incident, and consideration of the larger issues of the conflict would again be avoided.[72] Mussolini sealed this Italian position with a carefully drafted telegram to the secretary-general on 27 July, noting the Italian efforts of 14 and 23 July to get Ethiopia to agree to limit the work of the commission solely to the matter of responsibility. If Ethiopia agreed to these terms, said Mussolini, and if "the only object of the [council] meeting [will] be to consider the most suitable methods of enabling the Commission of Conciliation and Arbitration to resume its proceedings to advantage," then Italy would attend. If not, "the Italian Government will state its observations on the subject." Ethiopia replied to the League on the 28th, denying that it ever agreed to a limitation of the arbitrators' powers and fully endorsing the arguments presented by Potter and La Pradelle before the commission had ad-

[70] League, *Official Journal, 1935*, 972–3,5.

[71] Aloisi, *Journal*, 288–9; Villari, *Storia diplomatica*, 76, 120.

[72] Aloisi, *Journal*, 289; Villari, *Storia diplomatica*, 76; *U.S. Diplomatic Papers, 1935*, I, 618–9; Cohen, *La Société des Nations*, 92–3.

journed on the 9th. The Ethiopians maintained that the council should decide between the contentions of the two groups of arbitrators.[73] This Ethiopian telegram significantly omitted any demand that the council go into the broader reaches of the dispute. There was no call for help, no request that the articles of the Covenant be invoked to prevent the coming war. Ethiopia, missing a great opportunity, tacitly consented to the Italian demand that the council limit its discussion only to the technical matter of getting the commission back to work to settle an extraneous issue. Problems of war and peace were allowed once again to pass by default. The Ethiopian communication of the 28th, however, made the presence of an Italian delegate at Geneva more likely, and this evidently was the purpose behind its moderation.

Italy seemed to have won still another round. Mussolini told Aloisi to go to Geneva and to leave if the debate went beyond the Italian limits.[74] On the 30th, the eve of the council meeting, Mussolini wrote a significant article, published in *Il Popolo d'Italia* on the 31st, his frankest and bluntest public statement yet on the Italian-Ethiopian conflict.

The article was entitled "The Irrefutable Fact," and its purpose was to explain why Italy was preparing for action in Ethiopia. Most current arguments, Mussolini wrote, missed the point or were entirely extraneous to the real reason. There was slavery in Ethiopia, and slave trading continued despite the emperor's promises to the League to abolish it. Still, "it is not to abolish the commerce of slaves that Italy has prepared and is preparing for military action in its east African colonies. The abolition of slavery is not an objective, but will be a logical consequence, of our policy." Nor was the question of race behind Italy's preparations. First, the Ethiopians did not consider themselves Negroes, but Semites. Second, Italians had many black men fighting valiantly under the Italian flag: "We Fascists recognize the existence of races, their differences and hierarchy [*gerarchia*], but we do not intend to present ourselves to the world as flag bearers of the white race in antithesis to other races." Moreover, contrary to earlier statements, the bringing of civilization to Ethiopia was now regarded as only another side consequence of Italy's action.

The essential arguments, absolutely unanswerable and such to end all further discussion, are two: the vital needs of the Italian people

[73] League, *Official Journal*, 1935, 971-2, 976; Aloisi, *Journal*, 289.
[74] Aloisi, *Journal*, 290.

and their military security in east Africa. The first of these arguments has been specifically admitted by the British foreign minister [Hoare's speech of 11 July]. The second is the decisive one.

It is clear that the strategic situation of our colonies, precarious in normal times, would become untenable in exceptional times, if Italy found itself engaged in Europe, for instance. The solution of the problem must be total. An expansion which does not secure itself by arms, a protectorate which is not accompanied by military measures, is likely to end up as did that which followed Uccialli. On the other hand, so long as the Ethiopian military menace continues, the security of our colonies will be precarious. Italy is the sole judge of the limits of this security. In the case of danger we would have no aid of any sort from anyone. Indeed, the contrary would probably occur.

Put in military terms, the Italian-Abyssinian problem is immediately simple, with the force of a logical absolute. Put in military terms, the problem admits of only one solution — with Geneva, without Geneva, against Geneva.

In military domination, concluded Mussolini, the "policy of Fascist Italy has found its supreme historic and human justification." [75]

In London Samuel Hoare outlined to the American ambassador the plan of the Cabinet for the coming meeting of the council. The British delegation would go to Geneva to seek, first, the appointment of a fifth arbitrator and, second, a tripartite conference among the signers of the treaty of 1906. In both cases the British were aiming to keep the League out of the dispute and to provide opportunities for extra-League negotiations. Hoare believed that France would cooperate. By these means "at least there would be some delay and some possibility of negotiations in which the British would be willing to cooperate to obtain commercial advantages for Italy in Abyssinia and an extension of Italian right of way into Abyssinian territory, and, if necessary, to Italian economic advisers to Abyssinia, but in no case would the British agree to the destruction of the independence of Abyssinia." [76] Whether or not the British would act to prevent this destruction was still the all-important and unanswered question. The British government did not authorize Eden to say at Geneva that, in Austen Chamberlain's words, Britain was "prepared to fulfil [its] obligations under the Covenant if others will do the same." When Eden left London on 30 July for a preliminary meeting with Laval in Paris,

---

[75] Mussolini, *Opera omnia*, XXVII, 110–1.
[76] *U.S. Diplomatic Papers, 1935*, I, 620.

all he had to go on was a Foreign Office memorandum stressing the threat of the Italian-Ethiopian conflict to the League, to the European situation, to British-French relations, to the colonies of those two countries, and finally to Italy financially. The memorandum contained no constructive suggestions for solving the problem.[77] But it did represent a hardening of the British position, for, although it revealed no imagination and presented no proposals for bilateral or multilateral action, it did record the British government's reasons for opposing an Italian conquest of Ethiopia.

In France there was some talk about the possibility of applying article 12 of the Covenant to the dispute. This article required the contending parties to abjure war for a period of three months following an inquiry by the council or an arbitral award. The French felt an "almost breathless urgency" for some time in which the processes of conciliation could be put to work. It was known that Haile Selassie approved the invocation of article 12, if the cooling-off period could be guaranteed.[78]

The possibility of using article 12 does not seem to have been brought up in the Eden-Laval talks of 30 July. Indeed, nothing came of the conversations. Eden was hampered by the failure of the Cabinet to give him instructions specific enough to lay plans for either resistance or appeasement. Encountering such indefiniteness, Laval naturally dragged his feet. It was agreed to decide upon a course of action later in Geneva. Laval said he saw little chance of averting war. All Eden got from his stay in Paris was a warning from the Portuguese ambassador that anti-European nationalism would flare up throughout Africa if a war broke out between Italy and Ethiopia.[79]

On 31 July the delegates to the eighty-seventh (extraordinary) session of the council gathered in Geneva. Corridor diplomacy began at once, and it was in private negotiations that all the important decisions were made and the bargains struck. Aloisi made no concession on the 31st. He stayed firmly with the Italian position that the purpose of the meeting was solely to clarify the council's instructions of 25 May to the arbitral commission. Maintaining close consultation with Rome, Aloisi refused to agree to a broadening of the commission's sphere of competence.

---

[77] Avon, *Facing the Dictators*, 245–6; Guariglia, *Ricordi*, 249–50.
[78] *The Times* (London), 29 and 30 July 1935.
[79] Avon, *Facing the Dictators*, 246.

The private session of the council on the afternoon of the 31st was held only "because it was scheduled and not because an agreement had been reached." [80] Aloisi restated the Italian stand, that so long as the matter of Walwal was under arbitration the council could not examine the conflict. All that was at stake was the technical matter of arbitral procedure. Jèze demurred. Confronting the council, he said, was

> the problem of deciding whether this procedure is to be a dilatory procedure or a procedure aiming seriously at a settlement of the dispute between Ethiopia and Italy. The problem goes further than the appointment of a fifth arbitrator or the question of what is to happen in the event of the arbitrators failing to agree upon the appointment of the fifth arbitrator. The point is whether it is desired to continue to follow procedures which have so far yielded no result except that of aggravating a conflict which is every day more critical, or whether, on the contrary, the Council desires to take a decision to consider the situation as a whole with a view to ascertaining whether there is a possibility — and I may say at once, that the Ethiopian Government will co-operate in that effort — of finding a pacific solution.

This was the extent of Ethiopia's assertiveness. The government was fearful that Italy would withdraw from the League if Ethiopia stood on its rights: "It was clearly and strongly threatened that refusal [to acquiesce] would lead to abandonment of the arbitration, Italian withdrawal from the League, and war, and Ethiopian Government and its Agent felt, rightly or wrongly, that these consequences must be avoided as long as possible and practically at any cost." [81] Once again the Ethiopians had let pass an important opportunity to press their case. Eden said only that at this time he did not want to limit the agenda of the council session. Laval thought that "pending further developments" the council should restrict itself to considering the implementation of the resolutions of 25 May. All agreed that further meetings of the council should be postponed until private negotiations could be pursued. [82]

On the night of 31 July, Laval, with Eden's approval, submitted a plan to Aloisi. They agreed to Italy's desire to prevent the arbitration commission from discussing the problem of frontiers and the

[80] *U.S. Diplomatic Papers, 1935*, I, 621.
[81] Potter, *Wal Wal Arbitration*, 16.
[82] League, *Official Journal, 1935*, 964–6.

question of the ownership of Walwal. In return for this concession in Italy's favor on a substantive matter, the French and British asked Italy to permit the nomination of the fifth arbitrator. In addition, they asked Italy to accept the council's consideration of the entire Italian-Ethiopian conflict, on the condition that this comprehensive jurisdiction would in turn be delegated to Italy, France, and Britain who, as signatories of the 1906 treaty, would seek out a settlement among themselves.[83] To this last proposal Italy had two objections. It would mean admitting, for the first time, that the League could have an interest in the conflict as a whole. Such negotiations, secondly, would tend "to reaffirm the existence of British and French as well as Italian 'spheres of influence' in Abyssinia." [84] On the other hand, the Italians realized that if tripartite negotiations, so early sought by the British, could be held outside the League's jurisdiction, not only would this be a slap in the face for the League and a diplomatic disaster of the first magnitude for Ethiopia — both contrived and delivered by Britain and France, no less — but it would afford Italy a new mechanism for delay by forestalling League action at this time. No one would want to endanger the private negotiations of the leading powers of Europe by threatening Italy with League sanctions if it appeared that a settlement was in the offing. For these reasons the Italian government consented to the tripartite talks, and the British and the French consented to make them independent of the League.[85] Italy agreed to the appointment of the fifth arbitrator and the resumption of talks, and Britain and France agreed to have the purview of the arbitration commission narrowed, and its prestige and authority weakened.

The slap to the League was a hard one. At this critical moment its two leading members were willing to jettison its rules and ideals, to leave undeveloped its authority and effectiveness. In their own interests, Britain and France withdrew the problem from the international organization, to deal with it in secret bargaining as a colonial matter fit only for settlement among the interested powers. For Ethiopia, it was indeed a diplomatic disaster, for that nation was not consulted at any stage of the arrangements. Ethiopia's position before the arbitral commission was grievously undermined; a new delay was decreed

---

[83] Aloisi, *Journal*, 291.

[84] *U.S. Diplomatic Papers, 1935*, I, 622.

[85] Agreement was announced in a communiqué on 1 August, printed League, *Official Journal, 1935*, 969n.

before the League could consider the larger significance of the dispute; and the fate of Ethiopia was to be decided in secret by parties interested above all in the placation of Italy. No amount of window dressing could hide the insult to Ethiopia and the damage to the League. The fact that the arbitral commission would sit again could not conceal the profound blow dealt to its effectiveness and integrity.[86]

On 3 August the council met in public session. Two resolutions, drawn up and agreed to beforehand by France, Britain, and Italy, were presented for its approval. The first, conceding Italy's demands, stated that the question of frontiers did not fall within the competence of the commission. Thus the commission must not base its decision on a determination of who owned Walwal at the time the incidents occurred. It noted further that both sides had agreed to the appointment "without delay" of the fifth arbitrator. It hoped that the "procedure will have brought about the settlement of the dispute before September 1st, 1935." The second resoltuion stated: "The Council decides to meet in any event on September 4th, 1935, to undertake the general examination, in its various aspects, of the relations between Italy and Ethiopia." There was no mention of the agreement to enter into tripartite negotiations to the exclusion of the League and of Ethiopia.[87]

Ethiopia bowed to the fact that principle was being ignored, bowed to the political reality that weakness must give way to power, that small states count for less in international affairs than large states do. "For political reasons of expediency," Jèze said, "the Imperial Ethiopian Government is called upon to make a considerable sacrifice in the interests of world peace." Ethiopia would make this sacrifice, he noted, even though it weakened its case before the arbitration commission. Once it was forbidden to ask who held sovereignty over the wells of Walwal in 1934, Ethiopia lost the chance to present its strongest argument. Ethiopia, Jèze continued, did not withdraw its earlier contentions or consider them less valid. But, "to give the Council proof of its loyalty, its good faith, and even of its candour," Ethiopia would accept the council's resolutions and abide by the further deci-

[86] La Pradelle discusses the use of the ineffectual commission by the British and the French as an instrument of diversion to gain time for independent machinations in Le Conflit italo-étiopien, 169–72. On pp. 438–43, La Pradelle notes the fact that the council of the League failed to stand up to its legal and moral responsibilities to support the authority of the commission.

[87] League, Official Journal, 1935, 967–8.

sions of the arbitrators. Ethiopia hailed "with joy and gratitude" the second resolution, which committed the council for the first time to a general examination of the whole dispute — even though this would not take place until a month later.

Aloisi said only that Italy would abstain from voting on the second resolution. Laval praised the work of the council in facilitating the process of conciliation. His references to France's obligations under the Covenant were halfhearted and fell far short of a statement of support for the League that he and Eden had worked out before the council meeting.[88] Eden was content merely to outline the future. A further attempt would be made to settle the Walwal incident by the means of the treaty of 1928. "Independently of this procedure," the signatories to the treaty of 1906 would meet to seek a "solution acceptable to all for the difficulties of a more general nature." On 4 September, in any event, the council would meet "to deal with the whole question as it then exists." The representatives of the other twelve nations represented at the council remained silent, except for two colorless remarks by the delegates from Denmark and Argentina.[89] According to Avenol, almost every delegate was instructed to follow the British lead.[90]

> They knew well enough the gravity and danger of the situation: most of them knew that the safeguards of their own security were threatened. But they had been brought to believe that open recognition of the true facts, and open discussion of what their consequences might be, would exasperate the Italian dictator and destroy the chance that France and Britain might let find means to turn him from his purpose . . .
> There was yet another reason for the silence of the smaller powers. Not only were they anxious not to offend Italy; but they were also in complete uncertainty as to what the other great powers would do when the crisis came. The word Sanctions was on no one's lips; but it was in everyone's mind . . . The majority had, no doubt, a preference in favour of applying sanctions if the expected aggression took place. But they kept silence, since they dared not yet commit

[88] Geoffrey Thompson saw this as a "demonstration . . . of Laval's untrustworthiness." Eden told Thompson that Laval had shown his speech to Aloisi and the Italian advised that the "pungent last paragraph" be dropped. "Strangely," records Thompson, "Eden seemed satisfied with Laval's excuses." Thompson, *Front-Line Diplomat*, 105.

[89] The whole of the council meeting of 3 August is recorded in League, *Official Journal, 1935*, 967–70.

[90] Avon, *Facing the Dictators*, 248.

themselves to a policy which could not be followed unless the great powers were ready to play their part.[91]

There was no guidance from America. In a cautious statement on 1 August, President Roosevelt merely hoped "that an amicable solution will be found and that peace will be maintained." [92]

The two resolutions passed the council by unanimous vote, with Italy abstaining from voting on the second.

The Italians had given way on no important points. Once again they had succeeded in limiting the League's consideration of the conflict to a minor and extraneous issue — the Walwal arbitration — and this was to be taken up outside the framework of the League and without discussing the question of ownership. All this was accomplished without Italy's having to make a formal pledge not to resort to war.[93] Although a meeting to consider the general Ethiopian situation was scheduled for 4 September, that was another month away. This time was to be used by the Palazzo Chigi to concoct a new series of arguments for proving Ethiopia an unworthy member of the comity of civilized nations.[94] For Mussolini, Italian diplomacy at Geneva had gained one more month for military preparation.

It was another Italian triumph, and congratulations showered down upon Aloisi.[95] To the members of the council Haile Selassie sent what he called his thanks, and expressed the hope "that the efforts of the League will be successful in maintaining peace." [96] He was whistling in the dark, for what control over events did the League have?

[91] Walters, *History of the League*, II, 638, 639.

[92] *U.S. Diplomatic Papers, 1935*, I, 732–3; *New York Times*, 2 August 1935. This was the first formal statement that Roosevelt made on the Italian-Ethiopian conflict.

[93] There was an indirect pledge, however. By declaring its adherence to article 5 of the treaty of 1928, as stated in the first resolution, Italy tacitly agreed to "submit to a procedure of conciliation or arbitration . . . without having recourse to armed force."

[94] Guariglia, *Ricordi*, 249.

[95] Aloisi, *Journal*, 292, 294. The German government also sent him a eulogy. Eden later concluded: "I date [Britain's] Abyssinian failure from these weeks." *Facing the Dictators*, 245.

[96] League, *Official Journal, 1935*, 976.

Chapter 10

August: Against Geneva

The beginning of August found Italian military preparations well advanced. On 14 July Alfredo Dallolio, an army general and Fascist senator, had been named commissioner-general for war production. Men were being trained and outfitted, factories were working day and night, supply depots had been established, scores of private transport ships had been hired by the government, and a central communication center, the Naval Transport Office, was established in Naples, with offices in other principal Italian ports. All was being readied for the final mass movement of men and matériel, to be in position in Eritrea and Italian Somaliland by 1 October, the scheduled invasion date. Despite bitter rivalries among the ministries of colonies, navy, air, and war over their roles in the campaign, despite the corruption and profiteering that accompanied the hurried preparations, the Italians had succeeded in pulling together an enormous force for the Ethiopian venture.[1]

In Eritrea and Somalia, De Bono and Graziani had been working steadily to prepare these colonies as bases of operations. Not only did all building materials have to be sent out from Italy, but almost all construction had to be started from scratch. De Bono repeated over and over to Rome that he "absolutely could not rely on local resources for anything." Work had been slow, hampered by a shortage of labor and materials, and by the sickness and incompetence of the first groups of workers sent out from Italy.[2] Yet by August these

<hr />

[1] E. Polson Newman, *Ethiopian Realities* (London, 1936), 45–7; Lessona, *Memorie*, 158–64; Fermi, *Mussolini*, 328–9.

[2] Mussolini, *Opera omnia*, XXVII, 294; De Bono, *Anno XIIII*, 61, 65–6, 77. Ambassador Rosso in Washington admitted that sickness in Eritrea was a "very serious problem." *U.S. Diplomatic Papers, 1395*, I, 786. By mid-August an estimated 5,000 men with malaria and dysentery had been sent home. *The Times* (London), 13 August 1935.

difficulties had been largely overcome, particularly in Eritrea to the north, the planned launching site of the major advance. All-weather airstrips, encampments and hospitals, warehouses and barracks, and an elaborate water-supply system had been constructed to handle the invasion force. Most important, De Bono had built a bridge and double-laned road system by which to transport the Italian force from the port of Massawa to the highland centers of Asmara and Gura, the two principal camps planned for the army and air force respectively. Roads were then sent out to the Ethiopian border at the Mareb River, and advance camps were set up in September at Senafe and Adi Quala.

No less important was the reorganization of the two main Italian ports, Massawa and Mogadishu. In May 1935, before the Italian navy made its improvements, there was an average of eighteen ships in Massawa harbor, and it took some six days to unload a troopship and eighteen days to discharge cargoes. The situation was much worse at Mogadishu, where there was no harbor at all and ships had to anchor in an open bay beyond the reefs, at the mercy of monsoons. At Mogadishu some ships had to wait a full month before being un-loaded, for there was only one dock, one ten-ton crane, and one three-ton crane. By the end of August, harbor improvements had been made to the extent that, even with fifty ships in Massawa, troopships could be unloaded in one or two days, cargo ships in seven. At Mogadishu new docks were built and the harbor partly cleared, so that where before it had been possible to unload only a few tons a day, now 2,000 tons could be handled. There was still much confusion on the docks and inefficiency in the ports, but after August the Italians were able to transport all the men and war supplies they desired.[3] This was a major logistical achievement, and the real heroes of the Italian-Ethiopian campaign were the thousands of Italian men who worked in the thin air of the high plateaux and in the hot humid lowlands on the coast to build the roads, railways, airfields, and docks for the Italian army.

[3] By the end of September De Bono had an army of 170,000 Europeans, 65,000 natives, and 38,000 laborers assembled in Eritrea. In the course of the campaign, 360,000 men, 30,000 animals, 6,500 motor vehicles, and 3 million tons of supplies were sent from Italy to east Africa. A. Tosti, *Storia dell'esercito italiano, 1861–1936* (Milan, 1942), 287; Newman, *Ethiopian Realities*, 48. The story of the preparation of Italian Somaliland for war is told, with supporting documents, in Italy, Comando delle Forze Armate della Somalia, *La Guerra italo-etiopica: Fronte sud* (Rome, n.d.), vols. I and II. See also Graziani, *Il Fronte sud,* 79–85.

As military preparations moved into the final stages in the summer of 1935, the Italian government stepped up its efforts at internal political subversion within the Ethiopian empire. The lands of modern Ethiopia, defined only a generation before by the conquests of Menelik, contained subject peoples of various races and religions who, never assimilated, viewed the Amhara central government with suspicion and hostility. Despite his attempt to centralize administrative control of the distant provinces by the appointment of faithful governors, Haile Selassie, until the 1930s preoccupied with consolidating his own position in Addis Ababa, had not done much to win general popularity or to develop Ethiopian nationalism in the farther reaches of the empire. As recently as 1930 the troublesome northern Islamic Gallas had launched a full-scale revolt against him. Rebellions were put down in Gojam in 1932 and in northern Tigre in October 1934. The emperor's neglect of the peoples of the south gave them no reason to view their rulers in Addis Ababa with patriotic enthusiasm.[4] To take advantage of these dissatisfactions, the Italians instituted their political "policy of penetration."

The primary agents of the policy of penetration were the Italian consuls in Ethiopia. They acted on the orders of an especially constituted political bureau, under the supervision of the Italian military high command in east Africa. The head of the Ufficio Politico was Colonel Vittorio Ruggero, who until 1934 had been the military attaché in Addis Ababa. He was assisted by two old colonial officers of wide experience in Eritrea and Ethiopia. They maintained close

[4] In the middle of May 1935 Haile Selassie went to his family's province of Harar where he spent a month, returning to the capital in June. The purpose of this trip was to mend neglected fences, to seek support and approval in the southeast before the pressures in the north would demand his constant presence. In a land where personal loyalty on the local level still counted for more than national patriotism, only by a personal appearance could he hope to convince the leaders of the southeastern territories to put up some resistance to Graziani's army when it moved northward from Italian Somaliland. On 22 May the emperor held a great meeting of tribal leaders of the Ogaden and the chiefs of the Somalis. He stressed that Ethiopian independence and resistance to invasion was a common cause shared by Christian and Muslim alike. He appealed to their common interest in thwarting the conquest of their lands by European invaders. He spoke of Abyssinian friendship for the peoples of the Ogaden. He said he was ready to institute reforms in the area, to establish schools there. He repeated these appeals and promises to the most influential leaders of the Jijiga region. But it was clear to all that the emperor's concern and concessions were inspired only by his fear of an Italian invasion. Haile Selassie left Harar without the assurance that his last-minute appeals would be heeded. See Lessona, *Verso l'impero*, 102–9. Italian propaganda efforts in the south are noted in R. Greenfield, *Ethiopia, a New Political History* (London, 1965), 193–4.

contact with the Italian legation in Addis Ababa. After the summer of 1935, there was no lack of funds for propaganda and subversion.[5]

Centers for Italian activity were located throughout the empire — Tigre and the Danakil in the north, Gojam and the fertile area around Lake Tana in the west, Harar, the Ogaden, and Sidamo in the east and south. Wherever there was a record of discontent, wherever it seemed that chiefs or the native population would be susceptible to bribes or promises, there the Italians sent their propaganda. Encouraging separatism and playing on local antagonism to the central government, the Italians offered visions of a freer, richer life under Italian rule. Above all they tried to make sure that provincial chiefs would not lead their people against Italy and that the outlying inhabitants would not join the armies raised by loyal rases to support the emperor's guerrilla force.

Three regions, Tigre, the Danakil, and Gojam, received particular attention. Tigre held the key to Italian success. This vital northern province, fronting on the Mareb River and on Eritrea, contained the traditionally most important cities in Ethiopia, and it was the area in which the major Italian military offensive was to be launched. In and around Tigre were the most persistent rebels among the emperor's unruly subjects, the Azebu and Wallo Gallas, men who maintained a long-standing hatred for their Amhara rulers. Also in Tigre was the weakest link in the emperor's chain of commanders. Dejazmach Haile Selassie Gugsa[6] was a great-grandson of the Emperor Johannis and the son of Ras Gugsa Araya. As a member of this old and illustrious Tigrean ruling family, he harbored a deep-seated jealousy for the members of the Shoan dynasty who occupied the imperial throne. Haile Selassie was aware of potential trouble from this quarter, and when Ras Gugsa Araya died in 1932 the emperor divided the province of Tigre between two governors, Ras Seyum in the west and Haile Selassie Gugsa in the east. Gugsa greatly resented this, believing that he was being deprived of his legitimate patrimony. Despite the emperor's attempt to placate the dejazmach by giving him in marriage

[5] De Bono, *Anno XIIII*, 50–1, 249; Lessona, *Verso l'impero*, 110–4; Mussolini, *Opera omnia*, XXVII, 293. Italy had acquired from the mint in Vienna the dies for striking Maria Teresa thalers, the traditional currency in Ethiopia. Schuschnigg, *Ein Requiem in Rot-Weiss-Rot*, 243; *Le Temps*, 17 July 1935. One million newly minted thalers were sent to De Bono.

[6] Haile Selassie Gugsa was not a ras. Dejazmach is a lower rank. It was not until after his desertion in 1935 that he was given the title of ras — by the Italian government.

one of his daughters, Gugsa's anger and ambition did not abate. Indeed he was aroused further when Ras Seyum was appointed to head a unified military command for the province of Tigre.[7] "There was little sympathy between the two chiefs of Tigre; indeed, there was positive if not manifest enmity," noted De Bono. The Italians soon learned of the friction in Tigre. "Our intelligence agents and the whole personnel of the Consulate at Adowa," De Bono wrote, "wisely took advantage of this state of affairs to win Gugsa over to our side." In the summer of 1935 Gugsa threw in his lot with the Italians and for the next few months acted on their instructions. Since it was to the Italians' purpose that no action take place before their own preparations were complete, Gugsa was instructed to appear obedient to the emperor for the time being, but close contact was maintained so that "categorical instructions" could be given when the time came to act openly.[8] The importance of Gugsa to both Italy and Ethiopia was that, as the emperor's plan of defense developed, Gugsa and the 10,000 troops he commanded had a vital place within that plan. Gugsa's force was to hold Makale while the army of Ras Seyum, to the north, would fall back and join Gugsa; this combined force would then try to stem the Italian thrust. Two weeks before the Italian invasion, the emperor was warned of Gugsa's treachery. Haile Selassie refused to accept this fact, that his daughter's husband could turn against him. It was a serious mistake, for Gugsa's defection caused the collapse of the emperor's entire defensive scheme.[9]

The second major region in which the Italians pursued their policy of penetration was the Danakil. This desolate area had none of the strategic or historical importance of Tigre, but the Italians were thinking of sending a flanking force in from the port of Assab across the Danakil, and the Ethiopians were aware of this threat. Italy's political penetration of the area began soon after the Walwal incident. The Italian agent, acting originally on his own and using his own funds, was Baron Raimondo Francetti, a noted explorer of this region. An

---

[7] Waizero Zanaba Warq died in 1933, ending this connection to the emperor by marriage, but Gugsa had felt no affection for his father-in-law in any case. Ras Seyum was himself a natural grandson of Emperor Johannis and thus also of a hereditary Tigrean ruling family. He was related to the emperor through his daughter, who was married to the emperor's son, the crown prince.

[8] De Bono, *Anno XIIII*, 175–6; Lessona, *Verso l'impero*, 112.

[9] Steer, *Caesar in Abyssinia*, 63; L. Mosley, *Haile Selassie, the Conquering Lion* (London, 1964), 199.

armed band of soldiers was organized at Beilul; Assab was chosen as its base and coordinating center; and Francetti undertook to gain the favor of the neighboring tribes. The most important man in the area was the Sultan of Aussa, General Mohammed Yayo, who had recently succeeded his father. Francetti had been on excellent terms with the father, and he lost no time in ingratiating himself with the new sultan.[10] In July, reporting in Rome, Francetti said that he thought the sultan had come over to Italy's side and could henceforth be trusted as an ally. Mussolini accepted this opinion and, after Francetti's death on 7 August 1935, at once ordered the connection with Aussa renewed. The Italian high commissioner in east Africa did not share this optimism. De Bono told the Duce that Francetti had greatly exaggerated the success of his diplomatic mission. In truth, Mohammed Yayo was an indecisive man, and although he objected to Ethiopian encroachments into his territory, he was unwilling to commit himself to either side. Despite further Italian efforts, the policy of penetration in the Danakil was not a success.[11]

Gojam was the third area in which the Italians engaged in extensive political activity. This region, long the almost autonomous fief of Ras Hailu, had since 1932 been under the administrative responsibility of the emperor's personal representative, the loyal and brave Ras Imru. But among the native population the old separatist sentiment was still strong. Nearly isolated from the rest of Ethiopia behind the great sweeping curve of the Blue Nile, the Amharic people of Gojam viewed with scorn and anger the politicians of Shoa who claimed the heritage of Sheba, controlled the government at Addis Ababa, and who since 1932 held their old leader, Hailu, in prison. Italian propaganda, carried on by the consuls at Gondar and Debra Markos, tried to fan this resentment. The inhabitants of Gojam were assured that Italy felt the greatest sympathy for them, and they were exhorted to remember how the Ethiopian government treated Ras Hailu: "the Italian government would protect them, aid them, repair their ruined churches, their destroyed castles, build roads, protect commerce and agriculture from all oppression, respect their customs, families, and religion." In return the Italians appealed to the popula-

---

[10] In June Mussolini approved the idea that the sultan's two sons be enrolled in a military academy in Rome. Mussolini, *Opera omnia*, XXVII, 294.

[11] Lessona, *Verso l'impero*, 115–19; De Bono, *Anno XIIII*, 51–2.

tion of Gojam to make common cause with Italy and refuse to fight in the emperor's war. An Italian victory, they said, would mean the liberation of Gojam.[12]

The Italians had important successes in manipulating these areas of internal discontent and political weakness within the empire. But Italy's major goal was the decisive control of Ethiopia, which only military conquest could bring. If the old practice of subversion was important as a preliminary step, the means of assuring victory was to be found in the newly acquired might of the Italian air force.[13] On 23 July the air ministry completed its program for the Ethiopian campaign and ordered that 255 bombers and 52 scouting planes be sent out in stages to east Africa.[14]

As the result of the discussions at Geneva and of the resolutions of the council on 3 August, two sets of meetings were scheduled for the month of August. The arbitral commission was to sit again, to be held to the Italian terms of reference but with the appointment of a fifth member and under the interested eye of the League. The tripartite conference of the states signatory to the 1906 treaty was also scheduled to meet, with the British and French seeking to find a negotiated settlement of the dispute. Immediately after the council adjourned on 3 August, the Ethiopian-appointed members of the arbitral commission made an effort, at Geneva, to resume meetings at once. The Italian members did not agree, and the four members decided that the commission would reconvene some two weeks later, on 19 August, and not at Scheveningen or Geneva but at Paris.[15] In the meantime attention was turned to the preparations for the three-

---

[12] Lessona, *Verso l'impero*, 112–3.

[13] The great formations of cruiser squadrons led by Italo Balbo made the world conscious of the Fascist air force. These flights and aerial exhibitions of all sorts were a source of great pride to the Fascists, and Mussolini constantly associated the image of his regime with the progressiveness of modern air power. Despite the public image, when Balbo gave up the air ministry in 1933 the Italian air force was fit for nothing but exhibitions. The new undersecretary, General Giuseppe Valle, reorganized the force to give it fighting potential. With this, more serious attention was given to the military aspects of air power. See, e.g., an article by V. Giovine in the *Nouva antologia* of 16 August 1935, 380:622–4, in which the author notes that Italy, in mid-July, won the world's distance record for nonstop hydroplane flight with a flight of some 3,000 miles. Giovine concluded from this feat: "Italy is now better able to guard its colonies."

[14] De Bono, *Anno XIIII*, 177, 215. At the end of September 1935, there were 126 airplanes in east Africa.

[15] Potter, *Wal Wal Arbitration*, 16–7.

power negotiations, also to be held in Paris beginning on 16 August.

The success or failure of the tripartite talks depended on the attitude of Mussolini. At the beginning of August the Duce was in a recalcitrant mood. Mussolini's article of 31 July in *Il Popolo d'Italia*, we have seen, had expressed his resolve that the military solution to the conflict with Ethiopia had to be total — "with Geneva, without Geneva, against Geneva." Now to this determination was added a concern with what seemed to be a new development in Britain's policy. On 30 July, the British Foreign Office had sent its memorandum to Paris, for the purpose of giving Laval some background information for the talks with Eden. This memorandum contained no constructive proposals for the settlement of the conflict (and therefore was of no help to Eden in his effort to establish an agreement), but it did give a list of reasons why an Italian conquest of Ethiopia would displease the British. Although the memorandum did not pledge Britain to act to prevent the conquest, it did seem to indicate that the value of Italy as an ally was now being discounted; it might be in the British interest henceforth not to conciliate Mussolini but to oppose him. Laval passed the memorandum on to the Italians, and it deeply affronted them. The wording of the memorandum caused offense, as did the failure of the British to take seriously Italian plans. It included cavalier comments about the possibility of diverting Italian *opportunismo* from Ethiopia by encouraging Italy to "other adventures." It included unflattering references to Mussolini, to the Fascist regime, and to the Italian people. Most insulting of all, it implied that the Italians could be easily manipulated if they failed to comply with British wishes.[16]

This memorandum, coupled with Hoare's speech of 1 August,[17]

---

[16] Guariglia, *Ricordi*, 250.

[17] Hoare's speech of 1 August was made in the House of Commons on the day before the British Parliament went into recess until 22 October. For all its confusions, the speech was a strong statement of the British reasons for opposing an Italian-Ethiopian war: "The effect of a war between Italy and Abyssinia would, in our view, be wholly bad. Whether the war be long or short, whether the victor be Italy or Abyssinia, the effect would be harmful beyond exaggeration to the League and all the League stands for. . . . Outside Europe, the reactions, though they may not be so immediate, will be no less deplorable. . . . We are not unsympathetic to the Italian need for expansion. . . . If the Italian Government have any complaints to make against the Abyssinian Government let them make those complaints in the proper, regular manner. [Cheers] They will find the League ready to give full and impartial consideration to the case which they put before it. But these are issues which can be settled without recourse to war." *Parliamentary Debates*, 304 H.C. Deb. 5s., cols. 2927–36. Hoare, one

distressed the Italians. Aloisi wrote in his diary on 31 July when Laval first showed him the memorandum: "This is terrible for us. It clears up completely the intention of the British Cabinet in our regard. London, which treates us a little like fools, is uneasy for the League, for its colonial empire, and will prevent at all costs our making war." Aloisi sent a copy of the memorandum to Rome, where it "horrified everyone" and made Mussolini furious.[18] The German ambassador found the Duce, on 3 August, "serious and almost embittered." He was preoccupied with the implications of the British note. Mussolini said he would not accept a second Aduwa, Ulrich von Hassell reported, especially without a fight. Mussolini continued: "Some people had obviously not yet grasped the fact that Italy was now a different country from what she had been before. He had laid two mines, the Duce stated, one in Africa and one in Europe. He was prepared to explode them under anybody who refused to understand or believe that [Italy's demands and plans were serious]." [19]

To the old socialist Hubert de Lagardelle, a troubled Mussolini spoke of "vile and capitalistic Europe" whose great powers, Britain and France, were "trying to crush a poor and working people." [20] While the Italians were suspicious of British motives, they were more seriously concerned with the possible consequences of Britain's new harder position. From this time on, the specter of a war with Britain haunted Italian leaders. The old assumption that Britain would never fight was badly shaken. Aloisi wrote in his diary on 5 August: "the English note to France had hardened terribly the situation. The Duce thinks we will not be able to avoid conflict with England." [21]

The diplomats in the Palazzo Chigi thought they could divine the reasoning behind what seemed a new British willingness to confront Italy. The matter was more than simply the protection of British colonial interests. According to the analysis of men like Guariglia, Britain's ostensible determination to uphold the provisions of the Covenant against Italy stemmed from the influence on British foreign

---

must note, considered this speech as a statement of that part of his double policy leading to negotiated settlement. Templewood, *Nine Troubled Years*, 161. The speech was very badly received by the press in Italy as being vague, unconstructive, and malevolent.

[18] Aloisi, *Journal*, 290–1.

[19] *Documents on German Foreign Policy*, ser. C, IV, 533.

[20] Lagardelle, *Mission à Rome*, 141.

[21] Aloisi, *Journal*, 292.

policy of Sir Robert Vansittart. Vansittart, as was well known, was seeking to defend British interests against a rearmed Germany. One way to accomplish this was through the use of the strong sanctions prescribed in the Covenant. But large-scale sanctions had never yet been tried, and the British were now hoping to use Italy's invasion of Ethiopia as a test case to prove the effectiveness of sanctions and to prepare the way for their future use against Germany.[22]

A British disclaimer, in the form of a note to the Italian government in early August, said that the British did not want a conflict with Italy, that Britain's interest in supporting the League in this dispute was dictated largely by the pressure of public opinion at home, and that Britain would never take the initiative in establishing sanctions against Italy.[23] The Italians did not take this note seriously. The mistrust of Britain, the anger at being "betrayed," and the fear of being thwarted were now, in early August, too great to be so easily allayed. There was a pessimistic fatalism in Rome in the first two weeks of August, a feeling that no accommodation would be reached in the tripartite talks about to begin, and a growing concern that the Ethiopian adventure might lead to a war fought off the coast of Italy.

On 9 August Mussolini asked Badoglio to begin an immediate study of the problem of national defense "in the eventuality of having to cope with a situation of extreme tension with England."[24] Badoglio called a meeting of the chiefs of staff. The conclusion of the military leaders presented to Mussolini on the 14th was that, although Italy possessed a better army than Britain's, any war between the two countries would be fought on the sea and in the air near the Italian peninsula. In such a conflict the British would have an overwhelming advantage, for the British fleet was far superior to Italy's and the

[22] Guariglia, *Ricordi*, 255–6. Daniele Varè, a former Italian diplomat, in a speech at Chatham House in London on 19 November 1935, said that "no more cruel insult has ever been thrown at a proud and sensitive nation than the assertion, publicly and repeatedly made by [Britain's] responsible statesmen, than the Abyssinian question was 'a test case' for the League . . . Italy is the rat for vivisection, the guinea-pig, on which to try the vaccine of sanctions." D. Varè, "British Foreign Policy through Italian Eyes," *International Affairs*, 15:80–102 (January–February 1936).

[23] Guariglia, *Ricordi*, 109–10. In this note the word "sanctions" was used for the first time in a formal diplomatic message to Italy.

[24] This paragraph's discussion of the mid-August concern with the possibility of war with Britain rests on documents published in the Milan paper, *Corriere d'informazione*, 14–17 January 1946, as reported in Salvemini, *Prelude*, 255–6.

Italian air force, although equal in numbers to Britain's was composed to a large extent of obsolete planes. As a result, Britain would be able to inflict heavy damage on the Italian ports, cities, and industrial centers. Purely military calculations, therefore, showed that nothing but disaster for Italy would ensue from war with Britain at this time. But Badoglio assured Mussolini that "the country, indignant over British behaviour, would follow the Duce with enthusiasm," in whatever decisions he made.

On 5 August Aloisi met with Mussolini and Suvich to discuss future diplomatic strategy. Suvich had been slated to represent Italy at the forthcoming Paris talks, but Aloisi was substituted at Laval's request. An aide-mémoire by Aloisi made clear the extent of the opposition within the international community against Italy's Ethiopian campaign. Mussolini was totally pessimistic that anything would come of the tripartite conference in Paris. He refused to commit himself to any agreement which would give Italy less than 100 percent control of Ethiopia. The truth of the matter was, as Aloisi noted in his diary on the 8th, that the transactions in Paris would not succeed for the simple reason that Mussolini did not want them to. On the 9th the Duce presented Aloisi with instructions for the Paris talks: "I want no agreement unless I am conceded everything, Mussolini said, and that includes the decapitation of the emperor. For I am preparing for war and even for a general conflict. *What one must seek therefore is to gain time.*" On 11 August Mussolini received Aloisi for a final word before the diplomat left Rome: "You must act henceforth as a soldier rather than as a diplomat, as a Fascist rather than as a negotiator. Even if I am accorded everything I prefer to avenge Aduwa. I am already prepared." [25]

What he desired, Mussolini repeated, was to gain time, to use Italian diplomacy to forestall the coming meeting of the League council on 4 September from taking up and acting on the Ethiopian matter. Of greatest importance in Paris would be the talks with Laval. Aloisi was instructed to speak frankly to Laval and to tell him that, if France supported Italy over Ethiopia, Mussolini would stand by France in the region of the Danube and come to a treaty agreement with Yugoslavia. In this way, if France and Italy stayed together, Hitler could be barred from advancing to the southeast. The determining decision in this regard was France's. Mussolini sent a similar message to Vittorio

[25] Aloisi, *Journal*, 292–4.

Cerruti, recently transferred from Berlin as the new Italian ambassador in Paris.[26]

On 13 August, in the "anguished manner of a man who feels himself caught up and trapped by fate," Mussolini unburdened himself to the French ambassador. A campaign had already begun against Italy, Mussolini told Charles de Chambrun. Economic, financial, and moral sanctions were already being applied.

> English banks have suspended, by order, all credit in favor of our established financiers. We are no longer able to buy, on the London market, coal, tin, or copper, without gold payment, even though we are creditors of England. In New York, in a demonstration of Anglo-Saxon solidarity, it is the same for our purchases of cotton. A campaign is being directed against the lira in the Near East and Malta . . . Movements of troops in Palestine, Egypt, and Syria, without being aimed directly at us, give the same impression.[27]

What the British wanted, Mussolini said, was "to bring me, at any price, to a Fashoda." But "in a strangled voice" he added, "they will not succeed."

> My victory in Abyssinia is certain. I have 170,000 infantry soldiers there and continue to send troops. Cost what it may, I will avenge Aduwa and if England, putting the mark on its hostility, which is henceforth patent, closes the Suez Canal despite the treaties, under the pretext that the Covenant, in the superior interest of peace, supersedes the previous agreements, I will open the passage myself. Out of desperation I would not hesitate, if it were necessary, to make war on [the British].[28]

[26] Aloisi, *Journal*, 294; Salvemini, *Prelude*, 257. Mussolini had sweetened his request with an appreciation of Laval's diplomacy, which he published in the *Giornale d'Italia* on 5 August. Lagardelle, *Mission à Rome*, 144–5.

[27] It was reported that Italy was attempting to buy between 250,000, and 500,000 bales of cotton in America, and asking for a credit of $15–30 million. On 7 August the American Export-Import Bank forbade credits for the purchase of goods that looked like "munitions," applying in this case to cotton export to Italy. *The Times* (London), 8 August 1935; *New York Times*, 8 August 1935. *Le Temps*, 12 August 1935, reported that five English divisions were soon to be sent to reinforce the Sudan's Ethiopian frontier guard. In August English aircraft were observed over Greece, apparently en route to the Sudan.

[28] Chambrun, *Traditions*, 218–19. At Fashoda in 1898 France was humiliated when Britain forced the French government to recall its troops from the Sudan. The British government sent a report of the Mussolini-Chambrun conversation to Washington on 17 August, adding that "Italy is feeling the effect of economic difficulties and is nervous of economic pressure, which may, consequently, perhaps form an effective means of restraining her." *U.S. Diplomatic Papers, 1935*, I, 630–1.

Gaetano Salvemini wrote: "With a man like Mussolini, it was not possible to guess how far he was in earnest, how far he was bluffing, or how far he was being carried away by his own bluff." [29] There is much truth in the comment, and it is important to understand this element of Mussolini's character during these critical months of August and September. In the realm of diplomacy, bluffing will rarely succeed when directed against a nation whose own intent is clear and whose purpose is determined — the bluff will readily be called, and the bluffer exposed. On the other hand, faced with opponents who are unsure of themselves, whose determination is wavering, whose resistance is halfhearted, a bluff may well succeed. This brings us to the significance of Mussolini's statements to Chambrun. It was obviously absurd to believe that Mussolini could himself open a passage through the Suez Canal, for no British government would allow such action and Britain had the force to prevent it. Yet when Mussolini talked of waging war "out of desperation," this added a new dimension to the picture. It was clear that Mussolini was in earnest about the Ethiopian campaign, and apparent that he was in a difficult position. He had committed his regime to success in east Africa. He had undertaken major political and military gambles in conducting the campaign, at a time of great uncertainty in Europe.[30] Although no one knew whether Mussolini could succeed in conquering Ethiopia, there was no doubt that he was determined to try.[31] Now if Mussolini had all this at stake, might he not in fact be "carried away by his own bluff" and strike out against Britain or France or whoever opposed him? Who was to know whether or not Mussolini was bluffing when he spoke of going to war against Britain, or against France, if they forcibly resisted him? It is doubtful whether in mid-August Mussolini himself really knew what action he would be prepared to take in these circumstances. But

[29] Salvemini, *Prelude*, 255.

[30] Said Winston Churchill in a September speech: "To cast an army of nearly a quarter of a million men, embodying the flower of Italian manhood, upon a barren shore two thousand miles from home, against the good will of the whole world and without command of the sea, and then in this position embark upon what may well be a series of campaigns against a people and in regions which no conqueror in four thousand years ever thought it worth while to subdue, is to give hostages to fortune unparalleled in all history." *The Gathering Storm*, 173.

[31] There was much inexpert speculation during these days that Italian aircraft and men would not be able to function in the high altitudes of Ethiopia, that the Ethiopian army would slow down the Italian advance until the next rainy season, which would halt the invasion, and that Mussolini only wanted to make a *show* of force, after which he would stop, satisfied. These ideas were often used to justify not taking a strong stand against Italy.

his bellicose statements had a profound effect on Britain and France. Even though their superior forces could probably beat Italy's, did they want a war with Italy?

Mussolini's "bluff" inspired this question in Britain as the British Cabinet made its preparations for the forthcoming tripartite talks in Paris. The concern that Mussolini might be serious, that there would be war in the Mediterranean if Britain cut Italy's route to east Africa or blockaded the peninsula, caused the British to re-evaluate the part they were willing to play and the price they were willing to pay in this conflict. Laval said: "International morals are one thing; the interests of a country are another." [32] Was British interest incompatible with the application of League sanctions against Italy — if this led to war? Many Englishmen thought so.

Robert Vansittart, contrary to Italian belief, was not in favor of risking a single British ship against Italy. Focusing on the German question as "the overriding one in policy" for Britain, Vansittart believed that in the current incomplete state of British naval preparation every ship in the fleet must be kept to protect the British isles from Germany.[33] Knowing that any "rattling" of Italy would necessarily have to be done by the British navy alone, even if it were acting in a collective action under the auspices of the League, Vansittart desired to by-pass this "solitary side-show" and to avoid risking the consequences of Italian retaliation. Prime Minister Baldwin agreed.[34]

British preparations for the Paris talks began on Eden's return from the council meeting. Before leaving Geneva, on 3 August Eden gave a radio talk in which he pointed up the hope held both for the arbitral commission and for the tripartite talks. Of the latter, he said, there

---

[32] Avon, *Facing the Dictators*, 262–3.

[33] For a contemporary review of the weakness of Britain's armed forces, particularly the navy, see a speech given on 7 November 1935 at Chatham House by Lord Lloyd of Dolobran, "The Need for the Re-Armament of Great Britain," *International Affairs*, 15:57–79. (January–February 1936). Amery, *My Political Life*, III, 155–6, notes that the "Navy had not been lower in personnel for forty years."

[34] Vansittart, *Lessons*, 51; *The Mist Procession*, 522–3. Vansittart was particularly concerned over the navy's lack of air cover. Without British air support, "even Italy's wooden bombers can drop explosives down our cruisers' funnels." In January 1936 Baldwin told Thomas Jones: "I had repeatedly told Sam [Hoare] 'Keep us out of war, we are not ready for it.'" Baldwin noted the dangers: "our fleet would be in real danger from the small craft of the Italians operating in a small sea. Italian bombers could get to London. I had also Germany in mind. Had we gone to war our anti-aircraft munitions would have been exhausted in a week. We have hardly got any armament firms left." T. Jones, *A Diary with Letters, 1931–1950* (London, 1954), 159–60.

was "no question . . . of shirking a difficulty, or of mere acquiesence in dilatory manoeuvers. On the contrary, we have named a date by which either the negotiations must succeed, or else the Council will have to discharge the obligations placed upon it under the Covenant." [35]

On 6 August Baldwin, Hoare, and Eden met at 10 Downing Street. Eden was designated the principal British delegate to the Paris talks, and Vansittart was to accompany him.[36] Eden was instructed to maintain close relations with Laval and to draw up before the meetings a British-French program which might force the Italians "to face realities." Mussolini was to be told to moderate his demands, or "be prepared to see the League carry out the procedure of the Covenant." But Eden was not allowed to discuss with the French what this procedure was to be or how it was to be carried out. All he was told to do was to "proceed on the basis that we and the French both realized our obligations." [37] The realization of obligations, however, is not the same as a determination to act upon them. Eden was given nothing to support a policy of negotiation — success would be possible only if backed by the most formal and definite warnings to Italy.

But forceful resistance was not part of British policy, and there was a reason at hand to avoid it. On 6 August the British chiefs of staff were asked to analyze British armed strength in the Mediterranean in case of action against Italy. The reply came a few days later to Hoare and Vansittart from Ernle Chatfield, the First Sea Lord. The report offered no encouragement for a strong stand against Italy, then or later. In his correspondence with Hoare and Vansittart, Chatfield noted the unreadiness of the services. The consensus of opinion was that the British navy in the Mediterranean was too weak to confront Italy until reinforcements were sent out. Chatfield drew a political conclusion from this military estimate: it would be advisable for Britain to move cautiously in Paris. The chiefs of staff pointed out to the government that "sanctions, as ordained by the League, could not be effectively inflicted without leading to war." As Hoare remembers

[35] As an example of Italian propaganda, Virginio Gayda, in the *Giornale d'Italia*, mistranslated this speech and had Eden saying that, if the negotiations were not successful, "the League would have to fulfill its duties and *impose* the Covenant." Quoted in Salvemini, *Prelude*, 254–5.

[36] Italy objected to Eden's representing Britain at Paris, but agreed to accept him because of French urging. Villari, *Storia diplomatica*, 123. Hoare, whom the Italians hoped would come, was immobile in London, victim to severe arthritis. Templewood, *Nine Troubled Years*, 163.

[37] Avon, *Facing the Dictators*, 248–9.

it, the naval staff "could not have been more insistent with their warnings against diminishing or dissipating our limited strength." [38]

The position of the naval staff was clear and straightforward. They had "no hesitation, tactically," of engaging in battle in the Mediterranean, as soon as the necessary reinforcements were brought in from other waters. When that occurred the Admiralty was sure Britain could defeat Italy on the sea, and there was no question of Britain's ability to stop the Italian movement to Ethiopia. What distressed the navy was not the question of winning, but the cost and the purpose of such a conflict.

The cost to Britain's defense capability would be great. Any ships lost in battle with Italy could not be replaced for years. The naval conference in London in 1930 had limited the scope of expansion for Britain's cruiser force. The destroyer program was restricted, and Britain's need for capital ships was in arrears. The delays incurred under the old "ten-year rule" and economy-conscious governments meant that future naval development would probably be slow. Any ships lost in the Mediterranean, then, would drastically curtail Britain's capacity to fight elsewhere. This was a serious matter, for the naval staff had to think in global terms, of the security of the widespread territories of the empire and the maintenance of lines of communication between them. In the Far East, for example, a restless Japan required a strong and vigilant British force there to protect British interests. All of this made the Admiralty "hesitant" to engage in any hostilities with Italy, a country with which Britain had no national quarrel.

Indeed, according to the naval staff, Italy's friendship was at the moment extremely valuable to Great Britain. The potential German threat in the home waters, combined with the danger from Japan, meant that the navy had to stretch its resources to cover its "vast responsibilities" on seas both east and west. Given the restrictions on Britain's naval strength, it was, in 1935 and for the foreseeable future, "quite impossible to fight successfully in Europe and in the Far East simultaneously, unless a friendly (or neutral) Italy was ensured." In the words of Lord Chatfield: "The Mediterranean was our main line of communications with India, Australia and New Zealand. Any act

---

[38] Avon, *Facing the Dictators*, 249; Chatfield, *The Navy and Defence*, II, 87; Templewood, *Nine Troubled Years*, 191. While Chatfield's report may well have been "very pessimistic," it is too much to say, as Admiral Cunningham does, that it was defeatist. Lord Cunningham of Hyndhope, *A Sailor's Odyssey* (New York, 1951), 173.

therefore which was likely to create for us a hostile nation in the Mediterranean, of growing naval and air strength, was directly opposed to naval strategic interests."

The conclusion of the naval staff, then, was that while the navy was prepared to fight, and to win, a sea war with Italy, there was no adequate reason for such a conflict. This attitude reflected a distrust by the leaders in the Admiralty of the League of Nations' concept of collective security. Britain's own security, and the security of the Dominions, rested on the British fleet used in Britain's national and imperial interest, on the basis of calculations made in London. It was obvious that, to maintain the principles of the Covenant, the burden of enforcement would fall almost entirely on this fleet. And under the League's system, the deployment of British forces would be determined not by independent British decisions, but by decisions taken at Geneva and elsewhere by foreign states. To participate in collective security under the Covenant would involve Britain in unpredictable actions in areas likely to be remote from the needs of Britain's defense. It would involve a dissipation of British power which Britain could not afford. Great powers, Germany, Japan, and the United States, were not party to the League's agreements, and in any punitive action Britain might run the risk of antagonizing those nations. As Chatfield noted, reflecting the position of 1935, "at almost a month's notice our oldest friend might become our bitterest enemy." Was it worth the cost to Britain now to support the League if this meant risking war with Italy, and maybe worse, just to punish the country for a colonial action in far-off Ethiopia? Should Britain's own defensive force be weakened to protect an African kingdom in which Britain's interests were not immediately engaged? [39]

Until the middle of 1935, despite or perhaps because of preliminary discussions on the consequences of the use of sanctions, the British government simply had not considered seriously the possibility of a real conflict with Italy. Two things gave credence to this now, and caused the British grave concern. One was a violent campaign in the Italian press against Britain, meant to stir up support for the Ethiopian war. The other was the rumor that Mussolini might be provoked into a

---

[39] For an account of the views of the naval staff, from which the quotations and much of the argument above are drawn, see Chatfield, *The Navy and Defence*, II, 65–90.

"mad dog act," in which he would attack Malta and British naval units in the Mediterranean.[40]

Britain's naval and military weakness in the Mediterranean profoundly influenced British diplomatic preparations for the Paris talks. Hoare and Vansittart agreed that this factor "must govern our actions in Paris." They heeded the warnings of their service advisers. Hoare and Vansittart rejected the plan for a strong warning to Italy, tempering the "comparatively firm language" of the meeting of 6 August. They adopted instead a position calculated not to provoke the Duce. Vansittart wrote: "We shall have to be exceedingly cautious in Paris." British policy making had returned to its old uncertain course. Eden left London "dreading these conversations more than anything I have ever undertaken — vague instructions from home and a thieves' kitchen in Paris . . . I have scarcely any hope for good results." [41]

In preparation for the Paris talks, the British government, through its minister Sir Sidney Barton, had inquired of Haile Selassie what sacrifices Ethiopia was prepared to make to achieve a peaceful solution of the dispute. The emperor was faced with a difficult problem. He had determined to hold to his position as a member of the League, for it was Ethiopia's only hope. Haile Selassie was willing to make concessions to preserve the peace "as far as his honour and that of his country allowed." But he was under increasing pressure at home to stand firm against Italy. Many Ethiopians believed that the emperor had already given in too far and that he must now confront Italian demands squarely and reject them. The rases opposed any concession of Ethiopian territory. After careful deliberation with his advisers, Haile Selassie replied to Britain that he would agree to the British proposal of June to give Italy a portion of the Ogaden in return for access to the sea at Zeila. He further offered to give Italy a part of the low-lying and unfertile province of Aussa, which bordered on southern Eritrea, to reopen the matter of a road between Assab and Dessye, and to permit the construction of a road between Eritrea and the town of Gondar, which would give Italians access, if the Ethiopians allowed them to use it, to the high plateau and the region of Lake Tana. In return, the emperor asked for an international loan to develop a communication network and to further his reforms in law and administra-

[40] Templewood, *Nine Troubled Years*, 163.
[41] Avon, *Facing the Dictators*, 249.

tion. He said he was prepared to accept foreign experts from candidates chosen by the League to aid him in this work. He suggested finally that the 1906 tripartite agreement be replaced by a treaty that would include Ethiopia.[42] These concessions fell far short of Mussolini's demands, of course.

In Paris, at a meeting of the Council of Ministers on 8 August, Laval stated that he saw little hope for a pacific resolution of the conflict. His plan was "to assure our friendship with Italy, more yet our ties with England, and more yet our fidelity to the Covenant." [43] Other than this broad statement, Laval kept his own counsel. In France, as Flandin has explained, "it is the established custom that the president of the Council reports on the conduct of foreign policy, but does not consult the Council beforehand when he combines his functions as premier with those as foreign minister." [44]

The British delegation, Eden, Vansittart, Strang, and Thompson, arrived in Paris on 13 August. On the following day Eden and Vansittart met with Laval. The British purpose was solely to create a joint Anglo-French position — cooperation was an end in itself. There was no discussion of what this joint action would lead to, if and when it was established. Laval was told only that, if a satisfactory settlement could not be reached, Britain and France must agree to join in meeting the challenge to the Covenant. But Laval was of the opinion that the issue now lay mainly between Britain and Italy, and that France should play the role of a mediator between the opposing points of view. The British delegates spent most of their energies on the 14th in trying to convince Laval that, on the contrary, the great and urgent need was for France to form a common front with Britain. From a negative standpoint, the British argued, the collapse or discrediting of the League might well have as its consequence the withdrawal of Britain from participation in the affairs of Europe. The League was the rallying point for the British people, and if it were destroyed public opinion might force the government to turn away from the continent and to seek its own safeguards for the island and the empire. The British hoped that this possibility would disturb Laval. To give the argument a more positive turn, Vansittart, speaking "as a permanent official

[42] Virgin, *Abyssinia*, 159–60.
[43] Herriot, *Jadis*, II, 574.
[44] Flandin, *Politique française*, 183n.

representing the continuity of British foreign policy friendly over a long period to France, and with no political fences to guard," stressed the absolute importance to the peace of Europe itself that Britain and France stand together.[45]

On 15 August, Aloisi arrived in Paris. Meeting with Laval, he outlined Italy's demands and proposals:

1. A declaration by Britain and France in favor of Italian political and economic preponderance in Ethiopia.

2. A French declaration of policy on the necessity of Italy's demographic and economic expansion.

3. Italy would assure its continued cooperation at Geneva in League affairs, if the above demands were met and if an agreement were reached on the basis of a recognition by France and Britain of Italy's right to attain the objectives established by Mussolini.

4. Italy would recognize the rights of Great Britain in Ethiopia as established in the treaty of 1906.[46]

What Italy wanted, Aloisi told Laval, was a Class C mandate over Ethiopia. Laval replied that he could not accept the demand for a mandate and that points 1 and 3 were too vague as an initial basis for negotiation, although, in the absence of any complete British-French proposals, they would be accepted as a beginning. Laval proposed a treaty, to be signed by the four interested states, to give Italy some economic concessions and rights of technical assistance, plus rights of settlement in certain areas of Ethiopia. Cession to Italy of the Ogaden and the right to lay a railroad line to join the two Italian colonies were also mentioned as possibilities. In the absence of any objection, these proposals were sent off to be worked out more fully. Laval told Aloisi that Britain's resistance was not as great as Italy might suspect, and that both France and Britain were interested primarily in safeguarding the League and in avoiding war. In such a mood, Laval thought, the British would be prepared to agree to whatever economic concessions Italy desired. He assured Aloisi too that France had no economic interest in Ethiopia.[47] On that same day Laval asked the new Italian ambassador, Cerruti, to assure Mussolini of his support, but also to warn the Duce against war and against putting the League in jeopardy.[48]

[45] Avon, *Facing the Dictators*, 249–50; *U.S. Diplomatic Papers, 1935*, I, 625–8.
[46] Villari, *Storia diplomatica*, 184–5.
[47] *U.S. Diplomatic Papers, 1935*, I, 629; Aloisi, *Journal*, 295.
[48] See Askew, "The Secret Agreement," 47–8.

On the evening of the 15th Aloisi visited Eden and Vansittart. He spoke frankly, emphasizing Italy's firm determination. He stated uncompromisingly that economic concessions in Ethiopia would be of no use to Italy unless they were reinforced by Italian military garrisons. The British replied that, on this basis, no agreement was possible.[49]

On 16 August the first formal meeting was held. Eden, seconded by Laval, rejected the Italian demand that there should be a British-French endorsement of Italian political as well as economic preponderance in Ethiopia. Laval, seconded by Eden, returned to his tentative proposals of the day before that Italy be given economic concessions, some rights of technical advisement and assistance, and some opportunities for settlement of Italian nationals in Ethiopia. A first draft, formulated along these lines, was rejected by all parties and sent back for amendment to a staff of experts. That evening the new draft proposal was presented to Aloisi. It set forward a plan for the economic and administrative reform of Ethiopia under the collective assistance of three European nations, but recognized "the special economic interests" of Italy and guaranteed Italy the major role in the "economic development and administrative reorganization" of Ethiopia. The possibility of Italian settlement in Ethiopia was allowed, and many of the most important aspects of the economic, commercial, and administrative control of the country were covered. It was, in effect, a nonpolitical mandate for Italy over Ethiopia. The program did not exclude "the possibility of territorial rectifications," but it respected "the principle of the independence and sovereignty of Ethiopia." [50]

[49] Aloisi, *Journal*, 295; Avon, *Facing the Dictators*, 250.
[50] The full plan went as follows:

1. Ethiopia may apply to the League of Nations for promoting the collaboration and foreign assistance necessary for the economic development and administrative organization of the country.

2. This assistance should be collective.

3. Such assistance would be best carried out through the cooperation of the powers bordering on Ethiopia.

4. The work ought to be accomplished in one of the two following ways: (a) The Council of the League of Nations should delegate the mission of assistance and reorganization; the decision of the Council ought naturally to be taken with the agreement of Ethiopia. (b) The conclusion of a treaty between the four powers would be communicated to the Council for its approval and would replace the treaty of 1906.

5. In either case the matters to be treated under the new arrangement are the following: (a) concessions for the development of economic resources; (b) development of foreign commerce; (c) admission of foreigners for their settlement in suitable locations; (d) construction of ways of communication and public works in general; (e) modernization of administrative services, with special

It was a good and profitable plan for Italy.[51] If all Italy wanted was to exploit the economic potential of Ethiopia, and to maintain that country under its sphere of influence, the present scheme provided a way. The plan was complicated, Léger admitted to Aloisi, and the drafting was awkward. But it was this very complication which enabled Laval to achieve his objective of keeping the League from dominating the proposed settlement. Whereas the League was given the possibility of becoming the titular supervisory agency, the procedures were devised to reduce League interference so that in practice Italy, with British and French cooperation, would achieve virtually sole control under the terms of the proposal. As Léger outlined the future, the League would concede the work of reform to the three European powers, and Britain and France would then give Italy freedom of action. All Italy would have to admit was that Ethiopia was a member of the League.[52]

Before the final plan was presented, Laval, on the afternoon of the 16th, telephoned the French chargé in Rome and told him to inform Mussolini that the proposal shortly to be submitted represented the limit to which Britain and France would go to establish a basis for negotiated settlement. Laval cautioned Mussolini to examine the proposal with great care, for if the Duce rejected it Laval would probably have no more plans to offer and would range himself on the side of his British friends. This was a strong warning. During the day's negotiation, Laval and Léger had stood loyally with Britain.[53]

When Aloisi received the French-British draft on the evening of 16

---

reference to the legal system, prisons, public health, postal system, telegraphy, etc.; (f) public education; (g) antislavery measures.

6. The arrangement indicated above would respect the principle of the independence and sovereignty of Ethiopia, as well as the open-door principle in the economic sphere.

7. This program in no way excludes the possibility of territorial rectifications.

8. It is understood that the suggested arrangement ought to take into consideration the special economic interests recognized as Italian in the economic development and administrative reorganization of Ethiopia, without prejudice to the special rights recognized as French and British. Villari, *Storia diplomatica*, 123–4. Britain remained prepared to give the port of Zeila to the emperor as a face-saving device should he cede territory to the Italians.

[51] Hoare told the American chargé on 20 August that the proposal was "tantamount to a concession to Mussolini of all he had looked for earlier, and indeed had he accepted them, he might well have claimed a decisive victory." *U.S. Diplomatic Papers, 1935,* I, 633.

[52] Villari, *Storia diplomatica,* 125.

[53] Eden agreed it was the "ultimate offer." *U.S. Diplomatic Papers, 1935,* I, 629–31; Avon, *Facing the Dictators,* 250–1.

August, his first reaction was to reject it out of hand, for it did not meet Mussolini's demand for political control in Ethiopia. Aloisi was not even going to forward the proposal to Rome. But Laval's call had alerted the Italian government, and there was a possibility that Laval might follow his first message with a direct call to the Duce. To keep the game in motion, Aloisi relayed the proposal to Suvich. There was no reply from Italy for twenty-four hours. Much to the astonished resentment of the British and French, just as the proposal was being sent to him, Mussolini decided to leave Rome for a series of military reviews. He could not be reached all during the day of the 17th.[54] The conference did not meet on the 17th, and all parties waited impatiently and with declining hopes for the reply from Rome. Mussolini's response came that night, and Aloisi showed Laval the telegram on the morning of the 18th. Mussolini flatly rejected the French-British plan:

> The proposals are absolutely unacceptable from any possible point of view. Ten months ago they might have offered the basis for discussion, but even then they would have been rejected. Today, however, when Italy has sent to Africa an army of 280,000 men and spent 2 billion lire, such proposals are the equivalent of trying to humiliate Italy in the worst possible fashion.

Such "Genevan" proposals, Mussolini continued, threw "dust in the eyes of Italy" and increased Ethiopia's prestige. For these reasons, Italy rejected the new plan and declared that further discussion would be fruitless. The Duce said to thank Laval for his efforts and to tell him that, in spite of the lack of success, Mussolini did not intend to alter his "frank and concrete friendship" with France.[55]

The tripartite conference thus ended in failure.[56] British and French efforts to negotiate a peaceful settlement of the dispute were unsuccess-

---

[54] Laval tried to contact Mussolini by telephone, but with no success. Laval was convinced that Mussolini was deliberately avoiding him. Aloisi, *Journal*, 296; Avon, *Facing the Dictators*, 251; *U.S. Diplomatic Papers, 1935*, I, 633.

[55] Another objection Mussolini referred to later was that the elaborate division of titular responsibility, instead of being, as Léger argued, the means to Italian freedom, might become a fetter on Italian action. Italy could never be certain that at some time hence the other nations might not assert their legal rights and interests in Ethiopia and use the terms of the proposal as grounds for limiting Italian activity. The Italian note of 17 August is printed in full in Aloisi, *Journal*, 297, and in part in Villari, *Storia diplomatica*, 124–5. In his letter to Laval of 25 December 1935 Mussolini reviewed his objections to the proposal. Lagardelle, *Mission à Rome*, 280–1.

[56] A short meeting of the delegates was held on the 18th to formulate a press communiqué, and the conference was formally ended. For the communiqué, see Heald, *Documents on International Affairs, 1935*, II, 51.

ful. To resolve the conflict short of war, there remained the forth-coming meeting of the arbitration commission, set to begin on 19 August. And then, under the terms of the League council's second resolution of 3 August, the council was scheduled "to meet in any event on September 4th, 1935, to undertake the general examination, in its various aspects, of the relations between Italy and Ethiopia." But in the aftermath of the Paris talks, both Eden and Laval regarded an Italian-Ethiopian war as inevitable.

The British now took stock of the seriousness of the situation. "Anthony," Vansittart said to a "tired and petulant" Eden on the night of 18 August, "you are faced with a first class international crisis. We've got to reinforce the Mediterranean fleet." A letter to this effect was sent to Hoare, warning him that the resources of negotia-tion seemed almost exhausted and that, in the face of renewed French uncertainty, Britain should take its own precautionary measures. Orders calling up certain naval reservists were quietly issued.[57] Hoare asked Eden to telephone Baldwin, who was vacationing in his favorite re-treat, Aix-les-Bains, and to arrange a meeting of the Cabinet as soon as possible. The date was set for 22 August.

The British government was again up against the problem of choosing between Rome and Geneva. Only the most unreceptive, blindly optimistic official mind could fail to perceive that Mussolini was going ahead with the invasion of Ethiopia, that he could not be talked out of it, and that this aggression would be a clear and direct violation of several treaties, including the Covenant of the League.[58] The British people awoke to this fact with a jolt upon the collapse of the Paris talks. Some few had earlier realized the gravity of the devel-oping situation, but the majority of the populace did not become fully aware of the serious consequences of the dispute until mid-August.

[57] Thompson, *Front-Line Diplomat*, 107-8; Avon, *Facing the Dictators*, 253. Another precaution was taken during this period. Over the initial objections of Haile Selassie, who gave his Imperial Guard the responsibility of protecting foreigners in Addis Ababa, Geoffrey Thompson ordered a company of Punjabis from India as additional support for the guard at the British legation compound. These soldiers, 129 well supplied men, arrived in conditions of secrecy on 7 September.

[58] As I have shown above, the League provided no means by which a potential aggressor could be deterred before there was an actual "resort to war." No nation felt constrained to make up for this deficiency except through general, hence ineffectual, warnings. All acted on the assumption, legally correct, that war must first begin before it could be stopped.

Public opinion was, as with the Peace Ballot, in favor of British support and cooperation with the League. This was qualified by the contention that Britain should not act until the other nations of the League had gathered their forces and established the course of "collective" action. Britain, it was agreed, should do nothing that would involve the nation alone.[59] Popular opinion was based on the belief that the League was an entity sufficient to itself and possessed of political powers that could somehow cause an organized and active body of international support to spring full-blown into existence. This myth assumed that the League could achieve its ends completely without the inspiration and leadership of Great Britain. Even so great a political realist as Winston Churchill could write, long afterwards: "If, therefore, the League were prepared to use the united strength of all its members to curb Mussolini's policy, it was our bounden duty to take our share and play a faithful part. There seemed in all the circumstances no obligation upon Britain to take the lead herself." [60]

The government made little effort to explode this myth. The British people were not shown that their aspirations for the collective-security system could be fulfilled only through action that would involve rearmament in Britain, a firm British commitment to maintain the status quo on the continent, and, in the present instance, the risk of war with Italy. Winston Churchill also wrote:

> One thing was clear and certain. Half-measures were useless for the League and pernicious to Britain if she assumed its leadership. If we thought it right and necessary for the law and welfare of Europe to quarrel mortally with Mussolini's Italy, we must also strike him down. The fall of the lesser dictator might combine and bring into action all the forces — and they were still overwhelming — which would enable us to restrain the greater dictator, and thus prevent a second German war.[61]

When Baldwin's government eschewed this policy, the only alternatives remaining were appeasement and nonresistance. Appeasement, in the form of a negotiated settlement, had proved unsuccessful. And all that could be said for a policy of nonresistance is that it would

[59] For representative statements of this opinion, see Toynbee, *Survey of International Affairs, 1935*, II, 48–70, and the "great discussion" carried on in the letters column of *The Times* during the late summer and autumn of 1935.

[60] Churchill, *The Gathering Storm*, 167.

[61] Churchill, *The Gathering Storm*, 167.

prevent war between Italy and Britain. Yet this was the government's paramount concern, and it tipped the balance against resistance.

By 21 August the members of the Cabinet had reassembled, with maximum publicity being given to their urgent return to London. Statements were issued that put the stamp of emergency on this special meeting. Ramsay MacDonald said on the 21st: "I regard the present situation as the most serious thing we have had to face since 1914." [62] Before the Cabinet met, Hoare invited to the Foreign Office a wide range of opposition leaders. August 21st was the busiest day at Whitehall in four years, *The Times* reported: Winston Churchill, Lloyd George, Robert Cecil, Austen Chamberlain, Herbert Samuel, and George Lansbury, the veteran pacifist leader of the Labour Party's parliamentary opposition, all came to advise the foreign secretary. Everything they said bolstered the prevailing opinion that the League should be supported only if the action taken was collective. Whether from fear of war, from a desire to conserve British strength for the German danger, or from the ingrained resistance of the more pacifist-minded to admit that the only way to protect the League from destruction was by the use of righteous strength, no one wanted war with Italy and all continued to accept the notion that the process of collective security could somehow be made to work its miracles without the active leadership of Great Britain. Even Robert Cecil allowed himself to be put off after he had urged that the government should repeat a declaration of loyalty to the Covenant — for Hoare, responding in the negative, claimed that the government "was anxious at the moment to avoid getting out of step with the French." [63]

Here was the key to Britain's future policy. France's unwillingness to antagonize Italy was the perfect counterpart to Britain's unwilling-to act at all. The members of the British government could now refuse to accept the responsibility of leadership with a clear conscience: once it was agreed that Britain would act only "collectively," the initiative for action fell to the other interested members of the League, of whom France became then the determining force. Making its own actions dependent on the French enabled the British government to appear to its electorate as the champions of the principles of the League without assuming the burden of making those principles work. The notion of

[62] *U.S. Diplomatic Papers, 1935*, I, 635.
[63] Templewood, *Nine Troubled Years*, 160.

collective responsibility came to mean in practice how far the French were willing to go. Such was the potency of the myth of League power that it came to seem that French action was possible apart from British encouragement and guarantees. The new "policy" suited the British government. To "go no further than the French," said Vansittart, was "a limitation which made valor safe." [64] It reduced the chances of Britain's becoming involved in a conflict with Italy. It pleased the electorate. And no one pointed out that it was in fact less a policy than the evasion of one. An insistence on total British-French cooperation was shared by opponents as well as supporters of the government.[65]

The Cabinet met for nearly five hours on 22 August. With the breakdown of the Paris conference, it was obvious that the policy of a negotiated settlement was dead. What was required now was a decision on the action Britain was to take at the League meeting scheduled for early September. The Italian-Ethiopian conflict was formally inscribed on the agenda of the council, and all members would attend fully aware that the crisis was at hand. On the 18th Hoare wrote a letter to Neville Chamberlain, chancellor of the exchequer, which reveals the mind of the foreign secretary at this critical juncture:

> I believe that we have done everything possible to keep in step with the French and to do nothing to provoke the Italians. None the less, at the time of writing it looks to me as if the Italians will be entirely unreasonable, and as a result there will be a first-class crisis in the League at the beginning of September. It is urgently necessary for the Cabinet to consider what, in these circumstances, our attitude should be on two assumptions: (1) that the French are completely with us; (2) that the French have backed out. It is equally urgent for the Cabinet to consider what preparations should be made to meet a possible mad dog act by the Italians . . . On the one hand I was

[64] Vansittart, *The Mist Procession*, 532.

[65] See Templewood, *Nine Troubled Years*, 160. Churchill, in his interview on the 21st, told Hoare that "the Foreign Secretary was *justified in going as far with the League of Nations against Italy as he could carry France*; but I added that he ought not to put any pressure upon France because of her military convention with Italy and her German preoccupations; and that in the circumstances I did not expect France would go very far. Generally, I strongly advised the Ministers not to try to take a leading part or to put themselves forward too prominently." Churchill, *The Gathering Storm*, 169. Neville Chamberlain told Lord Lloyd at this time that the government had "first to act so that no charge could be against the Government of deserting the League. France, however, would not apply sanctions, and this would be Britain's chance to refuse to act alone and embark on a big naval reconstruction effort." Quoted in Amery, *My Life in Politics*, III, 174n.

anxious to suggest no action which would even give the impression of provocation to the Italians or of war to the British public. On the other hand, I have been very nervous of leaving undone anything that might make a mad dog act more dangerous . . .

As you may imagine I have received little or no help from other quarters. Stanley [Baldwin] would think about nothing but his holiday and the necessity of keeping out of the whole business almost at any cost. Ramsay [MacDonald] has written me a curious and almost unintelligible letter warning me of all the dangers that surround us, generally taking the side of the Italians and making the amazing suggestion that the Italians are likely to be our great Empire rivals in the future and will almost certainly be stronger than ourselves.

Outside the Cabinet public opinion has been greatly hardening against Italy. Papers like the *Birmingham Post* are getting restive over the arms embargo and over the ineffectiveness of the League. I see myself the making of a first-class crisis in which the Government will lose heavily if we appear to be repudiating the Covenant. When I say this, I do not mean that I have changed my views since we both discussed the question in London. What, however, I do mean is that if we adopt Stanley's attitude of indifference or Ramsay's alarmist and pusillanimous surrender to the Italians, we shall get the worst of every conceivable world. Our line, I am sure, is to keep in step with the French, and, whether now or at Geneva, to act with them.[66]

As the Cabinet met, all indications were pointing to strictly limited action on the part of France, at the most. Eden's cautious opinion from Paris on 16 August that the French "would stand to a firm line at Geneva, even if it led to economic sanctions," was undercut by the gloomy collapse of the tripartite talks. In their final conversation Laval warned Eden of the difficulty of France's situation. France counted on the military advantages of its Italian connection. Mussolini sent France an assurance of his loyalty and support in the message delivered by Aloisi on the 18th. This was an important consideration, and France would not quarrel with Italy unless it was absolutely certain, in advance, that Britain would come to France's aid on the continent. The tradition of Britain not to give categorical assurances made Laval unsure of Britain's policy in Europe, despite the Locarno agreements. To abandon the agreement with Italy, then, might leave France without an effective ally on the continent. Eden asked Laval what position France planned to take at the coming League meeting. Laval replied that he had not yet examined the problem, but "he

---

[66] Templewood, *Nine Troubled Years*, 164–5; Feiling, *Neville Chamberlain*, 267.

supposed some form of condemnation of Italy's act would be inevitable." He did not intend to turn his back on the League, Laval said, but the question of French support in resistance or in the imposition of sanctions was by no means settled. The French held that no discussion of sanctions should take place until after Italy had been formally named an aggressor by the League, for any premature discussion would only encourage Mussolini to seek economic ties with Germany.[67]

In these circumstances, the British Cabinet, by refusing to take the lead, perpetuated Britain's ambiguous position. It was publicly reported that the Cabinet had decided "to maintain the Government's attitude towards the League of Nations and the Covenant." Privately the British delegation was instructed to "keep in step with the French and follow closely the procedure laid down in the Covenant." [68] It is of great significance that the British government at this time failed to take the one step that would have enabled the French to support collective security at Geneva. The British refused to assure France of Britain's future support in Europe. What good to France was the League if even it, despite British claims, could not tie Britain to the continent? The effect was that, by withholding their assurances, the British made certain that France would not move against Italy.

The British government's pusillanimity is illustrated by another decision taken at the Cabinet meeting of 22 August. This was not to lift the British embargo of 25 July on the sale of arms to Ethiopia or to Italy. The prohibition, made against the advice of Eden and Sir Sidney Barton, had aroused considerable protest, for it favored Italy in practice by denying the Ethiopians what they so desperately needed. The embargo had been instituted for two reasons. One was that the British wished to do nothing that would antagonize Mussolini and hence prejudice the chances of a negotiated agreement. This reason now no longer held. The second reason, Britain's wanting to go along with the French embargo, was also weakened now, for Laval told Eden that, though he did not intend to lift the French embargo, he had no objection to the British raising theirs.[69]

The emperor had pointed out the inequity of the British and French embargoes in his interview with George Steer of *The Times* on 28 July.

[67] Avon, *Facing the Dictators*, 250–3; *U.S. Diplomatic Papers, 1935*, I, 636–8.
[68] Avon, *Facing the Dictators*, 255; *The Times* (London), 23 August 1935.
[69] Avon, *Facing the Dictators*, 252, 288–9.

On 12 August Tecle Hawariate, on instructions from Addis Ababa, sent a strong appeal to the secretary-general. His letter was circulated to the council members on the 14th, the eve of the Paris talks. It read:

Notwithstanding the resumption of the arbitral procedure, in conformity with the Council's decision of August 3rd last, the Royal Italian Government is continuing to send troops and ammunition to East Africa; it is ceaselessly manufacturing arms and implements of war, with the solemnly avowed intention of using them against the Ethiopian Empire.

There is no manufacture in Ethiopia, either public or private, of arms or munitions of war.

The Imperial Ethiopian Government today finds it absolutely impossible to obtain means of defence outside its own frontiers. Wherever it attempts to obtain them, it meets with prohibitions and export embargoes.

Is that real neutrality? Is it just?

Will the Council remain unmoved in face of this situation, which is growing steadily worse? Will it allow this unequal combat to continue between two Members of the League of Nations, one of which, all powerful, is in a position to employ, and declares that it is employing, all its resources in preparing for aggression, while the other, weak and pacific, and mindful of its international undertakings, is deprived of the means of organizing the defence of its territory and of its very existence, both of which are threatened? Will the Council assume responsibility, in the eyes of the world, for allowing preparations to continue unchecked for the massacre of a people which constitutes a menace to none? [70]

At Paris, on 18 August, Tecle Hawariate made a direct appeal to the British government to lift the arms embargo. All Ethiopia asked of the world, he told Eden, was the right to self-defense, and even that was being denied it by the existing prohibitions. Eden repeated this argument to London and urged the government to reconsider its stand. Lloyd George spoke to Hoare in the same vein on the 21st, pointing out that there was no need for the British government to get involved after revoking the embargo. "Just drop a hint to Vickers," he advised. "They will see to it." [71]

But nothing served to change the mind of the Cabinet. Fear of war with Italy meant that weight was given to threats in the Italian press

[70] League, *Official Journal, 1935,* 1601–2.
[71] Vickers was the British arms-manufacturing firm, Vickers-Armstrongs. Avon, *Facing the Dictators,* 253, 255.

that violent actions would follow if the British lifted the embargo.[72] There were at this time "strong representations" from the French government to avoid all anti-Italian acts until the League council met in September; despite Laval's disclaimer, the Cabinet decided to interpret the embargo in this light. On 22 August the Cabinet resolved "to maintain for the time being" the embargo on arms to Ethiopia.[73] The embargo was not lifted until after Ethiopia was invaded, and even then licensing was curtailed. This decision to deprive Ethiopia of the means for its defense was, Eden later wrote,

> not only inequitable, but a cardinal error of policy . . . [British] policy was determined by an optimistic belief that Mussolini might still come to terms, by reluctance to do anything which might goad the Duce into some rash act, and by an insufficiently clear view of whose side we were on. In fact, wishful thinking and a desire to appease were already doing their insidious work, with the usual disastrous consequences.[74]

There were no regrets in Italy over the collapse of the Paris talks. Virginio Gayda, editor of the *Giornale d'Italia* and a Fascist propagandist, noted that the conference had not been called by Italy and that the Italian delegation attended only to hear what the other two nations had to say.[75] The Paris proposals, regarded as the maximum concession Britain was prepared to make, were inadequate. The Italian government considered Mussolini's blunt and decisive rejection as the concluding act in its plan of negotiation for the sake of delay. The government now considered itself completely free from diplomatic restraints, and Mussolini declared himself "more satisfied now than at any other time." [76] On 20 August he telegraphed De Bono in east Africa: "The tripartite conference has failed. Now there is Geneva,

[72] At the Cabinet meeting of 22 August a special committee was set up to work with the Committee on Imperial Defence to make any necessary shifts of British forces in the event of hostile activity on the part of Italy in the Mediterranean. *U.S. Diplomatic Papers, 1935*, I, 638. There followed on 29 August the movement of the Mediterranean fleet from Malta to Alexandria. In August the Fascist publicist Virginio Gayda raised the cry: "Sanctions mean war." This warning was echoed by sections of the British press, notably Lord Rothermere's *Daily Mail*. Gayda further attacked the supporters of the League as "firemen incendiaries," who, "wishing to extinguish the small fire of a colonial war, threaten to cause thereby a terrible conflagration." *The Times* (London), 23 August 1935.

[73] *The Times* (London), 23 August 1935; *U.S. Diplomatic Papers, 1935*, I, 637.

[74] Avon, *Facing the Dictators*, 290.

[75] *The Times* (London), 20 August 1935.

[76] Aloisi, *Journal*, 298.

but the diplomatic situation is exhausted. You can draw the conclusion." [77]

There remained but four diplomatic chores for Italy to undertake. One was to complete the proceedings of the arbitration commission. The second was to minimize the effects of Mussolini's blunt talk wherever soft words might turn away wrath. Italy continued to encourage Laval's desire for friendship. Following upon the assurances of Italian loyalty that Aloisi had delivered on the 18th, Mussolini on 21 August drafted a message of thanks to the French premier for his conciliatory efforts at the Paris talks. Mussolini told Laval that Italy would consent to all France had asked: Italy would attend the coming council meeting at Geneva, the broadside press campaign against the British would be curtailed, and the French-Italian entente would be reinforced. Mussolini's message was drafted with the purpose of being useful to Laval in his efforts to apply a moderating pressure on the British.[78] Third, where stronger words did seem desirable, the British were warned in the Italian press that they had better watch their step. "Sanctions mean war," trumpeted Gayda. As we have seen, such threats had a profound effect on the British Cabinet's meeting of 22 August. The fourth diplomatic activity was the final preparation of an exhaustive memorandum for the forthcoming meeting of the council by which to prove the unfitness of Ethiopia for membership in the community of civilized nations, and so to diminish the moral sympathy and legal rights that Ethiopia was enjoying.

Diplomacy, however, was only a cover for the plan of armed invasion, and in the second half of August Italian military preparations moved into their final phase. Day after day new call-ups were announced for the armed services. Day after day Mussolini sped from place to place, reviewing and exhorting his troops. On 15 August another 150,000 men were ordered to report for duty. On 16 August it was announced that Galeazzo Ciano, the Duce's son-in-law and

[77] "Conferenza tripartita di Parigi è fallita. Ora c'è Ginevra, ma la situazione diplomatica è ormai esaurita. Puoi trarne le conclusioni." This secret telegram is printed in Mussolini, *Opera omnia*, XXVII, 295. De Bono, in his book, renders this message as "Conferenza niente concluso; c'è Ginevra che concludera lo stesso. Concludi" — "Conference came to no conclusion; Geneva will do the same. Make an end." It is this version that has become famous. De Bono, *La Preparazione*, 139; *Anno XIIII*, 190.

[78] Aloisi, *Journal*, 299.

minister of press and propaganda, had enlisted in the air force in the bomber command and was being sent to east Africa.[79] As many as fifteen steamers a day left Naples, "the Gate to Africa," loaded with supplies and men.[80] On the 23rd the Italian government announced the additional expenditure of 2.5 billion lire for the east African campaign. On 22 August Mussolini assumed supreme command of the great war maneuvers then beginning in the south Tyrol, in the Alto Adige, under the effective supervision of the undersecretary for war, General Federico Baistrocchi.

Before leaving Rome the Duce, on 26 August, called a dramatic emergency meeting of the Italian Council of Ministers, to be held on the 28th at Bolzano, the center of the maneuvers. The ministers attended in military uniform. The meeting was timed diplomatically to precede the meeting of the League council set for 4 September. The official communiqué of the Bolzano meeting, issued on 29 August, was restrained but firm in its warnings. An Italian delegation would attend the forthcoming session of the council and at Geneva would defend Italy's aims and actions with the aid of an extensive memorandum on the Ethiopian situation. The memorandum would reveal the retrogressive character and extent of disorganization of the empire and its history of continual aggression against its neighbors. The Fascist government considered the Ethiopian matter strictly a colonial question, which "should have no influence on the European situation, unless any one wants to run the risk of unleashing a new world war to prevent a great nation like Italy from bringing order to a vast country where the most atrocious slavery reigns and the conditions of existence are most primitive." The League was warned that "to speak of 'sanctions' means venturing onto a dangerous slope which may lead to the gravest complications." Italy announced that "long ago" it had taken the necessary measures to cope with the eventuality of military sanctions. Following the Italian argument that the motive behind British opposition was Britain's own interests in Ethiopia, the communiqué said in a conciliatory vein:

> Britain has nothing to fear from Italian policy toward Ethiopia. The policy of Italy does not threaten either directly or indirectly British imperial interests, and the tendentious fears that agitated certain quarters were simply absurd.

[79] Salvatorelli and Mira, *Storia d'Italia*, 794. Ciano was replaced as minister on the 22nd by Dino Alfieri.
[80] *The Times* (London), 21 August 1935.

Italy has a problem to solve with Ethiopia. It has none and wants none with Great Britain, with whom during the world war, at Locarno, and more recently at Stresa it achieved collaboration of undoubted importance for European stability.

The Bolzano communiqué ended by announcing a series of stringent financial measures designed to improve Italy's holdings of foreign exchange and to increase the revenue of the state and its financial control of industry.[81]

Another fact deserving notice in any discussion of Italian diplomacy in mid-August is a specific move made by Mussolini to improve his relations with Germany. The more opposition the Duce felt from his erstwhile allies, the more he felt need for assurance from Germany that Italy's Brenner frontier would be safe while Italy was involved in Africa. The more the Duce heard of the possible threat of economic or military sanctions, which might cut off the flow by sea of goods to Italy, the greater need he had for an entente with Germany which would allow Italy to procure food and fuel necessary for the peninsula's survival. To enhance the prospects for an Italian-German understanding, in mid-August Mussolini removed Vittorio Cerruti from his post at Berlin, where the ambassador was scarcely on speaking terms with the diplomats of the Wilhelmstrasse and even less well received by Hitler.[82] Cerruti was sent to Paris and replaced in Berlin by Bernardo Attolico, until then Italian ambassador in Moscow. His express purpose and first task, Attolico told Bernhard von Bülow of the German foreign ministry at their initial meeting on 19 August, was to improve the atmosphere between Berlin and Rome. This was easier said than done, however, for the Germans were determined to maintain their position of "wait and see." Bülow was cool to Attolico's overtures. Germany, he said, wanted nothing to do with Italy's conflict. Italy would have to be satisfied with German neutrality, the prevention of arms exports to Ethiopia, and no recruitment in Germany for the emperor's forces. The German press would not even take a pro-Italian line, for this might endanger the lives of German citizens living in Ethiopia.[83]

---

[81] Mussolini, *Opera omnia*, XXVII, 115–18. There is a good contemporary study of the economic aspects of this phase of the conflict by H. V. Hodson in Toynbee, *Survey of International Affairs, 1935*, II, 414–24.

[82] Wiskemann, *The Rome-Berlin Axis*, 49.

[83] *Documents on German Foreign Policy*, IV, 564–5. It is perhaps worth noting that Ulrich von Hassell, the German ambassador in Rome, was on leave from the first week in August until 28 September.

On 31 August Mussolini repeated his general warnings. In a speech to 100,000 soldiers gathered near Bolzano to celebrate the ending of the war maneuvers, the Duce said:

> During the month of September another two-hundred thousand men will be called into your ranks to bring the effectives of the Army up to the foreseen level of a million men. The world must realize yet once again that as long as this absurd and provacative talk about sanctions continues, we will not give up a single soldier, a single sailor, or a single airman, but we will raise all the armed forces of the nation to the highest possible level of strength.[84]

Bold words and stern warnings, a refusal to consider a compromise settlement, elaborate military preparations — all of this was used by the Fascist government to inspire support at home and, more important, to offer the rest of the world an impression of unswerving Italian determination to complete a conquest of Ethiopia that could not be stopped by argument. Mussolini realized the vulnerable position to which he had exposed his country. Only by a policy of bluff, predicated on the reluctance of Britain and France to destroy his regime, might Mussolini prevent sanctions, give the British and the French their excuse for avoiding action against him, and win in his gamble on the Ethiopian campaign.

The crucial period of the conflict was now beginning, and Mussolini, despite all his brave declarations, was realistic enough to hedge his bets. On or about 25 August he sent a message to De Bono:

> This is the last letter I will write to you before the action . . . I believe that after 10 September you should expect my word of command at any moment. By that time you will have in Eritrea two divisions of Blackshirts and another sixty airplanes. The forces are sufficient for the first rush and the winning of the established objectives. You will halt on the line conquered and take steps to organize the rear and await events on the international plane . . . You will celebrate Mascal in conquered territory.[85]

The line referred to ran from Adigrat through Aduwa to Aksum, the area from which the Italians were pushed in 1896, and it was to be extended as soon as possible to run roughly from Makale to the

---

[84] Mussolini, *Opera omnia*, XXVII, 118–9. It was as Lloyd George said: Mussolini was "not merely blustering and bluffing the nation out of its rooted fears; he is building up its fighting strength so as to give Italians the confidence that drives out fear." *Memoirs of the Peace Conference*, II, 528.

[85] Mussolini, *Opera omnia*, XXVII, 277; De Bono, *Anno XIIII*, 191. The Ethiopian religious holiday of Mascal was celebrated on 27 and 28 September.

Takkaze River. The conquest of this area would give Italy a prestigious victory. The "shameful scar" of Aduwa would at last be erased. Italy would have avenged itself against the old foe, and the "broadly psychological aspect of the question," as De Bono put it, would be resolved.[86]

What then? The most interesting part of Mussolini's letter is that after the initial military thrust, which would extend the Italian occupation only some hundred miles into Ethiopia, De Bono was ordered to "halt on the line conquered and take steps to organize the rear and await events on the international plane." Here is the crux of the matter. Once the aggression took place, it was obvious from the diplomatic activity of the preceding months that the League of Nations would be called into session with an effort made to apply article 16, the imposition of sanctions, against Italy. If sanctions were imposed, and if the British used their fleet to enforce them, Italian forces in Africa would be in serious and immediate trouble. Italian east Africa was almost unprotected. A royal decree of 2 September established a naval command for the Red Sea, the Gulf of Aden, and the Indian Ocean. But this force consisted only of two cruisers, two scouts, and two torpedo boats, hardly enough to face up to the British navy; the extent of their usefulness was in reconnoitering the coast. More than this, there were problems involved in conquering the Ethiopian armies. Mussolini was optimistic of a swift victory, but, according to one report, Italian military experts set the duration of a full-scale war at two years. Estimates elsewhere were considerably higher, and there was the possibility of an indefinite period of guerrilla warfare on the part of Ethiopia.[87] In June Ciano had told the British historian John W. Wheeler-Bennett that the Italian government counted on one year of war and five years of pacification.[88] The logistical problem during an invasion was another unknown. As a result, the initial Italian thrust could not be too deep — in case sanctions were applied

[86] See De Bono, *Anno XIIII*, chap. 12. The term "shameful scar" was contrived by Gabriele D'Annunzio in a letter to a young man, Agostino Lazzarotto, who was going to serve in the east African campaign. D'Annunzio's letter was published in the Italian press in July 1935. D'Annunzio regretted being of the generation that had suffered this defeat and called upon the young to erase the disgrace "without hesitation." "You go to conquer," he told the 'African Legionary,' and said that Italy's "new greatness is able to be accomplished only with a true Roman triumph over barbarism."

[87] Laval, looking to the precedent of Morocco, thought the war would last for many years. Gamelin, *Servir*, II, 174.

[88] U.S. Diplomatic Correspondence, 765.84/459.

and enforced, withdrawal might become necessary. In a secret message Mussolini also told De Bono that, if Italy became engaged with Britain, the troops in east Africa would have to renounce further offensive action and restrict themselves to defending Eritrea. But even if this drastic situation did not occur immediately, De Bono was instructed to "halt . . . and await events on the international plane." Something was bound to happen in Europe, for better or worse, and until the European situation cleared, some degree of caution was necessary.[89]

There were at this time many people in Britain and France who thought that, although nothing had yet come of proposals for a negotiated settlement, such a solution might still have a chance even after a limited Italian invasion. If Mussolini gained an initial victory, went a representative view, "and has the satisfaction of being able to claim that Adowa is avenged by occupying the very place where General Baratieri was defeated — he may feel that Italian honour is satisfied and that the considerable economic concessions which have already been offered to him and which will still be presumably available, may provide the basis of a settlement."[90] On 19 August Mussolini made a statement to the American chargé in Rome which gave some slight encouragement to this view. Ethiopia, the Duce told Alexander C. Kirk, had as its military plan

> to retreat before the Italian advance and then when the Italian lines were extended to launch attacks against those lines in the form of guerilla warfare. The Abyssinians were not taking sufficiently into account the Italian air force which would eliminate the chance of success of these tactics. Mussolini expressed complete confidence in the outcome of this military set-up and he intimated that he believed it would be brief. He indicated that following this phase negotiations for a final adjustment would be simple.

But any adjustment, Mussolini continued, would have to meet Italian demands. Economic concessions were without value, as were all four-power arrangements. What Italy demanded was "first and foremost the military occupation of the country."[91]

In all probability, Mussolini would have been forced to consider a compromise settlement after Italy's initial thrust *if* either European opposition or Ethiopian resistance were great enough to jeopardize

[89] De Bono, *Anno XIIII*, 202; Mussolini, *Opera omnia*, XXVII, 299.
[90] This quotation is from Salvemini, *Prelude*, 262.
[91] *U.S. Diplomatic Papers, 1935*, I, 741.

the Italian army. But if Ethiopia did fade before the Italian air offensive, and above all if Britain refused to act, there was no reason to suppose that Mussolini would halt Italy's advance longer than it took to test the wind. If he found it favorable, he would press on to total and unrestricted military conquest and pay no heed to the possibilities of a negotiated adjustment. Before the war the Italians had made no provisions for the conclusion of a limited settlement. To impose such a settlement on Italy would require, sooner or later, a stand of strong resistance to total conquest by Britain acting alone or with France, with or without the League. Unless this pressure were applied, Mussolini's "halt" would be no more than a pause.

Chapter 11

August: The Holy See, America, and a Verdict

Apart from Mussolini, the two most important men in Italy in 1935 were the king, Victor Emmanuel III, and the pope, Pius XI. The king never opposed Mussolini once the Ethiopian campaign had begun in earnest. In August Victor Emmanuel had some apprehensions in the wake of President Roosevelt's appeal to the Italian government and because of the grave uncertainties of the future, a nervousness shared with certain ranking members of the armed services, but this concern did not manifest itself in any attempt to restrain Mussolini.[1] The king, a meek, indecisive man, did not stray from his role as a loyal Italian, allowing the political fortunes of his country to be determined by the dictates of the leader of the Fascist Party and the head of the government.

In the months before October 1935, the position of the Holy See was marked by a clear unwillingness to become involved in the Italian-Ethiopian issue. Since the settlement of the "Roman question," the pope was re-established in his dual capacity as both a spiritual leader of a world-wide church and a parochial temporal prince. In his political capacity the pope, by article 24 of the Lateran Treaty of 1929, agreed that the papacy should remain "extraneous to the temporal competition between other states and to the international conferences summoned for such an object, unless the contending parties agree to appeal to its mission of peace." Tradition as well as treaty obligation led the Vatican to stand apart from what in the political sphere might be construed as a purely secular dispute. Never during the

[1] N. D'Aroma, *Vent'anni insieme: Vittorio Emanuele e Mussolini* (Rome, 1957), 233.

conflict did the Vatican "depart by word or action from formal neutrality" in its official political position.[2]

Yet neutrality does not mean indifference, and the pope and the diplomats of the Vatican were greatly concerned over the consequences of Italy's Ethiopian campaign. From January 1935 on, the Vatican was aware that Mussolini planned war against Ethiopia.[3] This posed a problem of extreme delicacy. The close relations between the Catholic Church and the country and government of Italy made it impossible for the Vatican to ignore the military and psychological preparations for war, so obvious throughout Italy during the first nine months of 1935. By the same token, it seemed that these close relations made it even more difficult, even if tradition and treaty had allowed it, for the papacy to take a strong stand against Mussolini. For four hundred years, in unbroken line, every pope had come from Italy. Pius XI was a loyal son of Lombardy and "loved his native land with an intense and personal love." For thirty-two years, as Achille Ratti, he had led a quiet life in the Ambrosian Library in Milan. At the end of World War I, he became apostolic delegate to the new state of Poland. Hardly had he arrived in Warsaw, fresh from his library and unused to the ways of international politics, when he was thrust into the turmoil of the Russian-Polish war. He was in Warsaw when Pilsudski repulsed the Red Army at the "miracle of the Vistula." He then returned to the see of Milan, was made a cardinal, and, the newest cardinal in the conclave, was elected pope as a compromise candidate in January 1922, nine months before Mussolini came to power.

> His brief diplomatic experience in Warsaw brought him to the throne with an imperfect and one-sided appreciation of contemporary European affairs. He didn't exaggerate the dangers of Communism, but he mistook the defenders of traditional Christian civilization against the new barbarism. He believed that democracy was too feeble and incoherent to serve as a dam against the Communist tide, and thus he turned to the new form of authoritarian government as offering the only hope of successful resistance.[4]

[2] D. Binchy, *Church and State in Fascist Italy* (London, 1941), 641.
[3] Charles-Roux, *Huit ans au Vatican*, 134.
[4] Binchy, *Church and State*, 85, 88. According to the Polish ambassador at the Vatican, Pius XI saw Soviet Russia as a factor in encouraging Britain to oppose Italy over the Ethiopian question, with the Communists hoping for a general upheaval in Europe. Szembek, *Journal*, 131.

The pope thus made the church's peace with Fascism and accepted Mussolini (for his work on the concordat) as a man of Providence, a man not deluded by liberalism.[5] There were occasional conflicts of interest, such as over the nature of Italian youth groups or, in 1931, the matter of Catholic Action or, later, protests against Mussolini's anti-Semitic decrees; but for the most part, in response to Mussolini's slogan of "Rome or Moscow," the majority of the Catholic clergy became, if not firm supporters of Fascism, at least reluctant to oppose the regime.[6] Not until just before his death in 1939 did Pius XI admit: "Late, too late, in my life, I have discovered that the dangers that threaten religion do not come only from one side; they come from the other side as well." [7]

Yet despite its ties with the Italian nation, its connections with the Fascist regime, and its formalized political neutrality, the Vatican viewed Mussolini's Ethiopian campaign with deep concern. In July the French ambassador had an audience with the pope. François Charles-Roux recorded that Pius XI was worried more about the risks of the failure of the Italian conquest than about its success. The pope said:

> I am very upset, very preoccupied, with this conflict. Already the repercussion on our Catholic interests in Ethiopia, and even in all of black Africa, have been made known to me. Catholic missionaries in Abyssinia are being denounced as spies. The situation is being used among the blacks to incite negroes against whites. A defeat of the Italian undertaking would be to the detriment of the interests of the European colonizers of Africa.[8]

As the summer progressed, and the days of war came nearer, the Vatican's concern increased. There was the fear that the demands of

[5] See Salvatorelli and Mira, *Storia d'Italia*, 419–94.

[6] See A. Jemolo, *Chiesa e stato in Italia dal risorgimento ad oggi* (Turin, 1955), 383–4. R. Webster describes the relations between the church and the Fascist state during Pius' last eight years as "idyllic," *The Cross and the Fasces* (Stanford, 1960), 114.

[7] This quotation, from one of Pius' last audiences, as reported in *Osservatore romano*, is found in Sforza, *Italy and Italians*, 77.

[8] Charles-Roux, *Huit ans au Vatican*, 135; see also *Le Temps*, 12 July 1935. The fact that the pope did not denounce Italian aggression was said to end the feeling among many Africans that Pius XI was their friend, and it caused a setback in many missionary activities of the church. W. Teeling, *The Pope in Politics* (London, 1937), 223. Perhaps in an effort to allay such feeling, in July Pius gave an audience, and extended warm greetings, to the pupils of the Ethiopian College, which had been founded in 1930 and which was the only pontifical college domiciled within the Vatican in 1935. The college had about 40 Ethiopian students. The Roman Catholic Church considered Coptic Ethiopia a non-Catholic state.

the situation were pushing Mussolini toward Berlin and an alliance with Nazi Germany. More important, the pope told the Belgian ambassador on 12 September, the pontiff was now concerned with the moral question involved in Italy's resorting to aggressive conquest behind the camouflage of the claim of preventive war.[9]

In the same article 24 of the Lateran Treaty that restricted political activities, the Holy See had reserved to itself "the right to make its moral and spiritual protest heard." Here, if condition need be found, was the clause through which the pope might speak out for the cause of justice and peace. Although it was the custom of the papacy not to denounce any particular war as unjust, for this would mean passing judgment on secular causes and events, peace was important to the church.

> The greater the war the greater the disaster to the Church, and in particular a European war in which Italy was involved would be a calamity of the worst kind. Hence it was in the interests of the Holy See, first, that a peaceful settlement of the quarrel should be found, and then, if this should prove impossible, that the conflict should be localized. All the efforts of Vatican diplomacy were related to one or the other of these objectives.[10]

The first public reference the pope made to the impending conflict came on 28 July, when the pontiff spoke in favor of the eventual beatification of Giustino De Jacobis, an Italian missionary and the first apostolic vicar to Ethiopia, who had died on his mission in 1860. The pope's words were meant to be a discreet warning to Mussolini.[11] He found it cause for concern, Pius said, that his panegyric in honor of De Jacobis, "this great Italian, this great Abyssinian by adoption," should come at a time when

> between Italy and Abyssinia there crossed a cloudy sky, of which no one is able to evade the presence, the significance, indeed the mystery, because there is yet more cloudiness to come . . . We trust, we will always continue to trust, in the peace of Christ within the reign of Christ, and, we cherish full faith that nothing will happen except according to truth, according to justice, according to mercy.[12]

[9] Charles-Roux, *Huit ans au Vatican*, 137–8.
[10] Binchy, *Church and State*, 640.
[11] Charles-Roux, *Huit ans au Vatican*, 135.
[12] *Discorsi di Pio XI*, D. Bertetto, ed. (Turin, 1960), III, 362–3. (Permission to quote granted by Casa Editrice SEI; all rights reserved, Società Editrice Internazionale.)

On 27 August at Castel Gandolfo, the pope addressed an international congress of Catholic nurses.

We long for peace and we pray to God that we may be spared from war. The mere thought of war . . . is terrifying. Already we see that abroad there is talk of a war of conquest, of a war of aggression. That is a hypothesis which we even fear to think of; it is a hypothesis which is truly disconcerting. A war which is only a war of conquest would be clearly an unjust war; it is something which passes all imagination, which would be beyond words sad and horrible. We are not able to think about an unjust war, nor admit its possibility, and we deliberately turn our mind from it. We do not believe, we do not wish to believe, in an unjust war. On the other hand, it is said in Italy that the war of which there is question would be a just war, because it is a war of defense, to secure the frontiers against repeated and incessant attacks, a war become necessary because of the expansion of a population which is daily increasing, that it is a war undertaken to defend or assure the material security of a country, that such a war justifies itself. It is, however, true, and we cannot but reflect on this truth, that if there is this need for expansion, if there is this need to defend the frontier and make it secure, we can only wish that some other means than war can be found to resolve these difficulties. What are these means? Obviously it is not easy to say, but we do not believe that it is impossible to find these other means. It is necessary to study the possibilities. One thing seems to us beyond doubt, that is, if the need for expansion is a fact with which we must reckon, the right of defense has its limits and its qualifications, and if the right of defense is to be blameless it must observe a certain moderation. In any event we pray to God to second the activity and industry of those far-sighted men who understand what the true welfare of peoples and of social justice demands, men who are doing all in their power, though not by means of threats, which can only irritate men's spirits and make the day by day situation more difficult and more menacing — of the men who are doing all that is possible, not with delays which represent only a waste of precious time, but with a truly human intention are doing their utmost to maintain peace, with the sincere intention of keeping war at a distance.[13]

This speech of late August was the pope's most complete and definite statement on the Italian-Ethiopian conflict before the outbreak of war. It was addressed not only as a warning to the Fascist regime but also as an encouragement to those who were seeking a negotiated settlement. Pius's speech was completely unexpected. The

[13] *Discorsi di Pio XI*, III, 379–80.

Italian ambassador to the Vatican tried in vain to keep it from being published in the *Osservatore romano*. When it came out, the repercussions in Rome were enormous.[14] The Fascist press did its best to distort the message to make it appear that the pope had given his unreserved approval to Italian arguments for expansionism. Three days later the pope himself wrote a rebuttal to this falsification, which appeared in the *Osservatore romano* on 30 August: "The Pope's thought is clear: the need to expand is not a right *per se*, but simply a fact of which note must be taken. Self-defence, on the other hand, constitutes a right, but the exercise of this right may be harmful if it does not observe certain limits and a certain moderation." [15] But the Italian government's representations to the Vatican's secretary of state, Cardinal Eugenio Pacelli, had their effect. Pressure was exercised on the pope to attenuate the harshness of his remarks and to counteract the bitterness they caused among the Fascist leaders.[16] On 7 September, speaking to a gathering of Catholic war veterans, the pope said that while he prayed for peace he hoped that "the hopes, the demands, the needs of a great and good people, which are [my] people . . . would be recognized and satisfied . . . but with justice and with peace." [17]

These quotations represent the extent of Pope Pius XI's public remarks on the Italian-Ethiopian conflict before the beginning of the war. Despite the pressing seriousness of the affair and his own concern, Pius made only one other effort to check the broadening dispute. Stricken by "nightmares and insomnia" in his worry for Italy, "now in a position where it is not able to advance or retreat," toward the end of September the pope sent to Mussolini some of the letters that had arrived at the Vatican, presumably expressing dismay at the coming of war, and suggested a private meeting together.[18] This overture came to nothing, and the new secular Roman imperialism went its way. The Holy See did not further warn or condemn the potential aggressor or offer succor to the intended victim;[19] nor did it support the efforts at mediation or the principles of international law

---

[14] Charles-Roux, *Huit ans au Vatican*, 136.
[15] *The Times* (London), 31 August 1935.
[16] Charles-Roux, *Huit ans au Vatican*, 137.
[17] *Discorsi di Pio XI*, III, 389.
[18] Charles-Roux, *Huit ans au Vatican*, 139–40.
[19] Ethiopia, always trying to ingratiate itself abroad, reportedly sent a message to the pope on 5 September thanking him for his prayers for peace. *The Times* (London), 6 September 1935.

as then accepted by most of the world. Unlike his predecessor Benedict XV, Pius XI gave no encouragement to the League of Nations,
whose ethical and juridical foundations corresponded so closely to
Christian precepts.[20]

The unwillingness of the papacy to intervene in this dispute may
be explained on an institutional level by its long-standing reluctance
to involve itself in secular affairs, and by the particular acuteness
of this reluctance when the issue involved the Italian state. But the
pope was only secondarily a temporal statesman. What cannot be as-
sessed in terms of law or politics is the fact that the Vicar of Christ, in
his primary capacity as a spiritual and moral leader, failed to speak
out more strongly against what was clearly an unjust war. As Daniel
Binchy writes, "even if the Vatican itself maintained a formal neutrality, its toleration of the chauvinist speeches and behavior of members of the Italian hierarchy and other prominent Italian ecclesiastics
constituted a direct encouragement to the Fascist leaders and an implicit support of the Fascist cause." [21]

The United States, in the second half of August, took three actions
in the Italian-Ethiopian question. One was Franklin D. Roosevelt's
message to Mussolini on the 19th; the second was the first neutrality
act, which became law on the 31st; and the third was the move of
the Department of State in forcing withdrawal of the so-called Rickett
concession.

In mid-August the American government was watching the development of the conflict with "care and concern." On the eve of the
tripartite conference in Paris, on 15 August, Secretary of State Cordell
Hull telegraphed the American chargés in London and Paris to learn
if there were any American action that might help the British or
French to find a peaceful settlement of the dispute — any American
action, that is, which would be within the limits of America's "estab-

---

[20] For Benedict's interesting remarks in support of the League, in his encyclical
Pacem Die of 23 May 1920, and for the problem of the relation between the church
and this new laic institution, see L. Sturzo, *Chiesa e stato: Studio sociologico-
storico* (Bologna, 1958, reissue), II, 163–4, 188–9.

[21] Binchy, *Church and State*, 643. See also Webster, *The Cross and the Fasces*,
122–3, 155–9. For an interpretation of the pope's public statements maintaining that
Pius XI was being deliberately ambiguous in order to avoid any outright criticism
of Mussolini's planned war against Ethiopia, see Salvemini, "The Vatican and the
Ethiopian War," in F. Keene ed., *Neither Liberty nor Bread* (New York, 1940),
191–200.

lished policy." A month before, Hoare suggested that Hull's statement of 12 July, which noted the still binding character of the Kellogg-Briand Pact, be conveyed directly to Mussolini by the American ambassador in Rome, to assure the Duce's awareness of the statement and to emphasize the legal aspect of the dispute. This proposal was now repeated. On the night of 16 August and on the day of the 17th, the Paris talks were in suspense as Aloisi awaited a reply from Rome on the British-French proposal. Now, if ever, American intervention might prove valuable. Both the British and the French delegations urged the American chargé in Paris to consider the possible effectiveness of an American move. Mussolini, Léger said, was "always relying on the hope that the United States would remain at least indifferent or disinterested." A strong stand by America at this point might bring home to Mussolini the true seriousness of his position. Coupled with the warnings from Britain and France, the members of the British delegation said, a firm statement by the United States might indicate to the Duce the "moral isolation" in which Italy would find itself if it made war on Ethiopia.[22]

Immediately upon learning of these appeals, Hull went to see Roosevelt. For some time the Department of State had been considering a message to Italy. Action in the name of the president would naturally carry more weight and reinforce the moves of the department. Roosevelt suggested a personal communication from him to Mussolini. Alexander Kirk, the chargé in Rome, was directed to seek an immediate interview with the Duce. On Kirk's suggestion the message was not to be made public. In it, Roosevelt expressed his "earnest hope" that the Italian-Ethiopian dispute would be resolved peaceably. War, he said, "would be a world calamity the consequences of which would adversely affect the interests of all nations." [23] It was a bland message.

Mussolini did not receive the American chargé until almost noon on the 19th. By this time his rejection of the Paris proposal was a day and a half old. Any hope that the American démarche would influence the Paris conference was thus dead even before the démarche

---

[22] *U.S. Diplomatic Papers, 1935*, I, 732, 735–7.

[23] C. Hull, *Memoirs* (New York, 1948), I, 421–2; *U.S. Diplomatic Papers, 1935*, I, 739. For a conection between the Italian-Ethiopian conflict and American interests in the Far East, see H. Braddick, "A New Look at American Policy during the Italo-Ethiopian Crisis, 1935–36," *Journal of Modern History*, 24:64–73 (March 1962).

took place. It is doubtful whether the note from Washington would have affected the conclusions of Paris in any case. Mussolini told Kirk that Italy was determined to "pursue her course regardless of opposition." The consequences to any nation that might interfere in a matter of vital interest to Italy, Mussolini added, "might prove disastrous." "It was now too late to avoid an armed conflict": preparations for war were so far advanced that any withdrawal would be a devastating blow to Italy's prestige, and this Mussolini would not tolerate. Italy's aim was not the revenge of Aduwa: "That was forty years ago and the circumstances were such that Italy herself need not harbor a necessity for revenge." But the Ethiopians had developed from their triumph at Aduwa a bellicose spirit, which had created an intolerable situation for Italy as a neighboring country. "This situation could only be met by a display of force and could only be remedied by inflicting a defeat on the Abyssinians." After an initial Italian victory, Mussolini indicated, perhaps negotiations might be resumed. What Italy demanded, however, was "first and foremost the military occupation of the country." Until this was conceded by all parties concerned, Italy would accept no proposals for settlement. As for the future in Europe, Mussolini told Kirk:

> Italy had prepared an exhaustive statement of her case which would be laid before the League of Nations. When that was presented the League would have to choose between Italy and Abyssinia. If Abyssinia were ejected from the League Italy would proceed with her plans in Abyssinia which . . . could then be regarded as having the character of high police measures enforced by arms. Abyssinia would by a brief demonstration of force be convinced of the power of Italy, the impression of the victory of Adowa would be wiped out and the undertaking would develop into a colonial enterprise.[24]

If the nations of Europe regarded the undertaking only as a colonial action and allowed Italy to settle the matter without interference, "there need be no danger to world peace." Interference or opposition, on the other hand, could only give rise to increased determination on the part of Italy.

So ended America's mid-August attempt to influence Italy. Kirk found Mussolini "in excellent health and spirits," radiating "calmness and confidence." Save for fluttering the king, the American démarche accomplished nothing.

[24] *U.S. Diplomatic Papers, 1935,* I, 740–1.

It is impossible to determine whether Mussolini actually meant what he said concerning a willingness to negotiate a settlement after a limited military advance and an initial prestige victory. But it seems clear that any negotiable moderation of Italian demands could come only after the threat of sanctions by the leading powers of Europe. As long as Mussolini maintained his conditions of ultimate military control in Ethiopia, terms only scarcely less severe than the goals to be gained by conquest, Britain and France could agree only if they were prepared to ignore the League. Nor could anyone determine the extent of Ethiopian resistance, which might still require an Italian conquest. Further, an "initial victory," one might have predicted, would only whet the Fascists' ambitions and make them even less willing to negotiate — in the absence, again, of a firm British-French stand.

Mussolini no doubt was speaking his mind more accurately when he appealed to the nations of the League to treat the conflict not as a matter of principle or as a matter of international law governing nations of equal standing, but as a purely colonial enterprise, entirely extraneous to the needs of Europe and to Italy's European position.

On 31 August 1935 President Roosevelt signed into law the first neutrality act, which had been rushed through Congress during the month of August in an effort to provide the president with some controlling legislation during the congressional recess. The hope was to keep America from becoming involved in the Ethiopian war and in the more general war that might follow in Europe if League sanctions were imposed against Italy. Mindful of the early years of World War I and the recent conclusion of the Senate investigation into the munitions industry — that traffic in arms was a cause of war — the neutrality bill authorized the president to proclaim, "upon the outbreak or during the progress of war," the existence of such a war and to prohibit exports to or for any belligerent country of "arms, ammunition, or the implements of war." [25]

The administration had serious reservations about the wisdom of this bill, the most serious being that it hampered the executive branch

[25] U.S. Department of State, *Peace and War, United States Foreign Policy, 1931–1941* (Washington, 1943), 266–71, gives the text. R. Divine, *The Illusion of Neutrality* (Chicago, 1962), chap. 4, and Harris, *The United States and the Italo-Ethiopian Conflict*, 25–9, 53–5, give discussions of the bill.

in its handling of foreign policy.[26] Once war was recognized, it became mandatory for the president to apply the embargo at once to all belligerent countries — he could not apply it selectively. He was prevented from trying out the effectiveness of a warning to a potential aggressor that its victim might be helped with arms shipments once hostilities began. Once war was recognized, regardless of the rights or wrongs of the situation, regardless of which country was the aggressor and which the victim, regardless even of the fact that this inability to make a distinction between nations might run counter to American national interests, it was now required that all belligerents would equally and simultaneously be prohibited arms from America. Out of a desire to eliminate any show of support or disfavor and hence involvement, this piece of legislation could not help but be unfair in practice.

On the other hand, under the terms of the neutrality act the president still had considerable discretionary latitude. The president was authorized, not directed, to proclaim the state of war under which the embargo would become mandatory. When and why this action should be taken was left to him. He might, for example, hold off the declaration until provisions were sent to Ethiopia, providing public opinion at home allowed of such a delay. Then too the bill permitted the president to define "the arms, ammunition, or implements of war" prohibited by the act. There was no reason why raw materials — petroleum, metals, and the elements of munitions manufacture so essential to Italy's campaign — could not be included by deeming them implements of war.[27]

The provisions of the neutrality act of 1935 said nothing concerning American behavior toward the League of Nations in case of war. America's reaction to the application of sanctions against Italy was left largely up to the president. He had no power to take those actions against a war-making state required of League members by article 16 of the Covenant; he could not, for example, prohibit the import of Italian goods into the United States. He did, however, have the power to cooperate actively in the imposition of the following League sanctions: the withdrawal of diplomatic representatives from Italy,

---

[26] See Roosevelt's statements issued on the day he signed the law, *Peace and War*, 278, and Hull's comments, in *Memoirs*, I, 412-7.

[27] For a discussion of this point, see the excellent monograph by R. L. Buell, "American Neutrality and Collective Security," *Geneva Special Studies*, 6.6:18-19 (Geneva, 1935).

nonrecognition of any Italian conquest, acquiescence in a naval blockade of Italy, in the closing of the Suez Canal, and in similar economic and financial actions.[28]

What action the president would take, of course, depended on his own attitude toward the issues involved. There was never much hope that Roosevelt or Hull would take a bold initiative in using America's power and influence to cooperate with the League in its application of collective security. The spirit of isolationism and noninvolvement in the affairs of Europe was still too strong. On the other hand, Roosevelt had an opportunity to come to the aid of the organ of international justice created by his predecessor by using his option for free interpretation of the act; he could have broadened the definition of "implements of war" to include those articles that might also be part of the League's economic sanctions against aggressors. Roosevelt did not follow this course. Rather, in a series of statements culminating with a presidential proclamation on 26 September, the list of things to be embargoed was defined narrowly as arms, ammunition, and such tools of destruction as tanks, aircraft, and warships. All other products remained free for American trade and profit.

When the neutrality bill was passed, and then defined as applying only to arms, some thought that Italy would suffer more than Ethiopia would, for Italy had the "shipping and money" to import arms from America while Ethiopia did not.[29] This was a shortsighted analysis. By the end of August, Mussolini's army was incomparably better equipped than Haile Selassie's, and the Italian troops could march to victory without one additional rifle from America. Italy had its own production plants for the implements of war, and as long as petroleum, steel, foodstuffs, fibers, and other materials of great military significance flowed freely into Italy, the kingdom could easily equip its own troops. The arms embargo was only a nuisance for Italy; for Ethiopia it spelled disaster. With the purchase of arms from France, Britain, and most of Europe already prohibited, America was one of the few sources still open. Ethiopia did not need the raw and finished materials which fueled and supplied the Italian army. Without its own

[28] For a discussion of the powers of the president to influence the course of future events by agreeing to respect the imposition of League sanctions, see Buell, "American Neutrality," 12–16. For considerations within the State Department, see Harris, *The United States and the Italo-Ethiopian Crisis*, 54–5.

[29] Hull, *Memoirs*, I, 414. The counselor to the Italian embassy in Washington, Rossi Longhi, protested that it was directed against Italy. *U.S. Diplomatic Papers, 1935*, I, 789.

means of manufacturing arms, what Ethiopia needed above all was exactly what was forbidden it under the terms of the neutrality legislation.

When the act was being drawn up, little or no heed was paid to the consequences it might have abroad. For the Americans it was a temporary piece of legislation which, according to its terms, was to remain in effect only until the end of February 1936. In Europe, however, coming at this critical time, the act had an impact that ultimately encouraged the forces of disorder and made more difficult, if not impossible, the task of those who were working for peace.

At the end of August, in the aftermath of the abortive Paris talks, the members of the League knew that they would soon be faced with the reality of an Italian act of aggression. According to paragraph 1, article 16, once any member of the League resorted to war in disregard of the Covenant,

> it shall *ipso facto* be deemed to have committed an act of war against all other Members of the League, which hereby undertake immediately to subject it to the severance of all trade or financial relations, the prohibition of all intercourse between their nationals and the nationals of the covenant-breaking State, and the prevention of all financial, commercial, or personal intercourse between the nationals of the covenant-breaking State and the nationals of any other State, whether a Member of the League or not.

The idea behind economic sanctions, and a condition of its effectiveness, was that the nations of the League would unite against a transgressor. It was the crux of the system of collective maintenance of peace, and it seemed an efficient way of punishment without the carnage of war. Yet in 1935 one crucial factor was lacking: the League did not include one of the greatest trading nations in the world. The success of economic sanctions against Italy in large measure was reduced to the question: would the United States render the League's application of sanctions futile by supplying Italy's economic needs? If the United States would place a general embargo against Italy, then success seemed assured, and others would rally to the League. If the United States allowed its trade to continue, sanctions must fail. No one in Europe took seriously the obligation under article 16 to restrict the commerce of non-League nations. A blockade against the United States, in the face of America's insistence on its rights of trade, might even mean war. The possibility of a conflict with Italy was bad enough; the idea of provoking war with America was wholly untenable.

The American government had never stated its intended policy toward an Italian-Ethiopian war, for it had prepared no program of action.[30] So the countries of Europe looked with eager eyes to catch whatever clues were offered. The neutrality legislation, passed at the end of August, was treated as a portent of the future. It did not answer the question of what the United States would do if the nations of the League found themselves at war with Italy. But the new act left to the American president's discretion the extension of the arms embargo to other states if they became involved in the war. There was now the likelihood, therefore, that the democratic nations of Europe, acting under the League, might find themselves cut off from certain American markets. More important, the gradual clarification of the act made it appear that what was to be embargoed was only arms, narrowly defined. Those other crucial commodities needed by Italy were not mentioned. The neutrality legislation, then, was interpreted in Europe as meaning that the United States would not cooperate in a trade embargo against Italy. The whole plan of economic sanctions became hollow.

On the other hand, League members in Europe were still not without power in this matter, not without effective means to resist, punish, or prevent an act of aggression against Ethiopia. The overwhelming forces that the British and French could assemble in the Mediterranean, the resources that determined diplomacy could still elicit from the nations of the League, these would have been more than sufficient to deter Mussolini, protect Ethiopia, and save the League — had there been the will to make them succeed. But the will was weak, and as a result the failure of the United States to assent even halfheartedly to the scheme of collective security was used by the timid and unwilling nations as an excuse to evade their own obligations under the Covenant.

On 31 August, a few days before the meeting of the League council, the world was startled by the announcement from Addis Ababa that Haile Selassie had signed, on the day before, a petroleum concession

[30] For a good account of the Department of State and the Italian-Ethiopian conflict, see Feis, *Seen from E.A.*, 218–83.

that gave a seventy-five-year exclusive right of exploration and development in the eastern half of Ethiopia to an American firm. The man behind this totally unexpected event was a colorful British promoter, Francis W. Rickett, and it was widely thought that British capital was behind the venture.[31] World reaction to the Rickett concession was immediate and intense. Throughout Europe and America, especially in Italy and among the anglophobic French, the conclusion was instantly drawn that the British and American interest in keeping the Italians out of Ethiopia was simply because Britain and America wanted to keep Ethiopia for themselves. Far from being a disinterested party in the dispute, Britain was only using the League to cover its own greedy ambitions. Reports that a deal over Lake Tana was also being attempted by Rickett encouraged this accusation of British imperialism, and an exaggerated belief in Ethiopia's oil resources made the whole story plausible. Italian propaganda efforts pulled out all stops in an effort to destroy the image of Britain's principled behavior. Arguing that the British were responsible for the substance of the concession and that the Americans had merely supplied the form — criticism of America was deliberately subdued — the Italian press asserted that the true needs of the Italian people were being thwarted by Anglo-Saxon capitalists.[32] It was noted that the concession covered the area allotted Italy in the treaty of 1906. If the British government were behind this new agreement, it would be in violation of that treaty.

This incident caused an uproar in London, Washington, and Geneva. The British government at once issued a statement denying any knowledge of Rickett's transaction. They restated that Britain had "no Imperial economic interests in Abyssinia except Lake Tsana" and that even there they were postponing any agreement so as not to aggravate the present Italian-Ethiopian dispute. Going even further, on the 31st the British government announced that their minister in Ethiopia was instructed to advise the emperor not to consent to the concession. Representations were made by Barton to the emperor, and on 3 September Haile Selassie issued a communiqué stating that the

[31] Sir Percival Phillips' scoop for the London *Daily Telegraph* is printed in part in Salvemini, *Prelude*, 281. A clearer account of the terms of the concession are found in the report from the American chargé in Addis Ababa, *U. S. Diplomatic Papers, 1935*, I, 778, and in *The Times* (London), 2 September 1935.

[32] An interesting collection of Fascist newspaper comments on this matter, accusing Britain, is noted in Salvemini, *Prelude*, 283–5. For some French comments, see *The Times* (London), 2 September 1935.

British government had not been involved "directly or indirectly."[33]

The concession was in fact made to a strictly American concern, a subsidiary created for this very purpose by the Standard Vacuum Oil Company. The company had moved into Ethiopia in a private commercial venture, inspired by the enthusiasm of Rickett. Its proposition was accepted by the emperor for two reasons. First, and less important, Haile Selassie was in desperate need of money, and a large advance by the new concessionaire was the only new source of revenue he could hope for in his country's fearful hour.[34] It was feared by those abroad who sought to minimize the conflict that the advance would be used for the purchase of arms, but in fact only a small part of it was to go for this purpose.[35] The second advantage of the Rickett concession was that it involved American interests in Ethiopia. It was this political advantage that determined the emperor's thinking. Grasping at a straw is the prerogative of a drowning man, and the emperor, with few other devices at his command, held to the hope that the Italians might be restrained if extensive American interests existed in a territory they were preparing to invade.

But it was precisely this point that proved fatal to the scheme, for it was contrary to America's policy of avoiding any commitment which might involve the United States in war. The American government was not consulted on the Rickett concession, and it was now unwilling to extend its protection. Ethiopia was clearly a sinking ship. Its fields, no matter how profitable their subsoil might be, were marked for war in the near future, and the American government wanted no responsibilities that might embroil the United States in this distant land. Representatives of Standard Vacuum Oil, who had haplessly tried to deny their parenthood of the subsidiary that Rickett represented, now listened sheepishly as the Department of State officially advised them to cancel their contract at once. Emphasis was put on the great embarrassment the agreement caused to "governments who are making strenuous and sincere efforts for the preservation of the peace." Stress was laid on the importance of the League meeting about to start in Geneva and to the "painful handicap under which . . .

[33] *U.S. Diplomatic Papers, 1935*, I, 779; *The Times* (London), 2 September 1935; Toynbee, *Survey of International Affairs, 1935*, II, 178–9.
[34] Representatives of the Standard Vacuum Oil Company later denied that any advance payment or loan was to be made to the emperor, and that Ethiopian profits would have to wait for royalties from actual production. *The Times* (London), 4 September 1935. No money ever changed hands.
[35] Steer, *Caesar in Abyssinia*, 72.

the British were now placed in view of the suspicions and recrimina-
tions arising out of the oil transaction." [36] This official American
position was published on 3 September and sent to London, Paris,
and Rome. Hull's pressure had immediate effect. The American oil
company withdrew promptly from the concession, and Haile Selassie's
hope of a last-minute reprieve disappeared. Despite a few more efforts
by Rickett and by an American speculator named Leo Chertok to
find backing, official disapproval in Britain and America doomed any
further Ethiopian concession to representatives of those countries.

The emperor accepted this turn of events with good grace. There
is no substance to the charge that he acted improperly or in defiance
of his treaty obligations. Ethiopia was not a party to the 1906 agreement, and the emperor's lands were still his to do with them as he
pleased. Haile Selassie did express his deep regret to the American
chargé. America, he noted, was politically disinterested in Ethiopia
and at the same time possessed of the technical skill and experience
that could assist in the economic development of Ethiopia. He had
extended the oil concession, the emperor said, as proof of his friendly
feelings and as a gesture of his appreciation for America's sympathetic
interest in his country. All of this was no doubt true, but the desire
of the American government, in common with the governments of
Britain and France, was not primarily to protect or improve the state
of Ethiopia, but rather to dampen the Italian-Ethiopian conflict without becoming involved. They sought to work not for the strengthening of Ethiopia's powers of resistance but rather for the moderation
of Italy's ambition. On 5 September Secretary of State Hull ordered
the American chargé in Addis Ababa to modify his message to the
emperor: the phrase that the United States still wanted to be "helpful
to Ethiopia" was to be changed to "helpful to the cause of peace." [37]

At the meeting of the League council on 3 August, Italy had agreed
to reactivate the deadlocked commission of arbitration with the appointment of a fifth member. This was a shrewd diplomatic move,
as we know. The Italians never conceded that the settlement of responsibility for the Walwal incident would in any way affect their plans
for the full-scale invasion of Ethiopia, but their willingness to go on

[36] U.S. Diplomatic Papers, 1935, I, 781–2; Hull, Memoirs, I, 423–4.
[37] U.S. Diplomatic Papers, 1935, I, 783–4.

talking before the commission created an illusion of progress toward a peaceful settlement. Accepting this illusion partly as a means to gain time for the direct negotiations with Italy by Britain and France, partly to postpone confronting the deeper issues now in play, the other nations at Geneva had credited Italy with a major concession and agreed to delay full consideration of the dispute by the council for yet another month. Italy scored a major triumph at almost no cost to itself, and the entire month of August was freed from League complications. But this was outweighed by a greater procedural victory. The terms of the first resolution of 3 August met Italy's demand for the limitation of the commission's sphere of competence, and the commission was instructed formally by the council not to examine the question of frontiers and ownership. It was to investigate only the *de facto* immediate circumstances of the squabble. The commission, idle since the impasse of 9 July, was to meet again, now with a strictly limited scope and with a new, and determining, member.

Immediately following the League council meeting, the Ethiopian-appointed members tried to secure a sitting of the commission in Geneva. The Italian members refused, and it was eventually decided to reconvene in Paris on 19 August, following the tripartite talks, which, as we have seen, ended in failure on 18 August. On the 20th, La Pradelle, Potter, Aldrovandi, and Montagna met once again. They extended an invitation to Nicolas Politis, Greek minister to Paris, to become the fifth member of the commission, and he accepted on the following day.

The recruitment of Politis occasioned some surprise, although it was already known in official circles that he was the commission's choice and that he was prepared to accept the post. What was surprising was that the Italian government should consent to his nomination. Politis was in excellent standing in Addis Ababa. Indeed, the Ethiopians had named him as their appointee to the original commission, only to find that the Greek government would not allow him to accept because of direct pressure from Rome.[38] Politis was a renowned jurist, and an old associate of La Pradelle's. But if these facts gave the Italians cause for doubt, other reasons led them to believe that the nomination of Politis might gain them important advantages. One was suggested by the Italian minister in Bucharest, Ugo Sola, when Politis' name was being considered. In March 1933, Sola said,

---

[38] *U.S. Diplomatic Papers, 1935*, I, 624; Berio, "L' 'Affare' etiopico," 193–4.

Politis had defined a situation of aggression in which the victim of this aggression had the right to respond with war, without being considered an aggressor itself. Many nations had subscribed to this condition at a conference in London in July 1933. There seemed a close parallel between the example given by Politis in this report of two years before and the Italian interpretation of the Walwal incident. If the present arbitral commission found Ethiopia guilty without extenuation in the Walwal incident, application of Politis' example might give Italy a formidable tool to support future diplomatic action. If all worked out as Sola thought, Italy could claim that its invasion was justified because of Ethiopian aggression, either at Walwal or at some spot where another incident could be contrived. If Politis, the source of this particular position, were a decisive member of the commission which found Ethiopia guilty, the felicity of the arrangement would be particularly complete.[39]

The question was whether or not Politis would be favorable to Italy. There could be no certainty about what the commission's verdict would be, but if the fifth arbitrator had to be accepted by both sides, Politis seemed to the Italians as good a bet as anyone else. Politis was Laval's nominee, and the French foreign minister had persistently urged the Italian government to accept the moderate Politis as the fifth arbitrator for its own good. Politis realized how close war was and wanted to do nothing to precipitate it. He, like Laval, realized that the Walwal problem was secondary to the main issue, and Politis was, Laval argued, prepared to use his influence as a mediator to find a solution acceptable to all parties. What was being considered was a mandate for Italy over Ethiopia, analogous to that held by France over Syria. The good offices of Politis might make such an arrangement acceptable both in Addis Ababa and in London, if the British were assured of protection for the sources of the Nile and for the general principles of the League. As for the decision to be reached by the arbitration commission, Politis seemed ready, according to his own and Laval's witness, to give the judgment to Italy, so long as Ethiopia was spared undue humiliation, for that could only make the emperor less able and less willing to concede anything to Italy.[40]

Persuaded of the benefits, the Italian government approved Politis' appointment. The Italian foreign office took care to impress upon

[39] Guariglia, *Ricordi*, 250–2.
[40] Guariglia, *Ricordi*, 252–4.

Politis the significance of his coming decision. The arbitral verdict, Pignatti and Aloisi told him, would be the specific determining factor in future Italian-Ethiopian relations. The verdict must be decisively in Italy's favor, for an ambiguous judgment would only encourage Ethiopia to further resistance and hence hasten the coming of war. These warnings seemed to fall on receptive ears. At any rate Politis told Aloisi on 16 August that he would not pronounce a judgment unfavorable to Italy.[41]

Politis was formally named the fifth arbitrator on 20 August, on the basis of an unusual distinction: he was "designated," not "appointed." The four-man commission, it was decided, would continue to meet as before, to hear arguments and testimony. The newly designated member would stand by; although he would not take part in the proceedings, he would have an opportunity to familiarize himself with the materials of the case. Then, when the need arose, when another deadlock came about, the fifth arbitrator would be "appointed" without further delay to associate himself formally and fully with the commission.[42]

In Paris on 20 August the commission, without Politis, resumed its work at the point where it had been interrupted a month and a half before. Jèze presented the Ethiopian case that the Italians had occupied Walwal illegally and that their uncompromising and aggressive attitude had led to the incident.[43] There followed a request from the Italian advocate that the commission hear from a series of Italian witnesses on the events in the Ogaden. The witnesses included former Governor Rava and Major Roberto Cimmaruta, the Italian commander at Walwal on that distant December day. Jèze protested that further representations were unnecessary, that the Italian witnesses, as officials of the state, were unreliable, and above all that any further delay would reduce the time needed for the fifth arbitrator's evaluation[44] Silvio Lessona, the representative of the Italian government, insisted that witnesses were essential to Italy's case. The members of the commission agreed, and on 23 August they left Paris for Bern

---

[41] Aloisi, *Journal*, 296.

[42] La Pradelle, *Le Conflit italo-éthiopien*, 546–7; Potter, *Wal Wal Arbitration*, 17.

[43] La Pradelle, *Le Conflit italo-éthiopien*, 446–73; Potter, *Wal Wal Arbitration*, 70–85.

[44] The League council resolution of 3 August had fixed a time limit for the commission's deliberations, determining that they must be completed by the evening of 3 September. See comments on this by Politis, Jèze, and Lessona in Potter, *Wal Wal Arbitration*, 149–50.

where the Italian witnesses were to be heard and examined (Ethiopia presented no witnesses). Oral testimony was taken on the 23rd, 24th, and 25th, and the two government agents submitted their final conclusions.[45] The formal presentation of cases ended on the 25th.

On the 25th the commission returned to Paris to begin deliberations on a verdict. On the 28th it became evident that a majority opinion could not be reached. So Politis sat in for the first time as a member of the commission in a meeting on the 29th. The five arbitrators then retired to meet *in camera* for several days. Draft proposals were considered, and a final compromise text was finally accepted, the work of Politis.[46] On 3 September the commission rendered its unanimous decision.

The scope of the verdict was strictly limited. It did not judge the question of sovereignty, physical or legal possession, frontiers, ownership in any form, or any matter on which there was a serious difference of opinion. The verdict was limited to a description of the *de facto* circumstances of the Walwal incident, and it assigned no responsibility to either party for the events of 5 and 6 December 1934. The incident, the commission members were "inclined to think," was "due to an unfortunate chain of circumstances; the first shot might have been accidental, [as were] numerous and frequent shots that preceded it." Since there was no guilty party, there was no mention of an arbitral award, reparations, or apologies. With regard to the various incidents that took place between 6 December 1934 and 25 May 1935, the commission concluded that those immediately following Walwal "were of an accidental character, while the others were for the most part not serious and of very ordinary occurrence in the region in which they took place." Thus, the verdict continued, "no international responsibility need be involved." [47] The decision was handed to the agents of the Italian and Ethiopian governments, transmitted by them to the secretary-general and then to the League, and the case of the Walwal incident was formally closed on 3 September, one day before the convening of the council.

The unanimous verdict of the commission was made possible only

[45] La Pradelle, *Le Conflit italo-éthiopien*, 473–546; Potter, *Wal Wal Arbitration*, 93–149.

[46] *U.S. Diplomatic Papers, 1935*, I, 642; La Pradelle, *Le Conflit italo-éthiopien*, 546–9; Potter, *Wal Wal Arbitration*, 18–9, 149–69.

[47] La Pradelle, *Le Conflit italo-éthiopien*, 599–607; Potter, *Wal Wal Arbitration*, 175–82.

by concentrating on the trivial matter of incidental responsibility and evading the controversial questions of sovereignty and trespass.[48] The effort of the commission was to avoid the issue of blame and was aimed at conciliation rather than arbitration. But at this late stage, when the Walwal affair had already faded into almost total insignificance, the commission's feeble compromise was of no value whatsoever in alleviating the present threat of war. Conciliation had never been a realistic possibility, and the day was past when the commission could serve a useful purpose by affording time for the independent exploration of a negotiated settlement.

For Ethiopia the commission's verdict was a minor victory. If Italy could not be branded an aggressor under the commission's limited *compromis*, at least the Italian charges were judged as unproved. Ethiopia, wrongly cast in the role of the defendant, was found not guilty.

For Italy the commission's decision was a great disappointment. All the hopes riding with Politis were dashed. "Politis has betrayed us," wrote Aloisi.[49] Italy was whitewashed, but the verdict was confined and equivocal. Italy could not base later diplomatic activity, or excuse its intended aggression, on the Walwal incident. Concern with Walwal ended abruptly, and the world's attention now turned to the meeting of the League council about to open.

[48] There was no doubt in the minds of Potter and La Pradelle that Ethiopia held legal sovereignty over Walwal, regardless of Italy's *de facto* occupation of the wells, and hence that under any fuller judgment Italy would have been considered the trespasser. La Pradelle, *Le Conflit italo-éthiopien*, 550–60; Potter, *Wal Wal Arbitration*, 29–33.

[49] Aloisi, *Journal*, 299.

Chapter 12

September: Positions before the League

The council session set for 4 September put an end to the nine-month-long attempt to seek a solution outside the League. At long last the evasions and delays practiced by Italy were ended, for the terms of the Covenant were now to be applied. For the first time, the council was formally bound to take up the dispute, in all its aspects. The coming session was "universally regarded as the most critical in the history of the League." [1] The League as an organization had little power to prevent a war from breaking out, but it did have effective means to punish Italy once a violation of the Covenant had occurred. The council was meeting on the eve of what everyone realized would be the *casus foederis* for punitive action by the League. If the League stood up successfully in the face of this challenge, there would be hope for its system of collective security. If it failed, the League would be dead as a politically significant institution. Of all the League's members only Britain had the power and authority to stop Mussolini decisively, to impose the sanctions demanded by the Covenant. Each nation looked to London for its cue; the policy of Britain would determine the outcome of the affair, for as Britain went so went the League.

Britain's preparation for the September council meeting began immediately following the mid-August collapse of the tripartite Paris talks. The government now had to decide whether and to what extent it would honor its obligation to the Covenant. On 22 August the Cabinet met to consider this specific problem. The session was dramatic, but the results were equivocal. Far from taking a clear stand, the British government decided to act only if, and only after, all the other nations in the League had prepared themselves to act. By in-

[1] *The Times* (London), 4 September 1935.

terpreting the Covenant in light of the notion of collective obligation, the British government sought to avoid responsibility. Further, the government determined not to move except in step with France. This meant inaction, for the French would act only with the assurance of further support from Britain. The Cabinet's policies, therefore, were in themselves enough to defeat the League. The infirmity of Britain's purpose is illustrated in the instructions given the British delegation leaving for Geneva: "to avoid trying to force nations to go further than they wished, and to be on our guard lest others might not in practice fulfill their commitments." [2] Evidence soon at hand exposed the fallacy in ascribing to other governments the same timidity and indecisiveness that motivated the British. Within a week, categorical statements of support for the League came from the foreign ministers of Norway, Sweden, Denmark, and Finland, meeting in Oslo, and from the permanent council of the states of the Little Entente, meeting in Bled.[3] These countries, and Spain, brought their declarations of loyalty to the specific attention of the British Foreign Office. They all looked to Britain to save the League. They were willing to stand against Italian aggression if Britain would but lead.

It was true that these states were weak and that the burden of any punitive action would fall mainly upon Great Britain. The fact that Britain's political and military pre-eminence would cause it to bear the burden revealed the emptiness of the government's argument that Britain would act only as an equal in a prearranged collective enterprise. It was obvious that the support of the smaller nations of the League would be of little or no practical effect in the imposition of sanctions. If Britain chose to act against Italy, the practical result of the demands made upon Britain would be the same whether Britain acted alone, as a leader of the League and champion of collective security, or only as a follower in the train of fifty other nations. In any case, if Britain acted it would have to carry the major load of resistance. The question the British government had to answer was whether it would act at all.

Yet the government still did not have a policy for the future. It seems fitting that beginning on 23 August, the day after the Cabinet meeting, daily prayers were started in Westminster Abbey to ask divine guidance

[2] Avon, *Facing the Dictators*, 255.
[3] *The Times* (London), 30 and 31 August 1935; S. Jones, *The Scandinavian States and the League of Nations* (Princeton, 1939), 259–60; F. Vondracek, *The Foreign Policy of Czechoslovakia, 1918–1935* (New York, 1937), 422.

for the country's statesmen.[4] Despite the need for decision, the British government could not choose between the contradictory alternatives. On the one hand, its members did not want to become involved, hoping to avoid the risk of a war with Italy. On the other hand, it would be hard, and perhaps unwise, to desert the League, to back down on the politically important pledges of support for the Covenant. As war grew nearer, there was increasing reason to believe that the British public was expecting and would support strong measures against Italy. On 5 September the Trades Union Congress carried by 2,962,000 votes to 177,000 a resolution calling for the use of "all the necessary measures provided by the Covenant to resist Italy's unjust and rapacious attack." This resolution was submitted to the Labour Party conference on 3 October and carried by another overwhelming majority, 2,168,000 to 102,000.[5]

The government of France, in the last week of August, was similarly undecided. The French could not resolve the bitter and perplexing dilemma of the contradiction between their traditional support of the League and their recently acquired defensive need of Italy. Through no desire of their own, these two facets of their foreign policy — once, it seemed, so complementary — now had developed into incompatible alternatives.[6] For the present the government sought to stay in the middle, to save what it could from the two extremes, and to moderate the attacks on both.

On 18 August, Laval outlined the French dilemma to Eden. France, Laval said, had made a treaty with Italy, the collapse of which would leave France without an effective ally in Europe. The assurance of support that Aloisi had brought from Mussolini only increased France's reluctance to antagonize Italy, for the import of this message was that the Duce was willing to keep his troops on the Brenner and protect France's flank. One fact and one alone could outweigh the military advantage of the Italian connection, and that was an ironclad assurance from Britain of support for France in Europe in case of a German attack. A British guarantee was the *sine qua non* for France's cooperation in resisting Italy through the League. In the absence of this, and

---

[4] *The Times* (London), 23 August 1935.
[5] Toynbee, *Survey of International Affairs, 1935*, II, 61, 63.
[6] Frenchmen tended to blame the British for having pulled France into this agonizing predicament, and they were suspicious of Britain's motives. See, e.g., Toynbee, *Survey of International Affairs, 1935*, II, 70–9; Flandin, *Politique française*, 179–82; Vaucher and Siriex, *L'Opinion britannique*, 91–4.

in light of Britain's traditional reluctance to state its policies in advance, Laval could not be certain of British support on the continent,
despite the Locarno Treaty. Laval implored Eden to make France's
position known in London. As for France's course at the coming
session of the council, Laval said he did not intend to turn his back
on the League. But beyond "some form of condemnation of Italy's
act," Laval was not yet prepared to forecast France's actions. For the
moment, he added, France would maintain its embargo on arms to
Italy and Ethiopia.[7]

The French viewed favorably the moderate statements issuing from
the meeting of the British Cabinet on 22 August and approved the
cabinet's decision to maintain the arms embargo as evidence that the
British government did not want, at least for the moment, to exasperate
Italy.[8] On the other hand, there was no hint of what Britain would do
next.

On 28 August Laval held a meeting of the French Council of Ministers to discuss the French position for the coming meeting of the
League.[9] The specific question was what France should do if sanctions
were proposed against Italy. Laval himself feared that sanctions meant
war. If sanctions were imposed with Britain in the lead, Italy would
retaliate with force, and Britain, he said, had no real power. The role of
France must be to moderate any British action which might force a
rupture with Italy. Laval solicitated opinions from his ministers.
Edouard Herriot, leader of Radical Party, was categorical. Even at
the risk of a break with Italy, France, in its own best interests, must
never separate itself either from the League or from Britain. As for
sanctions, there were sanctions of various kinds: it was necessary to
find those which would not result in the outbreak of a European war.[10]
Jean Fabry, minister of war, presented an opposing argument based on
his estimate of the needs of French security. Sanctions, Fabry said,
would mean the end of the Italian alliance, and this in turn would
cause the gravest strategic problems for France. It would force a

---

[7] Avon, *Facing the Dictators*, 251–2.

[8] *The Times* (London), 24 August 1935.

[9] Reports of this meeting are found in Herriot, *Jadis*, II, 574–5, and Fabry, *De la
Place de la Concorde*, 69–70.

[10] Laval could not afford to ignore Herriot's opinion, for the Radical Party was
the largest single party in the assembly (and the oldest in the nation), and it was
on Radical support that Laval's coalition government rested. While the Radicals
and the Radical Socialists were loyal to Laval and favored his domestic reforms,
their support depended on his conduct of foreign affairs.

complete reformulation of the military plans for the defense of the country. "We would lose," Fabry feared, "the liberty of the free employment of the army of the Alps, the assured tranquility in the Mediterranean, the free disposition of the army of Africa." France would be weakened "perhaps decisively," and put at a serious disadvantage should hostilities break out in Europe. Lacking a firm commitment to the continent, the British would hesitate to send their troops across the channel, and France would be left to face its risks alone. For these reasons, Fabry argued, sanctions must be avoided. This opinion was shared by the other ministers of national defense, François Piétri of the French navy, General Denain for the air force, and Gamelin, commander in chief of the French armies.[11] Laval closed the meeting saying he would never vote for sanctions. However, he would take Herriot with him to Geneva, and Herriot was given permission to speak at the Assembly meeting according to his own dictates.[12] Laval, who as both foreign minister and prime minister was in complete control of the formulation of French foreign policy, had decided not to set a plan for the meeting of the League. A great deal would depend on what the British resolved to do. Meanwhile Laval made an effort to impress again upon Mussolini the serious consequences of Italy's course. On 30 August he telegraphed the Duce to repeat his warning of 19 July and to inform Mussolini that, despite his friendship, France could not desert the League. Laval's appeals and cautions at the end of August accomplished nothing, however, for the Italian government would not respond to last-minute pleas.[13]

On 2 September Eden stopped in Paris en route to Geneva. He talked with Laval for an hour. In view of the fact that Britain and France were each preparing to base their future actions to a large extent on the policies of the other, it might have been expected that now, at last, the two would take this opportunity to coordinate ends and means. On the contrary, the British, in their slipshod fashion, made no real attempt to find out what the French were planning to do. And, the Cabinet having made no positive plans at its meeting on 22 August, Eden could not inform the French of Britain's own course. Far from being sent to coordinate policies, Eden arrived in Paris on the 2nd "with no in-

[11] Fabry, De la Place de la Concorde, 71.
[12] Herriot, Jadis, II, 574.
[13] Journal officiel, débats parlementaires, Chambre des Députés, 29 December 1935, 2865; Villari, Storia diplomatica, 185-7.

structions"; the British government "had simply come to no conclusion on the next move." [14]

The French could no longer afford to put up with such indetermination, although they themselves had gone for months without developing a "full understanding of a precise nature with the country that must be the basis of [France's] alliances." [15] At the beginning of September, therefore, Laval decided to clarify matters.[16] His problem was to discover whether, if France supported the League against Italy, France could then count on Britain to give an amount of defensive security equal to that lost. On 2 September Laval inquired informally if Eden could "give him the assurance that Britain would be as firm in upholding the Covenant, to the extent of sanctions in Europe in the future, as she appeared to be today in Abyssinia. [Laval] made is clear that he was referring to a comparable example of deliberate military aggression and a violation of the Covenant, and not merely a repudiation of treaties." [17] This was an important, and valid, question. In terms of their own national security, or the security of, say, eastern Europe, the French had a good case for making their action in the present conflict dependent on such a British guarantee. All Laval asked was that Britain apply the same standard to Europe, to France, as its statesmen appeared ready to apply to Ethiopia. The British, if their current pro-League enthusiasm were not just a politically inspired equivocation, should have been able to respond strongly in the affirmative, for Britain's long-range interests would be far more seriously affected by German aggression in Europe than by an Italian colonial excursion in remote Ethiopia. It is of the highest significance for an interpretation of British policy that Eden, on 2 September, found it "impossible" to promise unconditional support of the Covenant in the future, regardless of the outcome of the present dispute. He gave instead a vague and inconclusive reply to Laval, stating that Britain's obligations to support the Covenant would be increased if it were enforced now, and decreased if the Covenant were violated with impunity. This feeble response gave the French no reason to believe that resistance to Italy, as Eden urged, would result in any net gain for

---

[14] A. Johnson, *Anthony Eden* (New York, 1939), 271.
[15] This was Gamelin's definition of the "great error" of French policy in the Italian-Ethiopian conflict. Gamelin, *Servir*, II, 173.
[16] "Until then Laval had tacked," wrote Flandin. *Politique française*, 182.
[17] Avon, *Facing the Dictators*, 257–8.

France.[18] By the time the council of the League met on 4 September, therefore, no progress had been made in jointly contriving or co-ordinating British and French policies to deal with the menace of the Italian-Ethiopian conflict, and both Britain and France were still in the dark as to the other's intentions. On 10 September, having decided to clear up this alarming confusion in order to achieve some perspective for his own position, Laval formally asked the British Foreign Office: To what degree would France be guaranteed by Britain of an immediate and effective application of all the sanctions listed in article 16 of the Covenant if an aggression occurred in Europe? [19]

The eighty-eighth session of the League council convened on 4 September in Geneva. According to the resolution of 3 August, the purpose of this meeting was to undertake a general examination of all aspects of Italian-Ethiopian relations.

Mussolini permitted the Italian delegation to attend, although he was indifferent to the action of the League and believed that Italy had nothing to gain from further diplomacy at Geneva. War was only four weeks off, and unless Britain and France suddenly decided either to oppose fully or to appease fully, the Duce intended to go ahead with his invasion as planned.

Despite Mussolini, the professional diplomats at the Palazzo Chigi had great expectations for the meeting of the council. Since June, following a suggestion from Avenol, which Laval endorsed and Eden found interesting, the Italian foreign ministry had been preparing a memorandum to submit at the session. This project was the independent work of the Ethiopian department of the foreign office, whose diplomats had very little contact with Mussolini. Raffaele Guariglia, head of the Ethiopian department, did not have a single audience with the Duce during the entire Ethiopian conflict, and Mussolini rarely bothered to inform Guariglia's department of the diplomatic and military planning being carried on under his direction in the Palazzo Venezia.[20] Mussolini used the foreign ministry not to initiate or approve foreign policy, but only to provide the means to expedite the policy decisions he alone made. Now, with the preparation of the

[18] For a fatuous interpretation by Eden of the French position, see *U.S. Diplomatic Papers, 1935*, I, 640–1
[19] Flandin, *Politique française*, 182; Herriot, *Jadis*, II, 577–8.
[20] Guariglia, *Ricordi*, 214, 260–1.

memorandum for the League, the professional diplomats saw their chance to take a lead in the dispute. Lacking any special instructions from Mussolini, in the absence indeed of any particular interest on the part of the Duce, the authors of the memorandum hoped to have it used at Geneva as the instrument for bringing about a new turn in Italy's foreign relations.

The purpose of the memorandum was to furnish the basis for the Italian position that Ethiopia's "continual aggression" against its neighbors, its treaty violations, its barbaric customs, and its despotic, ineffective government made Ethiopia unfit to be a member of the League. If such a denunciation could be sustained, the Italians hoped that Ethiopia would be isolated within the League, perhaps even expelled, that the popular sympathy Ethiopia was receiving throughout the world would disappear, and that official opposition, based on the notion of the equality of nations, would be undermined by a demonstration of the illegitimacy of Ethiopia's claim to nationhood. If Ethiopia were put beyond the pale of international law, Italy's forthcoming invasion might come to be regarded less as a colonial conquest, less as unwarranted aggression, and more as a necessary civilizing mission undertaken in the interest of law, order, and humanity against a savage and dangerous troublemaker. Italy might then be allowed to complete its conquest without international opposition.[21]

The Italian memorandum was presented to the Council on 4 September. It was a voluminous printed work, with hundreds of supporting documents and a number of photographs depicting barbarities calculated to end any image of Ethiopia as a land of noble savages, of free and simple people.[22] The Italian arguments began with the contention that "despite her membership in the League of Nations, which requires the scrupulous observance of existing treaties and of the principles of international law, Ethiopia has systematically violated the treaties she has signed and has shown that she does not possess that degree of international organization which is indispensable to a member of the community of civilized nations." Ethiopia had blocked all Italian efforts to "develop and promote trade between the two countries," under the

---

[21] Guariglia, *Ricordi*, 241–3, 249, 258.

[22] For the interesting idea that in the malaise of the great depression, "with millions of white men uncertain as to the benefits of civilization," there was a heightened sympathy for Ethiopia, viewed as free, uncomplicated, and primitive, and an increased anger that Italy should try to impose "the machine age" on such a life, see *Time*, 6 January 1936, 13.

treaty of 1928, and prevented the Italians from cooperating in the administration or technical development of the country. The memorandum said that Ethiopia also failed to provide the proper administration of justice for foreigners, such administration being "a sure indication of the degree of civilization and progress achieved by a people." The second cluster of Italian charges involved the contention that Ethiopia had willfully threatened the security of Italy's colonies, and that the country's anti-Italian sentiments had led to a long series of affronts to Italian diplomats and injustices to Italian subjects. Contributing to this was the "chronic state of internal disorder in Ethiopia, and . . . the inability of that country to progress." The memorandum then argued that Italy, "who stands in most urgent and recognized need of colonial expansion, is also the Power which is suffering the greatest damage through the present situation in Ethiopia."

Third, the memorandum contended, Ethiopia was not a unified and organized state. The Semitic minority, led by Menelik, had taken to imperialism and brutally conquered adjacent lands to carve out the boundaries of modern Ethiopia. In the process, whole regions were depopulated by the highland imperialists. The survivors, of a different race, religion, and language from the Amharic minority, were held as repressed and enslaved subjects.

> It is surely in the interests of civilization that the Harrari, Galla, Somali, Sidama, and other peoples which have for centuries formed separate national entities, should be removed from Abyssinian oppression. To effect an immediate settlement of this grave problem is, indeed, to act in conformity with the spirit of the Covenant, which requires that colonization should be carried out only by advanced States which are in a position to ensure the development and welfare of the native peoples.

The memorandum continued that the central government, despite its harsh colonialism, was still incapable of creating that degree of civil organization that a modern nation-state must have. If the country could not be ruled successfully and properly because of the inability of its leaders, how, the Italians asked, could it be expected to fulfill its international responsibilities? For example, "Ethiopia has not fulfilled any of her obligations under article 23 of the Covenant," which obliged all members to endeavor to improve the conditions of life of the peoples under their control. Another example of Ethiopian backwardness and irresponsibility concerned the matter of slavery. Ethiopia was admitted to the League in 1923 only after it had promised to end the practice of slavery and slave trading within the empire. These promises were not kept. It followed then, Italy contended, that Ethiopia had failed to carry out the very conditions under which it had been accepted as a member of the League. Moreover, Ethiopia had systematically broken the agreements that governed the importation of arms into the empire.

Under the Covenant, the memorandum concluded, there was "a system of obligations and rights which are interdependent." To violate one's obligations was to forfeit one's rights.

> Ethiopia has shown that she does not possess the qualifications necessary to enable her to obtain, through participation in the League, the impulse required to raise herself by voluntary efforts to the level of the other civilized nations.
>
> By her conduct, Ethiopia has openly placed herself outside the Covenant of the League and has rendered herself unworthy of the trust placed in her when she was admitted to membership.

Italy, "rising to defend" the threats to "her security, her rights, and her dignity," was, far from violating the Covenant, rising also to defend "the prestige and good name of the League of Nations." [23]

There was a small flurry at the League. "No one could read or hear unmoved the long catalogue of slavery, cruelty, and injustice. Ethiopia had come to the Council as an accuser; she suddenly found herself unexpectedly in the dock, and her delegates were unable to produce a prompt reply to so many different charges." [24] Jèze, surprised and unprepared for this "violent indictment," put forward on the 4th Ethiopia's claim that the charges were groundless. Tecle Hawariate attacked the memorandum in the assembly on the 11th. The Ethiopian government did not present an official rebuttal until the 14th, when it submitted "preliminary observations" that contradicted some of the Italian facts but dwelt mainly on the "tendentious character of the accusation." [25]

Naturally the memorandum never mentioned Italy's persistent efforts

[23] The Italian memorandum is printed in League, *Official Journal, 1935,* 1355–1584.

[24] Walters, *History of the League,* II, 644.

[25] League, *Official Journal, 1935,* 1137, 1595–1601. See also the comments of Marcel Griaule, forwarded to the secretary-general by Tecle Hawariate on 14 September, in which Griaule tried to add some perspective by relating the Italian accusations to the history and social traditions of Ethiopia. *Ibid.,* 1587–95.

to undermine the emperor's authority and to cause civil discontent within the empire. As a one-sided attack, it gave a distorted picture of Ethiopia and dwelt on the shortcomings of Ethiopian society particularly repugnant to European eyes. But as a diplomatic device the Italian memorandum was a failure. It failed not because it contained errors of fact, for much of what Italy asserted was recognized as true, but because the facts it presented did not justify the conclusions drawn from them. The main argument for intervention in Ethiopia's internal affairs was to end the threat that Ethiopia's deliberate policy of "continual aggression" posed to Italy's colonial security. This argument, by itself, might have had some effect in furthering British or French appeasement of Italy, although any invasion based on it would still be a violation of the Covenant. But Guariglia and his coworkers, hoping to influence the opinion of the entire world against Ethiopia, added to the argument of security the contention that certain conditions within the Ethiopian state themselves warranted unilateral interference by Italy. To join these arguments was a mistake in logic and in political propaganda. It might be true that Ethiopia was a socially backward state, but to argue that Italy was justified in conquering the country to impose a more advanced civilization was to go against the popular view of international morality and the current standards of international law. To suggest that Italy's invasion would be in the best interests of the League was not only effrontery — it was ridiculous.

No fact or argument presented in the memorandum gave Italy the slightest moral or legal right to act unilaterally against Ethiopia. Nothing allowed Italy the freedom to cross Ethiopia's border without breaking the Covenant. All Italy's arguments for independent armed action could be better interpreted as arguments for collective peaceable action. If Italy was the victim of continual aggression, there were established means within the League for the settlement of the problem without resort to war. Yet for almost a year Italy had worked to prevent the League from formally and fully considering the Italian-Ethiopian conflict. Italy's first complaint against Ethiopia was not presented to the League until 4 September, and this latter-day championship of the Covenant was patently false. If Ethiopia deserved to be expelled from the League and stripped of a member's rights and privileges, the procedures of expulsion were laid down in the Covenant. If Italy wanted further civilization to come to Ethiopia, the proper method of helping a country toward internal reform was to cooperate with it, not to threaten it with national extinction.[26]

Italy's position in the memorandum and in Aloisi's presentation speech to the council on the 4th was clearly only a rationalization of its preparations for aggression. But only two voices were raised at the council table in opposition. On the 5th, Jèze spoke for Ethiopia. A "war of extermination" was about to begin, he said, with pardonable exaggeration. He denounced the memorandum as an example of "puerile tactics to attempt to discredit one whom it is intended to despoil or destroy."[27] In this moment of extreme peril, of mortal danger to Ethiopia, Jèze again placed Ethiopia's cause with the League.

> The League is the conscience of mankind. Ethiopia makes a supreme appeal to that conscience. She asks you to say that a Member of the League, menaced in her integrity, her independence, her existence, in defiance of the Covenant and of the most solemn treaties, will not be left without support. Do not refuse to Ethiopia, because she is weak while her aggressor is powerful, the effective aid promised her by the Covenant. Do not let it be written in the annals of history that, as a result of intimidation, or by connivance or selfish indifference, the nations abandoned a small people the very existence of which is menaced. Ethiopia refuses to believe that she must count only on the strength of her despair to defend her territory and her life.

Jèze appealed for the invocation of and action under articles 10 and 15 of the Covenant. He asked the council to appoint a committee of its members to find "effective proposals for preventing war." He affirmed Ethiopia's willingness to follow any advice given by the appropriate organs of the League for the reform of the country.[28] Ethiopia could do no more short of surrender. Aloisi, the Italian delegate, left the council table in the middle of Jèze's speech.

The only other voice raised in protest against Italy's position was that of Maxim Litvinov, delegate from the USSR. The Soviet Union

[26] Walter, *History of the League*, II, 644–5. The Italian memorandum was later roundly castigated by the report of the council's Committee of Thirteen, submitted on 5 October 1935. League, *Official Journal, 1935*, 1618–9.

[27] Jèze's strong words inspired the French to suggest he be removed from the Ethiopian delegation; the emperor and his advisers rejected the suggestion. Virgin, *Abyssinia*, 163–4.

[28] League, *Official Journal, 1935*, 1140–1; Virgin, *Abyssinia*, 162–3, notes Jèze's instructions.

had been admitted to the League only recently, and Litvinov looked to the system of collective security as Russia's best defense against a rearmed Germany. But an anti-German Italy was a necessary element in such a system, and the Soviet Union saw no purpose in antagonizing Italy. The USSR had no direct interest in African affairs, and, although the Soviet government could not depart too far from its role as the principal opponent of imperialism, it maintained a certain circumspection in denouncing European colonialist countries. On 14 September the Soviet Union issued a decree prohibiting the export of obvious war materials to Italy, though it allowed Italy to increase its purchases of oil, cereals, coal, and timber. Russian petroleum amounted to almost one quarter of all Italian oil imports.[29] At the current council meeting, however, Litvinov found in the Italian memorandum ample grounds for Russian concern.

Italy based its argument for interference in Ethiopia in part upon a disapproval of the conduct of the country's government. The Soviet Union was extremely sensitive to the fact that its own regime was hated and feared throughout the world, and no leader fostered the fear of foreign intervention more than Joseph Stalin. Litvinov therefore attacked the Italian memorandum in order to condemn the notion that a nation could be judged abroad on the basis of its domestic regime. He sought to show that such a judgment should never be allowed as an excuse for the intervention by other countries. The Italian delegate, Litvinov said before the council on the 5th, was inviting

> the Council to declare its disinterestedness in the conflict, its in-
> difference, and to pass it by, sanctioning the freedom of action
> which he requires for his Government; but in this way, while basing
> his proposal on the non-observance and the violation of its interna-
> tional obligations by the other party to the conflict, he invites the
> Members of the Council to repudiate in their turn their interna-
> tional obligations, to disregard the Covenant of the League of Na-
> tions on which, in no little degree, depends the whole edifice of in-
> ternational peace and the security of nations . . .
> I am certain that there is no one here who feels sympathy with

[29] V. Yakhontoff, *USSR Foreign Policy* (New York, 1945), 142; M. Beloff, *The Foreign Policy of Soviet Russia, 1929–51* (London, 1947), I, 200; A. Rubinstein, ed., *The Foreign Policy of the Soviet Union* (New York, 1960), 351. The Soviet Union's ambivalent role in the Italian-Ethiopian conflict destroyed its reputation among many black Africans as an anti-imperialist state. S. Yakobsen, "Russia and Africa," in I. Lederer, ed., *Russian Foreign Policy* (New Haven, 1962), 470.

the internal regime of Ethiopia as it is described in the documents submitted to us; but, as regards the internal regime, the countries of the world nowadays present a multifarious variety, and very few of them have preserved great likenesses between themselves. Nothing in the Covenant of the League entitles us, however, to discriminate between Members of the League as to their internal regime, the colour of their skin, their racial distinctions or the state of their civilization, nor accordingly to deprive them of privileges which they enjoy in virtue of their membership of the League, and, in the first place, of their inalienable right to integrity and independence. I venture to say that, for the development of backward peoples, for influencing their internal life, for raising them to higher civilization, other means than military may be found.

The League of Nations, Litvinov concluded, should "stand firm on the principles that there cannot be justification for military operations except in self-defence." [30]

Although Litvinov spoke with Russia's interest in mind as much as Ethiopia's, his remarks were considered in Rome as hostile to Italy. On 6 September Mussolini sent a telegram of protest, describing Litvinov's speech as a "grave blow" to Italian-Russian relations.[31] But Litvinov's was the only non-Ethiopian protest to Italy's memorandum and, coming from a government viewed with deep suspicion, it had little effect. There was no murmur against the Italian assertions from Britain, France, or any other state. The delegations were not silent because they were suddenly convinced of the righteousness of the Italian cause and the unworthiness of Ethiopia. Silence did not mean the realization of Italian hopes. On the contrary, most members of the League simply failed to take the memorandum seriously. Neither Britain nor France found it could use the memorandum's clumsy arguments as an aid in the appeasement of Italy or in the condemnation of Ethiopia. They felt no need to expose or belabor Italy's manifest insincerity. The Italian memorandum was greeted with almost complete indifference. It fell, Guariglia mournfully recorded, "in a void" — "No one paid attention to us." [32]

The delegates of Britain and France, we have seen, came to Geneva for the council session without definite plans. Both Eden and Laval, speaking on 4 September, were restrained in their remarks, general in their pledge of allegiance to the Covenant, and careful not to make any

---

[30] League, *Official Journal, 1935,* 1142.
[31] Guariglia, *Ricordi,* 260; Aloisi, *Journal,* 300–1.
[32] Guariglia, *Ricordi,* 259.

accusations toward Italy. There was no call to action, and the tones were those of conciliation. Eden and Laval stressed their desire to find a peaceful settlement of the dispute, and both expressed a resolve to find a way to avert war — as Laval said, to find "an equitable settlement . . . one affording Italy the satisfaction she can legitimately claim without disregarding the fundamental rights of Ethiopian sovereignty."[33] They held to the dream of a negotiated settlement and pursued it, as always, without being prepared to force Mussolini to agree by threatening him with sanctions.

The old search for a settlement began again, this time along the lines suggested in article 15 of the Covenant. The problem was to create a committee of the council to undertake a full-scale study of the dispute. Preliminary discussions took place "in the corridors." On 5 and 6 September Aloisi met with Laval and Avenol. Aloisi wanted the committee composed only of small nations and refused to consider the participation of Britain. The delegates of the smaller nations, however, men such as Salvador de Madariaga of Spain, Josef Beck of Poland, and Rüstü Aras of Turkey, specifically refused to take part if Britain were not a participant. Laval, working hard for conciliation, suggested turning the council itself, including Italy, into the investigating committee, but Aloisi rejected this arrangement. At this point the Italians decided not to discuss the question further. Following his dramatic walkout of the 5th, in the middle of Jèze's speech, Aloisi informed the president of the council that he would no longer sit at the table if the Ethiopian delegate were also there. His argument was that Italy and Ethiopia could not be considered equals. Aloisi's high-handed behavior elicited most unfavorable reactions from the other delegates. It irritated Laval particularly, for it exposed as futile all the elaborate efforts to pretend that the conflict was still subject to an amicable settlement through diplomatic means.[34]

The withdrawal of Italian opposition, however, made possible the formation of a committee, and at the council meeting of the 6th the president, Enrique Ruiz Guiñazú of Argentina, proposed that a committee of five, composed of Britain, France, Poland, Spain, and Turkey,

[33] League, *Official Journal, 1935*, 1133-5. Laval's speech caused surprise in Italy because it was so similar to Eden's. The Italian press had built up the opinion that Britain was Italy's only real enemy, that France would stand by Italy, and that there was no possibility of any British-French agreement. *The Times* (London), 6 and 14 September 1935.

[34] Aloisi, *Journal*, 300-1; Avon, *Facing the Dictators*, 259; Villari, *Storia diplomatica*, 132.

be appointed "to make a general examination of Italo-Ethiopian relations and to seek for a pacific settlement." This proposal was adopted,
with Aloisi absent from the council room and abstaining.[35] The council's first full consideration of the dispute hence resulted in the referral
of the problem to committee and the postponement of further action.
The Committee of Five, under the chairmanship of Madariaga, held
eleven meetings between 7 and 24 September, and on the 18th
presented a plan for peaceful settlement.

As might be expected, Italy paid no attention to the work of the
committee, for the needs of diplomacy gave way to the needs of war.
Italian military preparations were stepped up as the hour of invasion
approached. Every day thousands of troops left Naples for east Africa.
Prior to the day when Italy would cross the Mareb, prior to a
triumphal victory that would make Mussolini's reputation as a military conqueror, there was no hope for a negotiated settlement. Galeazzo
Ciano, now an aviator with the army in Eritrea, said in Asmara on the
8th that Italy considered "as closed forever the period of attempts at
pacific collaboration with Ethiopia," and added that the people of Italy
were "ready to assume the gravest responsibilities." On the same day
Mussolini left an enthusiastic audience with the words: "Noi tireremo
diritto" (we shall go straight ahead), a motto he henceforth used
often. On 10 September Mussolini planned the "mobilization of ten
million," a huge civilian demonstration called the "general assembly of
the forces of the regime." Instructions were issued for the simultaneous
gathering of nationwide rallies under his central direction. Details
were given for the bells, sirens, and drums which would summon the
people of Italy to this gigantic *adunata*. On the 14th it was announced
that the ecclesiastical authorities in Italy would cooperate in sum-
moning the people, and that to all the other signals would be added
the bells of the churches of the land.[36] A propaganda masterpiece was
being created, the most sensational public event in the history of the
regime. While the mechanics of the "general assembly" were carefully explained, its purpose and the date were concealed in order to
build up maximum suspense.

An Italian move of a different sort took place on 9 September. On
that day in Berlin, Hitler officially received the new Italian ambassador,
Bernardo Attolico. The reception was unusual. It had not been expected

---

[35] League, *Official Journal, 1935*, 1145.
[36] Salvemini, *Prelude*, 294; Mussolini, *Opera omnia*, XXVII, 123, 351–2.

until a later date; it was held on a Sunday; and Hitler came from Berchtesgaden for the event. One result of all this attention was that Attolico was obliged to attend the forthcoming Nazi Party congress, which his predecessor, Cerutti, had stayed away from the year before. In a prepared statement Attolico said that he sought closer ties for Italy with Germany and that "only advantages can come of good friendship." The French could not miss the significance of this Italian démarche. Their concern was not allayed by an official denial from Rome on the 11th that Italy had proposed the negotiation of an Italian-German nonaggression pact.[37] What we do not know is whether this display was an important step toward the creation of the Axis or mainly an effort to frighten the French into giving Italy fuller support in the Ethiopian issue.

The French did not need any reminders of the delicacy and difficulty of their situation. Laval sought to keep the matter flexible, in order to prevent permanent damage either to the League or to French-Italian friendship. Laval was willing to sacrifice Ethiopia for the stability of Europe, if the sacrifice could be carried out with a minimum of long-term complication. If it could be done without crippling the League's system of security as applied to Europe, then the League might be patched up, Italy reconciled to collective security in Europe, and France's pro-League and pro-Italian policies brought together again to resist Germany. And Mussolini seemed ready to condone France's equivocation, as long as France did not join any coalition against him. Laval's policy raised the question whether the League could in fact survive such a restrictive application of its principles and a selective use of its machinery of enforcement. It also left unanswered the question of what the French should do if they did finally have to choose between Italy and the League. The answer to this depended entirely on Great Britain. If Britain would come to the firm support of collective security in Europe, then France would gain by supporting the Covenant even at the heavy cost of losing Italy's friendship. If Britain remained aloof and uncommitted, then a strong and friendly Italy was of more value to France than an enfeebled League.

During the first week of September Laval tried to find out what Britain's future policy would be. On 2 September he had sought from

[37] *The Times* (London), 9 September 1935; Toynbee, *Survey of International Affairs, 1935,* II, 183.

Eden the assurance "that Britain would be as firm in upholding the Covenant, to the extent of sanctions in Europe in the future, as she appeared to be today in Abyssinia." Eden replied that he found it impossible to promise unconditional support for collective security in Europe. The meeting of the council gave no indication that the British meant to give up their isolationism. Hence there was no compelling reason for France to take up the championship of the League. The French were disturbed by Britain's apparent interest in applying the Covenant to a little known African state of no strategic importance, at the cost of overthrowing the present balance of power in Europe, while remaining unwilling to apply the same principles to the continent. On 10 September, Laval again formally inquired of the British government if it would guarantee an immediate and effective application of all the sanctions under article 16 of the Covenant if an act of armed aggression took place in Europe.[38]

On 9 September the sixteenth session of the assembly of the League opened in Geneva, providing an opportunity for direct British-French talks. The British sent a large delegation headed by Foreign Minister Hoare. On the 10th and 11th, Hoare, Eden, and Laval met at length to discuss "the question of how the mechanism of collective security should be put into operation." [39] Laval saw immediately that the British had no new proposals to offer and that their public statements in support of the League had to be weighed against their unwillingness to take the lead, to antagonize Mussolini, or to become actively embroiled in the political affairs of Europe. Although Hoare solemnly warned Laval that the Ethiopian case tested the efficacy of the Covenant, it was obvious that nothing had changed with Britain. On the 10th Hoare told Laval: "A double line of approach was essential. On the one hand, a most patient and cautious negotiation that would keep [Mussolini] on the Allied side; on the other, the creation of a united front in Geneva as a necessary deterrent against German aggression." [40] But these were only vague generalities. Hoare had no suggestions for implementing this "double line" and had prepared no alternatives. France received no guarantee for Europe.

Hoare was beset with the fear of precipitating an open military conflict with Italy. The British ambassador in Rome had just cabled

[38] Flandin, *Politique française*, 182; Herriot, *Jadis*, II, 577–8.
[39] Laval's description in his speech of 28 December 1935 to the French Chamber of Deputies. *Journal officiel, débats parlementaires*, 29 December 1935, 2863.
[40] Templewood, *Nine Troubled Years*, 168.

him: "In their present mood, both Signor Mussolini and the Italian people are capable of committing suicide if this seems the only alternative to climbing down. Rome today is full of rumours of an impending declaration of war on Great Britain." Laval was in full agreement with Hoare that the real menace to Europe came from a rearmed Germany, and he too feared the consequences of a British-Italian war. He frankly pursued his own policy in the Italian-Ethiopian question in order to keep Mussolini from "being driven into the German camp." The repercussions of the Italian-Ethiopian affair were getting broader and more dangerous every day. Although France could not desert Britain, in a British-Italian war the safety of France's Mediterranean coastline and colonies, and the forces of both Britain and France, would be jeopardized. Such a war would destroy the stability of Europe and, the French thought, precipitate a German attack. Mussolini told Laval that in a British-Italian conflict Italy would be forced to abandon the Brenner.[41]

Lacking a British guarantee of support on the continent, Laval tried to steer the British away from any thought of active resistance to Italy. Laval decided to encourage Hoare's predilection for a negotiated settlement, the search for which was being carried on at the time by the Committee of Five. Laval told Hoare that, contrary to Drummond's report, Chambrun had informed Paris that Mussolini had not finally decided on war, that the Duce had been impressed by the Paris talks, and that there remained room for further discussion, preferably outside the League.[42] The British did not commit themselves to any further negotiation, but Hoare was sympathetic to Laval's endeavors. Hoare records that he

> could not help admiring the quickness of [Laval's] versatile mind.
> More than once . . . he had been most helpful to Great Britain.
> Everyone knew him to be a cunning intriguer, but at the time there
> seemed a good chance of his wits once again being useful to us. Not
> only was he head of the French Government whose co-operation

---

[41] Templewood, *Nine Troubled Years*, 167, 169; Avon, *Facing the Dictators*, 260, 262.

[42] On the other hand, the American minister to Switzerland, Hugh Wilson, reported to Washington on the 14th that Mussolini had told Chambrun that he "damned the British for interference and stated that he [Mussolini] was willing to take them on, if they wanted, and could defeat them in the Mediterranean." *U.S. Diplomatic Papers, 1935*, I, 647.

was essential to us, but he was a personal friend of Mussolini, and seemed to have considerable influence in Rome.[43]

The momentous question Hoare and Laval faced in their conversations on 10 and 11 September was how to deal with their responsibilities as members of the League. Article 16 of the Covenant read:

> 1. Should any Member of the League resort to war in disregard of its covenants under Articles 12, 13, or 15, it shall *ipso facto* be deemed to have committed an act of war against all other Members of the League, which hereby undertake immediately to subject it to the severance of all trade or financial relations, the prohibition of all intercourse between their nationals and the nationals of the covenant-breaking State, and the prevention of all financial, commercial or personal intercourse between the nationals of the covenant-breaking State and the nationals of any other State, whether a Member of the League or not.
> 2. It shall be the duty of the Council in such case to recommend to the several Governments concerned what effective military, naval or air force the Members of the League shall severally contribute to the armed forces to be used to protect the covenants of the League.

Here was the final and decisive power of the League, the power to punish international criminals. If Italy committed an act of aggression, Britain and France would be obligated to impose economic and military sanctions. If the League failed to impose sanctions, it could not survive as an authoritative political organization.

The British, as we have seen, were not prepared to take the lead in imposing economic sanctions. On 28 August Hoare told the American chargé in London that "as to economic sanctions the British Government would not favor their employment until it knew the attitude of neutral countries not members of the League, and certainly until it was satisfied beforehand that the employment of economic sanctions would not conflict with United States policy." [44] An ultimate risk in sanctions lay in the logical need to proscribe America's trade with Italy. The United Kingdom, one of the great trading nations of the League, exported only 1.6 percent of its total exports to Italy in 1935 and imported from Italy only 1.1 percent of its total imports. This trade from Britain made up 7.2 percent of Italy's imports, and Italy exported 8.2 percent of its total sales abroad to Britain. In the same year, by con-

[43] Templewood, *Nine Troubled Years*, 168.
[44] *U.S. Diplomatic Papers, 1935*, I, 639.

trast, Italy imported 11.2 percent of its total imports from the United States and 18.3 percent from Germany, and sent 8.1 percent of its total exports to America and 16.2 percent to Germany.[45] In such circumstances, with such vital materials as petroleum, iron, and steel readily available from non-League members, economic sanctions against Italy was an uncertain business. Yet why not venture to impose them for the moral and political value they might have for the League, and because it was a treaty obligation?

The fact was that Hoare and Laval were worried about political consequences. Whether or not economic sanctions would hurt Italy or help the League, they wanted to act as moderately as possible to give Mussolini no reason for resentment. "We agreed," Laval recalled, "that such measures as financial sanctions or the embargo on arms should first be submitted to a committee which had not yet been set up, and then that other measures might be adopted, notably the refusal to buy from or sell to Italy." [46] This was caution itself: the proposal was limited in extent and would have to filter through a committee before taking effect. Economic sanctions would not cause much more strain in France than in Britain. France exported to Italy, in 1935, 3.8 percent of its goods sold abroad and imported 1.9 percent of its imports from the peninsula. French goods accounted for 6.0 percent of Italian imports, and 5.8 percent of Italian exports went to France.[47] Nevertheless, economic sanctions of any kind might anger Mussolini and be construed as an act of war.[48] Hoare writes that he and Laval "agreed that as we must, if possible, avoid provoking Mussolini into open hostility, any economic pressure upon which the League collectively decided should be applied cautiously and in stages, and with full account of the unescapable fact that the United States, Japan and Ger-

---

[45] The figures for 1934 are about the same. In 1934 the United Kingdom exported 2.4 percent of its total exports to Italy and imported from the peninsula 1.2 percent of its total imports. This trade made up 9.2 percent of Italy's imports and 10.1 percent of its exports. League of Nations, *International Trade Statistics, 1936* (Geneva, 1937), 303–48.

[46] *Journal officiel, débats parlementaires*, 29 December 1935, 2863.

[47] In 1934 France exported to Italy 3.1 percent of its goods sold abroad and imported 2.1 percent of its imports from Italy. This trade was 6.1 percent of Italy's imports and 6.7 percent of Italian exports. League, *International Trade Statistics*, 303–48.

[48] Avon, *Facing the Dictators*, 260. Hoare told Laval he did not even want to utter the word "sanctions" and preferred to speak of "measures of economic pressure." Herriot, *Jadis*, II, 594.

many were not Member States of the League." [49] The British, it will be noted, continued to deny their treaty obligations by affirming their notion of collective responsibility.

The prospect of military sanctions was a much more serious matter. Mussolini might survive a British and French economic boycott and, indeed, could use it to rally popular support. He could not survive British and French military interference. The British fleet dominated the routes to east Africa. With or without French assistance, the British could in a matter of hours cut the thin, exposed line that connected Italy with its army in the field. Some 200,000 of Italy's best soldiers would be stranded in the barren wastes of east Africa without the possibility of help, and Mussolini's regime would probably fall.[50] A blockade of the Italian peninsula by the British fleet would ruin the Italian economy, for more than 80 percent of Italy's imports came by sea.[51] In every regard, firmly applied military sanctions would be an unmitigated disaster for the Fascist government and immediately end the campaign against Ethiopia. As a threat they might still deter Mussolini; in action they would be decisive in upholding the principles of the Covenant and in saving the independence of Ethiopia. This was the League's trump card.

The success of military sanctions, like everything else the League attempted in this dispute, depended on the active participation of Britain and the cooperation of France. But, unknown to the rest of the League, the representatives of the governments of Britain and France, afraid to run the risk of war, now rejected the use of military sanctions. In their secret talks on 10 and 11 September Hoare and Laval agreed that war against Italy was simply too high a price to pay for the protection of Ethiopia or, in the present circumstance, for the maintenance of the universality of the Covenant. It was, wrote Hoare, "too dangerous and double-edged for the future of Europe." [52] More specifically, in Laval's words, he and Hoare "found ourselves instantaneously in agreement upon ruling out military sanctions, not adopting any measure of naval blockade, never contemplating the

[49] Templewood, *Nine Troubled Years*, 168–9.
[50] There was talk in Rome in mid-September of replacing Mussolini with Badoglio. Charles-Roux, *Huit ans au Vatican*, 139.
[51] D. Popper, "Strategy and Diplomacy in the Mediterranean," *Foreign Policy Reports*, 13:76 (June 1937).
[52] Templewood, *Nine Troubled Years*, 168.

closure of the Suez Canal — in a word, ruling out everything that might lead to war." [53] Economic sanctions were likewise affected by this private accord, the two statesmen agreeing that if sanctions came they "should be applied cautiously and in stages." Despite their obligations under the Covenant, then, the representatives of Britain and France agreed in advance to the selective use of the terms of article 16, deciding to apply at most and then in attenuated form only the economic and financial measures in paragraph 1 and to refuse to apply the terms of paragraph 2.[54] Although this agreement was provisional and not formally binding on either party, the question of freedom is academic: until the end of the Italian-Ethiopian conflict, British and French policy followed the course laid down at this time by Hoare and Laval.[55]

Britain, and France behind it, deserted the Covenant, and this is the major significance of the Italian-Ethiopian war. Influential Englishmen were afraid that the successful use of sanctions and the triumph of the League under British leadership would end Britain's political independence. Like a policeman required to quell all lawlessness, Britain would henceforth be involved deeply and endlessly in the troubled affairs of the European continent. One "prominent member of the British delegation" told the correspondent of the *Manchester Guardian* in Geneva that "it is of no use to blink the fact that, if sanctions succeed this time, we shall be morally bound to resort to them in the future in similar cases." [56]

The British-French agreement was a grievous blow to the League. Without the power of the British fleet, the forces the League could muster for deterrence or punishment would be only an impotent shadow of its potential. Nor was there any certainty that the League would survive this crippling blow to its authority and prestige. Hoare and Laval had agreed that they did not consider the League the

[53] This quotation is from a speech by Laval before the French Chamber on 28 December 1935. *Journal officiel, débats parlementaires,* 29 December 1935, 2863. See also his speech of 17 December, *ibid.,* 18 December 1935, 2647.

[54] Official statements confirming this agreement are found in Laval's note to the British government of 18 October 1935 — it is unpublished but extensive quotations appear in Dell, *The Geneva Racket,* 120–1, and its content is disclosed in Herriot, *Jadis,* II, 600–1. From the British side, see the statement by Lord Cranborne, undersecretary of foreign affairs, to the House of Commons on 2 March 1936, *Parliamentary Debates,* 309 H.C. Deb. 5s., col. 977.

[55] See the comments on this matter by Toynbee in *Survey of International Affairs, 1935,* II, 184–6.

[56] Dell, *The Geneva Racket,* 117.

primary instrument for maintaining the European peace. The fact that the agreement was taken in private and kept secret also put the League in a false and humiliating position. Laval, to his credit — and the French throughout were more honest with themselves and with others than the British were — wanted the agreements published and all misunderstandings concerning the extent of British-French commitment cleared away after war broke out, but the British rejected his call for frankness.[57]

While Hoare and Laval were secretly condemning the League to futile half measures, the rest of the world was waiting expectantly for their public pronouncements at the meeting of the League assembly. Greatest attention was focused on Hoare, for as the representative of the League's strongest and most influential member his words would determine future action. The question in everyone's mind was whether or not Britain would now break out of its isolation and commit itself to leading the League. "Rarely has an utterance by a foreign statesman been awaited with such anxiety," wrote the Paris correspondent of *The Times*.[58]

Hoare spoke before the assembly on 11 September, delivering the words without emphasis or emotion, his voice flat and toneless. The assembly hall became charged with excitement as Hoare's speech progressed, for it appeared to his hopeful listeners that a new turn in British policy was being revealed.

> I do not suppose that in the history of the Assembly there was ever a more difficult moment for a speech and a discussion . . . I will begin by reaffirming the support of the League by the Government that I represent and the interest of the British people in collective security . . . His Majesty's Government and the British people maintain their suport of the League and its ideals as the most effective way of ensuring peace, and [believe] in the necessity for preserving the League . . . No selfish or imperialist motives enter into our minds at all . . .
> The League is what its Member States make it. If it succeeds, it

[57] Dell, *The Geneva Racket*, 120; Herriot, *Jadis*, II, 601. See Laval's note to the British of 18 October 1935, which noted that "the French Government for its part has never felt the slightest difficulty in allowing the limits of its final decisions to be made known . . . It has always regretted to be unable to count on an indication of the same nature on the part of the British Government." Dell, *The Geneva Racket*, 121.

[58] *The Times* (London), 11 September 1935.

is because its Members have, in combination with each other, the will and the power to apply the principles of the Covenant. If it fails, it is because its Members lack either the will or the power to fulfill their obligations . . .

The obligations of the Covenant remain, their burden upon us has been increased manifold. But one thing is certain. If the burden is to be borne, it must be borne collectively. If risks for peace are to be run, they must be run by all. The security of the many cannot be ensured solely by the efforts of a few, however powerful they may be. On behalf of His Majesty's Government in the United Kingdom, I can say that, in spite of these difficulties, that Government will be second to none in its intention to fulfil, within the measure of its capacity, the obligations which the Covenant lays upon it . . .

We believe that small nations are entitled to a life of their own and to such protection as can collectively be afforded to them in the maintenance of their national life . . . And we believe that backward nations are, without prejudice to their independence and integrity, entitled to expect that assistance will be afforded them by more advanced peoples . . . It is not enough to insist collectively that war shall not occur or that war, if it occurs, shall be brought to an end. Something must also be done to remove the causes from which war is apt to arise . . .

I will take as an example the problem of the world's economic resources . . . The abundance of supplies of raw materials appears to give peculiar advantages to countries possessing them . . . Especially as regards colonial raw materials, it is not unnatural that such a state of things should give rise to fears lest exclusive monopolies be set up at the expense of those countries that do not possess colonial empires. It is clear that in the view of many this is a real problem; and we should be foolish to ignore it. It may be also that it is exploited for other purposes. None the less, as the question is causing discontent and anxiety, the wise course is to investigate it, to see what the proposals are for dealing with it, to see what is the real scope of the trouble and, if the trouble is substantial, to try and remove it.

The view of His Majesty's Government is that the [Italian-Ethiopian] problem is economic rather than political and territorial. It is the fear of monopoly — of the withholding of essential raw materials — that is causing alarm . . . So far as His Majesty's Government in the United Kingdom is concerned, we should, I feel sure, be ready to take our share in an investigation of these matters . . . Obviously, however, such an inquiry needs calm and dispassionate consideration, and calm and dispassionate consideration is impossible in an atmosphere of war and threats of war . . .

The attitude of His Majesty's Government has always been one of unswerving fidelity to the League and all that it stands for, and the case now before us is no exception, but, on the contrary, the continuance of that rule. The recent response of public opinion shows how completely the nation supports the Government in the full acceptance of the obligations of League membership, which is the oft-proclaimed key-note of British policy . . . In conformity with its precise and explicit obligations, the League stands, and my country stands with it, for collective maintenance of the Covenant[59] in its entirety, and particularly for steady and collective resistance to all acts of unprovoked aggression . . .

There, then, is the British attitude towards the Covenant. I cannot believe that it will be changed so long as the League remains an effective body and the main bridge between the United Kingdom and the Continent remains intact.[60]

The effect of Hoare's speech was immediate, general, and profound — an effect, F. P. Walters said, that "would be difficult to exaggerate." Britain, it seemed, after years of "uncertainty, timidity, opportunism . . . was ready to take her natural place as the leader of the League and all it stood for." [61] After all the ambiguities of British policy in the Italian-Ethiopian dispute, after all the months of delay, Britain at last, or so it seemed to Hoare's excited and approving audience, had made up its mind to stand unequivocally by the system of collective security. Paul Hymans of Belgium summed up the judgment of men of international experience who heard the speech: "The British have decided to stop Mussolini, even if that means using force." Eden, writing twenty-five years after the event, said: "To this day I consider that this was the only possible interpretation of the speech, if the words meant what they said." [62] Hoare's speech caused a surge of hope among the League's lesser members, such as no other event could have produced. G. M. Young wrote: "Never did [Britain's] name stand higher in Europe than at the close of that day." [63] Leopold Amery noted: "Italy was, in fact, at that moment without a friend . . . To such a lead from England all were prepared to follow." [64] The discouragement and sense of impending defeat that had clouded the past months were largely dissipated, and the smaller nations began to line up loyally behind

[59] At this point Hoare paused and repeated the word "collective." This sentence was delivered with emphatic tone and with repeated raps on the lectern for additional emphasis.
[60] League, *Official Journal*, Special Supplement No. 138, Records of the Sixteenth Ordinary Session of the Assembly, Plenary Meetings (Geneva, 1935), 43–6.
[61] Walters, *History of the League*, II, 648.
[62] Avon, *Facing the Dictators*, 262.
[63] Young, *Baldwin*, 210.
[64] Amery, *My Political Life*, III, 171–2.

Britain and behind a League whose future once again appeared bright.[65] The secretary-general had another reaction: Hoare's speech distressed Avenol. By placing the responsibility for collective security on each nation individually, Avenol feared that the Committee of Five's job of finding a compromise solution now was made even more difficult, perhaps impossible.

To what purpose did Hoare excite the members of the League and raise their hopes? Did he mean what he said? Had Britain really decided to save the League?

The most significant gap between the effect and the intent of Hoare's speech is disclosed by considering the emphasis he gave to "collective maintenance of the Covenant." These words were generally, wishfully, interpreted as meaning that Britain was now prepared to stand behind the League. If the British meant what they said about their "full acceptance of the obligations of League membership," then Britain must take the lead to make the Covenant work. But this was not the plan of the British government. Quite the contrary, Hoare himself interpreted these phrases in a narrow technical way, designed to excuse Britain's unwillingness to act. Hoare did not mind if his listeners gullibly misinterpreted his words and gave the British credit they did not deserve. Yet he was careful to preserve his own interpretation of the letter of the Covenant, in order to deny its spirit. He generalized the notion of collective obligation in order to evade Britain's particular responsibility. The nub of Hoare's speech, representing the view of the British government, was contained in the following sentences, which were deliberately emphasized:

> If the burden [of the Covenant's obligations] is to be borne, it must be borne collectively. If risks for peace are to be run, they must be run by all. The security of the many cannot be ensured solely by the efforts of a few, however powerful they may be.

Hoare's audience can be pardoned, in its excitement, for overlooking the significance of these words, for they were buried among Hoare's apparent message of encouragement. Hearing only the words they

[65] For accounts of the immediate reactions throughout the world to what *The Times* called "the most momentous, and, in the view of the overwhelming majority of those who heard it, the most satisfactory statement of British policy which has been heard in Geneva in years," see *The Times* (London), 12 and 13 September 1935. For a very interesting collection of editorial opinion from leading world newspapers on Hoare's speech, and a source to be consulted for editorial opinion on all phases of the Italian-Ethiopian conflict, see League of Nations, Section d'Information, *Revue des commentaires de la presse sur la Société des Nations*, a daily publication.

sought, Hoare's auditors failed to heed those clues that showed that British policy remained the same. By denying its position as the natural leader, Britain condemned the League to inaction.

Hoare professed himself "amazed" at the "universal acclamation" accorded his speech and wondered "what it was that had so greatly excited" his listeners. Hoare said he read the speech over and over again on the 11th, trying to find out what had caused the great outpouring of relief. From his own reading of the words, he claimed he could see nothing new, nothing that had not been already said in previous statements of British policy. In his memoirs he implies that the members of the League should have been completely aware already of Britain's reservations and its invincible unwillingness to take the lead.[66] But Hoare's retrospective analysis is in its turn misleading and inaccurate. The speech was in fact a carefully prepared deception. Hoare's talk of "collective obligation" was camouflage, an expression of resolution calculated to generate public enthusiasm. Hoare prepared his speech for a moment when, in his view, "bluff was not only legitimate but inescapable." Unwilling to stand against Mussolini, the British resorted, in Hoare's words, to a "revivalist appeal to the Assembly," hoping to instill "new life into its crippled body." [67] Hoare's idea was that if the League showed some flicker of life, Mussolini might be intimidated into surrendering his ambitions and peace would be maintained. Britain still would seem on the side of the League and not have to act on its obligations to the Covenant.

This tactic involved taking two extremely dangerous risks. If it failed — as it was sure to do — it would result in the most harmful consequences both for the League and for British-Italian relations. As a deterrent to Mussolini, the bluff was completely uncertain. Hoare knew that the rally of support for the League would last only a short time, until Britain's false position was revealed. He hoped that in that interval the apparent vigor of the League would somehow cause Mussolini to pause and negotiate. But when the British bluff was called, it would be for Mussolini final proof of Britain's infirmity of strength and purpose, proof that the lion was toothless. For the League, Hoare's tactic raised high hopes, but based them on false assumptions. Once it became evident that Britain would not honor its commitments, would not give the League the lifesaving support it appeared to be offering, once it was shown that the League's foremost member was acting in bad faith,

[66] Templewood, *Nine Troubled Years,* 169–71.
[67] Templewood, *Nine Troubled Years,* 166.

the League as an institution would be discredited and confidence in Britain would be irreparably destroyed.

The speech was drafted by Hoare with the help of Vansittart and Neville Chamberlain. Hoare took the speech to Baldwin in the garden at Chequers. The prime minister "gave it a quick glance," approving it offhandedly without any close analysis. Hoare did not bother to explain his plan to his chief. In Geneva Hoare showed the speech to Eden and to Eden's undersecretary, Lord Cranborne. He allowed them to think that its strength of tone represented a major move by the Cabinet toward firm support of the system of collective security. Hoare never revealed to them that it was a bluff.[68]

In any event, the British government was surprised by the popular reaction. Far from inciting a mild agitation to scare Mussolini into a more moderate mood, Hoare's speech created the general impression that the British were resolved to stop Mussolini even if it meant the use of force. The bluff went too far, for its very purpose was to prevent Britain from having to take any strong action against Italy. There would be no military sanctions, for that had been decided already in the Hoare-Laval talks preceding the speech. It was this private agreement, not the public pronouncement, which was, in Toynbee's words, "the historic event" at the sixteenth session of the assembly.[69] Hoare was amazed at the strong response, and it is interesting to note that in the midst of the world-wide acclamation only one member of the British government — Simon, curiously — sent Hoare a telegram of congratulations. That, wrote Hoare, was "the only comment I received from Whitehall." [70]

Hoare's speech was conceived as a continuation of his old double policy. Titular fidelity to the League was one part, but as an opera-

[68] Templewood, *Nine Troubled Years*, 167; I. Colvin, *Vansittart in Office* (London, 1965), 69; Macleod, *Neville Chamberlain*, 186. Eden notes that he and Cranborne "were both considerably surprised and concerned by its strength, which surpassed anything that the tone of discussions with our colleagues had revealed up to the time when I left London for a fortnight before . . . [Hoare] was not prepared to consider any major changes to moderate its force, arguing that the speech had been approved by his senior colleagues . . . I remained puzzled that Ministers should have supported such firm language, particularly in the light of their refusal to allow me to give warning to Laval earlier of our intention to fulfill the Covenant. I could only suppose that, while Cranborne and I had been at Geneva, they had been brought up against the character of the obstacle which faced them and had decided to make a clean leap over it." Avon, *Facing the Dictators*, 260–1.
[69] Toynbee, *Survey of International Affairs, 1935*, II, 185.
[70] Templewood, *Nine Troubled Years*, 171.

tive policy this was qualified by the condition of collectivity extended into ineffectiveness. It did have a role to play, however, if it succeeded in causing Mussolini to accept a negotiated settlement. To provide a favorable climate for this eventuality, Hoare decided that "the best hope lay in shifting the controversy from the political ground to the economic." In his speech he defined Britain's position in these terms: "the view of His Majesty's Government is that the [Italian-Ethiopian] problem is economic rather than political and territorial. It is the fear of monopoly — of the withholding of essential raw materials — that is causing alarm." If this position were accepted at Geneva, Hoare thought, the chances of coming to an agreement with Mussolini would be vastly increased, for economic fulfillment was a far less inflammable problem than political security and Mussolini might accept this chance to "withdraw from this threatening position." So Hoare revived an old and not too clear program of free access to raw materials taken from the Economic Conference of 1931. Vansittart and Neville Chamberlain gave their enthusiastic approval to including these arguments in the speech.[71] Anything to avoid war, to evade the risks war would entail for Britain. Hoare announced in Geneva that Britain was ready to cooperate in finding a solution of Italy's demands for raw materials if Mussolini would dispel the threat of war.

Italy made no response to Hoare's overtures, since of course his premises were all wrong. Italy's demands and Mussolini's interests in an invasion of Ethiopia were primarily political and territorial, not economic. Hoare's proposals offered Mussolini nothing in the way of satisfaction and, in any case, his talk of free access to raw materials was ignored in the general excitement caused by the other parts of the speech. Here too the British had miscalculated, for the effect of Hoare's speech taken as a whole was to concentrate everyone's attention on the political side of the dispute. His strong words, his bluffing words, were those that were heard. *Le Temps* on 13 September stated that Hoare's clear statement "effectively changed something in the international situation." What it changed was the attitude and resolve of the other members of the League. As nation

---

[71] Templewood, *Nine Troubled Years*, 165–6. Hoare's proposal is discussed in critical and wide-ranging detail in H. Hodson, "World Economic Affairs: (1) The Problem of Raw Materials," Toynbee, *Survey of International Affairs*, I, 340–88. A second notable effort to investigate the problem in response to Hoare's suggestion in his speech is J. DeWilde, "The International Distribution of Raw Materials," *Geneva Special Studies*, 7.5 (Geneva, 1936).

after nation at Geneva, and public opinion throughout the world, rallied to the League, the British government found itself being forced toward an extreme it had worked to avoid: support of the League against Italy. Of Hoare's speech Winston Churchill wrote: "It aroused everyone, and reverberated throughout the United States. It united all those forces in Britain which stood for a fearless combination of righteousness and strength . . . If only [Hoare] had realized what tremendous powers he held unleashed in his hand at that moment, he might indeed for a while have led the world." [72]

No one not privy to the secrets of government knew at the time of the private agreements of the 10th and 11th or of the British government's hypocrisy. The impression of British resoluteness was confirmed to all the world by the news, broken on the 12th, that a large section of the home fleet was arriving at Gibraltar, including the battle cruisers *Hood* (then the largest warship in the world) and *Renown*, accompanied by the Second Cruiser Squadron and a destroyer flotilla. Three weeks before, the Mediterranean fleet had moved from Malta to the eastern Mediterranean and now covered the sea route to east Africa through the Suez Canal. These naval deployments, and then the secret and dramatic transfer of the home fleet away from Channel waters, were viewed everywhere as proof that Hoare had meant what he said. Britain and Italy seemed truly on a collision course, with the League at stake. Churchill said:

> For the first and the last time the League of Nations seemed to have at its disposal a secular arm. Here was the international police force, upon the ultimate authority of which all kinds of diplomatic and economic pressures and persuasion could be employed. [With the movement of the fleet to the Mediterranean] it was assumed on all sides that Britain would back her words with deeds. Policy and action alike gained immediate and overwhelming support at home. It was taken for granted, not unnaturally, that neither the declaration nor the movement of warships would have been made without care-

[72] Churchill, *The Gathering Storm*, 173. Inspired by Hoare's speech, Cordell Hull made a plea for peace on the 12th, but this contributed little to the debate. *U.S. Diplomatic Papers, 1935*, I, 746–8. For reaction in the United States, see *New York Times*, 12 and 13 September 1935. The American ambassador to Switzerland noted on the 14th: "No one who listened to Hoare can escape the conclusion that Great Britain is determined that Italy shall not conquer Ethiopia and is prepared to take the initiative toward collective action when the time comes." *U.S. Diplomatic Papers, 1935*, I, 648.

ful expert calculation by the Admiralty of the fleet or fleets required in the Mediterranean to make our undertakings good.[73]

Now, from 11 to 16 September, the delegates of many of the member nations of the League made their way to the podium of the assembly to assert their willingness to stand by the Covenant.[74] Within a week the atmosphere of Geneva was changed, and the thought that collective security could succeed was no longer the opinion of a radical minority. The majority of the speakers had a common theme: if the Covenant was violated, their countries stood prepared to fulfill their obligations as members of the League. Finland, Sweden, Norway, Denmark, the Baltic states, the Netherlands, Belgium, and Portugal all gave their allegiance to the League. Haldvdan Koht of Norway coolly appraised the fact that, if the League failed in this case, it could no longer claim to be a political organization of any strength and would have to readjust the scope of its ambitions to nonpolitical concerns. The delegate from Yugoslavia spoke on behalf of the Little Entente, the delegate from Greece on behalf of the Balkan Entente, and both vowed their fidelity. Eamon de Valera expressed Ireland's determination to fulfill the letter and spirit of the League's charter, although he probably spoke for only a minority of his countrymen. Litvinov for the Soviet Union noted on the 14th that if the present assembly ended "with the certainty that the States whose representatives have addressed us here have formally and solemnly pledged their Governments to allow no new attempts against the League's Covenant . . . this Assembly may become a landmark in the new history of the League." [75] General Alfred Nemours of Haiti strongly pledged his Negro republic to the cause of the League, emphasizing the universality of the principles of the Covenant.[76] The other countries of Latin America were reluctant for the moment to declare themselves. Various delegates were silent not from a desire

[73] Churchill, *The Gathering Storm*, 173.

[74] League, *Official Journal, 1935*, Supplement No. 138, 46–84. Herriot called it "an admirable debate. For the first time since the discussion of the Protocol of 1924 the international conscience manifested itself; the world sought unity in reason." Herriot, *Jadis*, II, 584.

[75] Strictly speaking, the Italian-Ethiopian dispute was still before the council, and the members of the assembly were not stating their judgments but indicating the positions their countries would adopt in the case of a violation of the Covenant.

[76] Nemours' interesting position is elaborated in his collected speeches, *Craignons d'être un jour l'Ethiopie de quelqu'un* (Port-au-Prince, 1945). Nemours was known as the "Black Briand of Geneva."

to break faith with the League or to offer encouragement to Italy, but because distance hampered consultation with their governments or because they did not want to commit themselves until the last possible moment.[77] China, a recent victim, spoke feelingly for the League. Tecle Hawariate ended his moderate but earnest comments by commending Ethiopia's cause "to the sovereign protection of the League of Nations." Switzerland, Poland, and Spain remained silent, as did Austria and Hungary.

In the Commonwealth, the Union of South Africa and New Zealand gave their support to the apparent policy of Great Britain. Charles te Water of South Africa warned of danger to white civilization in Africa if the contagion of war spread from Europe to that susceptible continent. New Zealand was steadfast in its support of the Covenant and its opposition to appeasement. The representatives of Canada and Australia were more cautious. The Australians, concerned for the safety of the Suez Canal route, wanted to prevent any conflict between Britain and Italy, and so counseled appeasement. The Canadian government, reflecting the growing isolationism of the country, wanted to stay clear of any sanctions. The idea of League action that might lead to war was not popular in the nation, especially among the Roman Catholic French Canadians who had no desire to join in punitive measures against the home of the papacy on behalf of far-off Ethiopia. Canada was in the final weeks of a turbulent election campaign, in which domestic issues claimed most attention. Ernest Lapointe of the opposition Liberal Party, speaking for the majority of French Canadians, said on 9 September: "No interest in Ethiopia, of any nature whatever, is worth the life of a single Canadian citizen. No consideration could justify Canada's participation in such a war, and I am unalterably opposed to it." The main consideration raised by the crisis was of course the fate of the League of Nations, and on this matter the government equivocated. Canada's policy on this issue was shaped by Oscar Douglas Skelton, the undersecretary of state for external affairs, who was running the foreign ministry while the members of the government engaged in the election campaign. Skelton did not approve of the collective-security provisions of the Covenant; he wanted Canada isolated from European problems; and he was no

[77] Iraq is a case in point. "Uncertain as to what action Great Britain and other great powers would take, Iraq remained silent during debates on the Italo-Ethiopian dispute." A. Al-Marayati, *A Diplomatic History of Modern Iraq* (New York, 1961), 87.

friend to Great Britain. In an influential memorandum written at the end of August 1935, Skelton put forward the pros and cons of Canada's participation in League sanctions against Italy. Expressing his own opinion as he argued against involvement, Skelton contended that the sanctions provided for in the Covenant were no longer feasible. The League, he thought, should turn away from its untenable position as an enforcer of the peace, with which Canadian governments had never been in sympathy, and concentrate on its capacity for publicity and conciliation. Economic sanctions against Italy, Skelton wrote, would in any case not deter Mussolini from his purpose in Ethiopia and would likely lead to war. If economic sanctions failed, the League would be discredited. If they did succeed in hurting Italy, Mussolini might turn in desperation to an alliance with Nazi Germany, and Japan would take advantage of the great powers' preoccupation with Europe to complete its conquest of China. Skelton noted further that Britain's final position on the question of sanctions was yet uncertain: "in any case, each member of the League must decide for itself." And for Canada, if it followed the requirements of the Covenant, any effort to curtail trade between the United States and Italy "would be suicide." This position was the operative policy of the government in mid-September and, when the Canadian delegate to the League requested permission to speak in the excitement following Hoare's speech, permission was denied. As the general enthusiasm after the speech became more evident, however, Skelton changed his mind and the Canadian representative was authorized to make some vague remarks to the assembly on the 14th that committed Canada to nothing.[78]

Of all the speeches after Hoare's, the one most eagerly awaited was Laval's. Laval was surprised by the strength of Hoare's words — he had told Aloisi on the morning of the 10th that Hoare would be very moderate and in general conciliatory. Laval must have been impressed by the effect on French public opinion. Hoare's speech, wrote the Paris correspondent of *The Times* on 12 September, "completely monopolizes French attention." With Britain publicly proclaiming support of the Covenant, France could not but do likewise. On the 11th Laval sent a telegram to Rome, informing Mussolini that he could not abandon the League.[79] But not until forty-eight hours after Hoare

[78] For an excellent account of Canadian policy, see James Eayrs, *In Defence of Canada: Appeasement and Rearmament* (Toronto, 1965), 1–11.
[79] Herriot, *Jadis*, II, 579.

had spoken did Laval finally take the rostrum before the assembly. Not until Laval spoke on the 13th was it known "whether he would confirm or destroy the high hopes which the British statement had aroused." [80]

> France is loyal to the Covenant. She cannot fail to carry out her obligations . . . The Covenant is our international law. How could we allow such a law to be weakened? To do so would be contrary to our whole ideal, and it would be contrary to our interests to do so. France's policy rests entirely on the League. All our agreements with our friends and with our allies are now concluded through Geneva, or culminate at Geneva . . . Any attack on the League would be an attack on our security . . . Our obligations are inscribed in the Covenant; France will not shirk them.

With great cleverness Laval underlined the significance for France of Hoare's speech. He noted that Britain's general commitment to the Covenant covered the League's security system in Europe, that Hoare's remarks provided, in Laval's interpretation, a guarantee for France's protection as well as for Ethiopia's.[81]

> Sir Samuel Hoare told us, the day before yesterday, that it was the desire of the United Kingdom to associate herself unreservedly with the system of collective security. He affirmed that this desire was, and would continue to be, the guiding principle of the United Kingdom's international policy. His words have nowhere been received with more satisfaction than in France. No country can better appreciate and determine the scope of such an engagement. The spirit of solidarity in the matter of responsibilities of all kinds, in all circumstances, and at all times and places, which is implied for the future by such a statement, marks an epoch in the history of the League. I rejoice at this, and so does my country, which understands the vital necessity of close collaboration with the United Kingdom in defence of peace and for the safeguarding of Europe.

Laval had no unkind words for Italy, and his comments left the door open for a negotiated settlement of the dispute. He stressed especially the importance to him of French-Italian friendship.

---

[80] Walters, *History of the League*, II, 649.

[81] Herriot claimed that Hoare's speech of the 11th, especially the closing sentences, was the British reply to Laval's inquiry of the 10th as to whether Britain would apply the Covenant to Europe. Herriot, *Jadis*, II, 580–1. In his speech of the 13th Laval adroitly gave it this interpretation, which stirred up a "hornet's nest" in Britain among those who did not want to see Britain committed to coming to France's aid in every future crisis on the continent. See Salvemini, *Prelude*, 299–301; Villari, *Storia diplomatica*, 134.

On January 7 last, M. Mussolini and I, acting not only in the interests of our two countries, but also in that of the peace of Europe, reached a final settlement of all our differences. Conscious of the immense value of the Franco-Italian friendship, I have left nothing undone to prevent any blow to the new policy happily established between France and Italy.

At Stresa, together with the delegates of the United Kingdom Government, we found the head of the Italian Government imbued with the same desire and the same will to serve the cause of peace. I know he is prepared to persevere in this collaboration. I need say no more to show how much importance I attach to the maintenance of such solidarity in the interests of both of the European community and of general peace. I have spared no effort at conciliation. We all desire to reach an understanding, and, in the supreme effort being made by the Council, I shall have the satisfaction of once more fulfilling my duty as the representative of a Member of the League and that dictated to me by friendship. I still hope that the Council may shortly be able to carry out its mission of conciliation. The task is doubtlessly a difficult one, but I still do not think it hopeless.[82]

Laval's speech was well received by the assembly. Hoare stopped Laval as he was leaving the rostrum to congratulate him. In company with the majority of members of the League, France now too was pledged to maintain the principles of the Covenant and the system of collective security. Herriot said Laval's words "could not be more categorical." [83]

The strength and apparent resolution of the public stands taken at the League by Britain on the 11th and France on the 13th, the ensuing acclamation, and the menacing movements of the British fleet gave rise to the greatest concern Italian officials had felt so far. For the first time the possibility of active British opposition seemed real, and the disastrous consequences such resistance would have on the Fascist regime caused no little dismay. Suvich told Aloisi on the 11th that Hoare's speech was not being taken tragically in Rome, but Aloisi found this hard to believe. Italian concern deepened after the widespread affirmative response to Britain's position and after Laval's speech on the 13th. The government recognized and appreciated that Laval was doing his best for Italy within the limitations. Laval told Aloisi on the 11th that his task was always "that of minimizing with regard

---

[82] League, *Official Journal, 1935*, Supplement No. 138, 65–6.
[83] Herriot, *Jadis*, II, 583–4.

to the British the measures which they want now to adopt against Italy, and in searching always to satisfy the greatest possible degree of [Italian] demands." But, he added, "France is not able to disassociate itself from England." [84] This is what worried the Italians, for it now appeared that the British were hardening their line into truly serious opposition. On the 14th Vinci telegraphed from Addis Ababa that the British minister had again assured the emperor that Britain would prevent any action on the part of Italy.[85]

The first public official Italian response to the new situation came on 15 September, with the communiqué of the previous day's meeting of the Council of Ministers. Mussolini told the ministers, the communiqué recorded, that Italian military preparations in east Africa were "proceeding with greater intensity." Implicitly referring to British activity in the Mediterranean, Mussolini said that Italian armed power on land, air, and sea would "reply to any threat whatsoever, from wherever it may come." Mussolini discounted the importance of the speeches of Hoare and Laval, implying that they were merely token sentiments resulting from the general positions held by Britain and France toward the League. For this reason, he said, discounting the effects, they were received with "greatest calm" in Italy. On the other hand, Laval's reaffirmation of France's friendship with Italy was noted with approval, and a complementary assurance was given to the French.

> The Council of Ministers . . . notes with satisfaction the cordial words which M. Laval devoted in his speech to the Franco-Italian agreements of January 1935, and to the friendship that they confirmed; a friendship that Italy intends to develop and strengthen, not only in the interests of the two countries but also in the interests of European collaboration which cannot be broken by a conflict of a colonial character or by the employment of sanctions which were never specified and never applied in the much graver preceding controversy between members of the League of Nations.

As for the future, Mussolini warned that Italy was re-examining the conditions under which it would continue its membership in the

---

[84] Aloisi, *Journal*, 303. Italians spoke of Laval's policy as that of a tightrope walker (*la politica del filo teso*) between Britain and Italy. Mussolini had been warned by Laval on the 11th concerning his forthcoming speech, but the Italian people were stunned to learn that France was standing by Britain. Fascist propaganda had led them to believe that France was friendly and would never side with the arch-enemy.

[85] Villari, *Storia diplomatica*, 140.

League.[86] In one matter the communiqué was definite: "The Council of Ministers, after having ascertained that around the Italo-Ethiopian dispute are gathering all the forces of foreign anti-Fascism, feels it its duty to reconfirm in the most explicit manner that the Italo-Ethiopian problem does not admit of a compromise solution after the immense efforts and sacrifices made by Italy and after the irrefutable documentation contained in the Italian memorandum presented at Geneva." [87] Aloisi in Geneva surmised in his diary on the 14th that this "display of intransigence" was put forward to extract the maximum concessions from the Committee of Five. It had also a domestic political value for Mussolini. But Aloisi correctly noted that it contributed to a hardening of the situation and that, since positions were becoming firmer all around, "the critical period" of the dispute was beginning.[88]

On 15 September Mussolini gave an interview to the correspondent of the Paris journal *Matin*, which published it on the 17th. The Duce had warnings for both Britain and France. For the British he elaborated on the danger to the peace.

> We have had for many years a sincere and faithful friendship with the British people, but today we find it monstrous that a nation which dominates the world refuses us a wretched piece of ground in the African sun. Many times and in every way I have given the assurance to Great Britain that her interests in Abyssinia would be scrupulously safeguarded. But the interests for which she is so strongly opposing us are other interests and she does not say so. This is not a game of poker . . . We shall go straight ahead. Never from our side will come any act of hostility against a European nation. But if an act of war is committed against us, well, there will be war. Italy does not desire it, but she is not afraid of it. Instead of the losses involved in a simple colonial policing action, such as England and France have carried on in their turn, does one want millions of dead? I refuse to understand those people who, because a house is burning, decide to set the entire city on fire.

[86] Mussolini could adapt this question of membership to various circumstances. On the 17th he told the American ambassador that Italy would not withdraw from the League. *U.S. Diplomatic Papers, 1935*, I, 758. From this period Mussolini increasingly sought to picture Italy's position as "Italia contra mundum," or vice versa, although he still held the door open to Italy's "Latin sister." The League was presented as the organ of an international anti-Fascist conspiracy bent on preventing Italians from having what was justly theirs.

[87] Mussolini, *Opera omnia*, XXVII, 128–36.

[88] Aloisi, *Journal*, 305

For the French Mussolini had one warning. If France adopted military sanctions against Italy, the entire map of Europe might have to be recast. "We shall see how much it will cost to drive [Italy] into the ranks of those who claim a new distribution, and, who knows, perhaps greater justice." Mussolini's threat was clear: military sanctions would result in increased Italian-German friendship and create fertile ground for an upheaval in Europe.[89]

On the 16th, in an interview with the *Morning Post* of London, Mussolini took another tack. He tried to impress upon the British that there was no need for them to take extreme measures. He reviewed Italian attempts to come to an agreement with Britain. The Duce asserted he had always remained receptive to a discussion of ways to settle harmoniously Italy's demands in Ethiopia without endangering either British interests or the peace of Europe. But to the Italian overture of 29 January and to Mussolini's leading qualifications at Stresa, which should have provided an opening for discussion, the British returned only evasive replies or ignored them altogether. In the face of this persistent refusal to discuss the matter, and despite Britain's latter-day opposition, Mussolini had decided that Italy must act alone. An army had been sent to east Africa; two billion lire had been spent on preparations to gain a colonial empire for Italy. These steps had not been taken lightly. Italy was exercising its rights in the same fashion that Britain and France did when they won their empires, empires they now coveted jealously. Even small powers, like Belgium, the Netherlands, and Portugal, had overseas colonies. "As long as Italy is without the colonies necessary to her, she must remain a source of agitation." But once Italy gained a good empire, "then Italy will become a conservative nation like all colonial powers, and England and France will have nothing to fear, because Italy will then join them, in the nature of things, in the preservation of peace." The interviewer asked if Italy would accept a mandate over Ethiopia. Mussolini did not reply. The correspondent asked if war with Ethiopia was therefore inevitable. That, Mussolini said, "depends on Ethiopia and the League of Nations."[90]

The League, with the cooperation of Britain and France, was doing all it could to forestall the outbreak of war. Following its formation

[89] Mussolini, *Opera omnia*, XXVII, 136–9.
[90] Mussolini, *Opera omnia*, XXVII, 139–41.

on 6 September, the council's Committee of Five worked diligently to create a formula that would satisfy Italy without destroying Ethiopia's independence. On 18 September the chairman, Madariaga, handed to the representatives of Italy and Ethiopia at Geneva the committee's results.

During the deliberations of the committee, various of its members held conversations with Aloisi. Avenol, Madariaga, Laval, Beck of Poland, and Aras of Turkey all sought to assure the Italian of their good intentions and to point out the difficulties of their situation. They tried to determine exactly the extent of Italy's demands. Aloisi could tell them nothing officially. Italy was not represented on the committee and did not recognize its jurisdiction. But Aloisi informally told his questioners that Italy would insist on the disarmament of Ethiopia and that the committee's report take account of the arguments of the Italian memorandum of 4 September, including the contention that Ethiopia was not a single, homogeneous state but instead territorially, politically, and ethnically divided between the subject peoples of the lowlands and the Amharic conquerors of the plateau. Within the committee, Beck and Laval, supported by Avenol, made some effort to stretch the draft proposals into a generous interpretation for Italy. Eden and Aras held to a more restrained line.[91]

The result of the committee's work was a plan of international assistance for Ethiopia, an "international mandate" Madariaga called it in private.[92] Ethiopia's independence and territorial integrity were assured by the League. Italy's foremost argument against Ethiopia was that of disorder, of continual aggression, on the frontiers. Administrative reforms were suggested by the new plan aimed at removing the causes of the problem and hence eliminating this excuse for war.

The plan visualized a series of reforms, drawn up and supervised by the council of the League, for public administration and for the development of the economic and financial affairs of the country. Of prime importance was the reorganization and supervision of the Ethiopian police force in order to:

[91] Aloisi, *Journal*, 302, 304–6; Villari, *Storia diplomatica*, 132–5; Avon, *Facing the Dictators*, 264.
[92] Dell, *The Geneva Racket*, 123; see also Templewood, *Nine Troubled Years*, 172. For the report of the Committee of Five to the Council, including the text of the proposed basis for settlement and the Italian and Ethiopian replies, see League, *Official Journal, 1935*, 1620–7.

1. Prohibit and suppress slavery.

2. Strictly regulate the carrying of arms by persons not belonging to the regular army or to the police forces.

3. Police centers in which Europeans reside.

4. Ensure security in agricultural areas where Europeans may be numerous and where local protection may not be sufficiently developed.

5. Maintain order in the frontier territories of the empire to safeguard neighboring territories against incursions, particularly those bent on traffic in slaves, looting, and smuggling.

A mission of foreign specialists was to go to Ethiopia to oversee the reform projects, and foreigners were to be allowed to participate in the country's economic development. The principal advisers would be "appointed by the Council of the League with the agreement of the Emperor." Lesser officials and advisory agents would be appointed by the emperor. At the end of five years, the entire plan would be reviewed by the council. In a postscript it was stated: "the representatives of France and the United Kingdom have informed the Committee of Five that, with a view to contributing to the peaceful settlement of the Italo-Ethiopian dispute, their respective Governments are ready to facilitate territorial adjustments between Italy and Ethiopia by offering Ethiopia, if necessary, certain sacrifices in the region of the Somaliland coast." France and Britain noted further that "without wishing to impair the existing regime in regard to the treatment of foreigners and in regard to external trade, [they] are prepared to recognize a special Italian interest in the economic development of Ethiopia. Consequently these Governments will look with favor on the conclusion of economic agreements between Italy and Ethiopia." The condition here was that the recognized interests of Britain and France be safeguarded.

The proposals of the Committee of Five reached Rome on 19 September. Within the Italian government there were arguments for and against acceptance. Those who argued for acceptance feared that to reject the League's plan would harden Britain's will to resist. Grandi, on 19 September, sent word from London that British opinion was rallying behind Hoare's apparent show of strength; if the prestige of Britain and the safety of its empire were challenged by an Italian invasion, the British might respond with force.[93] Aloisi warned Rome

---

[93] Guariglia, *Ricordi*, 264–5.

on the 19th, 20th, and 21st that the choice for Italy lay between peace and war with Britain. The British fleet was mobilizing against Italy. Half a loaf was better than none, and in Italy's present "dilemma" Aloisi urged his government to accept the League's proposals. To do so, he contended, "would reconcile the demands of the British for the defense of their empire and those of [Italian] expansion" while avoiding the incalculable risks of war.[94]

There were also arguments in favor of acceptance based on the belief that Italy stood to gain positive benefits. The proposals of the Committee of Five, while they did not meet all Italian demands, had, as Guariglia said, "vast possibility of development." Madariaga at a later date spoke of the plan as "an empty framework into which could be put what one wanted." This line of reasoning was pursued on the 20th in a telegram to Lessona from Riccardo Astuto, the representative of the ministry of colonies with the Italian delegation in Geneva. Astuto noted that the "sphere of competence" designated for the council with regard to the administrative control of Ethiopia "covered at least 90 percent of all possible state activity," including finance, economic development, and above all maintenance of order. If Italians were the principal advisers in these areas, in the course of time Italy would gain the upper hand over all the sources of power in Ethiopia and achieve a virtual protectorate. The process would be slow, but it would be accomplished without the risk or cost of war and eventually might become complete. At the end of five years, say, such a situation would be semipermanent, and Italy would have a *de facto* mandate.[95] Even the increased settlement of Italians in Ethiopia, colonization under the auspices of the League, seemed allowed in the plan.

The question was whether Italy would be allowed to secure this position, and there were some reasons for optimism. The entire scheme was created to give Italy satisfaction. Madariaga told Aloisi that Britain and France specifically recognized Italy's special interest in the economic development of Ethiopia. As Hoare described this concession, Britain and France declared their readiness "to transfer to

[94] Aloisi, *Journal*, 307–8; Guariglia, *Ricordi*, 265–7, 269.
[95] Guariglia, *Ricordi*, 266–8; Villari, *Storia diplomatica*, 146–7, 251. Astuto's estimate is interesting in the light of Eden's statement to an Italian official on the 22nd that, while it was impossible to give Italy complete control over Ethiopia, the amount of control Italy was to be allowed was a question of "percentage."

Italy any rights that we possessed under the 1906 Treaty apart from our respective interests in Lake Tsana and the Djibouti Railway." [96] As in the case of the Paris proposals of mid-August, more was settled behind the scenes than appeared in print. On 12 September Laval informed Aloisi that Britain and France had agreed to furnish Italy with the necessary capital for the construction of public works in the colonies. This might possibly be extended to Italian undertakings in Ethiopia. On the same day Avenol told Aloisi that he believed Britain and France would not participate in the program of assistance, leaving the field free for Italy. Both countries were eager to see Italy pacified and would go the limit in interpreting the proposals to Italy's benefit. Hoare thought that they "were nearer to a compromise at this moment than at any other," and he viewed the League's plan as providing "a wide opening for the recognition of Italian special interests." Laval, on the 19th, telegraphed to Rome insisting that Mussolini accept the committee's proposals.[97]

Nonetheless Mussolini found enough reason for rejection. He had no certainty that Italy would be allowed a predominant position in the commission of advisers sent out by the League. Far from the tripartite arrangement of the mid-August Paris plan, in which the practical control was clearly to be Italy's, the present program was carefully stipulated in a framework of widespread collective responsibility. It was the League, not Italy, which was undertaking to reform Ethiopia. Mussolini reviewed his criticisms to Laval in a letter of 25 December.[98] The project was "contrary to the interests of Italy because it meant that the League would take possession of Ethiopia to the exclusion in practice of Italy." Italy's exclusion was assured by the provision that the advisers were to be named either by or with the consent of the emperor. Mussolini contended that in fact the proposals were put forward in a spirit of ill will toward Italy. (Suvich told Aloisi in September that the government in Rome thought the British were trying to deceive them with the plan and were deliberately preventing any significant Italian participation.[99]) Moreover, Mussolini objected, the Ethiopian army was allowed to remain intact

[96] Templewood, *Nine Troubled Years*, 172.
[97] Aloisi, *Journal*, 304; Villari, *Storia diplomatica*, 133; Herriot, *Jadis*, II, 586–8. Templewood, *Nine Troubled Years*, 172. Vansittart was surprised at the comprehensive extent of the plan, which went further than he had anticipated. *The Mist Procession*, 531.
[98] Mussolini, *Opera omnia*, XXVII, 282–3; Lagardelle, *Mission à Rome*, 281–2.
[99] Aloisi, *Journal*, 307–8.

and under the aegis of the emperor.[100] No provision was made for the supervision or control of the fundamental lawmaking authority. The Ethiopian government still retained, under the League's guarantee, these basic sources of power and independence. Above all, the proposals of the Committee of Five did not satisfy Mussolini's own need, a dramatic victory of revenge. They did not give him the satisfaction and political advantage of capping his regime with this triumphant conquest of a new empire.

Even before any plan was tendered, Mussolini had made up his mind to reject it. On 17 September he told American Ambassador Breckinridge Long:

> It is too late to talk of compromise. It is too late to withdraw any of my plans for operations in East Africa. I will proceed. I will not interfere with anyone. I do not expect anyone to interfere with me. But I will not permit interference. I have one million men under arms in Italy . . . It is too late. My plans have developed too far. My soldiers down there could not be controlled. They would act on their own account, and what could I do with my army of a million?

At the end of their long talk, Long summed up the Duce's position.

> He does not want an "out." He does not want a way of escape. He proposes to go straight ahead, in spite of everybody and against anybody . . . He is adamant. He is irrevocably determined and serenely calm and is riding into the face of a storm which will either ruin him and bring disaster to his country, or raise him actually to that pedestal where he is sentimentally placed by his fanatic adherents.
>
> One of his first remarks when I had finished speaking was, "What would I do with my army of a million?" And what would he do? To disband them would create merely a million unemployed. To stop war orders at the factory would throw others out of work and increase the number of idle, add possibilities for local discontent, and foment trouble. He now has no unemployed, everybody is busy, and the entire country organized. Economic necessity is driving him forward. Hope of fame and riches in Africa is lighting the way. The grandeur of Empire and the dream of glory buoy him up. His determination to fight his way through the encirclement of economic poverty and his fear of facing the social, economic and political phases of a *volte-face* have lined the road of his advance.[101]

---

[100] On 11 September Hoare told Laval that Britain "could not contemplate support for any proposal which would give Italy military control over Abyssinia." Avon, *Facing the Dictators*, 262.

[101] *U.S. Diplomatic Papers, 1935*, I, 652, 752–61.

On the 18th, after an account of the committee's plan had been leaked to the press, Mussolini told a correspondent of the *Daily Mail* that the proposals were "not only unacceptable but derisory." "In the scheme of an international administration and gendarmerie it seems that Italy is not to be represented at all. The suggestion apparently is that all the 200,000 Italian troops in East Africa should be brought home and told they have been sent out there for an excursion trip. That certainly will not be done in any case." [102] On the 19th an official spokesman in Rome declared that the plan was "quite unacceptable to Italy." On the 21st the Council of Ministers discussed the matter and rejected the proposals as not offering "a minimum basis sufficient for conclusive realizations which would take final and effective account of the rights and interests of Italy." The Italian rejection, Aloisi noted, was "courteous but complete." [103] On 22 September, acting on instructions from Rome, Aloisi presented the official Italian reply to the chairman of the committee, Madariaga.

Aloisi's reply was a clever, if extraneous, piece of diplomatic argument. It gave as grounds for rejection the very reasons Italy was using to justify the proposed conquest. The Committee of Five, Aloisi stated, failed to take into account the Italian memorandum of 4 Sep-

---

[102] Toynbee, *Survey of International Affairs, 1935*, II, 195–6. This interview is not recorded in Mussolini, *Opera omnia*. The leak that prompted Mussolini's comments came out in the *Manchester Guardian* under the byline of its Geneva correspondent, Robert Dell. The premature disclosure was widely credited in Britain as the cause of Mussolini's rejection. Mussolini also said on the 18th: "The suggestion is apparently made that Italy's need for expansion in East Africa should be met by the cession to her of a couple of deserts — one of salt, the other of stone. They are the deserts of Danakil and Ogaden . . . It looks as if the Committee of the League thinks I am a collector of deserts. I got 110,000 square miles of Saharan desert from the French a little while ago. Do you know how many inhabitants there are in that desolate area? Sixty-two." There had been a discussion on the 16th within the Committee of Five on ceding Italy the non-Amharic territories to the south and east of the plateau. No cessions were offered in the final proposal.

[103] Toynbee, *Survey of International Affairs, 1935*, II, 196; Mussolini, *Opera omnia*, XXVII, 142; Aloisi, *Journal*, 307. With totally unwarranted optimism Aloisi thought that Italy's rejection shut the door to further discussions but did not lock it. This sentiment was shared by Hoare, who believed that the committee's proposals had received a sympathetic hearing in Rome and had been rejected only because Mussolini's self-esteem had been wounded by the leak to the press. Despite the latest Italian rejection, Hoare wrote, "we remained convinced that the Report was not only sound, but capable of becoming the framework of an eventual settlement" — but not before a war broke out. On the 16th he told the American chargé in London that he expected Mussolini to take aggressive action in early October. Templewood, *Nine Troubled Years*, 172; *U.S. Diplomatic Papers, 1935*, I, 649.

tember and hence had based its proposals on false premises. Ethiopia was not a civilized state capable of reform through advice alone. Indeed, it was in such uncivilized disorder that it was not fit to be a member of the League. As the Italian memorandum had asserted, the sending of foreign specialists to Ethiopia resulted in the past only in increasing the power of the country to threaten its neighbors, not in improving internal administration. So long as the emperor was allowed to retain control of his army, and the government thus allowed to keep the country's major source of power, other reforms could not succeed. The basic problem stemmed from the fact that there was not one Ethiopia but two. The governing Amharas of the central plateau might be reformed administratively, but the subject peoples living on the frontiers needed not to be reformed but to be rescued. "Those peoples must be safeguarded once and for all from the misgovernment of a country which is not, and never will be, able to discharge in respect of them the mission incumbent upon a State that contains peoples of different races." All that was lacking in Aloisi's comments was the conclusion that only Italy (for whom Ethiopia was a "special and most dangerous enemy") could solve the problems of Ethiopia, and that this could be achieved only by total conquest.[104]

The plan did not reach the Ethiopian capital until the morning of 22 September, and the government delivered its reply to Madariaga on the 23rd. Addis Ababa viewed the plan as an infringement on large areas of Ethiopia's freedom. Still, the government believed that Italy would reject its terms. Thinking therefore that the plan would come to nothing, and eager to have the onus of blame fall solely on Italy, the emperor decided to appear cooperative. He accepted the plan of the council's Committee of Five and declared that Ethiopia was "prepared to open negotiations immediately." Tecle Hawariate took care to base Ethiopia's acceptance on the condition that "the assistance and collaboration of the League must be collective and international." Italy must not be allowed a paramount position. The Ethiopian delegate lost no opportunity to emphasize that the committee's proposals were predicated upon the full maintenance of Ethiopia's sovereignty, independence, and territorial integrity.[105]

On 23 September a spokesman for the Ethiopian government told

---

[104] The approved summary of Aloisi's verbal comments is printed in League, *Official Journal, 1935*, 1624–5.

[105] Virgin, *Abyssinia*, 166; *U.S. Diplomatic Papers, 1935*, I, 657–8; League, *Official Journal, 1935*, 1625–7.

a correspondent of the *Daily Telegraph* that the only territories Ethiopia was willing to cede (and these in return for appropriate compensation from Britain and France) were the Ogaden and Aussa. Ethiopia would agree to the construction of an Italian railway across the country, but only on the same terms as those held by France on the Djibouti line. Italy's demand for the disarmament of Ethiopia was rejected completely.[106] Haile Selassie knew that the possibility of mediation was gone and that there was no further hope for a negotiated settlement.[107] All that remained was somehow to prepare for war.

[106] Toynbee, *Survey of International Affairs, 1935*, II, 197.
[107] Virgin, *Abyssinia*, 167; Steer, *Caesar in Abyssinia*, 124.

Chapter 13

In the Shadow of War

The concentration and disposition of the British navy in the Mediterranean, coming on the heels of Hoare's speech to the League on 11 September, was taken by the world at large as proof of Hoare's contention that the British government would "be second to none in its intention to fulfill, within the measure of its capacity, the obligations which the Covenant lays upon it." This interpretation of the naval movements was wrong, for the British did not send their fleet to the inland sea to support the League, to deter Mussolini from invading Ethiopia, or to punish him if he did. The fleet was sent as a unilateral action unrelated to collective security, with the purpose of protecting British military and imperial interests, and of forestalling any Italian attack on British bases or ships. It was only a coincidence that this action came at the time when world attention was focused on Hoare's speech. The fleet's movement was based on the Admiralty's own judgment of the precautionary military measures needed to protect specific British interests. The two acts were not at the time part of a single or coordinated policy and were, initially, causally unrelated.

Ever since the first of August the Admiralty had been concerned over the weakness of its forces in the Mediterranean. Up to that time the possibility of a war with Italy was not taken seriously, and no preparations had been made. Sir William Fisher, who relieved Sir Charles Forbes as commander-in-chief of the Mediterranean fleet in the autumn of 1935, had earlier prepared for the Admiralty a memorandum on the lack of defenses at Malta, Britain's primary base in the Mediterranean, but he had been rebuked for wasting time and told that Italy came only fifth or sixth on the list of potential enemies.[1]

[1] D. Kelly, *The Ruling Few* (London, 1952), 228.

Malta was devoid of antiaircraft guns and so almost defenseless, although it lay less than a hundred miles off Sicily. Not until July and August did the specter of war with Italy rise to haunt the British, and then not as a result of any British plan to apply military sanctions — for no such plan was ever decided upon — but because it was feared that Mussolini might, on his own initiative, undertake a "maddog act" against Malta and the British fleet. The violent campaign against Britain in the Italian press, and the state of excitement in support of war created by Fascist propaganda, was what frightened the government in London.

This concern was valid. There were important naval officers in Rome who advocated, in July, a war against the then virtually defenseless British.[2] Britain had only thirty-seven ships in the Mediterranean, not enough to offset the highly regarded Italian offensive capability.[3] The Italians might take command of the passage dividing the eastern and western halves of the sea which was Britain's link to the Far East. Italy's smaller naval units, such as their much-feared swift torpedo boat, could concentrate in the straits and there have a tactical advantage over the larger capital ships of Britain.[4] In early September the Italian navy was deployed in practice maneuvers. Battle cruisers together with submarines and bombers acted to close the Strait of Messina, and sixty submarines and some forty torpedo boats maneuvered off Libya. There was talk of closing Gibraltar if Britain should close the Suez Canal.[5] At least, it was feared in London, from airbases and

---

[2] Aloisi, *Journal*, 349.

[3] The Italian navy was comprised of 4 battleships totaling 91,800 tons, 1 aircraft carrier of 4,900 tons, 23 cruisers totaling 163,227 tons, 103 destroyers, scouts, and torpedo boats totaling 108,644 tons, and 62 submarines totaling 47,931 tons. League of Nations, *Armaments Year-Book, 1936* (Geneva, 1936), 546. According to these official statistics, the total Italian tonnage was 416,562 tons — though Mussolini told Chambrun at the end of August that the Italian fleet had not yet reached 300,000 tons. Mallet, *Laval*, I, 99. For discussions of Italy's offensive capability, see C. Barcia Trelles, *Puntos cardinales de la política internacional española* (Barcelona, 1939), 437–52; Macartney and Cremona, *Italy's Foreign and Colonial Policy*, 4; Popper, "Strategy and Diplomacy in the Mediterranean," 67–9.

[4] Dr. Oscar Parkes, editor of *Jane's Fighting Ships*, found the Fascist "suicide boats" more alarming than any other Italian weapon and claimed that the torpedo boats and planes would play a more vital part in any conflict than the bigger ships. *Time*, 30 September 1935. British apprehension was increased by the braggadocio of a group of young Italian naval aviators who styled themselves a suicide club and vowed to fall on British ships as "living torches." Mussolini put an end to these displays of bravado as uselessly provoking bitterness in Britain. Lagardelle, *Mission à Rome*, 157.

[5] *Le Temps*, 10 September 1935. As a matter of fact, the Italian naval command

submarine pens in Sicily, Tripoli, and Sardinia Italian bombers, tor-pedo planes, and submarines might effectively block the British passage-way between the two halves of the Mediterranean and cause substan-tial losses to the British fleet either on the open sea or within its ports.

It was this latter possibility that the Admiralty dreaded. In the face of German naval rearmament, the restlessness of the Japanese in the Far East, and above all the heavy and extended demands of Britain's imperial obligations, the naval staff, in its report to the government in early August, had warned against "diminishing or dissipating our limited strength." [6] Furthermore, it was stated that the fleet would not be able to confront Italy until reinforcements were sent out. Chatfield told Eden and Hoare "to move cautiously" during the tri-partite talks in Paris in mid-August, and we have seen that on the basis of the Admiralty's report no strong stand was taken against Italy at that conference.

The Admiralty's concern grew in the following weeks, fed by the attacks on Britain in the Italian press.[7] As a precautionary measure, on 27 August it was announced that the garrisons of Malta and Aden were being brought up to normal strength, for the first time since the end of the world war. On 29 August, the Mediterranean fleet moved from the vulnerable port of Malta to the east, where it would be safer and where, it was noted, it could better command the ap-proaches to the Suez Canal. But the Admiralty's problems remained. Britain had no other base in the Mediterranean except Alexandria, and Alexandria was not a good port. It lacked repair facilities and was a thousand miles from the nearest dockyard and naval base at Malta. Alexandria's narrow-mouthed harbor, busy with foreign mer-chantmen, was in constant danger of being blocked. If this bottleneck were stopped, the warships inside would be caught in a trap. Worst

---

had not received any orders on what action to take in case of a war with Britain. As late as February 1936 the recently named commander-in-chief of the Italian fleet, Admiral S. Denti di Piraino, was still in Rome awaiting instructions. Aloisi, *Journal,* 348-9.

[6] Templewood, *Nine Troubled Years,* 191.

[7] The official explanation for Britain's naval deployment was that it was "not intended to imply any aggressive intention on the part of His Majesty's Govern-ment . . . [but was] a natural consequence of the impression created by the violence of the campaign against the United Kingdom which had been conducted by the Italian press during the last few weeks." This was Drummond's comment to Mussolini on 20 September, published in a Foreign Office communiqué, 22 September 1935. Cited in Toynbee, *Survey of International Affairs, 1935,* II, 254. This explanation has been ridiculed by many historians, but it is close to the truth.

of all, the fleet lacked ammunition and the British could not take satisfactory precautions to protect it while it lay cooped up in the crowded harbor. Since the British did not have an effective air cover, the lack of antiaircraft ammunition was critical. The Mediterranean fleet, just returned from the jubilee review (an undertaking that dislocated the year's program of cruises and exercises) had only enough ammunition to shoot for fifteen minutes.[8] In addition, the fleet's antisubmarine detection devices, the Asdics, did not work in the eastern Mediterranean because of the varying densities of the levels of sea water caused by the discharge of fresh water from the mouths of the Nile.[9]

Stronger measures were needed than simple local redeployment. During the first two weeks of September reinforcements were sent out, and on the 14th a large part of the home fleet moved from the North Sea to the Mediterranean. In Lord Chatfield's words: "Every available ship was assembled up the Straits that conceivably could be spared from Home Waters and distant stations."[10] This decision, it appears from the meager evidence available, was made by the Admiralty without consultation with the Foreign Office. Luigi Villari quotes "an eminent British admiral" as saying that the move was an unexpected "act of panic" by the Admiralty, whose fears were exacerbated by a telegram to London from Drummond reporting that, according to "a noted Fascist," Italy intended to attack "the British empire in the Mediterranean, to bomb Malta, invade Egypt, etc." This telegram is no doubt the same one that influenced Hoare to act so cautiously in his meeting with Laval on the 10th. It read: "In their present mood, both Signor Mussolini and the Italian people are capable of committing suicide if this seems the only alternative to climbing

---

[8] So Admiral Sir Charles Forbes, the Mediterranean commander-in-chief, told the British consul at Alexandria. Kelly, *The Ruling Few*, 227; Vansittart, *The Mist Procession*, 523. See also Viscount Cunningham of Hyndhope, *A Sailor's Odyssey* (New York, 1951), 171; J. Scott and R. Hughes, *The Administration of War Production* (London, 1955), 62. This shortage of ammunition was particularly serious if the Spithead review in mid-July was any indication of the quality of marksmanship. At Spithead, in a display of firepower, 320 dead shells were fired at a target ship, and only 56 shells made a hit. *Time*, 29 July 1935.

[9] Cunningham, *A Sailor's Odyssey*, 176.

[10] Chatfield, *The Navy and Defence*, II, 89. See also the strong criticism of this deployment of scarce resources by Basil Collier, *The Defence of the United Kingdom* (London, 1957), 41, and *Barren Victories: Versailles to Suez* (New York, 1964), 108.

down. Rome today is full of rumors of an impending declaration of war on Great Britain." [11]

Supplemented with ships from other waters, the two British fleets, clustered at the exits of the Mediterranean, Gibraltar and Alexandria, with a smaller group at Aden, presented an overwhelming force. It included 144 ships of war, totaling 800,000 tons, Drummond told Mussolini on the 20th. In the case of a war with Italy the earlier fear of torpedo boats was offset by a battle plan which envisioned an immediate night-time sweep of the west coast of Italy, striking at the peninsula and its harbors directly and trapping the Italian fleet in a widespread net.[12]

Drummond's announcement on 20 September of Britain's extraordinary build-up did not surprise Mussolini, for he had been informed of it by his secret service. The Servizio Informazioni Militiari gave as its opinion that the only effective strength of the British navy lay in concentration and that Britain's battleships were particularly exposed to air attack, since all but two were unprotected against bombers.[13] Villari, writing in 1942 or 1943, "presumed" the Italian government knew that the British fleet "had munitions sufficient only for half an hour's combat." [14]

Mussolini did not want a war with Britain: at this time he had everything to lose and nothing to gain, despite his belief that the Italian air force was capable of inflicting great damage on the British fleet. But he was irrevocably committed to the success of the Ethiopian campaign and it is not impossible that, had the threat from Britain become critical, out of desperation he might have retaliated. If his

---

[11] Avon, *Facing the Dictators*, 262; Templewood, *Nine Troubled Years*, 167. Villari makes this comment: "This was not the first nor the last time that the incompetence and the inexact information of the British Ambassador to Rome (after the departure of Sir Ronald Graham) contributed to undermining the good relations between Italy and Great Britain and prepared the field for future conflict." Villari, *Storia diplomatica*, 142.

[12] Cunningham, *A Sailor's Odyssey*, 176. The shortage of ammunition was a limiting factor, but Rear-Admiral Cunningham insists that he and his fellow officers in the Mediterranean fleet "had no fear whatever of the result of an encounter with the Italian navy."

[13] Vailati, *Badoglio risponde*, 257. It is said that Mussolini greeted a stunned Drummond with the comment: "I note, Ambassador, that the British fleet has entered the Mediterranean. I note also that now it will be up to us whether it will be able to leave." D'Aroma, *Vent'anni insieme*, 234.

[14] Villari, *Storia diplomatica*, 141. This was *not* known to the diplomats in the Palazzo Chigi, however. Guariglia, *Ricordi*, 270.

Ethiopian policy were challenged, Mussolini might have chosen to engage the British rather than be forced to back down.[15] He was in an exceedingly difficult position. The very continuation of the Fascist regime and his dictatorship were on the line at this moment. He told Hubert de Lagardelle: "I am playing all for all. If I lose, all is lost."[16] Pope Pius said on 27 September: "Italy has put itself in a position now where it is not able to advance or retreat."[17] If Mussolini gave in and withdrew the Italian army from east Africa, he would stand accused of cowardice and ineffectiveness. Even more, if he took the issue to war, and the British did not give way, his regime might be destroyed by a revolution consequent on the effects of war — for, regardless of the state of Italy's coastal defenses, the peninsula was exceedingly vulnerable to a blockade. Italy received 86 percent of its imports by the Mediterranean: 13 percent came through the Dardenelles, 17 percent through the Suez Canal, and 70 percent through the Straits of Gibraltar, all entrances controlled by League powers. "What is England's way (via) is Italy's life (vita)," said Mussolini.[18]

Mussolini's first action after learning of the British decision to send out the home fleet was to make a countermove. A communiqué from the Grand Council issued on 15 September, following a meeting held the night before, read: "In view of the unrest manifested by certain native exiles of Cyrenaica, our defenses in Libya are now being reinforced."[19] The menace of a planned attack by these Libyan refugees in Egypt was totally fictitious. The two Italian divisions were being sent out solely as a provocation, "to menace Egypt," as Marshal Enrico Caviglia wrote in his diary on 15 September. It was simply Mussolini's response to Britain's naval maneuvers. On the 19th Mussolini sent a secret message to De Bono ordering him to prepare "a plan of attack from Eritrea toward the Sudan and from Somalia toward

---

[15] At this point Mussolini apparently saw a chance that the British would give way after an initial defeat. He thought at least that Italian air power could keep the British from concentrating their forces against the Italian mainland. See Aloisi, *Journal*, 249.

[16] Lagardelle, *Mission à Rome*, 160.

[17] Charles-Roux, *Huit ans au Vatican*, 139.

[18] H. Schonfield, *Italy and Suez* (London, n.d. [1940]), 24.

[19] Mussolini, *Opera omnia*, XXVII, 128. The exiles in question were the Senussi, a religious sect that had resisted Italian occupation of Libya until it was "pacified" in 1932, when the survivors fled to Egypt.

Kenya. If the English are napping, we must confront them wherever we touch on their border." [20]

Such actions could not fail to arouse the greatest concern in London, for they threatened the British empire in places that were politically unstable as well as strategically important. In Egypt, a vital link in Britain's imperial chain, Italian subversion was already under way in a widespread campaign to disseminate anti-British propaganda throughout the Arab-speaking world. This campaign was run by the Near East branch of the government-sponsored Stefani news agency, the Agence Egyptienne Orientale, and was centered in Cairo. Italian propaganda, created as part of Italy's preparation for the Ethiopian campaign, was designed to fan sparks of nationalism and to encourage a demand for British withdrawal from Egypt.[21] Of itself this propaganda had little success. Egyptians were sympathetic to Ethiopia, a fellow African nation threatened by European domination. The source of the Blue Nile was considered safer in Ethiopian hands than in Italy's. The nationalist demands arising at this time did not mean that all Egyptians wished to see Britain leave Egypt immediately. Italy had overt imperial ambitions toward lands on both sides of Egypt and, while the danger of an Italian act of aggression against Egypt did not seem imminent to many Egyptians, an expanding Italy might someday offer trouble. "A desire to blackmail Great Britain was almost equally balanced by a desire to be protected by Great Britain." [22]

On the other hand, Egyptian nationalists saw in the Italian-Ethiopian conflict a condition for which they had long been waiting. Britain's involvement in the tense international situation, and its increasing concern for the security of British interests in Egypt, gave Egyptian nationalists the opportunity to reopen the long unsettled issue of Anglo-Egyptian relations. This group feared that in the case of a conflict with Italy, as long as relations between Britain and Egypt were not regulated by treaty, Britain might again exploit Egypt in the same highhanded manner that had caused so much resentment

[20] Mussolini, *Opera omnia*, XXVII, 297; Villari, *Storia diplomatica*, 141; Caviglia, *Diario*, 132.

[21] H. Schonfield, *The Suez Canal in World Affairs* (New York, 1953), 81; Martelli, *Whose Sea?*, 169, 173. Some documents on this activity are found among the files of the Ministero di Coltura Popolare, on deposit at the National Archives, Washington, D.C., Microcopy No. T-586, Job (Series) No. 26, frames D 12471-83.

[22] J. Marlowe, *A History of Modern Egypt and Anglo-Egyptian Relations, 1880–1953* (New York, 1954), 294. See *Le Temps*, 30 July, 4 August, 15 September 1935.

during and after World War I. In the late summer of 1935 the British were again building up their military forces in Egypt, and the Egyptian government appeared willing to cooperate without first insisting upon concessions. This led the nationalist Wafd party to declare in early September that cooperation should be given only if it could occur "between equals." The Wafd demanded that Britain agree by treaty to the re-establishment of parliamentary government in Egypt, to the abolition of the postwar "capitulations," and to entry of Egypt into the League of Nations. Nationalist parties continued to press their demands during the last months of 1935 and into 1936. Italy's war against Ethiopia, and the difficulties this created for the British government, provided the context in which Egyptian nationalism reasserted itself and in which negotiations took place that led to the British-Egyptian treaty of alliance of August 1936.[23]

The British were troubled by the news of 15 September that two Italian divisions were being moved into Libya. It is true that there were comments in the Italian press in August noting that Ethiopia, once conquered, would become a beachhead for Italian expansion into Egypt,[24] and a great new coastal highway designed for military transport was being constructed in Libya from the border of Tunisia to the border of Egypt ("La Litoranea" was begun in February 1935 and completed in April 1936). But until Mussolini's action of 14 September the British never seriously considered the possibility that, in a Mediterranean conflict, Italy might try to invade Egypt directly. The army had taken no precautions during the summer months of 1935. Summer leaves went on freely, and officers were often absent from the Egyptian establishment. The only existing plan of defense "contemplated solely war with *Japan* and the danger of sabotage to the Suez Canal, the idea being that Japanese agents might sink a ship across the Canal to stop British ships from going to the Far East."[25] In the face of Italian military activity in Egypt, an entirely new plan of defense now had to be drawn up.[26]

---

[23] M. Zayid, *Egypt's Struggle for Independence* (Beirut, 1965), 147–61; Avon, *Facing the Dictators*, 390–4.

[24] See M. Vaussard, *De Pétrarque à Mussolini: Evolution du sentiment nationaliste italien* (Paris, 1961), 293–4.

[25] Statement of General George Weir, the British army's commanding officer in Egypt, to David Kelly. *The Ruling Few*, 228.

[26] On the Italian side, on 30 September the governor of Libya, Italo Balbo, submitted "somewhat late" to Mussolini two military plans, one for the invasion of lower Egypt and one for the invasion of the Sudan. The latter was given

In Rome the arrival of the home fleet in the Mediterranean, the threatening concentration of British forces, and the prospect of a conflict with Britain led to a grave crisis within the Fascist regime. It was a "critical internal malaise," for it appeared that Mussolini's African adventure, far from leading to easy victories and political successes, might have as its only consequence a major war with the strongest naval power in Europe, backed by the League of Nations. Such an outcome had not been expected and was viewed with alarm by many of Italy's most influential men. Criticism of Mussolini came to the surface as the responsibility for Italy's terrible danger was laid at his feet. The suspicion was that he might commit the Italian nation to a disastrous and unnecessary war for the sake of his own pride and ambition. On 24 September the American ambassador reported that "conservative quarters" in Rome thought that if Mussolini suffered a naval defeat, was prevented from military action in east Africa, or had to recall the Italian troops, he would be forced out of office. Speculation on the Duce's future was widespread, and there was even talk in Rome about finding a successor. The name of Pietro Badoglio, Italy's leading career soldier, was mentioned. On 27 September the Pope told the French ambassador that he was suffering from nightmares and insomnia in his worry over the situation that Mussolini had created.[27]

The apprehension among the Italian general staff was the most telling of all. These professionals, responsible for Italy's defense, knew the country was not prepared for a war with Britain. The Duce's senior military advisers did not share his optimism that the Italian air force could deal effectively with Britain's navy. Proof of their concern for the future of Italy is a letter sent to Mussolini by Marshal Badoglio, who composed it after consultation with Admirals Burzagli, Cantù,

the greater chance of success, and Mussolini rejected the other: "A land attack against Cyrenaica by British forces is out of the question because of the lack of objectives." This information comes from what is purported to be Mussolini's secret correspondence, seized in April 1945 by the partisans and published in the Milan journal *Corriere d'informazione* on 16 and 17 January 1946 (quoted in Salvemini, *Prelude*, 310–1). Another argument against an Italian invasion of Egypt was that it would give the British a clear right to close the Suez Canal to Italian warships and troops. Schonfield, *Italy and Suez*, 48. According to a report from the American consul in Naples on 2 October, in case of war with Britain the Italian general staff planned to scrap the invasion of Ethiopia, keep only a guard force on its border, and move the army in Eritrea to the Sudan and Khartoum by way of Kassala. Egypt would be invaded at once by the two divisions in Libya. U.S. Diplomatic Correspondence, 765.84/1520.

[27] Charles-Roux, *Huit ans au Vatican*, 138–9; U.S. Diplomatic Correspondence, 765.84/342.

and Cavagnari. It was a "serious and authoritative warning not to launch the country into a catastrophic adventure." Badoglio wrote:

> [The British fleet] represents a force which in comparison with ours can be defined only as having "crushing superiority." It is not possible to hold any hope of winning in a battle against such a force, given that our Navy has only a small vanguard. A war of ambush, for example in a narrow sea like the Adriatic, is not possible in a sea like the Mediterranean. In fact no more than 12 or 15 of our submarines would be able to find themselves in ambush in a sea which is over 2,000 miles long. The problems of surveillance render almost nonexistent the probability of striking any good blow. On the other hand, the English battle fleet, escorted by a powerful mass of destroyers, is able to ramble about the Mediterranean inflicting whatever damage it wants on our scarcely defended coast.
>
> Nor is it possible to use the aviation which Valle [commander of the Italian air force] has described as in a state of crisis, and of which all the old units — the majority of the air force — would be out of use after several days of hard use. It is true that new squadrons are being constructed. But it is necessary to prepare the equipment and crews, and it is not possible to have positive efficiency until after a long period of training . . .
>
> [War with Britain] would lead us to a true catastrophe. We have 200,000 men in east Africa, and our naval force in those seas is such that it would be put out of action at once by the preponderant force England is gathering south of the Canal.
>
> It is impossible seriously to menace Egypt by increasing our forces in Cyrenaica, [for the extent and nature of the terrain] make action by a massed force of metropolitan troops in that sector impossible.
>
> In a conflict [with Britain] everyone will be against us. We have, it is true, mobilized a great part of the army, and it is certain that sufficient preparation will weaken the desire for action by less friendly neighbors. But if the army's divisions give us security on the land frontier, they are useless in a conflict with England.
>
> After having studied the problem profoundly, and having weighed the French spirit on my recent trip,[28] I conclude that no one will move to our aid, limiting themselves with a platonic declaration of

---

[28] Badoglio attended the French military maneuvers at Rethel in the middle of September at the invitation of Gamelin. Both men were upset by the threatened break between France and Italy. Gamelin insisted that Italy should act only within the framework of the League and asked Badoglio: "What do you care about the external form if you get the substance of things? Form comes in its own time and models itself on realities. But if you violate the form you will collide with the League and then everything will become uncertain." Badoglio agreed. "But he was not the master, any more than I," wrote Gamelin. *Servir*, II, 172-3.

friendship, and that most would be fully satisfied at our grave predicament.

Your Excellency has done enormous good for our country. You have the honor of the world. Your Excellency must not interrupt these great activities. The country should not be exposed to a disaster, the outcome of which is problematical. Your Excellency must certainly be able to find, among your inexhaustible resources, of which you have given shining proof, an honorable solution to the present anguishing problem which avoids a war with England.

After all this is said, I want to assure Your Excellency that we soldiers will fulfill our duty to the utmost.[29]

Mussolini now had no recourse but to find a way to deal with this omnious turn of events, this "much-feared crisis" in his regime.[30]

Mussolini fully recognized the seriousness of his position. He realized that the superiority of the British force made a last resort of any Italian attack on a direct British interest, whether Egypt, Malta, or the fleet itself. War could come about, therefore, only if the British imposed military sanctions against Italy.

Mussolini did not believe that the British would take their support of the League as far as war. So he had to prove the ultimate harmlessness of the British threat, prove that he could prevent an Italian-British war without capitulating and giving up his plans for imperial glory. He knew that the British were as apprehensive as the members of his own government were over the possible outbreak of war. Mussolini therefore proposed that the British and the French should promise not to apply military sanctions. In return, Mussolini would agree to renounce "certain military precautions" Italy had taken in view of the threat posed by the British fleet. This was meant to be interpreted as an assurance that Italy would not attack British interests in the Mediterranean and would withdraw the two divisions sent to Libya. The best means to an Italian-British détente, he implied, would be for the British to withdraw their naval force. On 18 September Suvich made these proposals to Chambrun. On the 19th Aloisi repeated them to Laval at Geneva, with the request that Laval pass them on to the British. This

---

[29] The letter was published in F. Rossi, *Mussolini e lo stato maggiore* (Rome: Tipografia Regionale, 1951), 24–6, and reprinted in Guido Gigli's appendix to Vailati, *Badoglio risponde*, 258–60. Mussolini wrote later: "In September when the British fleet steamed into the Mediterranean, Marshal Badoglio was very upset and considered that the game was up." *Storia di un anno*, 191.

[30] Mussolini, *Storia di un anno*, 191–2.

Laval did on the 20th, also suggesting to Eden that Mussolini be assured that Britain was not contemplating closing the Suez Canal or imposing a blockade. Eden in turn passed on what he had heard to London.[31]

The British responded at once. On the 20th Drummond told Suvich that British reinforcements in the Mediterranean "were not intended to imply any aggressive intention" and were taken as a "purely precaution-ary" measure in view of the violent campaign directed against Britain in the Italian press. On the 23rd the British were more explicit in their protestations of good will. On that date Hoare, "speaking as an old friend of Italy," sent a personal message to Mussolini. The note, de-livered by Drummond, assured the Duce that Hoare never intended to humiliate Italy and that, indeed, the British foreign secretary desired to see Italy strong and prosperous. Britain's naval movements should not be interpreted as menacing Italy. Above all, Hoare denied that the British government had ever considered military sanctions against Italy or the closing of the Suez Canal. Although Britain was prepared to act as part of a collective undertaking, Drummond said, any action would be limited to economic sanctions. Vansittart echoed these assurances to Grandi on the 27th.[32]

Mussolini's diplomacy had succeeded: domestic opposition faded with this dispelling of the fear that Britain would act in open resistance to Italy. Although the Italian divisions were not immediately with-drawn from Libya,[33] there was a significant relaxation of Italian-British tension. In Rome the much-feared crisis passed, and everyone breathed easier. Mussolini had proved his point that the British did not want to fight Italy to uphold the principles of the League.

If Britain was not prepared to enforce the Covenant, then, the only reason for the maintenance of a concentrated naval force in the Mediter-ranean, apart from the effect such a display might have on the British electorate, was the protection of British interests in the area. It was this reason that had inspired the movements of the fleets in the first place. Mussolini now worked to allay this worry, to cause the British to withdraw their still potentially dangerous force. In the communiqué

[31] Avon, *Facing the Dictators*, 265; Aloisi, *Journal*, 306–7.

[32] Villari, *Storia diplomatica*, 142–4; Toynbee, *Survey of International Affairs, 1935*, II, 254–5; Avon, *Facing the Dictators*, 267.

[33] Hoare noted this fact to Grandi on 30 September. He told the Italian am-bassador that when Italy withdrew its troops then Britain would re-examine its decision to send military reinforcements to Egypt. Vallari, *Storia diplomatica*, 145–6.

of the Council of Ministers meeting held on 28 September, the Italian government took note of the "cordial terms" of Hoare's recent message to the Duce and affirmed once again, as it had at Balzano a month before,

> that the policy of Italy has not immediate or remote aims which could be injurious to the interests of Great Britain. The British government has been informed, from 29 January to today, in a most legal manner, of the colonial objectives of Italian policy and of the interests which guide it, interests recognized in bilateral agreements with Great Britain itself. The British people ought to know . . . that the Italian government has told the British government of its constant readiness to negotiate further agreements that would put at rest all concern for legitimate British interests in east Africa. The Fascist government solemnly declares that it will avoid anything that might cause the Italian-Ethiopian conflict to spread to a larger terrain.[34]

The exchange between Italy and Britain in the last half of September gave satisfaction to both sides. For the British government, its "combination of pressure and friendly message" seemed to awake Mussolini to the danger of action against any British interest south of Sicily.[35] By assuring Mussolini that Britain was not preparing for military sanctions, that it would not act alone against Italy, the British government thought to reduce the danger of an attack on Malta and the fleet. Mussolini, on his part, could now proceed with his war, secure at home and with the virtual certainty that Britain, and hence the League, would not stop him. The crisis in his regime was over.

For all this, however, Mussolini could not afford to give up the political advantage that the threat of a hostile Britain gave him among the Italian people. His propaganda machine continued to encourage the idea of *Italia contra mundum*, of a selfish bullying Britain unjustifiably opposing Italy's legitimate national aims. The fact of the matter was that it was only the fear and hatred of Britain, the sense of facing a national danger, that brought Mussolini widespread popular support in the Italian-Ethiopian conflict.

A second diplomatic exchange was carried on during the last half of September, between the British and the French. The question was one

---

[34] Mussolini, *Opera omnia*, XXVII, 153.
[35] Hoare's words to Eden on 24 September. Avon, *Facing the Dictators*, 269. Hoare held onto the hope that the "somewhat altered atmosphere" was indicative of Mussolini's increased willingness to come to a negotiated settlement of the dispute.

of mutual assistance. On 10 September Laval formally asked the British government to what degree it would guarantee France of an immediate and effective application of the sanctions under article 16 of the Covenant, in the event of a treaty violation or an act of unprovoked aggression in Europe. In his inquiry Laval "referred in particular to the eventuality of a resort to force in Europe on the part of some European state, whether or not that state might be a member of the League of Nations." France's concern was obvious and reasonable. Before committing themselves to support the Covenant against Italy, the French needed to be certain that Britain, unilaterally or through the League, would support them against Germany; if, in other words, the British would live up to their obligations under the Treaty of Locarno. The question of whether, and under what conditions, the British were prepared to enforce the Covenant was kept in the air by Hoare's speech of the 11th, following his agreement with Laval on the day before. In his speech to the assembly on the 13th, Laval had made it clear that France was seeking a British guarantee.

On 17 and 24 September, Hoare gave preliminary oral replies to the French ambassador, Charles Corbin. A formal written answer was sent to Paris on the 26th. Britain's response disappointed and troubled the French. Hoare referred them to the general declarations of his speech before the League assembly. He repeated that Britain's fidelity to the Covenant was part of the established policy of the country. Yet to these broad assertions he added several specific, and disturbing, reservations. Hoare said that, though his general statements reflected the policy of the present ministry, such declarations could not be considered binding on future British governments. Above all, Hoare drew a "very clear" distinction between the applicability of sanctions in the case of armed aggression, on the one hand, and in the case of a treaty violation on the other. He noted that article 16 of the Covenant applied only to "a positive act of unprovoked aggression," and not merely to a failure to fulfill a treaty obligation. Of the latter Hoare stated that "elasticity is a part of security, and . . . the World is not static." "Further, in the case of a resort to force, it is clear that there may be degrees of culpability and degrees of aggression, and that consequently, in cases where Article 16 applies, the nature of the action appropriate to be taken under it may vary according to the circumstances of each particular case."

The French were distressed by, in Flandin's words, the "disquieting and renewed" emphasis Hoare placed on this interpretation of Britain's obligations. To France, whose stake in the matter was its national security and the stability of Europe, it appeared that the foreign secretary was repeating all the old evasions by which Britain had denied its responsibilities to Europe and had tried to camouflage its isolationism. The French drew the conclusion that not only would Britain not act alone, or take the lead in enforcing the full punitive machinery of the League, in Ethiopia's behalf, but also that the British government was serving notice that it would consider Germany's failure to hold to the stipulations of the Locarno agreement insufficient grounds for applying sanctions. The French decided they could count on no help from across the Channel. Since Hoare's attitude condemned the League to ineffectiveness and implied a withdrawal of Britain's protection as defined in the Treaty of Locarno, the French saw no reason to alienate their Italian friend over Ethiopia.

Before Hoare's response of the 26th, the British in their turn had posed a question to the French. Whereas it was agreed in London that no more than limited economic sanctions would be imposed on Italy for a violation of the Covenant, Drummond warned from Rome that Mussolini might regard a refusal by Britain and the smaller powers to accept Italian imports as a cause for war; Italy would not act hostilely, however, if France was also involved. Eager not to leave the French out of any dangerous situation, hoping for their support if trouble came, and interested in what France might do to prevent its arrival, Hoare on 24 September asked Corbin if France would come to Britain's aid, as provided by paragraph 3 of article 16 of the Covenant, if the British fleet or British bases and possessions were attacked by Italy while Britain was preparing to apply sanctions required under the same article 16.[36] Hoare's question specifically envisioned a hostile act *before* sanctions were applied. Laval delayed his reply until 5 October. He then affirmed France's intention of standing behind Britain and coming to its aid, but so cleverly did Laval word this reply that, to accept it,

---

[36] Paragraph 3 of article 16 read: "The Members of the League agree, further, that they will mutually support one another in the financial and economic measures which are taken under this Article, in order to minimize the loss and inconvenience resulting from the above measures, and that they will mutually support one another in resisting any special measures aimed at one of their number by the covenant-breaking State."

the British government would have to bind itself to the very action it had tried to evade in its own reply of the 26th.[37]

The final days of September thus passed in the dark shadow of war. The last attempt to find a negotiated settlement prior to the outbreak of war ended on the 22nd when Italy rejected the conciliatory proposals of the League's Committee of Five. On the 23rd Ethiopia declared its willingness to abide by the committee's suggestions, but the emperor had made this gesture believing that chances for negotiation were already dead. "The final effort of the League of Nations to preserve peace by discussion between the parties," as the emperor called it on the 23rd, ended in failure.[38] On the 24th the committee drew up an account of its work and Madariaga submitted it without comment to a meeting of the council on the 26th. The council received the report with the knowledge that the Italian invasion was about to begin. Despite this, there was still a degree of optimism at the League. Ignorant of the Hoare-Laval agreement of the 10th, ignorant of Britain's assurances to Rome, the more hopeful members of the League had before them Hoare's speech of the 11th and expected strong leadership from Britain, as proved, it seemed, by the British naval concentration in the Mediterranean.

Eden telegraphed from Geneva to London on the 24th: "There is no sign of any weakening in the overwhelming support for the Covenant which was a feature of the debate in the Assembly, nor any sign that members of the League would be unwilling to shoulder their obligations should the situation demand it." [39] But the British government did not intend to assume the leadership expected of it, or to make use of the enthusiasm Hoare's speech had aroused. Hoare, whose own health was far from good, continued with the policy of calculated and wistful inaction.[40] Members of the League, notably the British Domin-

---

[37] For discussions of these British and French exchanges, see Toynbee, *Survey of International Affairs, 1935*, II, 258–62; Flandin, *Politique française*, 182–3; Avon, *Facing the Dictators*, 268–9; Herriot, *Jadis*, II, 590–1; Mallet, *Laval*, I, 107, and Flandin's testimony in Assemblée Nationale, 1947 session, *Rapport . . . 1933 à 1945*, I, 148–9.

[38] Steer, *Caesar in Abyssinia*, 124.

[39] Avon, *Facing the Dictators*, 268.

[40] On 24 September Leopold S. Amery talked with Hoare and recorded in his diary: "His whole line was that it was far too late to change the policy when he took office, that we have got to see through the attempt to make the Covenant work, that we might get out by the failure of others to support us or, alternatively, that Mussolini might find his difficulties too great for him, and under

ions, looked to Eden for a strong stand on the 26th, but this was ruled out. On the night of the 24th, Hoare cabled Eden the following instructions:

> I trust that you will not allow any haste on the Council in regard to the discussion of sanctions. The feeling of the Government is that, though the efforts of the Committee of Five have proved unavailing and they have rightly remitted the matter to the Council, the latter should make a further effort to find a solution, and that it might not yet prove hopeless in view of the somewhat altered atmosphere produced at Rome by the combination of pressure and friendly message.[41]

The British government was ordering Eden to "allow" the council to go no further in asserting its authority than a strict methodical observance of the procedures of the Covenant. On the 26th the council accepted Madariaga's account of the failure of the Committee of Five to settle the conflict. The president of the council, Ruiz Guiñazú, said that the process of conciliation under article 15, the article governing the council's actions ever since the Covenant was applied to the conflict on 4 September, could still not be considered finished until a final report was submitted and adopted. He proposed as the next step that a new committee be established to draft this report, as stipulated in paragraph 4 of article 15.[42] The council's new agent was called the Committee of Thirteen and was composed of all the states represented on the council except Italy. Though the Committee of Five was to survive "for the purpose of judging, should any suggestions be made to it, whether

---

economic pressure come to reasonable terms soon after his war started, if not before. He refused to admit that ineffective economic sanctions must create the demand for effective ones and that these would bring us to the verge of war." A few days later Amery saw a "frankly cynical" Neville Chamberlain: "His whole view, like [Hoare's], was that we were bound to try out the League of Nations (in which he does not himself believe very much) for political reasons at home, and that there was no question of our going beyond the mildest of economic sanctions such as an embargo on the purchase of Italian goods or the sale of munitions to Italy. When I pointed out that this, unless Mussolini was stopped, meant open failure in the eyes of the world, he tried to ride off with the hope that Mussolini might find these measures embarrassing and was getting into hopeless financial difficulties anyway. If things became too serious the French would run out first, and we could show that we had done our best." Amery, My Political Life, III, 174.

[41] Avon, Facing the Dictators, 269.

[42] This paragraph read: "If the dispute is not thus settled, the Council either unanimously or by a majority vote shall make and publish a report containing a statement of the facts of the dispute and the recommendations which are deemed just and proper in regard thereto."

they might justify a further attempt at conciliation," it was universally realized that the establishment of the Committee of Thirteen was the first constitutional step toward the application of sanctions should an act of aggression occur.[43]

In Ethiopia the last week of September was the feast of Maskal. During this celebration of the end of the rains and the start of planting, the emperor appears twice before the people. The first occasion, the King's Maskal, is a religious ceremony. The second Maskal is the occasion for great popular festivities, for feasts, parades, and above all for the ostentatious display of martial skills. In this week in 1935 thousands upon thousands of soldiers poured into Addis Ababa to shout threats and deprecations againt Italy, to pledge their allegiance to the emperor, to cheer the memory of Aduwa and affirm the belief that victory over Italy could easily be won again.

Mock heroics might buoy the spirits of the army. The emperor, however, knew the true seriousness of the crisis. On the 23rd, the day of the King's Maskal, he learned of Italy's rejection of the proposals of the Committee of Five. Haile Selassie saw that there was no further hope for conciliation. That same day the emperor called George Steer of *The Times* to his palace for an interview. Haile Selassie said he had two special appeals to make to Great Britain. One was that Britain raise the embargo on the shipment of arms to Ethiopia; the other was that the British government grant Ethiopia a munitions loan, to be guaranteed by fixed sources of his government's income. Arms and a loan — Ethiopia's only chance for self-protection. Haile Selassie said of the loan that he could think of "no step of more advantage to peace." [44]

On the 25th Ethiopia sent a telegram to the council of the League. There was no where else to turn, and the emperor had a faith in the power of diplomacy that obstinately transcended past and present disappointments. To the council the emperor announced, as an earnest of Ethiopia's pacific intentions, that "several months ago we gave orders to our troops along our frontiers to withdraw thirty kilometres from the frontier and there to avoid any incidents that might serve the Italians as a pretext for aggression." He actually had given orders for this withdrawal as early as the spring of 1935.[45] The action had an

[43] League, *Official Journal, 1935*, 1201–2, 1605–19; Walters, *History of the League*, II, 652; Aloisi, *Journal*, 308. The Committee of Thirteen reported on 5 October 1935, at a time when the situation was radically changed.

[44] Steer, *Caesar in Abyssinia*, 124–7.

[45] League, *Official Journal, 1935*, 1602; Virgin, *Abyssinia*, 166.

earlier parallel in the French retreat of ten kilometers on 30 July 1914 along the whole of the German border, and it was undertaken for the same reason. "The act of withdrawal," writes Barbara Tuchmann about the French move, "done at the very portals of invasion, was a calculated military risk deliberately taken for its political effect."[46]

In his telegram of the 25th the emperor also reminded the council of his previous request "for the despatch of impartial observers to establish the facts in regard to any aggression or other incident that might occur in order to fix the responsibility therefor." The Committee of Thirteen took this request under consideration to see "whether the actual circumstances would permit [the observers] to discharge their mission," and a subcommittee was set up. The British gave no help. London advised Eden "not to be too cordial towards the proposal and that in any event there should be no British observers." The reason given was an unwillingness to provoke Mussolini. On 2 October the subcommittee reported that to send out a team of observers would involve enormous difficulties.[47]

On 26 September the emperor received a report from his delegation at Geneva. It stated that opinion in Geneva was unanimous: war was inevitable. The emperor replied that he would order a general mobilization if the delegation thought this opinion correct. The delegation replied that it considered war to be not only certain but imminent, and this message reached Addis Ababa on the 28th.[48] That night the emperor sent another telegram to the president of the council of the League. He spoke of Ethiopia's desire for peace and the country's readiness to continue its collaboration with the council. He drew attention to the seriousness of the Italian threat. In its abbreviated fashion the emperor's telegram continued:

> Earnestly beg Council to take as soon as possible all precautions against Italian aggression since circumstances have become such that we should fail in our duty if we delayed any longer the general mobilization necessary to ensure defense our country. Our con-

[46] B. Tuchmann, *The Guns of August* (New York, 1962), 84–5. The emperor's announcement perplexed Rome. On the 28th the ministry of colonies asked De Bono if the emperor's assertion were true. De Bono replied it was not. De Bono, *Anno XIIII*, 215–6. The communiqué of the Council of Ministers meeting on the night of the 28th called the withdrawal a disguise for strategic preparation. Mussolini, *Opera omnia*, XXVII, 352.

[47] League, *Official Journal, 1935*, 1602; Avon, *Facing the Dictators*, 270; Villari, *Storia diplomatica*, 148.

[48] Steer, *Caesar in Abyssinia*, 129–30.

templated mobilization will not affect our previous orders to keep our troops at a distance from the frontier and we confirm our resolution to co-operate closely with the League of Nations in all circumstances.[49]

On the night of 28 September the emperor signed the mobilization decree, but he did not issue it then. Haile Selassie did not order a general mobilization until five hours after the Italians had bombed Aduwa.[50]

In Italy's east African colonies, final preparations for the attack were concluded. The concentration of supplies in Eritrea left General Graziani poorly prepared in Italian Somaliland. The southern front lacked men, materials, and munitions. Graziani told DeBono that, as a consequence, he would have to restrict his sphere of operations to a limited area in the Ogaden.[51] DeBono pointed this fact out to Mussolini, noting that in view of the distance between the two fronts synchronized action was both impossible and unnecessary. De Bono did not mind having the limelight. Mussolini replied on the 28th, telling De Bono to pick the day when action would begin. He ordered Graziani to remain absolutely on the defensive: the thrust would all be in the north, an avenging drive by De Bono into the Ethiopian heartland. DeBono chose 5 October as the date for the invasion.[52] On the 29th he asked the Duce if a declaration of war was to be made. Mussolini replied on the same day: "No declaration of war in the first instance. In the face of the general mobilization which the Negus has already officially announced in Geneva it is absolutely necessary to end any delay. I order you to begin advance early on the 3rd, I say 3rd October." On the 30th Mussolini

[49] League, *Official Journal, 1935,* 1603.

[50] Steer, *Caesar in Abyssinia,* 130. In the middle of September, the powerful old war minister, Ras Mulugeta, increasingly impatient with the emperor's diplomatic caution and his reliance on the League and foreign advisers, issued his own order for mobilization. This order was printed and left on the desks of the emperor's foreign advisers. Colson protested at once, and Haile Selassie, who had not known of Mulugeta's order, commanded its suppression. *Ibid.,* 123.

[51] De Bono, *Anno XIIII,* 218–9; Graziani, *Il Fronte sud,* 144, 147–8, 161. Steer, after a tour of Harar and the Ogaden, had the opposite opinion, of which he informed the emperor. Steer did not think the small Ethiopian forces in these areas could hold out against what seemed to him an overwhelming Italian force in Italian Somaliland. Steer, *Caesar in Abyssinia,* 120–1. See also Whitaker, *And Fear Came,* 29.

[52] De Bono, concerned about the poor communications between Massawa and the high plateau, wanted to postpone hostilities for as long as possible. Mussolini was advised to begin operations quickly, to remedy the pessimism and bad morale among the troops, and he pressed for immediate action. Lessona, *Memorie,* 179.

sent a further order to DeBono: "In view of the approaching events the strictest orders should be given by you personally to all the commanders: Inexorable decision against the armed forces, respect and humanity for the unarmed defenseless population." [53]

In Rome the diplomats and propagandists of the Fascist government prepared the general arguments to justify Italy's war of invasion. Their basic theme was "continued aggression," as presented in the Italian memorandum of 4 September. To this was now added a specific reason for action, the sham contention that the emperor had ordered a general mobilization of the Ethiopian army and that this presented a direct and immediate threat to Italy.[54] The emperor's telegram to the League of 28 September claiming that his army had withdrawn from the frontiers embarrassed Italy, for it undermined the argument of continued aggression. The Ethiopian action was emphatically denied in *Il Popolo d'Italia* on 1 October. On 2 October the whole range of Italian justifications was developed in an article in the same newspaper, together with the threat that Italy might leave the League if sanctions were imposed. On 3 October Suvich cabled the secretary-general of the League protesting the "warlike and aggressive spirit" in Ethiopia which, Italy falsely contended, "found its latest expression" in an imperial order for general mobilization. As a result of this so-called threat, the Italian government "has found itself obliged to authorize the High Command in Eritrea to take the necessary measures of defence." [55] On 2 October, in an effort to pacify Britain and France, Mussolini sent a message to Hoare proposing the simultaneous and reciprocal demobilization of their Mediterranean forces. Mussolini added that there remained open the possibility of an Italian-British agreement, "not only with regard to British interests in Africa, but also with regard to a solution of the Italian-Ethiopian conflict satisfactory to Italy." Cerruti was instructed to relay this message to Laval, adding that Italy would meet the public reaction against it at Geneva with calm and that Italy desired to remain in the League as long as its dignity was not harmed.[56] Aloisi was struck by Mussolini's statement on the 1st that, if he could

[53] Mussolini, *Opera omnia*, XXVII, 297–8; De Bono, *Anno XIIII*, 218–9.
[54] Guariglia, *Ricordi*, 272; Aloisi, *Journal*, 310–1.
[55] League, *Official Journal*, *1935*, 1603. Suvich based his claim on the emperor's telegram of 28 September, but this was a deliberate Italian misreading of the text. The emperor spoke there only of "contemplated mobilization."
[56] Guariglia, *Ricordi*, 273.

be guaranteed possession of the "great vassal regions" of Ethiopia, the conflict could be settled.[57]

Italy's propaganda arguments were blunted on 2 October by the revelation that on the day before an Italian motor column had penetrated into Ethiopian territory south of Mount Mussa Ali in the province of Aussa. This fact was discovered by French pilots on patrol from Djibouti, and the French ambassador in Addis Ababa informed the emperor.[58] Again, and for the last time before the invasion, Haile Selassie turned to the League. In a telegram to the secretary-general for transmission to the League members, the emperor reported this violation of Ethiopia's frontier. He added: "Proximity to sea in this region and its easy access through territory of French Somaliland make it possible for Council either to send observers or to obtain confirmation of this violation of Ethiopian territory through Government of French Somaliland." This complaint, quickly denied by Italy, was soon overtaken by greater events.[59]

On the morning of 2 October, Mussolini called on the king at the Quirinale palace. According to Mussolini's later account, Victor Emmanuel told him that he was well aware of the difficulties of the enterprise, and that he had noted the fears of "many generals and admirals." The king continued: "Well then, now that the British are in our sea and believe to have us frightened, so an old king says to you: 'Duce, go ahead: I am behind you . . . Forward, I say to you!' " [60]

At 3:30 P.M. on this day, the sound of sirens, bells, and guns announced throughout Italy the coming of that masterpiece of Fascist propaganda, the "national mobilization of the forces of the realm," planned since 10 September. At the signal Fascist party members donned their uniforms and dashed to their meeting places.[61] At 5:15 a second signal was sounded, announcing that all the people of Italy

---

[57] Aloisi, *Journal*, 310.

[58] Steer, *Caesar in Abyssinia*, 130–1, gives a good account of this episode.

[59] League, *Official Journal, 1935*, 1603, 1604.

[60] D'Aroma, *Vent'anni insieme*, 235. Another who expressed his support to Mussolini at this time, and who offered his services, was V. E. Orlando, former leader of the liberal opposition. Chabod, *A History of Italian Fascism*, 78, wrote: "It was a great mistake on the part of the British to make popular a war which otherwise would have been anything but that."

[61] For the role of the Fascist Party in stirring up excitement and in assuring the success of the rallies, see D. Germino, *The Italian Fascist Party in Power* (Minneapolis, 1959), 23–5. For a description of this vast national assembly, see *Il Popolo d'Italia*, 3 October 1935, reprinted with comments from other journals in Mussolini, *Opera omnia*, XXVII, 353–60.

should gather in the squares of their towns. At 6:30 the Duce appeared on his balcony overlooking a cheering crowd packed into the Piazza Venezia. His words were broadcast by loudspeakers to every corner of the peninsula. Mussolini had come to announce the outbreak of war and to appeal for the united support of the Italian people.

Blackshirts of the revolution! Men and women of all Italy! Italians throughout the world, across the mountains and across the seas! Listen!

A solemn hour is about to strike in the history of the Fatherland. Twenty million Italians at this moment gathered in the squares throughout the whole of Italy. It is the most gigantic demonstration in the history of mankind. Twenty million persons: a single heart, a single will, a single decision. This manifestation is to demonstrate that the identity between Italy and Fascism is perfect, absolute and unchangeable . . .

For many months the wheel of destiny, under the impulse of our calm determination, has been moving towards its goal. In these last hours the rhythm has become more swift and cannot now be arrested. Not only is an army marching towards its objectives, but forty million Italians are marching in unison with this army, all united because there is an attempt to commit against them the blackest of all injustices, to rob them of a place in the sun. [After all the Italian sacrifices in the World War] when it came to sitting around the table of the mean peace, to us were left only the crumbs from the sumptuous colonial booty of others. For twenty years we have been patient while around us tightened ever more rigidly the ring which sought to suffocate our overflowing vitality. With Ethiopia we have been patient for forty years. Now, enough!

At the League of Nations, instead of recognizing the just rights of Italy, they dare speak of sanctions. Now, until there is proof to the contrary, I refuse to believe that the true people of France can associate themselves with sanctions against Italy . . . Until there is proof to the contrary, I refuse to believe that the true people of Great Britain want to spill blood and push Europe on the road to catastrophe in order to defend an African country universally stamped as unworthy of taking its place with civilized peoples.

At the same time, we must not pretend not to know the eventualities of tomorrow. Against sanctions of an economic character we will oppose our discipline, our sobriety, and our spirit of sacrifice.

To military sanctions we will respond with military measures.

To acts of war we will respond with acts of war.

Let no one think to deflect us without first having had a hard fight. A people who are proud of their name cannot adopt a different language or a different attitude. But let it be said again in the most categorical manner — as a sacred pledge which I take at this moment before all Italians — we will do everything possible to prevent this colonial conflict from assuming the character and bearing of a European conflict.[62]

At 5:00 on the morning of 3 October 1935, with no declaration of war, vanguards of three of De Bono's army corps crossed the Ethiopian frontier, and Italian planes bombed Aduwa and Adigrat. The Italian-Ethiopian war had begun.

The response of the League was swift and uncompromising. Within a week Italy was declared an aggressor state, declared to have violated its obligations under the Covenant and thereby "to have committed an act of war against all other Members of the League." Involved in accepting this verdict was the legal duty of each member state to apply the sanctions against Italy needed to restore the peace. The testing time of the League had come.

There was, among most of the lesser states of the League, a genuine willingness to cooperate in upholding the Covenant, if a strong lead were given them by Britain and France. Although important countries such as the United States, Germany, and Japan were outside the League, 70 percent of Italy's foreign trade was with League members. Supporters of the League thought there was a chance that a promptly applied economic boycott of Italy by League members alone, if Ethiopia could hold out until these sanctions took effect, might be enough to force Italy to give up the war. De Bono's offensive had come to a halt after its initial thrust and did not start up again despite Mussolini's insistent commands. In mid-November the Fascist functionary was replaced by the professional soldier Badoglio, but Badoglio could not begin his advance until January 1936. If during this time sanctions were applied firmly, the pressure might be enough to cause Italy to come to terms. Some sanctions were instituted. An arms embargo, a prohibition against loans and credit to Italians, the stopping of imports from Italy, these were put quickly into operation and worked to undermine the Italian economy. There was a surge of support for the League — in Britain the government won its election in November pledging to support the Covenant — and optimism grew in Geneva.

Yet on the critical question of extending sanctions to prohibit exports to Italy of coal, steel, and, above all, oil, the leaders of the League

[62] Mussolini, *Opera omnia*, XXVII, 159–60.

delayed, and this delay was crucial. In London and Paris the horror of broadening the conflict and the fear that Mussolini might be provoked into reacting violently against them overrode British and French commitments to the system of collective security. While the other sanctionist nations awaited the strong leadership they expected, Laval and Hoare hedged and, contrary to their obligations at Geneva, in December negotiated a secret plan for the partition of Ethiopia that they thought would appease Mussolini. When the Laval-Hoare plan was divulged to the public, the hopeful spirit of Geneva was destroyed and the belief that Britain would stand by the Covenant evaporated. Eden replaced the discredited Hoare as foreign secretary but this did not repair the damage, for the British government, it soon was clear, was not going to extend the embargo against Italy to include the vital resources of modern war, coal, steel, and oil. Then, on 7 March 1936, encouraged by the weakness he saw around him, Hitler marched into the demilitarized Rhineland in violation of the treaties of Locarno and Versailles. Britain and France, hoping to salvage something in their relations with Italy, began to try to make their peace with Mussolini. No further sanctions were implemented. The League's attempt to stop aggression by nonmilitary means collapsed. And armed resistance to Mussolini had been precluded by Britain and France from the beginning.

As the danger of crippling sanctions disappeared, the Italian offensive went rapidly ahead. Badoglio had at his disposal all the forces of modern warfare: mechanized armor, air power, and poison gas. The Ethiopians could not withstand this onslaught, and 2 May 1936 Haile Selassie fled his country. The emperor's dramatic appearance before the League assembly on 30 June 1936, though it struck hard at the conscience of the world, came too late for his cause. On 5 May Marshal Badoglio had entered Addis Ababa, and on 9 May 1936 Ethiopia had been proclaimed part of a new Italian empire. On 15 July 1936 sanctions against Italy came to an end. The League of Nations had not kept the peace, had not protected one of its members, had not deterred or punished an aggressor, and by its failures at the time of the Italian-Ethiopian war the League as a political institution was humiliated and doomed.

Bibliography

Index

Bibliography

Abraham, E. "Abyssinia and Italy — The Case for Ethiopia," (*Journal of the (Royal) African Society*, 37:374-7 (October 1935).

Africanus (pseud.). *Etiopia 1935: Panorama geo-politico*. Rome: Ardita, 1935.

Agostino Orsini di Camerota, Paolo d'. *L'Italia nella politica africana*. Bologna: Cappelli, 1928.

—— *Perchè andiamo in Etiopia?* Rome: Cremonese, 1936.

Alfieri, Dino. *Dictators Face to Face*. D. Moore, trans. London: Elek, 1954.

Aloisi, Pompeo. *Journal, 25 juillet 1932 — 14 juin 1936*. M. Vaussard, trans. Paris: Librairie Plon, 1957.

Alype, Pierre, *L'Empire des Négus*. Paris: Plon, 1925.

Amery, Leopold S. *My Political Life*. 3 vols. London: Hutchinson & Co. Ltd., 1953-1955.

Anchieri, Ettore. *Antologia storico-diplomatica*. Milan: Instituto per gli Studi di Politica Internazionale, 1941.

Araldi, V. *Il Patto d'Acciaio*. Rome: Bianco, 1961.

Askew, William C. "The Secret Agreement between France and Italy on Ethiopia, January 1935," *Journal of Modern History*, 25:47-8 (March 1953).

Attlee, Clement R. *As It Happened*. London: Heinemann, 1954.

Auer, Paul de. "The Lesson of the Italo-Abyssinian Conflict," *New Commonwealth Quarterly*, 1:1-19 (March 1936).

Avenol, Joseph. "The Future of the League of Nations," *International Affairs*, 13:143-58 (March-April 1934).

Avon, Earl of (Anthony Eden). *The Eden Memoirs: Facing the Dictators*. London: Cassell & Co., 1962.

Badoglio, Pietro. *La Guerra d'Etiopia*. Milan: Mondadori, 1936.

—— *The War in Abyssinia*. London: Methuen, 1937.

Baldwin, Arthur W. *My Father: The True Story*. London: George Allen and Unwin, 1955.

Baldwin, Stanley. *This Torch of Freedom*. London: Hodden and Stoughton, 1935.

Barcia Trelles, C. *Puntos Cardinales de la politica internacional española.* Barcelona: Fe, 1939.

Bardens, Dennis. *Portrait of a Statesman.* New York: Philosophical Library, 1956.

Barzini, Luigi. "Benito Mussolini," *Encounter,* 23:16–27 (July 1964).

Bastianini, Giuseppe. *Uomini, cose, fatti.* Milan: Vitagliano, 1959.

Bastin, Jean. *L'Affaire d'Ethiopie et les diplomates, 1934–1937.* Brussels: Universelle, 1937.

Beauvoir, Simone de. *The Prime of Life.* P. Green, trans. Cleveland: World, 1962.

Bechtel, Guy. *Laval vingt ans après.* Paris: Laffont, 1963.

Beer, George L. *African Questions at the Paris Peace Conference.* L. H. Gray, ed. New York: Macmillan, 1923.

Beer, Max. *The League on Trial.* W. H. Johnston, trans. Boston: Houghton Mifflin, 1933.

Beloff, Max. *The Foreign Policy of Soviet Russia, 1929–1951.* 3 vols. London: Oxford University Press, 1947–1953.

—— *The Great Powers: Essays in Twentieth Century Politics.* New York: Macmillan, 1959.

Benjamin, R. S., ed. *Eye Witness.* New York: Alliance, 1940.

Bentwich, Norman. *Ethiopia, Eritrea, and Somaliland.* London: Gollancz, n.d. [1945?].

Berkeley, George F. *The Campaign of Adowa and the Rise of Menelik.* London: Constable, 1902.

Berio, Alberto. "L' 'Affare' etiopico," *Rivista di studi politici internazionali,* 25:181–219 (April-June 1958).

Berretta, Alfio. *Amedeo d'Aosta.* Milan: Eli, 1956.

Bersellini, M. *Italia e Francia, per la nuova ascesa della civiltà latina.* Milan: Commerciale, 1935.

Bertonelli, Francesco. *Il Nostro mare,* 2nd ed. Florence: Bemporad, 1931.

Binchy, Daniel. *Church and State in Fascist Italy.* London: Oxford University Press, 1941.

Birkenhead, Earl of. *Halifax: The Life of Lord Halifax.* London: Hamish Hamilton, 1965.

Bitetto, Prince Carlo Cito de. *Mediterranée-Mer Rouge: Routes imperiales.* Paris: Grasset, 1937.

Blondel, Jules-Francois. *Au fil de la carriere: Recit d'un diplomate, 1911–1938.* Paris: Hachette, 1960.

Blum, John M. *From the Morgenthau Diaries: Years of Crisis, 1928–1938.* Boston: Houghton Mifflin, 1959.

Blum, Léon. *L'Histoire jugera,* 2nd ed. Montreal: Arbre, 1943.

Bonis, Umberto de. *La Lega delle nazioni.* Milan: Zucchi, 1937.

Bonnet, Georges. *Le Quai d'Orsay sous trois républiques.* Paris: Fayard, 1961.

Bottai, Giuseppe. *Vent'anni e un giorno,* 2nd ed. Rome: Garzanti, 1949.

Bova, Pasquale. *Il Criterio "razziale" nella politica imperiale d'Italia.* Naples: Capocci, 1937.

Bowman, Isaiah. *The New World: Problems in Political Geography,* 2nd ed. New York: World, 1928.

Braddick, H. "A New Look at American Policy during the Italo-Ethiopian Crisis, 1935–36," *Journal of Modern History,* 34:64–73 (March 1962).

Broad, Lewis. *Sir Anthony Eden.* London: Hutchinson, 1955.

Brogan, D. W. *The Development of Modern France, 1870–1939.* London: Hamish Hamilton, 1940.

Brook-Shepherd, Gordon. *Dollfuss.* London: Macmillan, 1961.

Budge, E. W. Wallis. *A History of Ethiopia.* 2 vols. London: Methuen, 1928.

Buell, Raymond L. "American Neutrality and Collective Security," *Geneva Special Studies,* VI, 6. Geneva: Geneva Research Council, 1935.

———— "The Suez Canal and League Sanctions," *Geneva Special Studies,* VI, 3. Geneva: Geneva Research Council, 1935.

Bullock, Malcolm. *Austria, 1918–1938; A Study in Failure.* London: Macmillan, 1939.

Butler, J. R. M. *Lord Lothian (Philip Kerr), 1882–1940.* New York: St. Martin's, 1960.

Buxton, David. *Travels in Ethiopia.* London: Drummond, 1949.

Caioli, Aldo. *L'Italia di fronte a Ginevra.* Rome: Volpe, 1965.

Cameron, Elizabeth R. "Alexis Saint-Léger Léger," in Craig and Gibert, eds., *The Diplomats, 1919–1939.* Princeton: Princeton University Press, 1953, pp. 378–405.

———— *Prologue to Appeasement: A Study in French Foreign Policy.* Washington: American Council on Public Affairs, 1942.

Campbell-Johnson, Alan. *Eden: The Making of a Statesman.* New York: Washburn, 1955.

Il Cardinale Ildefonso Schuster. Milan: Viboldone, 1958.

Castelli, Giulio. *La Chiesa e il Fascismo.* Rome: Arnia, 1951.

Cato (pseud.). *Guilty Men.* New York: Stokes, 1940.

Caviglia, Enrico. *Diario, aprile 1925 — marzo 1945.* Rome: Casini, 1952.

Cecil, Lord Robert. *A Great Experiment.* London: Cape, 1941.

Cerruti, Elisabetta. *Ambassador's Wife.* New York: Macmillan, 1953.

Chabod, Federico. *A History of Italian Fascism.* M. Grindrod, trans. London: Weidenfeld and Nicolson, 1963.

Chamberlain, Austen. "The Permanent Bases of British Foreign Policy," *Foreign Affairs,* 9:533–46 (July 1931).

Chambrun, Charles de. *Traditions et souvenirs.* Paris: Flammarion, 1952.

Charles-Roux, François. *Huit ans au Vatican, 1932–1940.* Paris: Flammarion, 1947.

Chatfield, Lord Ernle. *The Navy and Defence,* II: *It Might Happen Again.* London: Heinemann, 1947.

Cheesman, R. E. *Lake Tana and the Blue Nile.* London: Macmillan, 1936.

Cheever, D., and H. F. Haviland, Jr. *Organizing for Peace*. Boston: Houghton Mifflin, 1954.

Christopoulos, G. *La Politique extérieure de l'Italie fasciste*. Paris: Rodstein, 1936.

Churchill, Randolph. *The Rise and Fall of Sir Anthony Eden*. London: MacGibbon and Kee, 1959.

Churchill, Winston S. *The Second World War*, I: *The Gathering Storm*. Boston, Houghton Mifflin, 1948.

Ciano, Galeazzo. *Ciano's Diary, 1937–1938*. Andreas Mayor, trans. London: Methuen, 1952.

—— *Diario, 1937–1938*. Bologna: Cappelli, 1948.

—— *L'Europa verso la catastrophe*. Milan: Mondadori, 1948.

Cimmaruta, Roberto. *Ual Ual*. Milan: Mondadori, 1936.

Clonmore, Lord. *Pope Pius XI and World Peace*. New York: Dutton, 1938.

Clifford, E. H. M. "The British Somaliland-Ethiopia Boundary," *Geographical Journal*, 87:289–302 (April 1936).

Clough, Shepard B. *The Economic History of Modern Italy*. New York: Columbia University Press, 1964.

Codignola, Arturo. *Rubattino*. Bologna: Cappelli, 1938.

Cohen, Armand. *La Société des Nations devant le conflit italo-éthiopien (décembre 1934-octobre 1935), politique et procedure*. Geneva: Droz, 1960.

Cole, Hubert. *Laval*. New York: Putnam, 1963.

Collier, Basil. *Barren Victories: Versailles to Suez, the Failure of the Western Alliance, 1918–1956*. New York: Doubleday, 1964.

—— *The Defence of the United Kingdom*. London: Her Majesty's Stationery Office, 1957.

Collombet, E. *L'Ethiopie moderne et son avènement à la communauté internationale*. Dijon: Belvet, 1935.

Conti Rossini, Carlo. "L'Etiopia e' incapace di progresso civile," *Nuova antologia*, 303:171–7 (16 September 1935).

Coon, Carlton S. *Measuring Ethiopia and Flight into Arabia*. Boston: Little, Brown, 1935.

Cooper, Alfred Duff. *Old Men Forget*. London: Hart-Davis, 1953.

Coppola, Francesco. "La Società delle nazioni e l'Italia," in G. Volpe et al., *Le Ragioni dell'Italia*. Rome: Reale Accademia d'Italia, 1936.

Cora, Giuliano. *Attualita del trattato italo-etiopico del 1928*. Florence: Stet, 1948.

—— "Un Diplomatico durante l'era fascista," *Storia e politica*, 5:88–93 (January-March 1966).

—— "Il Trattato italo-etiopico del 1928," *Rivista di studi politici internazionali*, 15:205–26 (April-June 1948).

Craig, Gordon. "Totalitarian Approaches to Diplomatic Negotiation," in A. O. Sarkissian, ed., *Studies in Diplomatic History and Historiography in Honour of G. P. Gooch*. New York: Barnes and Noble, 1961, pp. 107–25.

—— and Felix Gilbert, eds. *The Diplomats, 1919–1939*. Princeton: Princeton University Press, 1953.

Criscuolo, Luigi. *After Mussolini . . . What?* New York: Wisdom, 1936.

Croce, Benedetto. *A History of Italy, 1871–1915*. C. M. Ady, trans. Oxford: Oxford University Press, 1929.

Cunningham of Hyndhope, Lord. *A Sailor's Odyssey*. New York: Dutton, 1951.

Curato, Federico. *La Conferenza della pace*. 2 vols. Milan: Istituto per gli Studi di Politica Internazionale, 1942.

Dalby, Louise. *Léon Blum, Evolution of a Socialist*. New York: Yoseloff, 1963.

Dalton, Hugh. *The Fateful Years: Memoirs, 1931–1945*. London: Muller, 1957.

D'Aroma, Nino. *Vent'anni insieme: Vittorio Emanuele e Mussolini*. Rome: Cappelli, 1957.

Deakin, F. W. *The Brutal Friendship: Mussolini, Hitler and the Fall of Italian Fascism*. London: Weidenfeld and Nicolson, 1962.

Dean, Vera M. "The League and the Italian-Ethiopian Dispute," *Geneva Special Studies*, VI, 8. Geneva: Geneva Research Council, 1935.

De Begnac, Yvon. *Palazzo Venezia: Storia de un regime*. Rome: La Rocca, 1950.

Debicki, Roman. *Foreign Policy of Poland, 1919–1939*. New York: Praeger, 1962.

De Bono, Emilio. *Anno XIIII*. B. Miall, trans. London: Cresset, 1937.

—— *La Preparazione e le prime operazioni*, 3rd ed. Rome: Istituto Nazionale Fascista di Cultura, 1937.

Degras, Jane, comp. *Calendar of Soviet Documents on Foreign Policy, 1917–1941*. London: Royal Institute of International Affairs, 1948.

—— *Soviet Documents on Foreign Policy, 1917–1941*. 3 vols. London: Oxford University Press, 1951–1953.

Dell, Robert. *The Geneva Racket, 1920–1939*. London: Robert Hale, n.d. [1940].

Delzell, Charles F. *Mussolini's Enemies: The Italian Anti-Fascist Resistance*. Princeton: Princeton University Press, 1961.

De Tarr, Francis. *The French Radical Party: From Herriot to Mendes-France*. London: Oxford University Press, 1961.

De Wilde, J. "The International Distribution of Raw Materials," *Geneva Special Studies*, VIII, 5. Geneva: Geneva Research Council, 1936.

DiNolfo, Ennio. *Mussolini e la politica estera italiana, 1919–1933*. Padua: Cedam, 1960.

Divine, Robert A. *The Illusion of Neutrality*. Chicago: University of Chicago Press, 1962.

Dolobran, Lord Lloyd of. "The Need for the Re-Armament of Great Britain," *International Affairs*, 16:57–79 (January-February 1936).

Donosti, Mario. *See* Luciolli, Mario.

Dorigo, P. P. *Ginevra o Roma?* Pisa: Nistri-Lischi, 1934.

Du Bois, W. E. B. "Inter-Racial Implications: A Negro View," *Foreign Affairs,* 14:82–92 (October 1935).

Dupuis, C. "Lake Tana and the Nile," *Journal of the (Royal) African Society,* 35:18–25 (January 1936).

Eayrs, James. *In Defence of Canada: Appeasement and Rearmament.* Toronto: University of Toronto Press, 1965.

Eden, Anthony. *Facing the Dictators. See* Avon, Earl of.

—— *Foreign Affairs.* London: Faber and Faber, 1939.

Ethiopia. Ministry of Justice. *Documents on Italian War Crimes.* 2 vols. Addis Ababa: Ministry of Justice, 1949–50.

Fabry, Jean. *De la Place de la Concorde au course de l'Intendance.* Paris: Editions de France, 1942.

Favagrossa, Carlo F. *Perchè perdemmo la guerra.* Milan: Rizzoli, 1946.

Federzoni, Luigi. "Hegemony in the Mediterranean," *Foreign Affairs,* 14:387–98 (April 1936)

Feiling, Keith. *The Life of Neville Chamberlain.* London: Macmillan, 1946.

Feis, Herbert. *Seen from E.A., Three International Episodes.* New York: Knopf, 1947.

Fermi, Laura. *Mussolini.* Chicago: University of Chicago Press, 1961.

Fischer, Louis. *Men and Politics: An Autobiography.* New York: Duell, Sloan and Pearce, 1941.

Flandin, Pierre-Etienne. *Politique française, 1919–1940.* Paris: Nouvelles, 1947.

Foot, Michael R. *Armistice, 1918–1939.* London: Harrap, 1940.

—— *British Foreign Policy since 1898.* London: Hutchinson's University Library, 1956.

Fornari, G. "La Crisi italo-etiopica del 1914," *Rassegna italiana,* 28:617–26 (December 1951), and 29:33–40 (January 1952).

France. Assemblée Nationale, 1947 session. *Rapport fait au nom de la commission chargée d'enquêter sur les événements survenus en France de 1933 à 1945. Annexes (dépositions).* No. 2344, C. Serre, recorder. 9 vols. Paris, n.d. [1951–1952].

—— Chambre des Députés. *Journal officiel, débats parlementaires.* Paris, 1935–36.

—— *Haute Cour de Justice. Procès du Maréchal Pétain.* Paris, 1945.

—— Ministère des Affaires Etrangères. *Bulletin périodique de la presse italienne.* Paris, 1935.

—— Ministère des Affaires Etrangères. *Documents diplomatiques français, 1932–1939,* 2nd series, I (1 January–31 March 1936). Paris, 1963.

—— Sénat. *Annales du Sénat, débats parlementaires.* Paris, 1935.

François-Poncet, André. *The Fateful Years: Memoirs of a French Ambassador in Berlin, 1931–1938.* J. LeClercq, trans. New York: Harcourt, Brace, 1949.

—— *Au palais Farnèse: Souvenirs d'une ambassade à Rome, 1938–1940.* Paris: Fayard, 1961.

Frassati, Alfredo. "Il Pericolo abissino e inghilterra, francia, ed italia," *Nuova antologia*, 25 (1 April 1899).

Gamelin, Général Maurice. *Servir: Le Prologue du drame, 1930–août 1939.* Paris: Plon, 1946.

Ganterbein, James, ed. *Documentary Background of World War II, 1931 to 1941.* New York: Columbia University Press, 1948.

Garosci, Aldo. *La Vita di Carlo Rosselli.* 2 vols. Florence: Edizioni U., n.d. [1945?].

Garratt, G. "Abyssinia," *Journal of the (Royal) African Society*, 36:36–50 (January 1937).

Gathorne-Hardy, G. M. "The League at the Cross-Roads," *International Affairs*, 15:485–505 (July-August 1936).

—— *A Short History of International Affairs, 1920–1939*, 4th ed. London: Oxford University Press, 1950.

—— and Mitrany, D. "Territorial Revision and Article 19 of the League Covenant," *International Affairs*, 14:818–36 (November-December 1935).

Gayda, Virginio. *Italia e francia: Problemi aperti*, 4th ed. Rome: Giornale d'Italia, 1939.

—— *Italia, Inghilterra, Etiopia.* Rome: Sud, 1936.

Gehl, Jürgen. *Austria, Germany, and the Anschluss, 1931–1938.* London: Oxford University Press, 1963.

Gemma, Scipione. *Storia dei trattati, 1815–1948*, 3rd ed. Florence: Barbera, 1949.

Gentizon, Paul. *Difesa dell'Italia.* Rocca S. Casciano: Cappelli, 1949.

Géraud, André. "British Vacillations," *Foreign Affairs*, 14:584–97 (July 1936).

—— Pertinax (pseud.). *Les Fossoyeurs.* 2 vols. New York: Editions de la Maison Française, 1943.

—— "France and the Anglo-German Naval Treaty," *Foreign Affairs*, 14:51–61 (October 1935).

—— "Gamelin," *Foreign Affairs*, 19:310–31 (January 1941).

Germany. *Documents on German Foreign Policy, 1918–1945.* M. Lambert et al., eds. Vols. II, III, and IV of Series C. Washington: U.S. Government Printing Office, 1959, 1962.

Germino, D. L. *The Italian Fascist Party in Power.* Minneapolis: University of Minnesota Press, 1959.

Giannini, A. *I Rapporti italo-inglesi.* Milan: Istituto per gli Studi de Politica Internazionale, 1940.

Gigli, Guido. "Sguardo ai rapporti fra Badoglio e Mussolini fino alla crisi etiopici del 1935-36." Appendix 1, pp. 255-60, in V. Vailati, *Badoglio risponde.* Milan: Rizzoli, 1958.

Giglio, Carlo. "Article 12 of the Treaty of Uccialli," R. Caulk, trans., *Journal of African History*, 6:221–31 (1965).

—— "L'Inghilterra e l'impresa di Massaua," *Nuova antologia*, 456:251–77 (November 1952).

Gilbert, Felix. "Ciano and His Ambassadors," in Craig and Gilbert, eds., *The Diplomats, 1919–1939*. Princeton: Princeton University Press, 1953, pp. 512–36.

—— "Two British Ambassadors: Perth and Henderson," in Craig and Gilbert, eds., *The Diplomats, 1919–1939*. Princeton: Princeton University Press, 1953, pp. 537–54.

Giovine (pseud.). "Aeronautica," *Nuova antologica*, 308:622–4 (16 August 1935).

Giraud, Emile. *La Nullité de la politique internationale des grandes démocraties, 1919–1939*. Paris: Sirey, 1948.

Goiffon, Paul. *Les Clauses coloniales dans les accords franco-italiens du 7 janvier 1935*. Lyon: Rion, 1936.

Graham, Robert A. *Vatican Diplomacy: A Study of the Church and State on the International Plane*. Princeton: Princeton University Press, 1959.

Grandi, Dino. "The Foreign Policy of the Duce," *Foreign Affairs*, 13:553–66 (July 1934.)

Graziani, Rodolfo. *Il Fronte sud*. Milan: Mondadori, 1938.

Great Britain. Foreign Office. *Correspondence respecting Abyssinian Raids and Incursions into British Territory*. Cmd. 2553 (1925), Abyssinia No. 1 (1925). London, 1925.

—— *Correspondence respecting the Agreement between the United Kingdom and Italy of December 14–20, 1925, in regard to Lake Tsana*. Cmd. 2792 (1927), Abyssinia No. 1 (1927). London, 1927.

—— *Documents on British Foreign Policy, 1919–1939*, 3rd series, III–VI; 2nd series, VI. E. L. Woodward, R. Butler, et al., eds. London, 1950–1953, 1957.

—— House of Commons. *Parliamentary Debates: Official Report*, 5th series, vols. 298–312. London, 1935.

Greenfield, Richard. *Ethiopia: A New Political History*. London: Pall Mall, 1965.

Grispo, Renato. "Il Patto a quattro — la questione austrica — il ponte di Stresa," in Augusto Torre et al., *La Politica estera italiana dal 1914 al 1943*. Rome, 1963, pp. 118–58.

Guariglia, Raffaele. *Ricordi, 1922–1946*. Naples: Edizioni Scientifiche Italiane, 1950.

Gunther, John. *Inside Europe*, 13th ed. New York: Harper, 1936.

Hancock, W. K., and M. M. Gowing. *British War Economy*. London: Her Majesty's Stationery Office, 1949.

Harrigan, W. "Nazi Germany and the Holy See, 1933–1936: The Historical Background of *Mit brennender Sorge*," *Catholic Historical Review*, 47:164–98 (July 1961).

Harris, Brice, Jr. *The United States and the Italo-Ethiopian Crisis*. Stanford: Stanford University Press, 1964.

Heald, Stephen, ed. *Documents on International Affairs, 1935*. 2 vols. London: Oxford University Press, 1936.

Herriot, Edouard. *Jadis*, II: *D'une guerre à l'autre, 1914–1936*. Paris: Flammarion, 1952.

Hertslet, Edward. *The Map of Africa by Treaty*, 3rd ed. 3 vols. London: His Majesty's Stationery Office, 1909.

Hess, Robert L. *Italian Colonialism in Somalia*. Chicago: University of Chicago Press, 1966.

—— "Italy and Africa: Colonial Ambitions in the First World War," *Journal of African History*, 4:105–26 (1963).

Hiett, Helen. "Public Opinion and the Italo-Ethiopian Dispute: The Activity of Private Organizations in the Crisis," *Geneva Special Studies*, VII, 1. Geneva: Geneva Research Council, 1936.

Hillson, Norman. *Geneva Scene*. London: Routledge, 1936.

Hilton-Young, Wayland. *The Italian Left: A Short History of Political Socialism in Italy*. London: Longmans, Green, 1949.

The History of "The Times," IV, part 2: *The 150th Anniversary and Beyond, 1912–1948*. New York: Macmillan, 1952.

Hoare, Samuel. *See* Templewood, Viscount.

Hodson, H. V. "The Economic Aspects of the Italo-Abyssinian Conflict," in Arnold J. Toynbee, *Survey of International Affairs, 1935*, II. London: Oxford University Press, 1936, pp. 414–42.

—— "The Problem of Raw Materials," in Arnold J. Toynbee, *Survey of International Affairs, 1935*, I. London: Oxford University Press, 1936, pp. 340–88.

Hollis, M. Christopher. *Italy in Africa*. London: Hamish Hamilton, 1941.

Hoskins, H. "The Suez Canal in Time of War," *Foreign Affairs*, 14:93–101 (October 1935).

Huddleston, Sisley. *Popular Diplomacy and War*. Rindge, N.H.: Smith, 1954.

Hughes, H. Stuart. "The Early Diplomacy of Italian Fascism, 1922–1932," in Craig and Gilbert, eds., *The Diplomats, 1919–1939*. Princeton: Princeton University Press, 1953, pp. 210–33.

—— *The United States and Italy*. Cambridge, Mass.: Harvard University Press, 1953.

Hughes, Philip. *Pope Pius the Eleventh*. London: Sheed and Ward, 1937.

Hull, Cordell. *Memoirs*. 2 vols. New York: Macmillan, 1948.

Institute of World Affairs. *Proceedings*, XIII and XIV. Los Angeles, 1936, 1937.

Istituto per gli Studi di Politica Internazionale. *Annuario di politica internazionale (Europa, 1935)*. Milan, 1936.

—— *Il Conflitto italo-etiopico: Documenti*. 2 vols. Milan, 1936.

Italy. Comando delle Forze Armate della Somalia. *La Guerra italo-etiopico: Fronte sud*. 4 vols. Rome, n.d.

—— Ministero degli Affari Esteri. *I Documenti diplomatici italiani*. 6th series (1918–1922), I, R. Mosca, ed., Rome, 1955. 7th series (1922–1935), I–IV, R. Moscati, ed., Rome, 1953–1962.

—— Personal Papers of Benito Mussolini, Together with Some Official Records of the Italian Foreign Office and the Ministry of Popular Culture, 1922–1944. National Archives Microcopy No. T-586, 316 rolls. National Archives, Washington, D.C. (These documents include, from the Ministero degli Affari Esteri, secret position papers entitled *Situazione politica nel 1935* on various countries, including Great Britain and Germany.)

Italy and Abyssinia. Rome: Società Editrice di Novissima, 1936.

Italy and the Treaties. Rome: Pallotta, 1936.

Jacini, Stefano. *Il Regime fascista*. Cernusco sul Naviglio: Garzanti, 1947.

Jemolo, A. C. *Chiesa e stato in Italia dal risorgimento ad oggi*. Turin: Einaudi, 1955.

Jesman, Czeslaw. *The Ethiopian Paradox*. London: Oxford University Press, 1963.

—— *The Russians in Ethiopia: An Essay in Futility*. London: Chatto and Windus, 1958.

Jones, A. H. M. and E. Monroe. *A History of Ethiopia*. Oxford: Oxford University Press, 1960.

Jones, Samuel S. *The Scandinavian States and the League of Nations*. Princeton: Princeton University Press, 1939.

Jones, Thomas. *A Diary with Letters, 1931–1950*. London: Oxford University Press, 1954.

Keene, Frances, ed. *Neither Liberty nor Bread: The Meaning and Tragedy of Fascism*. New York: Harper, 1940.

Kelly, David. *The Ruling Few, or, The Human Background to Diplomacy*. London: Hollis and Carter, 1952.

Kemp, P. K. *Key to Victory: The Triumph of British Sea Power in World War II*. Boston: Little, Brown, 1957.

Kennan, George F. *Russia and the West under Lenin and Stalin*. Boston: Little, Brown, 1961.

Kent, G. "Pope Pius XII and Nazi Germany: Some Aspects of German-Vatican Relations, 1933–1943," *American Historical Review*, 70:59–78 (October 1964).

King-Hall, Stephen. *Our Times, 1900–1960*. London: Faber and Faber, 1961.

Kirby, S. Woodburn. *The War Against Japan*, I: *The Loss of Singapore*. London: Her Majesty's Stationery Office, 1957.

Kirk, Dudley. *Europe's Population in the Interwar Years*. Princeton: League of Nations, 1946.

Kirkpatrick, Ivone. *Memoirs: The Inner Circle*. London: Macmillan, 1959.

—— *Mussolini: A Study in Power*. New York: Hawthorn, 1964.

Koren, William. "The Italian-Ethiopian Dispute," *Geneva Special Studies*, VI, 4. Geneva: Geneva Research Council, 1935.

Lagardelle, Hubert de. *Mission à Rome: Mussolini*. Paris: Plon, 1955.

Langer, William L. "A Critique of Imperialism," *Foreign Affairs*, 14:102–19 (October 1935).

———— "The Struggle for the Nile," *Foreign Affairs*, 14:259–73 (January 1936).

La Pradelle, Albert de. *Le Conflit italo-éthiopien*. Paris: Editions Internationales, 1936.

Larmour, Peter J. *The French Radical Party in the 1930's*. Stanford: Stanford University Press, 1964.

Latinus, pseud. *L'Italia e i problemi internazionali*. Milan: Istituto per gli Studi di Politica Internazionale, 1935.

Laval, Pierre. *The Diary of Pierre Laval*. New York: Scribner's, 1948.

———— *Le Procès Laval: Compte rendu sténographique*. Paris: Albin Michel, 1946.

Lawford, Valentine. *Bound for Diplomacy*. London: Murray, 1963.

League of Nations. *Armaments Year-Book, 1935* and *1936*. Geneva, 1935, 1936.

———— *International Trade Statistics, 1936*. Geneva, 1937.

———— *Money and Banking 1935/36*, II: *Commercial Banks*. Geneva, 1936.

———— *Official Journal, November 1926*. Geneva, 1926.

———— *Official Journal, 1935*. Geneva, 1935.

———— *Records of the Sixteenth Ordinary Session of the Assembly. Plenary Meetings. Text of the Debates. Official Journal, Special Supplement No. 138*. Geneva, 1935.

———— *Review of World Trade, 1936*. Geneva, 1937.

———— Section d'Information. *Revue des commentaires de la presse sur la Société des Nations*. Geneva, daily, 1935.

———— *Statistical Year-Book of the League of Nations, 1936/1937*. Geneva, 1937.

Lechenberg, H. P. "With the Italians in Eritrea," *National Geographic Magazine*, 68:265–96 (September 1935).

Legionarius (pseud.). *Las Razones por las cuales Italia levanta graves quejas contra Abisinia*. Rome: Ardita, n.d.

Leonard, J. "The Effect on Employment of Economic Sanctions on National and World Prosperity," *Proceedings of the Institute of World Affairs*, 13:221–5. Los Angeles, 1936.

Leroux, Eugène-Louis. *Le Conflit italo-éthiopien devant la S.D.N.* Paris: Librairie Technique et Economique, 1937.

Lessona, Alessandro. "L'Eritrea e la Somalia nei fini dell'espansione," *Rassegna italiana*, 35:119–27 (September–October 1933).

———— *Memorie*. Florence: Sansoni, 1958.

———— *Verso l'impero*. Florence: Sansoni, 1939.

Lewis, Ioan M. *The Modern History of Somaliland*. London: Weidenfeld and Nicolson, 1965.

Lewy, Guenter. *The Catholic Church and Nazi Germany*. New York: McGraw-Hill, 1964.

Litvinov, Maxim. *Against Aggression*. New York: International, 1939.

Livingstone, Dame Adelaide. *The Peace Ballot: The Official History*. London: Victor Gollancz Ltd., 1935.

Lloyd George, David. *Memoirs of the Peace Conference*. 2 vols. New Haven: Yale University Press, 1939.

Lothian, Lord. "The Place of Britain in the Collective System," *International Affairs*, 12:622–50 (September-October 1935).

Louis, Wm. Roger. "Great Britain and the African Peace Settlement of 1919," *American Historical Review*, 71:875–92 (April 1966).

Lowe, C. J. "Anglo-Italian Differences over East Africa, 1892–1895, and Their Effects upon the Mediterranean Entente," *English Historical Review*, 81:315–36 (April 1966).

Luciolli, Mario (Mario Donosti, pseud.). *Mussolini e l'Europa: La Politica estera facista*. Rome: Leonardo, 1945.

Ludwig, Emil. *Talks with Mussolini*. E. and C. Paul, trans. Boston: Little, Brown, 1933.

Lugard, Lord. "Africa and the Powers," *Journal of the (Royal) African Society*, 35:4–17 (January 1936).

—— "The Basis of the Claim for Colonies," *International Affairs*, 15:3–25 (January-February 1936).

Luther, E. W. *Ethiopia Today*. Stanford: Stanford University Press, 1958.

Macartney, M. H. H. *One Man Alone: The History of Mussolini and the Axis*. London: Chatto and Windus, 1944.

—— and P. Cremona. *Italy's Foreign and Colonial Policy*. London: Oxford University Press, 1938.

McCormick, Anne O'Hare. *Vatican Journal, 1921–1954*. M. T. Sheehan, ed. New York: Farrar, Straus and Cudahy, 1957.

MacCullum, E. P. *Rivalries in Ethiopia*. Boston: World Peace Foundation, 1935.

MacGregor, R. M. *Order or Disorder? Studies in the Decline of International Order, 1918–1936*. London: Duckworth, 1939.

MacGregor-Hastie, R. *The Day of the Lion: The Life and Death of Fascist Italy, 1922–1945*. London: MacDonald, 1963.

MacLean, Robinson. *John Hoy of Ethiopia*. New York: Farrar and Rinehart, 1936.

Macleod, Iain. *Neville Chamberlain*. London: Muller, 1961.

Mallet, Alfred. *Pierre Laval*. 2 vols. Paris: Dumont, 1955.

Magistrati, Massimo. "La Germania e l'impresa italiana di Etiopia (Ricordi di Berlino)," *Rivista di studi politici internazionali*, 17:562–606 (October-December 1950).

Mallory, Walter, ed. *Political Handbook of the World, 1935, and 1936*. New York: Council on Foreign Relations, 1935, 1936.

Mandelstam, André. *Le Conflit italo-éthiopien devant la Société das Nations*. Paris: Sirey, 1937.

Mantoux, Paul, et al. *The World Crisis*. London: Longmans, Green, 1938.

Marayati, Abid Al-. *A Diplomatic History of Modern Iraq*. New York: Speller, 1961.

Marcus, H. G. "The Last Years of the Reign of the Emperor Menilek, 1906–13," *Journal of Semitic Studies*, 9:229–34 (Spring 1964).

Marcus, John T. *French Socialism in the Crisis Years, 1933–1936.* New York: Praeger, 1958.

Margueritte, V. *The League Fiasco.* Mrs. N. MacFarlane, trans. London: Hodge, 1936.

Mariam, Mesfin Wolde. "The Background of the Ethio-Somalian Boundary Dispute," *Journal of Modern African Studies,* 2:189–219 (July 1964).

Marlowe, John. *A History of Modern Egypt and Anglo-Egyptian Relations, 1880–1953.* New York: Praeger, 1954.

Martelli, George. *Italy Against the World.* London: Chatto and Windus, 1937.

—— *Whose Sea? A Mediterranean Journey.* London: Chatto and Windus, 1938.

Mathew, David. *Ethiopia: The Study of a Polity, 1540–1935.* London: Eyre and Spottiswoode, 1947.

Matthews, H. L. *The Fruits of Fascism.* New York: Harcourt, Brace, 1943.

Maugini, A. "L'Azione colonizzatrice dell'Italia nel l'Africa Orientale," *Nuova antologia,* 302:491–506 (16 August 1935).

Megaro, Gaudens. *Mussolini in the Making.* Boston: Houghton Mifflin, 1938.

Melly, John M. "Ethiopia and the War from the Ethiopian Point of View," *International Affairs,* 15:103–21 (January-February 1936).

Mennevée, Roger. *Les Origines du conflit italo-éthiopien et la Société des Nations.* Paris: Documents Politiques, 1936.

Messing, S. "Changing Ethiopia," *Middle East Journal,* 9:413–32 (Autumn 1955).

Micaud, Charles A. *The French Right and Nazi Germany.* Durham: Duke University Press, 1943.

Micklem, Nathaniel. *National Socialism and the Roman Catholic Church.* London: Oxford University Press, 1939.

Miller, J. K. *Belgian Foreign Policy between Two Wars, 1919–1940.* New York: Bookman, 1951.

Monelli, Paolo. *Mussolini: The Intimate Life of a Demagogue.* B. Maxwell, trans. New York: Vanguard, 1954.

Monfreid, Henry de. *Ménélik, tel qu'il fut.* Paris: Grasset, 1954.

Monti, A. *Gli Italiani e il canale di Suez.* Rome: Vittoriano, 1937.

Mori, Renato. "L'Impresa etiopica e le sue ripercussioni internazionali," in Augusto Torre et al., *La Politica estera italiana dal 1914 al 1943.* Rome, 1963, pp. 159–87.

Morié, Louis J. *Histoire de l'Ethiopie.* 2 vols. Paris: Challamel, 1904.

Mosca, Oreste. *Nessuno volle i miei dollari d'oro.* Naples: Scarfoglio, 1958.

Mosley, Leonard. *Haile Selassie: The Conquering Lion.* London: Weidenfeld and Nicolson, 1964.

Mowat, Charles L. *Britain Between the Wars, 1918–1940.* London: Methuen, 1956.

Muggeridge, Malcom. *The Sun Never Sets: The Story of England in the Nineteen Thirties.* New York: Random House, 1940.

Mussolini, Benito. "La Dottrina del Fascismo," *Enciclopedia italiana*, XIV, 846–51. Milan: Treves, 1932.

—— *Memoirs, 1942–1943*. R. Klibansky, ed. F. Lobb, trans. London: Weidenfeld and Nicolson, 1949.

—— *Opera omnia di Benito Mussolini*. E. and D. Susmel, eds. 36 vols. Florence: Casa Editrice La Fenice, 1951–1963.

—— Personal Papers. *See* Italy.

—— *Storia di un anno (Il tempo del bastone e della carota)*. Verona: Mondadori, 1944.

Mussolini, Rachele. *Benito il mio uomo*. Milan: Rizzoli, 1958.

Mussolini, Vittorio. *Vita con mio padre*. Rome: Mondadori, 1957.

Navarra, Quinto. *Memorie del cameriere di Mussolini*. Milan: Longanesi, 1946.

Nagle, T. H. *A Study of British Public Opinion and the European Appeasement Policy, 1933–1939*. Wiesbaden: Chmielorz, 1957.

Nemours, Général Alfred. *Craignons d'être un jour l'Ethiopie de quelqu'un*. Port-au-Prince: College Vertières, 1945.

New Statesman and Nation. "The Abyssinian Dispute: The Background of the Conflict," X:321–6 (7 September 1935).

Newman, E. W. Polson. *Ethiopian Realities*. London: Allen and Unwin, 1936.

—— *Italy's Conquest of Abyssinia*. London: Butterworth, 1937.

Nicolson, Harold. "British Public Opinion and Foreign Policy," *Public Opinion Quarterly*, 1:53–63 (January 1937).

—— "Has Britain a Policy?" *Foreign Affairs*, 14:549–62 (July 1936).

—— *King George the Fifth*. London: Constable, 1952.

—— "Modern Diplomacy and British Public Opinion," *International Affairs*, 16:599–618 (September-October 1935).

Niliacus (pseud.). "L'Etiopia di oggi," *Nuova antologia*, 300:43–53 (1 March 1935).

—— "Etiopia schiavista," *Nuova antologia*, 302:161–9 (16 July 1935).

Nolte, Ernst. *Three Faces of Fascism*. L. Vennewitz, trans. New York: Holt, Rinehart and Winston, 1966.

Not To Be Repeated: Merry-Go-Round of Europe. New York: Long and Smith, 1932.

Orestano, Francesco. *Saggi giuridici*. Milan: Bocca, 1941.

Ormesson, Wladimir de, et al. Anglo-French Conference, Bouffémont, December 1935: *La Sécurité collective à la lumière du conflit italo-ethiopien*. Geneva: Entr'aide Universitaire Internationale, 1936.

Ortega y Gasset, Eduardo. *Etiopia: El Conflicto italo-abisinio*. Madrid: Pueyo, 1935.

Packard, Reynolds and Eleanor. *Balcony Empire: Fascist Italy at War*. New York: Oxford University Press, 1942.

Pankhurst, Richard. "The Ethiopian Army of Former Times," *Ethiopian Observer*, 7:118–43 (1963)

—— "The Ethiopian Slave Trade in the Nineteenth and Early Twentieth

Centuries: A Statistical Inquiry," *Journal of Semitic Studies,* 9:220-8 (Spring 1964).

Pankhurst, Sylvia. *Eritrea on the Eve.* Essex: "New Times and Ethiopian News," 1952.

Paul-Boncour, Joseph. *Entre deux guerres.* 3 vols. Paris: Plon, 1945.

Pegolotti, B. *Corsica, Tunisia, Gibuti.* Florence: Vallecchi, 1939.

Pellizzi, Camillo. *Italy.* London: Longmans, Green, 1939.

Perham, Margery. *The Government of Ethiopia.* London: Faber and Faber, 1948.

Pernot, Maurice. "Franco-Italian Relations," *International Affairs,* 13:508-22 (July-August 1934).

Pertinax. *See* Géraud, André.

Pesanti, G. "Alcuni aspetti del mondo muovo," *Gerarchia,* 15:389-402 (May 1935).

Pétain, Maréchal Henri P. "La Sécurité de la France," *Revue des deux mondes,* 8th ser., 27:i-xx (1 March 1935).

Peterson, Maurice. *Both Sides of the Curtain.* London: Constable, 1950.

Petrie, Charles A. *The Life and Letters of the Right Hon. Sir Austen Chamberlain.* 2 vols. London: Cassell, 1939, 1940.

Piazza, Giuseppe. *La Nostra pace coloniale.* Rome: Ausonia, 1917.

Pigli, Mario. *Etiopia, l'incognita africana.* Padua: Cedam, 1935.

Pignatelli, Luigi. *La Guerra dei sette mesi.* Naples: Mezzogiorno, 1961.

Pini, Giorgio. *Filo diretto con Palazzo Venezia.* Bologna: Cappelli, 1950.

Pius XI. *Discorsi di Pio XI.* Domenico Bertetto, ed. 3 vols. Turin: Società Editrice Internazionale, 1960.

Polanyi, Karl. *The Great Transformation.* New York: Farrar and Rinehart, 1944.

Popper, D. H. "Strategy and Diplomacy in the Mediterranean," *Foreign Policy Reports,* XIII, 6. New York: Foreign Policy Association, 1937.

Potter, Pitman B. *The Wal Wal Arbitration.* Washington: Carnegie Endowment for International Peace, 1938.

Prochazka, Baron Roman von. *Abissinia: Pericolo nero.* Milan: Bompiani, 1935.

Quaranta, Ferdinando. *Ethiopia: An Empire in the Making.* London: King, 1939.

Quaroni, Pietro. "Le Diplomate italien," in K. Braunias and G. Stourzh, eds., *Diplomatie unserer Zeit.* Graz: Styria, 1959.

—— *Ricordi di un ambasciatore.* Milan: Garzanti, 1954.

Ranshofen-Wertheimer, Egon. *The International Secretariat.* Washington: Carnegie Endowment for International Peace, 1945.

Rava, Maurizio. "L'Inghilterra e l'Etiopia, date e fatti," *Nuova antologia,* 303:74-90 (1 September 1935).

—— "Il Programma dell'Etiopia e la guerra contro l'Italia," *Nuova antologia,* 302:339-47 (1 August 1935).

Reale, Egidio. *La Politique étrangère du fascisme des accords de Rome à la proclamation de l'empire.* Paris: Alcan, 1937.

Rey, Charles F. *Unconquered Abyssinia as It Is Today*. London: Seeley, Service, 1923.

Reynaud, Paul. *Au coeur de la mêlée, 1930–1945*. Paris: Flammarion, 1951. Eng. trans.: *In the Thick of the Fight, 1930–1945*. J. D. Lambert, trans. New York: Simon and Schuster, 1955.

—— *La France a sauvé l'Europe*. Paris: Flammarion, 1947.

—— *Mémoires*, I: *Venu de ma montagne*. Paris: Flammarion, 1960.

Ribbentrop, Joachim von. *The Ribbentrop Memoirs*. O. Watson, trans. London: Weidenfeld and Nicolson, 1954.

Riddell, Walter A. *Documents on Canadian Foreign Policy, 1917–1939*. Toronto: Oxford University Press, 1962.

Ridley, Francis A. *Mussolini over Africa*. London: Wishart, 1935.

Roberts, Carl Bechhofer. *Sir John Simon*. London: Hale, 1938.

Roberts, Henry L. "Maxim Litvinov," in Craig and Gilbert, eds., *The Diplomats, 1919–1939*. Princeton: Princeton University Press, 1953.

—— "The Diplomacy of Colonel Beck," in Craig and Gilbert, eds., *The Diplomats, 1919–1939*. Princeton: Princeton University Press, 1953.

Robertson, John H. (J. Connell, pseud.). *The "Office": A Study of British Foreign Policy and Its Makers, 1919–1951*. London: Wingate, 1958.

Romains, Jules. *Seven Mysteries of Europe*. G. Brée, trans. New York: Knopf, 1940.

Rossi, Cesare. *Trentatre vicende mussoliniane*. Milan: Ceschina, 1958.

Rossi, Francesco. *Mussolini e lo stato maggiore (Avvenimenti del 1940)*. Rome: Tipografia Regionale, 1951.

Rossi dell'Arno, Giulio de'. *Pio XI e Mussolini*. Rome: Corso, 1954.

Rosso, Augusto. *Italy's Conflict with Ethiopia: The Facts in the Case*. New York: American League for Italy, 1935.

Rothermere, Viscount. *Warnings and Predictions*. London: Eyre and Spottiswoode, 1939.

Rouard de Card, Edgard. *L'Ethiopie au point de vue du droit international*. Paris: Pedone, 1928.

Rousseau, Charles. *Le Conflict italo-éthiopien devant le droit international*. Paris: Pedone, 1938.

Roux, Georges. *Mussolini*. Paris: Fayard, 1960.

Rowse, A. L. *All Souls and Appeasement*. London: Macmillan, 1961.

—— *The End of an Epoch: Reflections on Contemporary History*. London: Macmillan, 1948.

Royal Institute of International Affairs. *Great Britain and Egypt, 1914–1951*. London, 1952.

—— *The Italian Colonial Empire*. Information Department Papers No. 27. London, 1940.

—— *Italy and Abyssinia*. New York, 1935.

Rubenson, Sven. "The Protectorate Paragraph of the Wichale Treaty," *Journal of African History*, 5:243–83 (1964).

—— "Some Aspects on the Survival of Ethiopian Independence in the

Period of the Scramble for Africa," in *Historians in Tropical Africa*, Proceedings of the Leverhulme Inter-Collegiate History Conference, September 1960. Salisbury, Southern Rhodesia: University College of Rhodesia and Nyasaland, 1962.

Rubinstein, Alvin Z., ed. *The Foreign Policy of the Soviet Union*. New York: Random House, 1960.

Salter, Lord Arthur. *Memoirs of a Public Servant*. London: Faber and Faber, 1961.

—— *Personality in Politics*. London: Faber and Faber, 1947.

Salvatorelli, Luigi. *Vent'anni fra due guerra*. Rome: Italiane, 1941.

—— and Giovanni, Mira. *Storia d'Italia nel periodo fascista*, 3rd ed. Rome: Einaudi, 1959.

Salvemini, Gaetano. "Can Italy Live at Home?" *Foreign Affairs*, 14:243–58 (January 1936).

—— *Mussolini diplomatico, 1922–1932*. Bari: Laterza, 1952.

—— *Prelude to World War II*. London: Victor Gollancz Ltd., 1953.

—— "Twelve Years of Fascist Finance," *Foreign Affairs*, 13:473–82 (April 1935).

—— "The Vatican and the Ethiopian War," in F. Keene, ed., *Neither Liberty nor Bread*. New York: Harper, 1940, pp. 191–200.

Sanderson, G. "The Foreign Policy of the Negus Menelik, 1896–1898," *Journal of African History*, 5:87–97 (1964).

Sandford, Mrs. D. [Christine]. "Ethiopia: Reforms from Within versus Foreign Control," *International Affairs*, 15:183–201 (March-April 1936).

—— *Ethiopia under Haile Selassie*. London: Dent, 1946.

Sava, George. *A Tale of Ten Cities*. London: Faber and Faber, 1942.

Scaetta, H. "Geography, Ethiopia's Ally," *Foreign Affairs*, 14:62–70 (October 1935).

Schaefer, Ludwig F. *The Ethiopian Crisis: Touchstone of Appeasement?* Boston: D. C. Heath, 1961.

Schanzer, Carlo. *L'Acquisto delle colonie e dritto pubblico italiano*. Rome: Loescher, 1912.

Schmidt, Carl T. *The Corporate State in Action: Italy under Fascism*. New York: Oxford University Press, 1939.

—— *The Plough and the Sword: Labor, Land, and Property in Fascist Italy*. New York: Columbia University Press, 1938.

Schonfield, Hugh J. *Italy and Suez*. London: Hutchinson, n.d. [1947].

—— *The Suez Canal in World Affairs*. New York: Philosophical Library, 1953.

Schuschnigg, Kurt von. *Ein Requiem in Rot-Weiss-Rot*. Zurich: Amstutz, Herdeg, 1946.

Schwarz, Herbert. *Die Entwicklung der völkerrechtlichen Beziehungen Äthiopiens zu den Mächten seit 1885*. Breslau: Märtin, 1937.

Schwebel, Stephen M. *The Secretary-General of the United Nations*. Cambridge, Mass.: Harvard University Press, 1952.

396   BIBLIOGRAPHY

Scott, J., and R. Hughes. *The Administration of War Production*. London: Her Majesty's Stationery Office, 1952.

Scott, William E. *Alliance Against Hitler: The Origins of the Franco-Soviet Pact*. Durham: Duke University Press, 1962.

Selby, Walford. *Diplomatic Twilight, 1930–1940*. London: Murray, 1953.

Seldes, George. *Sawdust Caesar*. New York: Harper, 1935.

Sellassié, Guèbré. *Chronique du règne de Ménélik II, roi des rois d'Ethiopie*. 2 vols. Tèsfa Sellassié, trans. Paris: Maisonneuve Frères, 1930.

Serra, E. "Mussolini, l'Etiopia e un segreto di Sir Samuel Hoare," *Nuova antologia*, 477:481–8 (April 1960).

Sforza, Count Carlo. *Contemporary Italy*. D. and D. deKay, trans. London: Muller, 1946.

―――― *Italy and Italians*. E. Hutton, trans. New York: Dutton, 1949.

Shepardson, Whitney H., and William Scroggs. *The United States in World Affairs, 1934–1935*. New York: Harper, 1935.

Sillani, Tomaso. *L'Africa orientale italiana e il conflitto italo-etiopico*. Rome: La Rassegna Italiana, 1936.

Simon, Lord John. *Retrospect*. London: Hutchinson, 1952.

Simon, Kathleen. *Slavery*. London: Hodder and Stoughton, 1929.

Simoni, Leonardo. *Berlino, ambasciata d'Italia, 1939–43*. Rome: Migliaresi, 1946.

Slocombe, George. *A Mirror to Geneva: Its Growth, Grandeur and Decay*. New York: Holt, 1938.

Soulié, Michel. *La Vie politique d'Edouard Herriot*. Paris: Colin, 1962.

Soward, F. H., J. F. Parkinson, N. A. M. MacKenzie, and T. W. L. MacDermot. *Canada in World Affairs: The Pre-War Years*. Toronto: Oxford University Press, 1941.

Starhemberg, Prince Ernst R. *Between Hitler and Mussolini*. London: Hodder and Stoughton, 1942.

Steer, George. *Caesar in Abyssinia*. Boston: Little, Brown, 1937.

Steiner, H. Arthur. *Government in Fascist Italy*. New York: McGraw-Hill, 1938.

Stolper, G. "European Kaleidoscope," *Foreign Affairs*, 14:216–26 (January 1936).

Strang, Lord William. *Britain in World Affairs*. New York: Praeger, 1961.

―――― *Home and Abroad*. London: Deutsch, 1956.

Sturzo, Luigi. *Chiesa e stato: Studio sociologico-storico*. 2 vols. Bologna: Zanichelli, 1958, reissue.

Suvich, Fulvio, et al., *Il Processo Roatta*. Rome: Universale de Luigi, 1945.

Szembek, Comte Jean. *Journal, 1933–1939*. J. Rzewuska and T. Zaleski, trans. Paris: Plon, 1952

Tabouis, Geneviève. *Perfidious Albion — Entente cordiale*. J. A. D. Dempsey, trans. London: Butterworth, 1938.

―――― *They Called Me Cassandra*. New York: Scribner's, 1942.

―――― *Vingt ans de "suspense" diplomatique*. Paris: Albin Michel, 1958.

Taylor, A. J. P. *The Origins of the Second World War.* New York: Atheneum, 1962.

—— *The Trouble Makers: Dissent over Foreign Policy, 1792–1939.* Bloomington: Indiana University Press, 1958.

Teeling, L. William. *The Pope in Politics.* London: Dickson, 1937.

Temperley, Arthur C. *The Whispering Gallery of Europe.* London: Wm. Collins Sons, 1938.

Templewood, Viscount (Samuel Hoare). *Ambassador on Special Mission.* London: Wm. Collins Sons, 1946.

—— *Nine Troubled Years.* London: Wm. Collins Sons & Co. Ltd., 1954.

Terlinden, Vicomte Charles. *Le Conflit italo-éthiopien et la Société des Nations.* Liege: Desoer, 1936.

Thayer, John A. *Italy and the Great War: Politics and Culture, 1870–1915.* Madison: University of Wisconsin Press, 1964.

Thomas, Ivor. *Who Mussolini Is.* Oxford: Oxford University Press, 1942.

Thompson, A. "The Water Problems of Abyssinia and Bordering Countries," *International Affairs,* 14:769–79 (November-December 1935).

Thompson, Geoffrey. *Front-Line Diplomat.* London: Hutchinson, 1959.

Thomson, David. *Two Frenchmen: Pierre Laval and Charles de Gaulle.* London: Cresset, 1951.

Tittoni, Tommaso, and V. Scialoja. *L'Italia alla conferenza della pace.* Rome: Libreria di Scienze e Lettere, 1921.

Torre, Augusto, et al. *La Politica estera italiana dal 1914 al 1943.* Rome: RAI, 1963.

Torrès, Henry. *Pierre Laval.* N. Guterman, trans. New York: Oxford University Press, 1941.

Toscano, Mario. "Il Diario del Barone Aloisi," *Rassegna italiana,* 395:428–35 (October 1957).

—— "Eden a Roma alla vigilia del conflitto italo-etiopico," *Nuova antologia,* 478:21–44 (January 1960).

—— "Eden's Mission to Rome on the Eve of the Italo-Ethiopian Conflict," in A. O. Sarkissian, ed., *Studies in Diplomatic History and Historiography in Honour of G. P. Gooch.* New York: Barnes and Noble, 1961, pp. 126–52.

—— *Francia ed Italia di fronte al problema di Gibuti.* Florence: Studio Fiorentino di Politica Estera, 1939.

—— *Lezioni di storia dei trattati e politica internazionale.* Turin: Giappichelli, 1958.

—— *Le Origini diplomatiche del patto d'Acciaio,* 2nd ed. Florence: Sansoni, 1956.

—— *Il Patto di Londra.* Bologna: Zanichelli, 1934.

Tosti, Amedeo. *Pietro Badoglio.* Verona: Mondadori, 1956.

—— *Storia dell'esercito italiano, 1861–1936.* Milan: Instituto per gli Studi di Politica Internazionale, 1942.

Tournès, R. "The French Army, 1936," *Foreign Affairs,* 14:487–98 (April 1936).

Toynbee, Arnold J. *Survey of International Affairs, 1935*. 2 vols. Title of vol. II: *Abyssinia and Italy*. London: Oxford University Press, 1936.

Tuchmann, Barbara. *The Guns of August*. New York: Macmillan, 1962.

Ullendorff, Edward. *The Ethiopians*. London: Oxford University Press, 1960.

United States. Department of State. Diplomatic Correspondence pertaining to the Italo-Ethiopian Conflict. National Archives, Washington, D.C.

—— *Foreign Relations of the United States: Diplomatic Papers. 1934*, II: *Europe, The Near East, Africa. 1935*, I: *General, The Near East, Africa. 1935*, II: *British Commonwealth, Europe. 1935*, III: *The Far East. 1936*, I: *General, British Commonwealth*. Washington, 1951–1953.

—— *Peace and War: United States Foreign Policy, 1931–1941*. Washington, 1943.

Vailati, Vanna. *Badoglio risponde*. Milan: Rizzoli Editore, 1958.

Vansittart, Lord Robert. *Lessons of My Life*. London: Hutchinson, n.d. [1943].

—— *The Mist Procession: The Autobiography of Lord Vansittart*. London: Hutchinson, 1958.

Varè, Daniele. "British Foreign Policy through Italian Eyes," *International Affairs*, 15:80–102 (January-February 1936).

—— *Twilight of the Kings*. London: Murray, 1948.

—— *The Two Impostors*. London: Murray, 1949.

Vaucher, Paul, and Paul-Henri Siriex, *L'Opinion britannique, la Société des Nations, et la guerre italo-éthiopienne*. Paris: Centre d'Etudes de Politique Etrangère, 1936.

Vaussard, Maurice. *De Pétrarque à Mussolini: Évolution du sentiment nationaliste italien*. Paris: Armand Colin, 1961.

Vedovato, Giuseppe. *Gli Accordi italo-etiopici dell'agosto 1928*. Florence: Rivista di Studi Politici Internazionali, 1956.

Villari, Luigi. "Abyssinia and Italy: The Italian Case," *Journal of the (Royal) African Society*, 34:36–73 (October 1935).

—— *The Expansion of Italy*. London: Faber and Faber, 1930.

—— "Italian Foreign Policy," *International Affairs*, 14:320–45 (May-June 1935).

—— *Italian Foreign Policy under Mussolini*. New York: Devin-Adair, 1956.

—— *Italy, Abyssinia, and the League*. Rome: Dante Alighieri Society, 1936.

—— *Storia diplomatica del conflitto italo-etiopico*. Bologna: Zanichelli, 1943.

Virgin, General Eric. *The Abyssinia I Knew*. N. Walford, trans. London: Macmillan, 1936.

Volpe, Gioacchino, et al. *Le Ragioni dell-Italia*. Rome: Reale Accademia d'Italia, 1936.

Vondracek, Felix J. *The Foreign Policy of Czechoslovakia, 1918–1935*. New York: Columbia University Press, 1937.

Wagnière, Georges. *Dix-huit ans à Rome, 1918–1936.* Geneva: Jullien, 1944.

Walters, F. P. *A History of the League of Nations.* 2 vols. London: Oxford University Press (auspices of the Royal Institute of International Affairs), 1952.

Ward-Price, George. *Extra-Special Correspondent.* London: Harrap, 1957.

Waterfield, Gordon. *Morning Will Come.* London: Murray, 1944.

Watt, D. C. *Personalities and Policies: Studies in the Formulation of British Foreign Policy in the Twentieth Century.* South Bend: University of Notre Dame Press, 1965.

—— "The Secret Laval-Mussolini Agreement of 1935 on Ethiopia," *Middle East Journal,* 15:69–78 (Winter 1961).

Waugh, Alec. "History Text Books as a Factor in International Relations," *International Affairs,* 15:877–96 (November-December 1936).

Waugh, Evelyn. *They Were Still Dancing.* New York: Farrar and Rinehart, 1932.

—— *Waugh in Abyssinia.* London: Longmans, Green, 1936.

Webster, Richard A. *The Cross and the Fasces: Christian Democracy and Fascism in Italy.* Stanford: Stanford University Press, 1960.

Weir, Lauchlan M. *The Tragedy of Ramsay MacDonald.* London: Secker and Warburg, 1938.

Werth, Alexander. *The Destiny of France.* London: Hamilton, 1937.

—— *The Twilight of France.* D. W. Brogan, ed. New York: Harpers', 1942.

Wheeler-Bennett, John, and Stephen Heald. *Documents on International Affairs, 1935.* 2 vols. London: Oxford University Press, 1936.

Whitaker, John T. *And Fear Came.* New York: Macmillan, 1936.

White, Freda. *The Abyssinian Dispute.* London: League of Nations Union, 1935.

Williams, Francis. *A Pattern of Rulers.* London: Longmans, 1965.

Wilson, Arnold T. *The Suez Canal: Its Past, Present, and Future.* London: Oxford University Press, 1933.

—— *Thoughts and Talks.* London: Longmans, Green, 1938.

Wilson, Hugh R. *Diplomat between Wars.* New York: Longmans, Green, 1941.

Wilson, Hugh R., Jr. *For Want of a Nail: The Failure of the League of Nations in Ethiopia.* New York: Vantage, 1959.

Windsor, Duke of. *A King's Story.* New York: Putnam, 1951.

Wiskemann, Elizabeth. *The Rome-Berlin Axis: A History of the Relations between Hitler and Mussolini.* London: Oxford University Press, 1949.

Woolbert, Robert G. "Feudal Ethiopia and Her Army," *Foreign Affairs,* 14:71–81 (October 1935).

—— "Italy in Abyssinia," *Foreign Affairs,* 13:499–508 (April 1935).

—— "The Peoples of Ethiopia," *Foreign Affairs,* 14:340–4 (January 1936).

—— "The Rise and Fall of Abyssinian Imperialism," *Foreign Affairs,* 14:692–97 (July 1936).

Work, Ernest. *Ethiopia: A Pawn in European Diplomacy*. New Concord, Ohio: Privately printed, 1935.

Woolf, Leonard. *The League and Abyssinia*. London: Hogarth, 1936.

Wrench, John Evelyn. *Geoffrey Dawson and Our Times*. London: Hutchinson, 1955.

Wright, Quincy. "The Test of Aggression in the Italo-Ethiopian War," *American Journal of International Law*, 30:45–56 (1936).

—— and G. Kidd. "Reform of the League of Nations," *Geneva Special Studies*, V, 7–8. Geneva: Geneva Research Council, 1934.

Yakobson, Sergius. "Russia and Africa," in I. J. Lederer, ed., *Russian Foreign Policy: Essays in Historical Perspective*. New Haven: Yale University Press, 1962, pp. 453–88.

Yilma, Princess Asfa. *Haile Selassie, Emperor of Ethiopia*. London: Low, Maston, 1936.

Yokhontoff, Viktor. *USSR Foreign Policy*. New York: Coward-McCann, 1945.

Young, G. M. *Stanley Baldwin*. London: Hart-Davis, 1952.

Zaghi, Carlo, ed. *Crispi e Menelich, nel diario inedito del conte Augusto Salimbeni*. Turin: Industria Libraria Tipografica, 1956.

—— *Le Origini della colonia Eritrea*. Bologna: Cappelli, 1934.

Zayid, Mahmud. *Egypt's Struggle for Independence*. Beirut: Khayats, 1965.

Zimmern, Alfred. *The League of Nations and the Rule of Law, 1918–1935*. London: Macmillan, 1936.

—— "The League's Handling of the Italo-Abyssinian Dispute," *International Affairs*, 14:751–68 (November-December 1935).

—— "The Testing of the League," *Foreign Affairs*, 14:373–86 (April 1936).

Zoli, Corrado. "L'Avvaloramento agraira dell'Eritrea," *Rassegna italiana*, 26:203–17 (May-June 1930).

—— *Cronache etiopiche*. Rome: Sindacato Italiano Arti Grafiche, 1930.

—— *Espansione coloniale italiana, 1922–1937*. Rome: Arnia, 1949.

Index of Names